Above left: Thomas Gray in 1748, by
John Giles Eccardt
By courtesy of the National Portrait Gallery,
London

Above right: Robert Merry in the
1780s, after a portrait by Hugh Douglas
Hamilton, from *The British Album* (1790)

Left: Percy Bysshe Shelley in 1819, by
Amelia Curran
By courtesy of the National Portrait Gallery,
London

A GOLDEN RING

By the same author

Edgell Rickword: A Poet at War

Charles Hobday

A GOLDEN RING

*English poets in Florence
from 1373 to the present day*

PETER OWEN
LONDON & CHESTER SPRINGS

PETER OWEN PUBLISHERS
73 Kenway Road, London SW5 0RE
Peter Owen books are distributed in the USA by
Dufour Editions Inc. Chester Springs PA 19425-0007

First published in Great Britain 1997
©1997 Charles Hobday

A catalogue record for this book is available from the British Library

ISBN 0 7206 1051 6

Printed and bound in Great Britain by Biddles of Guildford and King's Lynn

My dear Helen,

Florence is a city that has meant a great deal to both of us, not only for its beauty, its art, its history and its memories of the poets, but also for more personal reasons. It was there that we first met — at the bottom of the Borgo Pinti, to be precise. As you knew the city better than I did, on a later visit you pointed out Casa Guidi to me, and thereby gave me the idea for the title of this book. While I was writing it we spent a month there, hunting down English poets. Together we climbed up to the villa at Arcetri where Milton talked with Galileo, and wished that we had taken the bus from the Porta Romana. Together we clung to our seats while a ramshackle bus lurched down the mountainous road from Vallombrosa, and the driver nonchalantly chatted with every passenger who got on. Together we tracked Shelley along the paths of the Cascine. Together we tramped along the lanes below Fiesole in search of the villa where Landor threw his cook out of the window. Together we found the house in the Via della Chiesa where he died, and we persuaded the tenant of his flat to move her washing, which was hiding the tablet to his memory. Together we took our lives in our hands to visit his grave and that of Elizabeth Barrett Browning. Together we identified the house in the Via de' Bardi where Lawrence chased a bat round his room.

Yes, this book is just as much your baby as mine. Now that it has at last been born, to whom else could I dedicate it?

Contents

Acknowledgements

I wish to express my gratitude to Lawrence Pollinger Ltd and the Estate of Frieda Lawrence Ravagli for permission to quote from the poems and prose works of D. H. Lawrence; to the National Portrait Gallery, London, for permission to reproduce portraits of Milton, Gray, Shelley, Landor, and Robert and Elizabeth Browning, and a photograph of Lawrence; to the British Library for permission to reproduce a portrait of Chaucer; to the Librarian of Colby College, Waterville, Maine, for permission to reproduce a photograph of Eugene Lee-Hamilton; to Giusti di Becocci, Florence, for permission to reproduce paintings of Dante, Galileo and the Piazza della Signoria and a photograph of an Etruscan sculpture; to the Ministerio per i Beni Culturali e Ambientali, Rome for permission to reproduce prints of the Cascine and a demonstration in 1847; to the staffs of the British Institute, Florence, the Italian Cultural Institute, London, the British Library, the London Library and the Kensington Central Library; and to Christine, who typed an untidy manuscript, for her skill and patience.

List of Illustrations

Front endpapers

Geoffrey Chaucer, from an early-fifteenth-century manuscript of Thomas Hoccleve's *De Regimine Principum* (Harley Ms. 4866, f.88)

By permission of the British Library

John Milton in 1629, by an unknown artist

By courtesy of the National Portrait Gallery, London

Thomas Gray in 1748, by John Giles Eccardt

By courtesy of the National Portrait Gallery, London

Robert Merry in the 1780s, after a portrait by Hugh Douglas Hamilton, from *The British Album* (1790)

Percy Bysshe Shelley in 1819, by Amelia Curran

By courtesy of the National Portrait Gallery, London

Between pages 204 and 205

Dante and medieval Florence, from a fifteenth-century painting by Domenico di Michelino in Florence Cathedral

By permission of Giusti di Becocci, Florence

Galileo in old age, by Giusto Sustermans

By permission of Giusti di Becocci, Florence

The Piazza della Signoria, Florence, in the mid-eighteenth century, by Bernardo Bellotto

By permission of Giusti di Becocci, Florence

The Cascine, Florence, in which Shelley wrote 'Ode to the West Wind', from a lithograph of 1848 by Lindemann Frommel

By permission of Soprintendenza ai beni storici e artistici di Firenze

The Villa Gherardesca, Landor's home near Fiesole, from John Forster's *Walter Savage Landor: A Biography* (1869)

The demonstration of 12 September 1847, which the Brownings witnessed and Mrs Browning described in *Casa Guidi Windows*, crossing the Ponte Santa Trinità, from a contemporary print
By permission of Soprintendenza ai beni storici e artistici di Firenze

Mrs Browning's tomb in the Protestant cemetery, Florence, from a photograph by Helen Hobday

An Etruscan bronze sculpture of a chimera in the Museo Archeologico, Florence, which D. H. Lawrence admired
By permission of Giusti di Becocci, Florence

Back endpapers

Walter Savage Landor in 1855, by Robert Faulkner
By courtesy of the National Portrait Gallery, London

Robert Browning in 1859, by Field Talfourd
By courtesy of the National Portrait Gallery, London

Elizabeth Barrett Browning in 1859, by Field Talfourd
By courtesy of the National Portrait Gallery, London

Eugene Lee-Hamilton in about 1900, from a photograph
By permission of the Librarian of Colby College, Waterville, Maine

D. H. Lawrence in 1929, from a photograph by Ernesto Guardia
By courtesy of the National Portrait Gallery, London

Preface

Ever since Chaucer visited Florence on a diplomatic mission and discovered the poetry of Dante, Petrarch and Boccaccio, English poets have
been conducting a love affair with the city. At least four major poets —
Chaucer, Milton, Shelley and Browning — derived inspiration from it, as
also did such outstanding poets of the second rank as Gray, Landor,
Elizabeth Barrett Browning and Lawrence. Even undeniably minor poets
such as Robert Merry, Isabella Blagden and Eugene Lee-Hamilton produced their best work while living there. Some, notably Landor and the
Brownings, chose to settle in or just outside Florence; others, including
Milton, Gray, Merry, Shelley and Lawrence, stayed there for months or
even years. A surprising number not only lived but died there; the city's
Protestant cemetery probably contains the remains of more English poets
than any other burial-place outside the United Kingdom — one might
almost say, outside Poets' Corner.

Florence had much to offer them: the beauty of its setting and its
architecture; Dante's poetry and Boccaccio's tales; a succession of
painters such as few cities, if any, have equalled; masterpieces of classical
sculpture, side by side with those of Donatello, Michelangelo and Cellini;
its music (opera originated in sixteenth-century Florence); the science of
Galileo; the scholarship of its academies; its historians and political theo-
rists; its republican traditions; its Etruscan heritage; its festivals; the song
of its nightingales; its flowery Tuscan countryside. From all of these
English poets have drawn inspiration, and some of the greatest English
poems — The Canterbury Tales, Paradise Lost, 'Ode to the West Wind', The
Ring and the Book — owe a debt to Florence. No other foreign city, it can
be argued, has contributed so much to English poetry. Jerusalem and
Athens have supplied poets with symbols of an ideal society, but it is
Florence where they have chosen to live, and to which they have given
their hearts.

1

Geoffrey Chaucer

On 1 December 1372 a diplomatic mission set out from London, in order to negotiate with the Doge of Genoa and his council on the selection of an English seaport for the use of Genoese merchants. The mission consisted of two Genoese citizens in the service of King Edward III, Jacopo Provano and Giovanni de' Mari, and an Englishman, Geoffrey Chaucer, squire in the royal household, soldier, diplomatist and poet. They were accompanied by Provano's son, improbably named Saladino, a guard of two Genoese crossbowmen, three king's messengers and several servants. Before leaving London Chaucer received an advance of 100 marks (£66.67) for his expenses, which were reckoned at a mark a day.

He was an appropriate choice for this particular mission, for he had one foot in the commercial world of the City and the other in the court, the centre of government. The son of a well-to-do vintner, he was born in the early 1340s, almost certainly in London, and by 1357 he had entered the service of the Countess of Ulster, wife of the King's third son, Prince Lionel. He served in the French campaign of 1359–60 and was taken prisoner, King Edward contributing £16 towards his ransom. In the spring of 1366 he visited Navarre, on what may have been his first diplomatic mission. By the following September he was married to one of Queen Philippa's ladies, and by June 1367 he was a member of the King's household. According to an Elizabethan biographer, he visited Italy for the first time in June 1368, when he was present at Prince Lionel's second marriage, to the daughter of Galeazzo Visconti, Lord of Milan, but this story is hard to reconcile with contemporary evidence on his movements in that year. Meanwhile he was becoming known at court as a poet. By 1372 he was clearly a rising man, with a distinguished career before him.

He may have been selected for the mission to Genoa because he knew Italian, although this was not essential. French and Latin, with which he had been familiar since childhood, were international languages; in England and Italy alike all nobles and most merchants knew French, and it was taken for granted that every educated man read and spoke Latin. Whether before or after 1372, however, Chaucer certainly acquired sufficient knowledge of Italian to read the works of Dante, Petrarch and Boccaccio with pleasure and appreciation. There were no Italian grammars or dictionaries, and he must have learned the language directly from Italian speakers. He had plenty of opportunities for doing so; over 100 Italian businessmen are known to have been active in London in the 1370s, and Provano and de' Mari were by no means the only Italians in the royal service. English scholars, like the Clerk of Oxenford in *The Canterbury Tales*, studied at Italian universities. To someone as familiar as Chaucer was with French and Latin, it would not have been difficult to pick up a working knowledge of Italian, as French and Italian resembled each other, and both resembled Latin, more closely than they do today. From a comparison between passages in *Troylus and Criseyde* and those in Boccaccio's *Il Filostrato* from which they are translated, a modern scholar has drawn the conclusion that Chaucer's knowledge of Italian was intimate enough to enable him to convey the subtleties of his original.[1]

As England and France were at war, after crossing to Calais, then in English hands, Chaucer and his companions probably travelled through Flanders, up the Rhine, across Switzerland, and through the St Bernard or the Mont Cenis Pass into Italy. Moving at the rate of twenty-five miles or so a day, or perhaps a little more slowly as it was winter, they may have reached Genoa in the first half of January 1373. They do not seem to have taken long in coming to an agreement with the Doge's council, for in March de' Mari was already back in Bruges hiring mercenaries. Instead of returning immediately to England, however, Provano and Chaucer went on to Florence. Why, we do not know; of the five documents in Latin and one in French which are our only sources of information on his mission to Italy, only three mention his visit to Florence, and none of them states its purpose. Two suggestions have been put forward. In the previous August, King Edward had approached the Florentine banking house of the Bardi for a loan, and Provano and Chaucer may have been required to settle the details. If they were, they would have found their negotiations very delicate indeed, for Edward's failure to pay debts totalling a million and a half gold florins in the 1340s had temporarily ruined the Bardi and helped to set off a disastrous chain of bankruptcies. On the other hand, the visit may have been connected with an agreement which Provano had signed in December 1371 with two Florentine merchants for the supply of ships for King Edward's service. Whatever its purpose, it was evidently an afterthought, and new instructions had been sent to them after they had set out. Chaucer's 100 marks proved insufficient to cover his expenses, and on 23 March he was obliged to borrow 220 florins from Provano.

From Genoa they probably travelled south along the coast, turning east at Viareggio or Pisa. As they approached Florence, after a week or so on the road, Chaucer may well have been impressed by the citizens' luxurious villas in the surrounding countryside; the chronicler Giovanni Villani estimated that within six miles of the city there were more than twice as many mansions as in Florence. When the city itself came into sight Chaucer would have been struck by its irregular skyline. Many of its noble families still lived in tall fortified towers similar to those for which San Gimignano is famous, although the number of towers had been drastically reduced since the 1250s, when there were said to be 300 of them, and their height had been restricted to 100 feet. In addition, there were Giotto's campanile, the towers of the Palazzo del Popolo (now the Palazzo Vecchio), the Palazzo del Podestà (the Bargello), 57 parish churches, 5 monasteries, 24 nunneries and 10 friaries, 15 city gates, and the 73 towers, over 100 feet high, of the city walls.

Fourteenth-century Florence was one of the greatest industrial and financial centres in the world, combining the roles which the City of London and Manchester were to play in Victorian times. In 1338 it contained about 200 workshops employing over 30,000 people. Wool imported from England and Portugal was washed in the Arno, combed, carded, spun, woven, shorn and dried in the Ognissanti quarter and San Frediano parish across the river, then dyed in the Santa Croce district in the rich reds, blues, yellows and browns for which Florence was famous. The profits of Florentine cloth and Florentine banking (there were eighty banks in the city in 1338) largely paid for the rebuilding, maintenance or adornment of the Duomo, the Baptistery, Orsanmichele and San Miniato, and for the upkeep of the city's thirty almshouses and hospitals, with over 1,000 beds for the poor and sick. They also contributed to the support of the schools, in which, according to Villani, 8,000 to 10,000 boys and girls learned to read and write, 1,000 to 1,200 were taught mathematics in six business schools and 550 to 600, destined for the law, medicine or the church, studied grammar and logic in four higher schools. Although he may have exaggerated, Florence probably had the highest level of literacy in Europe: one-quarter or even one-third of the male population. Florentines' pride in their city was eloquently expressed by the humanist Chancellor of the Republic Coluccio Salutati, who wrote, thirty years after Chaucer's visit:

> What city, not merely in Italy, but in all the world, is more securely placed within its circle of walls, more proud in its palazzi, more bedecked with churches, more beautiful in its architecture, more imposing in its gates, richer in piazzas, happier in its wide streets, greater in its people, more glorious in its citizenry, more inexhaustible in wealth, more fertile in its fields?[2]

And yet, despite its prosperity, Florence had already entered upon a long decline. During the thirteenth century its population had rapidly expanded. Although the old Roman walls had been replaced in 1172 by a much longer circuit, by 1284 the city had already outgrown it, and it was decided to build a third circuit. When this was completed it enclosed over 1,500 acres or nearly 2.5 square miles, including the industrial suburbs on both banks of the Arno. In the 1340s, however, disaster struck. Florence was a well-fed city (every year, Villani boasted, it consumed 4,000 oxen and calves, 60,000 sheep, 20,000 goats, 30,000 pigs and 55,000 to 65,000 flasks of wine), but it was not immune to famine. The harvest of 1346 was believed to be the worst for a century, and Villani estimated that 4,000 Florentines died of starvation in the following year. The Black Death, which reached Florence in March 1348, killed perhaps 80,000 of the population of 120,000, who were already weakened by famine. New outbreaks of plague in 1363 and 1374 and famines in 1352–3 and 1369–70 also took their toll. As it was the poor who supplied the bulk of the victims, so great was the shortage of labour that a decree issued in 1363 authorized the importation of unlimited numbers of foreign slaves, provided they were pagans, so that Chaucer may have been surprised to see Tartars and Mongols in the streets. When he arrived in the spring of 1373 Florence contained about 60,000 people – well above London's 40,000 or so, but only half its population thirty years earlier. So far from the population expanding to fill the area enclosed by its new walls, the large open spaces remaining were used for smallholdings, gardens, orchards, vineyards and even cornfields.[3]

Florence's crisis went deeper than a falling population. Its republican constitution had taken shape in the second half of the previous century, after the triumph of the Guelfs (the supporters of the Pope in his struggle with the Emperor) over the Ghibellines (supporters of the Emperor). The reforms of 1282 entrusted the government of the city to the priors of the major guilds, and the Ordinances of Justice in 1293 excluded from public office those magnates who were not members of the guilds. In 1343 the minor guilds had also won the right to representation on the Signoria, the supreme executive body. This extension of the regime's political basis was resented by the old-established families, whether of noble or merchant origin, which had formed the ruling oligarchy in the past. Against them were ranged the 'new men' who, having made fortunes in business, were forcing their way into the ruling class with the support of the artisans and shopkeepers of the minor guilds. The patricians fought back through the Guelf party organization, which attempted to exclude their opponents from power by labelling them as Ghibellines, although the Ghibelline party was extinct and the term had become merely one of political abuse. The situation was complicated by religious divisions. Papal expansion in central Italy seemed to threaten Florence itself, and aroused suspicions that the Church was plotting with the staunchly papalist Guelf party to bring about an oligarchic coup. Among the people moved the Fraticelli, who strove to practise St Francis's rule of evangelical poverty in all its rigour and denounced the Pope as Antichrist. The Church might persecute them as heretics, but their ardour impressed many Florentines, and some politicians saw in them a potential ally against papal aggression. Outside the struggle stood the *Ciompi*, the propertyless wage-earners in the textile and other industries, who were rigorously excluded from the city's political life. In 1373 they had been unusually quiet for some years, but they were watching their betters' squabbles with interest and listening to the subversive sermons of the Fraticelli. In the five years after Chaucer's visit, all the city's tensions – political, religious and economic – were to come to a head: a depression in the cloth industry, many bankruptcies, plague, famine, war with the papacy and violent political conflict, culminating in the uprising of the *Ciompi* and the revolutionary upheaval of 1378–82.

Chaucer arrived back in London on 23 May 1373, presumably having left Florence about the middle of April. He had probably spent at least six weeks there, which would have given him ample time to form a clear idea of the situation. He would have found many aspects of Florentine politics of interest. That a city should be governed by its guilds, or at least by their richer members, would have seemed natural to Chaucer the London vintner's son. What would have surprised Chaucer the royal servant was the Florentines' hatred of monarchy, which precluded acceptance even of a doge as head of state, and limited membership of the Signoria to a two-month term. Other features of Florentine life would have seemed more familiar to him, such as the bitter factional struggles inside the ruling class, widespread anticlericalism, the labour shortage caused by the Black Death and the consequent industrial unrest. England, like Florence, was entering a period of crisis; within a few years Wyclif's poor priests were to parallel the Fraticelli, and the Peasants' Revolt that of the *Ciompi*. Chaucer probably came to the conclusion that Florence, like England, was suffering from 'lack of steadfastness'.

Some biographers have depicted Chaucer as gazing open-mouthed at the higher civilization of Florence. That is debatable. Any comparison between fourteenth-century Florence and London is difficult; whereas much of Boccaccio's Florence survives, fires (and especially that of 1666), rebuilding, the dissolution of the monasteries, Protestant iconoclasm and German and Irish bombing have left hardly anything of Chaucer's London above ground between the Tower and Westminster Hall except St Bartholomew's and the Temple church. The two cities had much in common, but in town planning Florence had the advantage. In both most of the streets were narrow alleys, winding and stinking, but whereas in London Cheapside was the only exception, in Florence a programme of modernization had been in progress for nearly a century. New streets had been laid out, built broad and straight, and old ones had been widened and straightened. A slum quarter had been demolished to create the Piazza della Signoria. Whereas only one bridge served London, Westminster, Southwark and Lambeth, Florence had four spanning a comparatively short stretch of the river. Florence enjoyed the advantage that abundance of good building stone was easily available, and was used for palace and slum alike, at a time when the smaller houses of London, and some of the larger ones, were built of wood. If Florence suffered from disastrous floods (that of 1333 had swept away three of the four bridges), it was far less vulnerable to fire than London.

But was the Florence of 1373 artistically superior to London? Did Chaucer find the unfinished Duomo, its dome planned but not yet begun, more impressive than Old St Paul's with its spire 489 feet high? How did the Franciscans' and the Dominicans' churches in London compare with Santa Croce and Santa Maria Novella? The disappearance of almost all Gothic London makes it virtually impossible to answer such questions, but one can make tentative guesses. Chaucer must have been impressed by the mosaics in the Baptistery vault and the use of marbles of different colours in the Campanile, to which London could produce no parallel. He may have seen the frescos in Santa Croce and Santa Maria Novella, though we cannot tell what his reactions would have been. Nothing is left of the wall paintings which were common in London's churches and palaces except some fragments in Westminster Abbey, and the high quality of the best of these suggests that he was familiar with paintings that would stand comparison with most of what Florence could produce. One feature at least of Florentine building must have surprised him — the tendency to leave churches unfinished. Accustomed to seeing decoration lavished on the west fronts of the greater English and French churches, he must have been amazed to find that the façades of the Duomo and Santa Maria Novella were only half built and that of Santa Croce not even begun, although work on all three churches had started between 70 and 130 years earlier.

Whatever his reactions to Florentine art and architecture, there is no doubt that Chaucer was profoundly impressed by the work of the three great Florentine poets: Dante, Petrarch and Boccaccio. He must have owned copies of Dante's *La Divina Commedia* and Boccaccio's *Il Filostrato* and *Il Teseida*, and there is also evidence that he had read other Italian or Latin works by all three. He no doubt heard of some, at least, of these works while in Florence, but he did not necessarily bring back copies of all of them. It is more likely that he acquired some of his Italian books during a later visit to Italy in 1378, when he was sent on an embassy mission to Bernabo Visconti, Lord of Milan. During this visit he was also required to contact an Englishman, Sir John Hawkwood, the tanner's son from Essex who had become famous as a *condottiere*, presumably in the hope of attracting him back to the service of his native country. If this was his mission he was unsuccessful, for Hawkwood (whose unpronounceable name the Italians softened to the more musical Giovanni Acuto) entered the service of the Florentine Republic, which after his death rewarded him with a painted monument in the Duomo.

Dante had been dead for over fifty years when Chaucer arrived in Florence, but Petrarch and Boccaccio were still alive, and there has been a great deal of speculation on whether he met either or both of them. It has been argued that when the Clerk of Oxenford claims to have learned the tale of Griselda at Padua from 'Fraunceys Petrak, the lauriat poete'[4] Chaucer is speaking from his own experience. It is true that at the time of his visit Petrarch was at Padua, having fled from his rural home at

Arquà because war was raging in the neighbourhood, but that Chaucer, while engaged on a diplomatic mission, ran the risk of entering a war zone on the off chance of meeting a poet whom he admired passes rational belief; moreover, Petrarch's voluminous correspondence contains no reference to such a meeting. Boccaccio lived at Certaldo, only about twenty miles from Florence, and often visited the city, but the fact that Chaucer never mentions him makes it improbable that they ever met.

Paradoxically, one thing which Chaucer learned in Italy was an increased respect for the English language. Throughout western Europe Latin, the language of the Church, and French, the language of courts, enjoyed far greater prestige than the vernacular languages. In northern and western England, remote from the court, the native tradition of vernacular verse was vigorously alive, but in the London area the position was different. Chaucer's friend John Gower wrote his first long poem in French and his second in Latin before plucking up courage to write his *Confessio Amantis* in English. Chaucer himself may have begun his career by writing lyrics in French; the poems headed 'Ch' in a late-fourteenth-century manuscript at the University of Pennsylvania may be his.[5] In Italy some poets, such as the troubadour Sordello, had written in Provençal, and still others wrote in a mixture of French and Italian in which the French element predominated. It was Dante who, in his *De Vulgari Eloquentia*, vindicated (in Latin) the claim of the vernacular languages to be accepted as a medium for poetry, and proceeded to prove his case by writing the *Divina Commedia* in the language of his native Florence. Even so, the battle was not yet won. Petrarch wrote more than nine-tenths of his surviving work in Latin, and affected to despise the vernacular poems on which his reputation rests. His friend and admirer Boccaccio, after writing the *Decamerone*, devoted his later years mainly to Latin compilations. But in 1373 an event occurred that marked the triumph of the vernacular. While in Florence Chaucer may have heard of a proposal for a course of public lectures on the *Divina Commedia*. Dante thereby was recognized as a classic, on the same level as the great poets and philosophers of the ancient world and the great theologians of modern times. Not long after Chaucer left, Boccaccio was appointed to deliver the lectures, and despite some criticism chose to do so not in Latin, but in Italian.

Chaucer's discovery of Italian poetry encouraged him to experiment with metrical forms. His staple medium hitherto had been the octosyllabic couplet; now he tried his hand at forms used by Dante, Petrarch and

Boccaccio. He introduced two short passages of *terza rima*, the metre of the *Divina Commedia*, into *A Balade of Pity*, but soon gave up the attempt, finding, as he remarked in *The Complaint of Venus*, that 'ryme in Englissh hath such skarsite'. More stimulating was his study of *Il Filostrato* and *Il Teseida*, both written in the *ottava rima* stanza (abababcc). Chaucer never tried this form, for the same reason that he gave up *terza rima* — the scarcity of rhyming words made it too difficult — but it did suggest to him the use of the seven-line stanza (*ababbcc*), which we know as rhyme royal. French poets had sometimes used this stanza in ballades, but it had not previously been used for a long poem. From his point of view it had the advantage that it enabled him to produce similar effects to those of otta-va rima, but required only one rhyme instead of two to be repeated three times. There is a modern parallel in W. H. Auden's 'Letter to Lord Byron', in which, while closely imitating the 'airy manner' of *Don Juan*, he substi-tuted rhyme royal for *ottava rima*.[6] The third Italian form, the sonnet, presented even greater difficulty than *ottava rima*, in that it required two rhymes to be used four times. Chaucer did adapt one sonnet of Petrarch's in *Troylus and Criseyde*, where it appears as 'Cantus Troili', but, instead of attempting to reproduce its rhyme scheme, he expanded it into three rhyme-royal stanzas.

Victorian scholars divided Chaucer's career into a French period, when he imitated or translated French lyrics and dream allegories, an Italian period, when he fell under the influence of the great Florentines, and the English period of *The Canterbury Tales*. In reality, he drew upon English and French models throughout his career, and Italian models dur-ing his 'English' period. He translated passages from Dante, Petrarch and Boccaccio, imitated others, and borrowed stories from them, yet what-ever he borrowed he made very much his own. He always referred to Dante, for example, with great respect, calling him 'the wise poete of Florence' and 'the grete poete of Ytaille'. The following lines from 'The Prologue of the Second Nun's Tale' are a translation from St Bernard's prayer to the Virgin, with which Dante opens the final canto of the *Paradiso*:

> Thow mayde and mooder, doghter of thy sone
>
> . . . .
>
> Thow humble and heigh over every creature,
> Thow nobledest so ferforth oure nature

That no desdeyn the Makere hadde of kynde
His sone in blood and flessh to clothe and wynde.

Withinne the cloistre blisful of thy sydis
Took mannes shap the eterneel love and pees

. . . .

Assembled is in thee magnificence
With mercy, goodnesse, and with swich pitee
That thou that art the sonne of excellence
Not oonly helpest hem that preyen thee,
But often tyme of thy benygnytee
Ful frely, er that men thyn help biseche,
Thou goost biforn and art hir lyves leche.[7]

Chaucer's treatment of Dante was not always so reverent, however. In Canto IX of the *Purgatorio* Dante dreams that he is carried off by an eagle with golden feathers from Mount Ida, as Ganymede was. In *The House of Fame* Chaucer is similarly carried off by an eagle and recalls the precedent of Ganymede, but the effect is very different. In Dante the episode is completely serious; in Chaucer it is comic, as when the eagle complains of his weight and he wonders whether Jove intends to make a star of him. More surprising is his use of two more lines from St Bernard's prayer in *Troylus and Criseyde*, where they are translated:

Whoso wol grace and lyst the nought honouren,
Lo, his desir wol fle withouten wynges.[9]

These lines, which would not be out of place in the Second Nun's prayer to the Virgin, are in fact addressed to Cupid, and are spoken by Troilus on going to bed with Criseyde for the first time. Dante would probably have regarded such a use of his lines as bordering on blasphemy.

Chaucer's only description of hell, the Summoner's picture, in the prologue to his tale, of the fate awaiting friars in the next world, is less remote in spirit from Dante than would appear at first glance. Dante's humour could be Rabelaisian enough at times, as in the conclusion of Canto XXI of the *Inferno*, which some translators have found embarrassing. Chaucer's narrative is probably intended as a good-humoured parody of the final Canto of the *Inferno*; Satan is there described as chewing Judas, Brutus and Cassius in his three mouths, so why should not the other orifices in his body also be used for the punishment of notorious sinners? Dante compares Satan's huge wings to ships' sails; in Chaucer his tail is 'brodder than of a carryk is the sayl'.[9] Chaucer admired, even reverenced Dante, but his reverence did not preclude a joke on occasion at Dante's expense.

His version in 'The Monk's Tale' of the story of Ugolino, Conte della Gherardesca, in Canto XXXIII of the *Inferno* is his longest borrowing from Dante, but only eleven of its fifty-six lines are translations, and the details and tone of the story are transformed. The historical Ugolino was an unscrupulous politician who in the wars of the Guelfs and Ghibellines betrayed each side in turn. In 1288 the Pisans imprisoned him in a tower, with two of his sons and two of his grandsons; some months later they threw the key of the tower into the Arno and left all five to starve to death. Chaucer retains some details from Dante's version of the story (Ugolino's silence on hearing the door locked, his gnawing his hands, his sons' appeal to him to eat their flesh), but others he completely alters. In historical fact, Ugolino's sons and one of his grandsons were grown men and the other grandson was about fifteen; Dante, while vague about their exact ages, suggests that they were much younger. Misled by this, Chaucer makes his Hugelyn's fellow prisoners three little boys, the eldest of whom is scarcely five. The tone of the story is thus completely changed: the sheer horror of Dante's narrative becomes a sentimental pathos. On realizing that the prisoners are to be starved to death, Dante's Ugolino does not weep or say a word but 'turns to stone within'. The reaction of Chaucer's Hugelyn is feeble by comparison:

> 'Alas!' quod he, 'allas, that I was wroght!'
> Therwith the teeres fillen from his eyen.[10]

His sons' appeal to Ugolino to feed upon their flesh, although grotesque, is deeply moving; the similar appeal in Chaucer, put into the mouths of two little boys, is merely incredible. Chaucer's alterations to Dante's story are all for the worse.

Chaucer seems to have been familiar with the *Divina Commedia* before he had thoroughly mastered Boccaccio's poems. *The House of Fame*, which probably dates from the mid-1370s, is steeped in Dante, whereas its echoes of *Il Teseida* are few and slight. By the early 1380s, however, he had carefully studied both *Il Teseida* and *Il Filostrato*, of which it has been said that he 'made more use . . . than of any other group of texts in any language'. His two longer narrative poems, *Troylus and Criseyde* and 'The Knight's Tale', take their plots from them, and *Il Teseida* also supplied him with material for *The Parliament of Fowls* and *Anelida and Arcite*. What he took from Boccaccio, however, he handled with the same freedom as his borrowings from Dante. Much of *Troylus and Criseyde* is translated from *Il Filostrato*, sometimes closely, sometimes freely, but such borrowings make up less than a third of the poem. His combination of material from Boccaccio and other poets with original work is most strikingly apparent in the conclusion of the poem. Boccaccio's cynical sneers at women's fickleness jarred on him; such a story, he felt, deserved a more dignified conclusion. After mentioning Troilus' death at Achilles' hands, therefore, he added three stanzas in imitation of a passage in *Il Teseida* describing the flight of Troilus's soul to the next world. These stanzas echo the lines in the *Paradiso* in which Dante looks down upon the earth with contempt from the heaven of the fixed stars, and from then on the spirit of the poem is that of Dante rather than Boccaccio. Whereas Boccaccio at this point warns young men to put no trust in women, Chaucer appeals to 'yonge fresshe folkes, he or she' to turn from 'worldly vanyte' to the love of Christ, and the final stanza translates literally Dante's great lines on the Trinity:

> Quell' uno e due e tre che sempre vive
> e regna sempre in tre e'n due e'n uno,
> non circunscritto, e tutto circunscrive

which became in English:

> Thow oon and two and thre eterne on lyve,
> That regnest ay yn thre and two and oon,
> Uncircumscript and al mayst circumscryve. [11]

But it is not what Chaucer took from Boccaccio, Dante and his other sources that makes *Troylus and Criseyde* a great poem, but what he added of his own. *Il Filostrato* is the work of a poet in his early twenties; *Troylus and Criseyde* that of a man in his forties who has attained complete mastery of his craft and has had a far wider experience of life. The psychological treatment of the lovers, and especially Criseyde, is greatly deepened, and Pandarus is completely transformed into one of the great comic figures of English literature. Yet, while the poem is far richer in comedy than *Il Filostrato*, it also possesses a high seriousness that its model cannot attain.

Although Chaucer drew more upon Boccaccio than upon any other poet, he never mentions him by name, as he does Dante and Petrarch, and claims to have taken the story of *Troylus and Criseyde* from a book in Latin by a certain Lollius. Several explanations of this fact have been put forward: that he had met Boccaccio in Florence and disliked him; that he disapproved of his 'debasement of courtly language'; that his manuscripts of *Il Teseida* and *Il Filostrato* did not give the author's name; that he could not think of a way of Anglicizing the name Boccaccio as he Anglicized 'Petrarca' into 'Petrak', although his disciple John Lydgate found no difficulty in turning it into 'Bochas'. None of these suggestions is very convincing. Probably he was adhering to the established convention that a story on a classical theme should be attributed to an ancient Latin source, rather than a modern one in a vernacular language. In so doing he was following the example of his predecessors who had told the story. Guido delle Colonne, who based his *Historia Trojana* on Benoît de Sainte-Maure's *Roman de Troie*, cites the ancient writers Dares and Dictys as his sources, but nowhere mentions Benoît. Although Boccaccio drew upon both Benoît and Guido he gives credit to neither, but claims to be following 'antiche lettere'. He could therefore hardly complain when Chaucer treated him as he had treated his own sources. As for the name Lollius for a writer on the Trojan war, Chaucer seems to have taken it from a misunderstood line in Horace, 'Troiani belli scriptorem, Maxime Lolli', which was supposed to indicate that Horace's friend had written on the subject.[12]

It is still disputed whether Chaucer was familiar with Boccaccio's *Decamerone*. If he did read it, he would certainly have enjoyed it. Both writers, as was not uncommon in the fourteenth century, combined anticlericalism and a vein of scepticism with orthodox piety; Boccaccio in later life repudiated the licentious stories in the *Decamerone*, just as Chaucer retracted 'the tales of Canterbury, thilke that sownen into synne'.[13] Four of the *Canterbury Tales* – the Reeve's, Clerk's, Franklin's and

Shipman's tales – are stories that had already been told by Boccaccio. Chaucer took 'The Clerk's Tale' of the patient Griselda from Petrarch's Latin version of Boccaccio's story, 'The Franklin's Tale' probably from Boccaccio's *Filocolo* rather than from the *Decamerone*, and 'The Reeve's Tale' from a French fabliau. This leaves 'The Shipman's Tale' as his one probable borrowing from the *Decamerone*. The difference between the two is enlightening. In Boccaccio's story of Gulfardo and Ambruogia (Day VIII, Story 1) what happens is everything and the characters' personalities are of no importance, except insofar as they contribute to the action. In Chaucer the very thin story is less important than the subtle characterization of the monk, the merchant and his wife, who are presented as fully rounded human beings.

Chaucer's visit to Florence was an event of no political importance, but for him and for English poetry it was very important indeed. His reading of Dante and Boccaccio offered him new models for matter, form and style. Even when he wrote a dream allegory in octosyllabics, *The House of Fame*, he poured new Tuscan wine into this old bottle. Knowing his limitations, he did not attempt to imitate Dante's subject matter, but his reading of Dante widened his horizons and kindled his poetic ambitions. Boccaccio made him conscious of the potentialities of the romance, which in its English form he seems to have regarded with contempt, and encouraged him to give it the dignity of epic in 'The Knight's Tale' and *Troylus and Criseyde*. In Dante he found a model for 'a poetic that allowed easy passage from high to low style and deemed nothing too common, no image too homely'.[14] On that April day when he rode out of Florence, with the *Divina Commedia* and perhaps Boccaccio's two poems in his baggage, he must have been conscious, like Dante's Ulysses, of new worlds awaiting exploration.

Geoffrey Chaucer

DE HUGELINO COMITE DE PIZE
from THE MONKES TALE

Off the Erl Hugelyn of Pyze the langour
Ther may no tonge telle for pitee.
But litel out of Pize stant a tour
In which tour in prisoun put was he,
And with hym been his litel children thre –
The eldeste scarsly fyf yeer was of age.
Allas, Fortune, it was greet crueltee
Swiche briddes for to putte in swich a cage!

Dampned was he to dyen in that prisoun,
For Roger, which that bisshop was of Pize,
Hadde on hym maad a fals suggestioun
Thurgh which the peple gan upon hym rise,
And putten hym to prisoun in swich wise
As ye han herd, and mete and drynke he hadde
So smal that wel unnethe it may suffise,
And therwithal it was ful poure and badde.

And on a day bifil that in that hour
Whan that his mete wont was to be broght,
The gayler shette the dores of the tour.
He herde it wel, but he spak right noght,
And in his herte anon ther fil a thoght
That they for hunger wolde doon hym dyen.
'Allas,' quod he, 'allas, that I was wroght!'
Therwith the teeres fillen from his eyen.

His yonge sone that thre yeer was of age
Unto hym seyde, 'Fader, why do ye wepe?
Whanne wol the gayler bryngen oure potage?
Is ther no morsel breed that ye do kepe?

---

langour: starvation; *dampned*: condemned; *suggestioun*: accusation; *unnethe*: barely; *therwithal*: in addition; *wont*: accustomed; *doon*: make; *potage*: broth

I am so hungry that I may nat slepe.
Now wolde God that I myghte slepen evere!
Thanne sholde nat hunger in my wombe crepe.
Ther is nothyng but breed that me were levere.'

Thus day by day this child bigan to crye,
Til in his fadres barm adoun it lay
And seyde, 'Farewel, fader, I moot dye.'
And kiste his fader, and dyde that same day.
And whan the woful fader deed it say,
For wo his armes two he gan to byte.
And seyde 'Allas, Fortune, and weylaway!
Thy false wheel my wo al may I wyte.'

His children wende that it for hunger was
That he his armes gnow, and nat for wo,
And seyde, 'Fader, do nat so, allas,
But rather ete the flessh upon us two.
Oure flessh thou yaf us, take oure flessh us fro,
And ete ynogh. 'Right thus they to hym seyde,
And after that, withinne a day or two,
They leyde hem in his lappe adoun and deyde.

Hymself, despeired, eek for hunger starf.
Thus ended is this myghty Erl of Pize.
From heigh estaat Fortune awey hym carf.
Of this tragedie it oghte ynough suffise;
Whoso wol here it in a lenger wise,
Redeth the grete poete of Ytaille
That highte Dant, for he kan al devyse
Fro point to point, nat o word wol he faille.

---

wombe: stomach; *levere*: more desirable; *barm*: breast; *say*: saw; *wyte*: blame; *wende*: thought; *gnow*: gnawed; *yaf*: gave; *starf*: died; *carf*: cut off; *highte*: is called; *devyse*: describe

GEOFFREY CHAUCER

Cantus Troili
from Troylus and Criseyde, Book I

If no love is, O God, what fele I so?
And if love is, what thyng and which is he?
If love be good, from whenes cometh my wo?
If it be wykke, a wonder thenketh me
Whenne every torment and adversite
That cometh of hym may to me savory thynke,
For ay thurst I, the more that ich it drynke.

And yf that at myn owene lust I brenne,
Fro whennes cometh my waylyng and my pleynte?
If harm agree me, wherto pleyne I thanne? —
I not; ne whi unweri that I feynte.
O quyke deth, O swete harm so queynte,
How may of the yn me swich quantite,
But if that I consente that it be?

And if that I consente, I wrongfully
Compleyne, iwys. Thus possed to and fro,
Al sterles withinne a bot am I
Amyd the see, bitwyxen wyndes two
That in contrarye stonden evere mo.
Allas, what is this wondre maladye?
For hete of cold, for cold of hete, I deye.

---

wykke: evil; *thenketh me*: it seems to me; *savory thynke*: seem sweet; *lust*: desire; *brenne*: burn; *agree*: pleases; *not*: know not; *quyke*: living; *queynte*: strange; *iwys*: certainly; *possed*: tossed; *sterles*: rudderless; *in contrarye stonden*: blow in opposite directions

31

2

John Milton

After Chaucer left Florence, no major English poet came to the city for over 200 years. Sir Thomas Wyatt, who set out from Venice in 1527 with the intention of going there, was captured on the way by the Spaniards, then at war with the Pope, and after escaping or being released went on to Rome. Philip Sidney visited Florence in 1574, but his visit was short and seems to have exercised little influence on his poetry. Henry Wotton, the author of a handful of well-turned lyrics, spent about a year in Florence at various times between 1592 and 1602, and found it 'a paradise inhabited with devils'.[1] It was not until the summer of 1638, when John Milton arrived, that Florence received a visitor whose experiences there were as important for English poetry as Chaucer's had been.

While Milton was still at school his father hired private tutors to teach him French and Italian at home. Although French literature seems to have had little appeal for him, he early developed a passion for Italian poetry, stimulated by his friendship with Charles Diodati, a member of a distinguished family of Italian Protestant refugees. While at Cambridge he kept up his studies of the Italian poets – first and foremost Dante and Petrarch, but also more modern writers such as Giovanni della Casa, a copy of whose sonnets he bought for tenpence in 1629. Under their influence he began writing sonnets in the strict Italian form which he referred to in a letter as the 'Petrarchian stanza',[2] rather than the easier English form, and remained faithful to it throughout his life. He even tried his hand about 1630 at writing five sonnets in Italian, four of them addressed to a young Italian lady named Emilia and the other to Diodati. In another poem dating from the early 1630s, 'Upon the Circumcision', he followed exactly the intricate thirteen-line stanza form of the hymn to the Virgin with which Petrarch concluded his *Canzoniere*. To Milton as to Chaucer, Italian verse forms presented a challenge which he could not resist.

From his early years Milton was a dedicated Protestant, as his violently anti-papal poem 'In Quintum Novembris', written when he was seventeen, makes obvious. It may therefore appear paradoxical that he should admire poets as intensely Catholic as Dante and Petrarch, and imitate so Catholic a poem as Petrarch's hymn to the Virgin. Because they were sincere in their Catholicism, however, Dante and Petrarch were harsh critics of unworthy priests and Popes. An Italian critic has written of Dante:

> The Florentine intellectual who received his religious education between Santa Croce and Santa Maria Novella, between Franciscans and Dominicans, with an ever-increasing sympathy for the charitable poverty of the Franciscan Spirituals, who dreamed of a Church totally and devoutly dedicated to the edification and salvation of souls . . . could not bear the thought that the papal Curia, the great religious orders, the Popes themselves, should be a prey to simony, nepotism, temporal power and politico-military expansionism, and his moral disdain explodes into fury against Boniface VIII (see Canto XIX of the *Inferno*), his adversary in life, who is here chosen as the negative symbol of theocracy and its degeneration.

Petrarch denounced the corruption of the papal court at Avignon in Sonnets CXXXVI–CXXXVII so violently, apostrophizing it as 'putta sfacciata' (translated by Milton as 'impudent whore'), that publication of these sonnets was forbidden by the Inquisition. Because of their criticism of the papacy, Dante and Petrarch were honoured in the Protestant world as forerunners of the Reformation. John Foxe in his *Actes and Monuments* noted that 'in canto the thirty-second of his Purgatory [Dante] declareth the Pope to be the Whore of Babylon', and that Petrarch 'seemeth plainly to have thought the Pope was Antichrist'. A Puritan such as Milton could therefore admire and imitate them with a safe conscience. When in 'Lycidas' he put his condemnation of the Laudian clergy into St Peter's mouth, he probably had in mind Peter's denunciation of unworthy Popes as 'rapacious wolves in shepherd's clothing' in Canto XXVII of the *Paradiso*. He also praised Dante and Petrarch on moral grounds in *An Apology against a Pamphlet*, contrasting 'the two famous renowners of Beatrice and Laura, who never write but honour of them to whom they devote their verse, displaying sublime and pure thought, without transgression,' with those poets who speak 'unworthy things of themselves, or unchaste of those names which before they had extolled'.[3]

After leaving Cambridge in 1632, Milton devoted the next six years to a programme of intensive reading in preparation for his future career, whether in the Church, as his father expected, or as a poet, as he himself hoped. The entries in his commonplace book show that Italian writers made up a large part of his reading. He read or reread Dante's *Divina Commedia* and *Convivio*, and carefully noted the Italian's opinions on questions which he himself found of interest: the avarice of the clergy, suicide, sloth, education, usury, royal and papal authority, the nature of true nobility. He read Ariosto's *Orlando Furioso*, both in Italian and in Sir John Harington's translation, Boccaccio's *Vita di Dante* and Tasso's *Gerusalemme Liberata*. In a letter to Diodati he reported in 1637 that, after being 'occupied for a long time by the obscure history of the Italians under the Longobards, Franks and Germans',[4] he proposed to pass on to the history of the individual states, and asked to borrow a history of Venice. It was with a mind saturated in Italian literature and culture that in May 1638 he set out on his journey – it might almost be called a pilgrimage – to Italy.

Travel in Italy was easier for Englishmen in the 1630s than it had been for many years. Under Elizabeth I England had been at war with Spain, which ruled Lombardy, Naples and Sicily, and in both the Papal States and the Spanish possessions English Protestants were in danger from the Inquisition. Only in tolerant Venice could English visitors feel at ease. After the conclusion of peace in 1604 tension relaxed, and the papal authorities adopted a more indulgent attitude; John Mole, imprisoned for life in 1608, was the last Englishman to be persecuted in Rome for his opinions. War with Spain broke out again in 1624, but with the restoration of peace in 1630 the last serious obstacle to travel to Italy was removed. Charles I's marriage in 1625 to the Catholic Henrietta Maria aroused hopes for the conversion of both the King and his subjects, and in Rome young Englishmen, and especially those of good family, were courted and caressed. Milton, whose grandfather had been a Catholic recusant, seems to have been regarded as a possible convert. Among the complimentary verses published with his 1645 collection is a Latin couplet signed 'Selvaggi'; the only person of this name known is David Codner, an English Benedictine attached to Henrietta Maria's suite, who passed himself off as an Italian called Matteo Selvaggio. It is possible that he knew Milton, gave him advice on his Italian tour, and tried to win his confidence by praising his verse. While in Rome, Milton was entertained at the English College, was shown over the Vatican library, and received flattering attentions from Cardinal Francesco Barberini (the nephew of the Pope, Urban VIII), who was well known for his hospitality to English visitors. In the Grand Duchy of Tuscany, of which Florence was the

34

capital, Englishmen were especially welcome, for Ferdinando II, the ruling Grand Duke, was anxious to expand trade with England. His natural geniality, and perhaps his well-known weakness for handsome young men, also contributed to make him welcome visiting Englishmen; when Sir John Reresby and a friend visited the Grand Duke's villa at Poggio a Caiano, Ferdinando, 'according to his usual civility to strangers, sent us two dishes of fish (being Friday) and twelve bottles of excellent wines, to our inn'.[5]

It was at this time that the *giro d'Italia*, as part of the Grand Tour, assumed the form which it long retained. Travellers sailed from Marseilles to Genoa, and thence south by land or sea to Livorno (Leghorn). Through Pisa, Florence and Siena they made their way to Rome for a lengthy stay, and after a visit to Naples they returned to Rome for the Holy Week and Easter ceremonies. They then crossed to Loreto, to see the Virgin's house, allegedly carried there from Nazareth through the air by angels, and its treasures; journeyed through Bologna to Venice, arriving in time to see the Doge wed the sea on Ascension Day; and so homeward via Milan, Geneva and Paris. Milton followed this route, but with certain significant exceptions. He spent only a few days in Paris, and does not seem to have halted anywhere else in France. On the other hand, he lingered for about two months in Florence – much longer than was customary; John Evelyn, although a conscientious sightseer, spent only five days there, and another day or two on his return journey. Milton stayed in Rome for nearly four months in all, but he left before Holy Week; Evelyn, who was no Puritan, disliked the 'heathnish pomp' and 'unimaginable superstition' of the ceremonies, and Milton's reaction would have been even stronger. He did not visit the Holy House at Loreto, which he regarded as a fraud; in *Areopagitica* he cites 'any lay Papist of Loreto' as a type of superstitious credulity.[6] Instead he returned to Florence for another two months, interrupted only by a few days' excursion to Lucca, the home of the Diodati family. Of the year or so which he spent in Italy, about a third was passed in Florence.

The city's political status had been transformed since Chaucer's visit. After the defeat of the democratic revolution of 1378–82, power had been concentrated in the hands of a few great families, and from there it was but a step to the rule of a single family, the Medici, who took control in 1434. Twice expelled, they were twice reinstated by Spanish troops. With the conquest of Siena in 1557 virtually the whole of Tuscany passed under their control, with the exception of the tiny Republic of Lucca, and in 1569 they assumed the title of Grand Duke. Reresby summed up the situation in 1657 as follows:

> The government of Tuscany, as I said, is monarchical, and more absolutely so than any other principality in Italy, the prince laying what taxes he pleases upon the people, and having always a good competent standing force to keep them in subjection; of this his guards commonly quarter in the city, which mostly consist of High Duch and Switzers; the rest, which are four regiments, lye quartered upon the frontiers of his dominions'.[7]

The estimable qualities of Ferdinando II, whose temperament was not that of a tyrant, did not alter the fact that the proud Florentine Republic was now held down by foreign mercenaries.

In the later sixteenth century Florence enjoyed internal and external peace such as it had seldom known. In this atmosphere economic life revived. Florence, which before the Black Death had been the third largest city in Italy, had declined by 1550 to the seventh or even the ninth place, but with the new prosperity a slow recovery began. There were ominous signs on the horizon, however. The outbreak of the Thirty Years' War was followed in the 1620s by a catastrophic crash and a depression which continued till the end of the century. The population had risen from 59,000 in 1530 to 70,000 a century later, but the great plague of 1630–33 killed one Florentine in ten. Prosperity in Tuscany was confined to the port of Leghorn, the trade of which was in English and Dutch hands. The city to which Milton came was unmistakably in decline.

These political and social changes were reflected in the city's buildings. In the century before Milton arrived most of the outstanding new buildings had been put up to glorify the house of Medici. Having purchased the Pitti Palace, the Medici enlarged it and had the Boboli Gardens laid out behind it. The Palazzo della Signoria, no longer the Grand Duke's principal residence, became the Palazzo Vecchio. Vasari built the Uffizi to house the Grand Duke's bureaucracy, and linked it with the Pitti Palace by the elevated gallery across the Ponte Vecchio. Down the river Ammanati rebuilt the Ponte alla Carraia and the Ponte Santa Trinità, and connected them by the Lungarno along the north bank. As an insult to the republicans, the Column of Justice was raised on the spot where Cosimo I learned of the defeat of the exiles at Montemurlo; the Florentines called it the Column of Infamy, and said that the figure of Justice stood too high for poor men to reach it. As the central shrine of the Medici cult, the grandiose Chapel of the Princes was begun in 1604; Reresby noted that ''tis now fifty years since it was first begun, and yet not half finished'.[8] It was not completed until 1737, the year in which the last of the Medici rulers died.

Milton has left no record of his reactions to the buildings of Florence and the works of art which they contained. It was the city's intellectual life which impressed him, as conducted in its academies — 'a Florentine institution', he called them, 'which deserves great praise not only for promoting humane studies but also for encouraging friendly intercourse'. Academies, which were by no means confined to Florence, were societies combining literary or scientific with social activities. Some were official bodies under the patronage of the local ruler, such as the Florentine Academy founded by Cosimo I in 1540, and the Accademia della Crusca, founded in 1582 by seceders from the Florentine Academy, which sought to maintain the purity of the language by sifting the bran (*crusca*) from the wheat. It had made itself responsible for the production of a dictionary, the first edition of which had appeared in 1612 and the second in 1623. In a biography of Milton published in 1734 Jonathan Richardson claimed that 'so remarkable was he for his knowledge in the *Italian* Tongue that the *Crusca* (an Academy Set up for the Reducing, and keeping the *Florentine* Language to its First Purity) made no Scruple to Consult Him, Whom they had receiv'd an Academician, on Difficult and Controverted Points'.[9] Milton was never a member of the Accademia della Crusca, but the story may have some foundation; he was interested in linguistic questions, and discussed them with his friend Benedetto Buonmattei, who was a member.

Side by side with these official bodies there were some twenty private academies, of which some were devoted to serious literary studies, some were mutual admiration societies of literary dilettanti, and some were merely social clubs. Milton attended a meeting of one academy, the Svogliati or 'Lazybones', on 16 September 1638 and, according to its minutes, read 'a very learned Latin poem in hexameters'. After his return to Florence he was present at three successive meetings, on 17, 24 and 31 March 1639, at the first two of which he read Latin poems. He later described the poems which he had read on these occasions as 'some trifles which I had in memory, composed at under twenty or thereabout . . . and other things, which I had shifted in scarcity of books and conveniences to patch up amongst them'.[10] The poem in hexameters may have been one of his college exercises, 'Naturam non pati Senium' or 'De Idea Platonica', or the poem to his father, 'Ad Patrem'; it was certainly not 'In Quintum Novembris'. It is difficult to believe, however, that even Milton could repeat from memory poems ranging in length from 39 to 120 lines, and it seems more likely that he had brought copies with him. At the meetings in March 1639 he could have read 'Ad Salsillum' or the epigrams addressed to the singer Leonora Baroni, which he had written in Rome, or 'Mansus', written in Naples. He almost certainly attended meetings of another academy, the Apatisti or 'Dispassionate', of which several of his friends were members, and probably other clubs as well.

The activities of these groups had their lighter side. 'The members would go out of town in spring and picnic by the flower-decked bank of the Arno, improvising sonnets or epigrams or *rispetti*, which some of them had carefully prepared beforehand, or playing wild practical jokes in their youthful exuberance or producing outrageous satires.'[11] When Milton speaks in 'Epitaphium Damonis' of lying stretched out on the grass beside the Arno, listening to Menalcas competing with Lycidas in song and himself joining in the contest, he may be recalling a real event, rather than repeating the commonplaces of pastoral verse.

His fullest account of his Italian tour appeared in *Pro Populo Anglicano Defensio Secunda*, written as a reply to a pamphlet which had attacked his moral character. Listing his Florentine friends, he wrote. 'Time will never destroy my recollection – ever welcome and delightful – of you, Jacopo Gaddi, Carlo Dati, Frescobaldi, Coltellini, Buonmattei, Chimentelli, Francini, and many others.' That he named them in this context clearly implied that he regarded their friendship as itself a reply to his opponents' aspersions; like Yeats he could say, 'my glory was I had such friends'.[12]

He begins his list with Jacopo Gaddi, a wealthy aristocrat, minor poet, author of historical and biographical essays, and 'intellectual and social arbiter of the city, second in importance only to the Grand Duke himself', who 'knew everybody and was known by everybody'. His collections of paintings, sculptures, Egyptian and classical antiquities, books, manuscripts, jewels and medals, and his botanical gardens, containing plants from all over Europe, were famous. Evelyn, copying from a French guidebook, noted that 'Signor *Gaddi* is a letter'd person and has divers rarities statues, & Pictures of the best Masters, & one bust of Marble as much esteem'd as the most antique in *Italy*. Many curious Manuscripts: his best paintings are a Virgin of *del Sarto* mention'd by *Vasari*, a *St. John* of *Raphael* & an *Ecce homo* of *Titian*.'[13] He was well known for his generous hospitality to visiting foreigners, and may have entertained Milton as his guest at his palace in the Piazza Madonna. He had founded the Svogliati, which usually met in his houses and gardens in Florence and Fiesole.

Milton's closest friend in Florence was Carlo Roberto Dati, who when they first met was nearly nineteen. A former pupil of Galileo and the mathematician and physicist Evangelista Torricelli, he combined scientific with literary interests, and in later years published works on astronomy and linguistics as well as a long poem, *La Pace*, and a scholarly work on the ancient Greek painters. He was already a member of the Apatisti and the Platonic Academy, and was later to be elected to the Svogliati, the Accademia della Crusca (of which he became the secretary in 1647) and the Florentine Academy. Agostino Coltellini, a twenty-five-year-old advocate and poet, was the founder of the Apatisti, who met at his house in the Via dell' Oriuolo. Little is known of his friend Pietro Frescobaldi, but the fact that Milton named him immediately after Dati suggests that he highly respected him. Benedetto Buonmattei at fifty-seven was the oldest of the group, and had been a priest for thirty years. He was something of a collector of academies, being a founder-member of the Apatisti and a member of the Florentine Academy, the Accademia della Crusca, the Svogliati and five others. He had published in 1623 a treatise on grammar, *Della Lingua Toscana*, and was revising it for the third edition. Milton's interest in this work is shown by a letter which he wrote to Buonmattei on 10 September 1638, suggesting that for the benefit of foreigners he should include in the new edition notes on pronunciation and details of the best Italian writers. Buonmattei had been appointed the first reader in the Tuscan tongue at Pisa University in 1632, and since 1637 had held a similar post at Florence University. Valerio Chimentelli, who was just eighteen in the summer of 1638, had been an infant prodigy; when he took an oral examination in logic and philosophy in Santa Croce at the age of twelve, he displayed a learning which amazed the onlookers. He had been a member of the Apatisti since 1635. Antonio Francini is remembered solely for his ode in praise of Milton, who published it in the 1645 edition of his poems.

One friend whom Milton did not include in his list was the poet Antonio Malatesti, presumably because he was thought not quite respectable. He had in fact dedicated to Milton a series of mildly improper sonnets, *La Tina* — a fact which was to shock Victorian writers and biographers. His Rabelaisian sense of humour, however, did not exclude Malatesti from Florentine literary society; he was a member of the Apatisti, and Galileo, Coltellini and Chimentelli contributed commendatory poems to his book *La Sfinge*. Milton, whose own jokes could be broad enough, was certainly not offended by the dedication; when writing to Dati in 1647 he included Malatesti among the friends to whom he sent greetings.

The impression that Milton made upon his Florentine friends is recorded in Francini's poem and in the prose testimonial which Dati wrote. They praise his virtues, his good looks, his command of seven languages, his eloquence, his memory, his literary genius, and his knowledge of history and science. In that summer of 1638 he must have been a striking personality, a handsome young man of twenty-nine (but looking younger), of medium height, well-proportioned, with light brown hair, grey eyes and a fair complexion, 'of a very cheerful humour . . . extreme pleasant in his conversation'. [14]

One quality that must have endeared him to Florence and Florence to him was his knowledge and love of music, which all his early biographers emphasize. 'He had a delicate tuneable Voice & had good skill: his father instructed him: he had an Organ in his house: he played on that most.' 'He had an excellent Ear and could bear a part both in Vocal & Instrumental Music.' ''Tis said he Compos'd, though nothing of that has been brought down to Us. He diverted Himself with Performing, which they say he did Well on the Organ and Bas-Viol.' He sent back 'a Chest or two of choice Musick-books of the best Masters flourishing about that time in *Italy*', including Claudio Monteverdi, Luca Marenzio, Orazio Vecchi, Antonio Cifra and Carlo Gesualdo, Prince of Venosa. Italy led Europe in music, and Florence was a major musical centre, where opera had been born from a combination of the spectacular musical entertainments presented at the Medici court and the theoretical discussions of the groups of composers known as the Camerate. Both the Camerate and composers such as Monteverdi, Marenzio and Gesualdo had been concerned with the problem of how a musical setting could provide an emotional equivalent to the words, which also interested Milton, as his sonnet to Henry Lawes suggests. The association in his mind between music and Florence is apparent both in this sonnet, in which he compares Lawes to the Florentine musician Casella, and in the reference to 'immortal Notes and Tuskan Ayre' in his sonnet to Edward Lawrence.[15]

His relations with his Florentine friends were complicated by religious differences. They were Catholics, and there is no reason to doubt that all of them, with the possible exception of Malatesti, were as sincere in their beliefs as Milton was in his. Buonmattei was a priest, Chimentelli took orders in later life, and Dati was the brother of a bishop. Shortly after Milton's visit Coltellini became first a consultant and then censor to the Florentine Inquisition − a post which he held for more than forty years. He left his library to the Theatine monks, and was buried in their church. The papers read at meetings of the Svogliati and the Apatisti were pious in tone, and sometimes dealt with theological questions and the lives of saints. Even in Counter-Reformation Italy, however, it was possible to be a devout Catholic without being a bigot. Coltellini, for example, discharged his duties as censor with what has been described as 'remarkable broad-mindedness', and wrote a poem to a Jewish friend emphasizing that they both worshipped the same God. Dati commented on the persecution of Galileo that 'just as it had been asserted that Galileo was not competent to speak on theology, so priests as such were not competent to speak on philosophy − that some indeed were capable of every stupidity and indeed enormity'.[16]

Milton's Florentine friends were very conscious of the limitations imposed upon freedom of thought, speech and the press by the double tyranny of State and Church. 'The Counter-Reformation snuffed out whatever original thought was still permitted by the newly established dictatorship of Cosimo de' Medici . . . In these fields in which Florentines had been the most active and the most creative in the brilliant period from 1402 to 1527, the Renaissance was dead by the 1580s.' Warned by Galileo's fate, the academies avoided discussing scientific questions; it was not until 1657 that the Accademia del Cimento was founded to promote experimental science, with Ferdinando II and his brother Leopoldo as its patrons and Dati among its members. The Svogliati sometimes met in the Spanish Chapel of Santa Maria Novella, under the fresco depicting the Dominican Inquisitors as the black and white hounds of the Lord, *Domini canes*. It was in the adjoining church that the Dominican Fra Tommaso Cacini had preached in 1614 a sermon declaring that mathematics was the work of the devil, that mathematicians should be banished from all Christian states, and that the idea of a moving earth was very close to heresy. Nor was it only the Church that threatened intellectual freedom. Spies abounded in Florence, and intellectuals could never be certain that one or other of their colleagues might not denounce them to the Grand Duke. Throughout the seventeenth century Machiavelli's city did not produce a single work of any value on history or political theory. History had to be rewritten to avoid offending the Grand Dukes, as well as the Church; a history of the Medici family published in 1610 attributed to them virtually every achievement in the history of Florence. By 1630 'rhetoric and hagiography had at last extinguished all remnants of historiographic speculation'. Milton recorded that

> I have sat among their learned men (for that honour I had) and been counted happy to be born in such a place of philosophic freedom as they supposed England was, while themselves did nothing but bemoan the servile condition into which learning amongst them was brought; that this was it which had damped the glory of Italian wits; that nothing had been there written now these many years but flattery and fustian.[17]

Milton's phrase 'flattery and fustian' comes remarkably close to the modern historian's 'rhetoric and hagiography'.

Milton continues with his well-known reference to his visit to 'the famous Galileo, grown old, a prisoner to the Inquisition for thinking in astronomy otherwise than the Franciscan and Dominican licensers thought'.[18] The wording suggests that he was not familiar with the details of the case, for the persecution of Galileo was the work of the Jesuits and the Dominicans; the Franciscans had nothing to do with it. There has been some speculation about who gave Milton an introduction to Galileo. Dati seems the obvious answer, but a number of other names have been put forward. Galileo corresponded with many of the most original minds in Europe, and he and Milton were linked by an international network of Protestant and liberal Catholic writers, scholars and scientists. Before leaving England Milton had received a letter of advice from his friend Sir Henry Wotton, who when ambassador to Venice had sought to bring it into an alliance with England against Spain and the papacy. In this he cooperated closely with Paolo Sarpi, theological counsellor to the Republic and a friend of Galileo. Milton later made copious notes on Sarpi's *History of the Council of Trent*. In Paris he visited the Dutch jurist and poet Hugo Grotius, who corresponded with Galileo, and probably met

Elia Diodati, an uncle of Charles Diodati. Elia's circle of friends included the French philosopher Pierre Gassendi and the Neapolitan Utopian, revolutionary and poet Tommaso Campanella; all three were among Galileo's correspondents. On his return journey Milton visited in Geneva Elia's brother Giovanni Diodati, Calvinist theologian and translator of the Bible into Italian, who had worked with Wotton and Sarpi to promote religious reform in Venice.

Exactly when and where Milton met Galileo is uncertain. Since his condemnation in 1633 Galileo had been living under house arrest in his villa at Arcetri, just outside Florence, which he was forbidden to enter. After his sight began to fail, however, he was permitted in March 1637 to stay in his son Vincènzo's house, just inside the Porta San Giorgio, while receiving medical treatment. He became completely blind in the following December, but was allowed to remain there, as his health was still poor. In January 1639 he returned to Arcetri, which was his home until his death three years later. If Milton visited him during his first stay in Florence, in August or September 1638, he would have found him at his son's house, a tall building (now No.11) in the steep and narrow Costa San Giorgio; if, on the other hand, the visit took place early in 1639, after his return from Rome, he would have been taken to Il Gioiello ('The Gem'), Galileo's villa. He may, of course, have visited him at both houses. Il Gioiello is an attractive two-storey house, built round three sides of a courtyard, with a turret at one corner. A lifelike bust set in an outer wall looks down on the Via dei Pian dei Giullari and the buses which periodically arrive from the Porta Romana. On a hilltop opposite stands the astrophysical observatory of the University of Florence – a monument which Galileo would probably have appreciated more.

The conversation when they met was not necessarily on scientific subjects, for Galileo's interests included all the arts. His father, Vincènzo Galilei, had been a lutanist, a composer and a musical theorist, and had played a leading part in the activities of the Camerate. From him Galileo had learned to play the lute and the organ, and in his blindness he found comfort in playing his lute. Before he lost his sight he had been a highly competent painter, and had developed a wide knowledge of art; among his friends had been the painter and architect Lodovico Cardi, known as 'Il Cigoli', from the castle where he was born, who said that Galileo had taught him all he knew about perspective. In addition to his scientific works, themselves masterpieces of Italian prose, he wrote lively verse satires and critical studies of Dante, Ariosto and Tasso. According to his pupil and biographer Vincènzo Viviani, even in his last years

> his conversation was full of wit and conceits, rich in grave wisdom and penetrating sentences. His subjects were not only the exact and speculative sciences but also music, letters and poetry. He had a wonderfully retentive memory and knew most of Virgil, Ovid, Horace and Seneca; among the Tuscans Petrarch almost whole, the rhymes of Berni and all of the poem of Ariosto, who was his favourite author.[19]

He and Milton could have found plenty to talk about, and when they tired of talking he may have entertained his guest by playing his lute, or sent for the wine of which he often received gifts from his friends.

Their meeting may have suggested to Milton his visit to the monastery of Santa Maria di Vallombrosa, eighteen miles from Florence, where Galileo had been educated. The lines in *Paradise Lost* which provide the sole evidence for such a visit – 'Thick as Autumnal Leaves that strow the Brooks / In *Vallombrosa*, where th' *Etrurian* shades / High overarcht imbowr'[20] – occur only a dozen lines after a reference to Galileo, as if the mention of him had brought Vallombrosa into Milton's mind. If this is so, he must have met Galileo in 1638, for it was clearly in the autumn of that year that he visited Vallombrosa. It has been questioned whether the visit ever took place, on the ground that the trees around the monastery are coniferous, but the woods contain beeches as well as pines and firs, and it is difficult to imagine why Milton should have introduced such a reference if he was not drawing on personal experience. By the time Wordsworth came there in 1837 the monks, anxious not to disappoint English visitors, could point out Milton's lodging and the lonely spot where he retired to meditate. The monastery stands amid thickly wooded hills, 3,000 feet above sea level, and the approach is so steep that he and his friends probably rode there on mules. Of the present building the thirteenth-century campanile, the fifteenth-century defensive tower and the sixteenth-century library were already there, but the façade of the church was still under construction, and the courtyard through which the visitor now approaches it was not built until over a century later. What Milton did there is left to our imagination; he doubtless inspected the library with interest, and the story that he played the organ in the church may well be true.

During the later stages of his tour he learned that Charles Diodati had died in August 1638, and after his return to England he wrote an elegy for him: 'Epitaphium Damonis'. Like 'Lycidas', the elegy for Edward King which he had written two years before, it took the form of a pastoral; unlike 'Lycidas', it was in Latin. Diodati had meant far more to Milton than King, and when his deepest feelings were involved, as now, he preferred to write in a learned language rather than to wear his heart upon his sleeve. He also intended the poem for his Italian friends and, besides recalling Diodati's Tuscan descent, introduced a complimentary reference to Dati and Francini. When he was satisfied with the poem he had it privately printed, and sent copies to his friends in Florence, as he later explained in a letter to Dati, 'so that it might be, however small a proof of talent, by no means an obscure proof of my love for you, at least in those few little verses inserted – as it were inlaid – there'.[21]

Dati wrote a letter of thanks, and followed it with two other letters, none of which reached Milton. In 1645 Milton published his poems, English, Italian and Latin, in a double volume. He would have liked to send Dati a copy of the Latin poems, but unfortunately these included 'In Quintum Novembris' and five epigrams on the Gunpowder Plot, all strongly anti-Catholic in tone. Fearing that he might offend his friends, and even bring them into danger from the Inquisition, he let the matter rest.

Early in 1647, eight years after he left Florence, he finally received a letter from Dati. Milton's reply, written on 21 April, eloquently conveys the strength of his feelings for Florence and his friends there. His separation from them, he wrote, had been very painful for him, and had 'fixed those stings in my heart which even now rankle whenever I think that, reluctant and actually torn away, I left so many companions and at the same time such good friends and such congenial ones in a single city – a city distant indeed but to me most dear'. After mentioning the publication of his poems, he continued:

> I shall shortly send you that part of the poems which is in Latin; and I should have sent it of my own accord long since, had I not suspected that they would be unpleasing to your ears because of those words spoken rather sharply on some pages against the Roman Pope. Now I beg you to obtain from my other friends (for of you I am certain) that same indulgence to freedom of speech which, as you know, you have been used to granting in the past with singular kindness – I do not mean to your Dante and Petrarch in this case, but to me.

He concluded the letter with greetings to 'Coltellini, Francini, Frescobaldi, Malatesti, Chimentelli the younger, and any other of our group whom you know to be especially fond of me — in short to the whole Gaddian Academy.'[22]

Dati replied on 1 November, expressing his 'boundless joy' that 'remembrance of me is kept so fresh and affectionate in the most generous soul of John Milton'. As a hint that the promised book had not yet arrived, he added, 'I am anxiously awaiting your poems, in which I believe that I shall be given ample reason for admiring the fineness of your wit, save in those, however, which are in dispraise of my religion, and which, although coming from the lips of a friend, can only be excused, not praised.' A month later he wrote to acknowledge the receipt of two copies of 'your most learned poems, than which there could not have come to me a dearer gift'. Local news followed: the Grand Duke had appointed him Lecturer in Humane Letters to the Florentine Academy, and Chimentelli Professor of Greek Literature at Pisa University. He ended the letter with affectionate greetings from Frescobaldi, Coltellini, Francini, Vincènzo Galileo and 'many others'.[23]

If other correspondence followed it has not survived, but Milton certainly wrote official letters to Florence in his capacity as Secretary for Foreign Tongues to the Council of State. In the first of these, dated 20 January 1652, he gracefully complimented Ferdinando II on his hospitality to 'certain youths, the noblest and most honourable of our nation, who either journey through your cities or sojourn there to improve their studies'.[24]

Florence was never far from his memory; his fullest account of his stay there appears in *Defensio Secunda*, written in 1654. In *Paradise Lost* he frequently looks back to his Italian tour, and especially to Florence. His friendship in Naples with Giovanni Battista Manso, the friend and patron of Tasso, whom Milton classed with Homer and Virgil as one of the three supreme masters of epic poetry, gave him the idea of writing an epic on Arthur or some other 'king or knight before the conquest'. By 1642 at latest he was also planning a verse drama on the fall of man, for which his model, at least in part, seems to have been Giambattista Andreini's *Adamo*. When he finally decided that his poem on the Fall should be in epic, not in dramatic form, and should be written in blank verse, he again had an Italian model, in Tasso's *Le Sette Giornate del Mondo Creato*, written while he was enjoying Manso's patronage. It is possible that in the conception

and writing of *Paradise Lost* Milton was also influenced, perhaps unconsciously, by memories of paintings which he had seen in Italy, such as
Masaccio's fresco of the expulsion from Eden in Santa Maria del
Carmine, or Michelangelo's ceiling in the Sistine Chapel. Some details in
the poem may have been suggested by Italian paintings; his angels, for
example, have gorgeously coloured wings, like those in Fra Angelico's
paintings in San Marco. Is it a coincidence that these passages occur in
close proximity to references to Galileo and his telescope, as if one memory of Florence had called up another? Echoes of Italian poetry can also
be detected in the poem. In the description of Eden references to 'eternal spring' and the rape of Proserpina appear together; similar references
in Dante's description of the Terrestrial Paradise are separated by nearly
100 lines but were probably linked in Milton's mind by the appearance of
the word 'primavera' in both.[25]

Above all, his mind frequently turned back to Galileo; as so much of
the action of *Paradise Lost* takes place in outer space, this is not surprising.
Satan's shield is compared to

> the Moon, whose Orb
> Through Optic Glass the *Tuscan* Artist views
> At Ev'ning from the top of *Fesole*,
> Or in *Valdarno*, to descry new Lands,
> Rivers or Mountains in her spotty Globe.[26]

The markings on the moon, at which he may have gazed through Galileo's
telescope, clearly fascinated Milton, for he returns to the subject several
times. In this passage he has let his imagination run away with him;
although Galileo had announced in his *Sidereus Nuncius* his identification of
mountains on the moon higher than those on earth, he had said nothing
about rivers. There are rivers on the moon, however, in Canto XXXIV of
Ariosto's *Orlando Furioso*, a passage which Milton had quoted in *Of
Reformation Touching Church-Discipline in England*.[27] There may be another
association of ideas here, as in the reference to Vallombrosa a few lines
below; Galileo greatly admired Ariosto, and had written an essay maintaining that he was a greater poet than Tasso. It is highly probable that he
discussed Ariosto with Milton, and that henceforth Galileo and Ariosto
were associated in his mind.

This theory is strikingly confirmed in Book III of *Paradise Lost*, in which

Satan travels from the realm of Chaos through the universe to the earth. In such descriptions Milton was at a disadvantage for, despite his meeting with Galileo, he took little interest in recent developments in astronomy. The Ptolemaic system, which placed an immovable earth at the centre of the universe, had been abandoned after 1600 by most English scientists in favour of either the Copernican system or a combination of Tycho Brahe's system, whereby the sun and moon revolved around the earth and the planets revolved around the sun, with William Gilbert's theory of the rotation of the earth. Milton, however, when educating his nephews in the 1640s, several years after his encounter with Galileo, used as his most up-to-date astronomical textbook the *Sphaera Mundi* of Joannes de Sacrobosco, an exposition of the Ptolemaic system written about 1250. In *Paradise Lost*, written about 1658–63, when the Copernican system was ousting the Tychonic, Milton avoided committing himself to any one conception of the universe; it has been disputed whether he was ignorant of the existence of the Tychonic system, or whether his references to a geocentric system are meant to cover both the Ptolemaic and the Tychonic. In either case, he lagged far behind contemporary scientific opinion.

On emerging from Chaos Satan walks on 'the firm opacous Globe / Of this round World, whose first convex divides / The luminous inferior Orbs'[28] – in other words, the Primum Mobile, the outermost of the nine crystal spheres which made up the Ptolemaic universe. Even in the 1660s, it is clear, Milton still thought in terms of the Ptolemaic system.

At this point in the poem he introduces an invention of his own, the Paradise of Fools, located beyond the Primum Mobile, which after the fall of man is to be occupied by

> all things vain, and all who in vain things
> Built thir fond hopes of Glorie or lasting fame,
> Or happiness in this or th' other life
>
> . . . .
>
> All th' unaccomplisht works of Natures hand,
> Abortive, monstrous, or unkindly mixt
>
> . . . .
>
> Embryo's and Idiots, Eremites and Friers
> White, Black and Grey, with all thir trumperie.[29]

There is no doubt that this conception was suggested to Milton by Canto XXXIV of *Orlando Furioso*, in which Astolfo, in his search for Orlando's lost wits, visits the moon, where everything lost on earth is to be found. Ariosto's catalogue of the things Astolfo discovers there is primarily comic, though containing elements of social and anticlerical satire; Milton's similar catalogue is primarily an anti-Catholic satire, but contains elements of grim humour. We owe a debt of gratitude to Ariosto for this passage of light relief.

In his description of Satan's journey through the universe to the sun Milton refuses his endorsement to any of the rival systems:

> Thither his course he bends
> Through the calm Firmament; but up or downe
> By center, or eccentric, hard to tell.

At the climax of this section, where Satan lands on the sun, comes a second reference to Galileo in the poem:

> There lands the Fiend, a spot like which perhaps
> Astronomer in the Suns lucent Orbe
> Through his glaz'd Optic Tube yet never saw.

Galileo was not the only astronomer in the early seventeenth century to use the telescope to observe sunspots, but there is no doubt that it is he whom Milton has in mind. In his description of sunset in Book IV:

> the Sun now fall'n
> Beneath th' *Azores*; whether the prime Orb,
> Incredible how swift, had thither rowld
> Diurnal, or this less volubil Earth
> By shorter flight to th' East, had left him there,

he again leaves it to the reader to choose between a geocentric or a heliocentric universe.[30]

Galileo is mentioned by name in Book V — the only contemporary of Milton's so honoured in *Paradise Lost*:

> by night the Glass

49

> Of *Galileo*, less assur'd, observes
> Imagind Lands and Regions in the Moon.

Yet in the very lines where he pays Galileo this honour Milton shows himself sceptical of his theories. The word 'imagind' suggests that, like Simplicio in Galileo's *Dialogue Concerning the Two Chief World Systems*, a work which he had read, Milton believed that 'the appearances you speak of, the mountains, rocks, ridges, valleys, etc., are all illusions'. Later in Book V Raphael explains to Adam that all created things need to be fed, and that the air feeds the moon,

> Whence in her visage round those spots, unpurg'd
> Vapours not yet into her substance turnd.

The fact that this theory is put into an archangel's mouth suggest that Milton meant it to be accepted. After this retreat to pre-Galilean astronomy, however, he refers in Book VII to Venus's 'horns', thereby paying tribute to Galileo's discovery that Venus has phases like the moon. [31]

The rival systems between which he hesitated are debated at length in Book VIII. After hearing Raphael's account of the creation, Adam sensibly enquires why the heavenly bodies should travel such enormous distances every day merely to supply light to the earth, when it would be a better arrangement if the earth revolved round the sun. Raphael, while assuring Adam that there is nothing wrong in scientific inquiry, suggests that God left these problems unsettled so that astronomers could amuse him with their 'quaint Opinions wide'. He first defends the Ptolemaic system with specious arguments, then admits that Adam may be right, and concludes by advising him to enjoy life and leave scientific problems alone. In Book X Milton states that after the fall God ended the perpetual spring which existed in Eden, but offers alternative explanations of how it was done: whether by tilting the earth's axis if the sun is the centre of the universe, or by altering the sun's course if the earth is. [32] He also leaves open the question, much debated at the time, whether life exists on other planets, and especially on the moon. In Galileo's *Dialogue* Salviati, while not ruling out the possibility that forms of life 'very different and entirely unimaginable by us' exist on the moon, holds that 'plants and animals similar to ours would not be produced there', for two reasons: for fifteen days in every month the moon is continually exposed to the heat of the sun, and there are no rains there, 'because if clouds collected in any part of it, as around the earth, they would hide some of the things on the moon that we see with the telescope'. Milton, who speculates several times in *Paradise Lost* on the possibility of life on other worlds, makes Raphael directly contradict Galileo when arguing that there may be life on the moon:

> Her spots thou seest
> As Clouds, and Clouds may rain, and Rain produce
> Fruits in her soft'nd Soile, for some to eate
> Allotted there.

This presumably is a repetition of Raphael's earlier theory that the markings on the moon are 'vapours' on which the moon feeds. Despite his fascination with Galileo, Milton's science remained 'mainly classical in origin, medieval in implication, literary in function'.[33]

Milton described Florence in 1654 as 'that city which I have always admired above all others because of the elegance, not just of its tongue, but also of its wit'. His four months spent there were a landmark in his life.

> In the private Academies of Italy, whither I was favoured to resort, [he wrote in 1642], perceiving that some trifles which I had in memory, composed at under twenty or thereabout (for the manner is that every one must give some proof of his wit and reading there), met with acceptance above what was looked for; and other things, which I had shifted in scarcity of books and conveniences to patch up amongst them, were received with written encomiums, which the Italian is not forward to bestow on men of this side the Alps; I began thus far to assent both to them and divers of my friends here at home, and not less to an inward prompting which now grew daily upon me, that by labour and intense study (which I take to be my portion in this life), joined with the strong propensity of nature, I might perhaps leave something so written to aftertimes as they should not willingly let it die.

It was not vanity alone which persuaded him in 1645 to publish the 'written encomiums' of Dati, Francini and other Italian friends with his poems. But he learned other things in Florence besides confidence in his own powers. His conversations with his friends and his visit to Galileo taught him the necessity of 'the liberty to know, to utter, and to argue freely according to conscience'. He left Florence in the spring of 1639 a man dedicated, not only to poetry, but also to 'liberty's defence, my noble task'. [34]

John Milton
from EPITAPHIUM DAMONIS

Go home unfed, my lambs, your master has no time for you now.

Alas, what passion for roaming lured me to traverse
Towering cliffs and snowy Alps to unknown shores?
Was it so important to see buried Rome,
Even if Rome had still remained the city
Tityrus left his flocks and pastures to see,
That I must desert you, a friend so precious to me,
Putting so many deep oceans, so many mountains,
Forests, crags and roaring torrents between us?
Surely I might have touched your hand at the end,
Closed your eyes as you lay peacefully dying
And said 'Goodbye! Remember me, as you ascend to the stars.'

Go home unfed, my lambs, your master has no time for you now.

Though I shall never tire of remembering you,
Young Tuscan shepherds, devotees of the Muses,
Here too were Grace and Wit; and, Damon, you too were a Tuscan,
Tracing descent from the Lucumo's ancient city.
O how delighted I was, beside the cool murmuring Arno,
Stretched in the poplar grove where the grass is softest,
Plucking now the violets, now the myrtles above me,
When I heard Lycidas competing in song with Menalcas!
I too dared enter the contest, nor I think did I greatly
Displease you, for I have here still beside me your presents,
Pipes with waxen stops, winebowls and osier baskets,
And Dati and Francini, both of Lydian blood,
Both renowned for eloquence and learning,
Have taught their beech-trees to re-echo my name.

Go home unfed, my lambs, your master has no time for you now.

Translated from the Latin by Charles Hobday

Antonio Francini
ODE TO JOHN MILTON, AN ENGLISH GENTLEMAN

Up with me, Clio, through the air,
Till of the stars a coronet I twine!
No more the Greek god fair
On Pindus or Helicon has leaves enough divine:
To greater merit be greater honours given,
To heavenly worth rewards from heaven.

To Time's voracious maw
High virtue ever cannot remain a prey,
Nor can Oblivion's jaw
Tear from the memory its honoured day.
To my lyre's bow an arrow strong and sound
Let Virtue fit, and Death shall bite the ground.

All in the ocean deep
Doth England, with great surges girdled round,
Fit isolation keep,
For that her worth exceeds all human bound.
This land bears men of such heroic breed
That among us they pass for gods indeed.

To Virtue in exile
Give they a faithful refuge in their breast;
All else to them is vile;
Only in this they find their joy and zest.
Repeat it thou, Giovanni, and make plain
By thy true virtue how true is my strain.

Far from his native land
The artist's burning passion Zeuxis drew,
When he heard the rumour grand
Of Helen, which Fame's golden trumpet blew;
And, to depict her beauty at its fairest,
From fairest forms he culled the very rarest.

So the ingenious bee
Extracts with pains the honey for her cells
From lily or from pea
And from the rose and all the meadow-bells;
So diverse chords sweetly combine in one,
And various voices make a unison.

All truest glory loving,
Milton, from thine own clime, through various parts,
A pilgrim thou camest roving,
In each to seek out sciences and arts.
Kingly-great Gaul it hath been thine to see,
And now the worthiest wights of Italy.

A workman nigh divine,
Virtue alone regarding, hath thy thought
Beheld in each confine
Whoso still treads the noble path he ought,
Then of the best selecting yet the best
To form the image of one perfectest.

Our native Florentines,
Or who in Florence have learnt the Tuscan tongue,
Whose memory still shines
Throughout the world, eternalized in song, —
These thou wouldst master for thy private treasure,
Making their converse in their works thy pleasure.

In Babel's proud-built tower
For thee in vain did Jove all speech confound,
That jargon-shattering hour
When the huge ruin mounded the flat ground;
For, besides English, thou canst purely speak
Spanish, French, Tuscan, Roman, and old Greek.

The secrets most profound
Which Nature holds concealed in earth and heaven,
Whose darksome depths to sound

To earthly genius it is hardly given,
Thou knowest clearly; and, to crown the whole,
Of moral virtue thou hast reached the goal.

Beat not for thee Time's wings!
Let him stand moveless; crushed in one the years
Whose rolling sequence brings
Damage too much to what man most reveres;
In that all deeds worthy of verse or story
Thy memory clasps in simultaneous glory.

Give me thy own sweet lyre,
Wouldst thou I spoke of thy sweet gift of song,
By which thou dost aspire
To take thy place in the celestial throng.
Thames will attest this, seeing that she can
Rival Permessus, having thee her swan.

I, who, by Arno's stream,
Try to express thy merit in fit ways,
Know that I mar my theme,
And humbly learn to reverence, not to praise:
My tongue I then refrain, and let my heart
In silent wonder do her better part.

Translated from the Italian by David Masson[35]

3

Thomas Gray

On the whole Horace Mann, the British chargé d'affaires at the court of the Grand Duke of Tuscany, found life satisfying. His duties, which mainly consisted of keeping an eye on the Pretender's court in Rome and making himself useful to visiting members of the British upper classes, were not arduous. Florence had a lively social life, in which his official position allowed him to play a prominent part. The only drawbacks to this existence were the dilatoriness of the Treasury in paying his salary, which obliged him to live on money borrowed from his father, and his sufferings from piles. Early in December 1739, however, he was confronted with an unusually heavy responsibility, for he was expecting the arrival of Horace Walpole, the twenty-two-year-old son of the Prime Minister, Sir Robert Walpole, and his travelling companion, a Mr Gray. In any circumstances the British representative in Florence would have been eager to ensure that the Prime Minister's son enjoyed his stay there, but Mann was particularly anxious to make a good impression. The Manns and the Walpoles were distant cousins, and it was to Sir Robert's patronage that Robert Mann owed the many contracts and official appointments which had enabled him to make his fortune, and his son Horace to obtain his post at Florence. An unfavourable report from the younger Walpole would have brought Mann's diplomatic career to an abrupt end. In fact, he need not have worried; Walpole and Mann were immediately on such excellent terms that after Walpole left Florence, although they never met again, they kept up a regular correspondence until Mann's death forty-five years later.

Walpole and Gray came from very different social circles, but there were resemblances between their home backgrounds which permanently affected their psychology. Relations between Sir Robert and Lady Walpole had not been happy, and Sir Robert had made no secret of his *affaire* with Maria Skerrett. Lady Walpole lavished her affection upon her youngest son, who passionately returned her love and deeply resented his father's treatment of her. After her death in 1737 Sir Robert's marriage to his mistress deepened the gulf between his son and himself, but the second Lady Walpole's death only three months later relieved the situation. Father and son gradually drew closer together; Horace Walpole in his maturity combined reverence for his mother's memory with a fierce loyalty to his father. Gray's father, a scrivener and exchange-broker, was mentally unbalanced and often violent; his mother, who ran a millinery business with an unmarried sister, adored her son, the only survivor of twelve children. It is not surprising that there was a strong homosexual element in the make-up of both Walpole and Gray. Both struck their contemporaries as somewhat effeminate in their ways. Each had a circle of friends many of whom, like themselves, were lifelong bachelors. Walpole sought out the society of women much older than himself; his tragedy *The Mysterious Mother* deals with incest between a woman and her son. In 1760 Gray had the opportunity to marry a beautiful, intelligent and wealthy woman twelve years his junior, Henrietta Jane Speed, who was obviously in love with him, but he preferred his lonely bachelor rooms at Cambridge. At the age of fifty-three he underwent perhaps the most intense emotional experience of his life when he fell passionately in love with a twenty-four-year-old Swiss, Charles-Victor de Bonstetten.

Gray and Walpole had met at Eton, where together with two other boys, Richard West and Thomas Ashton, they formed a group which they called the Quadruple Alliance. All four wrote verse, but West was recognized by the others as the best poet among them. Both Gray and West later wrote poems looking back nostalgically on their days at school. To Gray, the shy and sensitive boy from an unhappy middle-class home, the friendship of Walpole, the witty and sophisticated son of the most powerful man in England, must have been an intoxicating experience, and there can be little doubt that he fell in love with him. Walpole's feelings for Gray were cooler but still affectionate.

In 1734 Gray was admitted at Peterhouse College, Cambridge, and Ashton at King's, where Walpole joined him in the following year. West went up to Oxford, where he suffered acute loneliness in the absence of his friends. Gray and Walpole studied Italian under Girolamo Bartolomeo Piazza, a former Dominican friar who after settling in England had been converted to Anglicanism. Gray clearly enjoyed his Italian studies. 'I learn Italian like any dragon,' he wrote to West in March 1737, 'and in two months am got through the 16th book of Tasso, whom I hold in great admiration: I want you to learn too, that I may know your opinion of him; nothing can be easier than that language to any one who knows Latin and French already, and there are few so copious and expressive.'[1]

From Tasso Gray passed on to the study of Dante, a poet little appreciated in England or even in Italy in the early eighteenth century. Ignoring literary fashions, he learned to admire the *Divina Commedia* with a passion which remained with him throughout his life. The opening line of the 'Elegy', as he himself admitted, was suggested by Dante's 'squilla di lontano / Che paia il giorno pianger che si more' ('the distant bell that seems to mourn the dying day').

He was particularly impressed, like Chaucer before him, by the episode of Ugolino of Pisa, of which he made a blank-verse translation, probably while still at Cambridge. When in 1762 he heard the undergraduate Norton Nicholls quote Dante he at once entered into conversation with him and recommended him to read the Ugolino episode. Walpole, on the other hand, never learned to appreciate Dante; as late as 1782 he described him as 'extravagant, absurd, disgusting, in short a Methodist parson in Bedlam'.[2]

Gray left Cambridge in 1738, intending to read for the Bar, but when early in the following year Walpole invited him to join him on a tour of France he welcomed the opportunity to escape, if only temporarily, from studies which he was finding increasingly irksome. Walpole's continued affection for him was manifested not only in the invitation and his offer to pay all the expenses of the tour, but also in the fact that he made a will, without Gray's knowledge, bequeathing him all his possessions.

They left England in March and made their way slowly through France. In October Walpole received a letter from Sir Robert giving him permission to go on to Italy. 'All the scheme of spending the winter in the south of France is laid aside', Gray wrote to his father, 'and we are to pass it in a much finer country. You may imagine I am not sorry to have this opportunity of seeing the place in the world that best deserves it.' They had a terrifying journey over the Alps, 'as well armed as possible against the cold, with muffs, hoods, and masks of beaver, fur-boots, and bear skins', during which Walpole's fat little black spaniel Tory was carried off by a wolf before their eyes. They were glad to rest for a week at Turin, although they thought the city dull; here they made the acquaintance of the young Earl of Lincoln and his tutor, Joseph Spence, Professor of Poetry at Oxford and friend of Pope. After a week in Genoa ('a charming place, and one that deserved a longer stay'), they travelled via Parma, Modena ('an ill built melancholy place') and the Lombard countryside ('one of the most beautiful imaginable') to Bologna, where they spent twelve days. And so across the Apennines, which they found 'not so horrid as the Alps', to Florence, where they arrived on 16 December.[3] They were met at the Porta San Gallo by Mann's servant, who conducted them to his master's house.

Mann lived at the Casa Ambrogi in the Via dei Bardi, almost opposite the Uffizi. The house no longer exists, having been blown up by the retreating Germans in 1944 in order to block traffic across the Ponte Vecchio. After his promotion to resident he leased the Palazzo Manetti, at Via San Spirito 23/25, as his official residence in August 1740, and had the royal arms put over the door, so that Walpole referred to the house as 'the King's Arms'. He kept on the Casa Ambrogi ('my sweet apartment over the river') as a guest-house for visiting notables, and it was here that Gray and Walpole stayed for most of the time they were in Florence. They were delighted with their lodgings, and Mann's kindly hospitality won their hearts. Walpole wrote to his cousin Henry Conway in July 1740, 'I am lodged with Mr Mann, the best of creatures. I have a terreno all to myself, with an open gallery on the Arno, where I am now writing to you. Over against me is the famous Gallery; and, on either hand, two fair bridges. Is not this charming and cool?'[4]

In some respects Florence had changed little since Milton's visit a century before. The population had increased by only a few thousand, and the new buildings were mostly churches and convents. Politically the situation had been transformed. It had long been obvious that the Grand Duke, Gian Gastone, would not father an heir, and the great powers had agreed to recognize Don Carlos, the younger son of the King of Spain, as his successor. When the War of the Polish Succession ended, however, Carlos became King of Naples and Sicily, which he had already overrun; the unsuccessful candidate for the Polish throne received Lorraine, which was to pass to France on his death; and Francis, Duke of Lorraine, was given the reversion of Tuscany as a consolation prize, together with the hand of the Emperor's daughter Maria Theresa. Francis, who succeeded Gian Gastone in 1737, made only one visit to Florence in the twenty-eight years of his reign; it lasted four months, and to celebrate the occasion an ancient column in the Piazza San Marco was taken down and a triumphal arch was erected outside the Porta San Gallo. In his absence power was wielded by a Council of Regency, headed by the Grand Duke's plenipotentiary, Prince Marc de Craon, to whom Walpole and Gray were presented on the day after their arrival. 'The princess, and he, were extremely civil to the name of Walpole,' Gray wrote to his mother, 'so we were asked to stay to supper, which is as much as to say, you may come and sup here whenever you please; for after the first invitation this is always understood.' Two days later Walpole was presented to the last of the Medici, Gian Gastone's sister Anna Maria, 'a stately old lady', who 'received him with much ceremony, standing under a large black canopy'.[5] These courtesy visits made, he and Gray settled down to a protracted stay as Mann's guests.

Gray was a conscientious sightseer and took careful notes on the paintings in the Palazzo Pitti and the classical sculptures in the Uffizi. His tastes were those of his age; he admired the great Renaissance masters, and still more the fashionable seventeenth-century painters Guido Reni and Carlo Maratti. Walpole, on the other hand, soon became bored. 'I see several things that please me calmly, but *à force d'en avoir vu* I have left off screaming Lord! this! and Lord! that!' he wrote to West when they had been in Florence little more than a month. 'To speak sincerely, Calais surprised me more than anything I have seen since. I recollect the joy I used to propose if I could but once see the great duke's gallery; I walk into it now with as little emotion as I should with St Paul's.'[6]

The advent of Carnival relieved his boredom. 'I have done nothing but slip out of my domino into bed, and out of bed into my domino,' he wrote to West on 27 February 1740. 'The end of the Carnival is frantic, bacchanalian; all the morn one makes parties in masque to the shops and coffee-houses, and all the evening to the operas and balls. *Then I have danced, good gods, how I have danced!*'[7] Gray, who was not a dancing man, said nothing of the Carnival in his letters, and presumably took little part in the celebrations.

After Carnival came Lent, which both found trying. Gray told his mother in March that 'the diversions of a Florentine Lent are composed of a sermon in the morning, full of hell and the devil; a dinner at noon, full of fish and meager diet; and in the evening, what is called a Conversazione, a sort of assembly at the principal people's houses, full of I cannot tell what'. To make matters worse, the weather became too cold for sightseeing. Walpole complained to West that

in Italy they seem to have found out how hot their climate is, but not how cold; for there are scarce any chimneys, and most of the apartments painted in fresco; so that one has the additional horror of freezing with imaginary marble. The men hang little earthen pans of coals upon their wrists, and the women have portable stoves under their petticoats to warm their nakedness.'[8]

To escape from the cold and boredom, Gray and Walpole left for Rome on 21 March. The Pope had died a few weeks before, and they looked forward to witnessing his successor's coronation, as well as the Holy Week ceremonies. Gray was thoroughly in his element in Rome, inspecting classical sites and copying Latin inscriptions. They visited Naples, and saw the excavations which had just begun at Herculaneum. Walpole, however, soon became bored again. The Conclave showed no sign of reaching a decision; he was made far less fuss of than in Florence, for Rome was the residence of the Pretender and his court, and Jacobite influence was strong in Roman society; and Rome was notoriously unhealthy in summer. He therefore decided to return to Florence, although Gray would gladly have remained in Rome indefinitely. As Walpole explained to Conway, 'intend I did to stay for a new Popedom, but the old eminencies are cross and obstinate, and will not choose one, the Holy Ghost does not know when. There is a horrid thing called the *mal 'aria*, that comes to Rome every summer and kills one, and I did not care for being killed so far from Christian burial.'[9]

After they returned to Florence on 8 July, Gray settled down to enjoy life at the Casa Ambrogi, despite his regrets at leaving Rome. 'We are settled here with Mr Mann in a charming apartment,' he wrote to his father.

> The river Arno runs under our windows, which we can fish out of. The sky is so serene, and the air so temperate, that one continues in the open air all night long in a slight nightgown without any danger; and the marble bridge is the resort of every body, where they hear music, eat iced fruits and sup by moonlight.

Walpole's letters give a similar picture of a *dolce far niente* existence

> We have operas, concerts, and balls, mornings and evenings. I dare not tell you all one's idlenesses; you would look so grave and senatorial, at hearing that one rises at eleven in the morning, goes to the opera at nine at night, to supper at one, and to bed at three! But literally here the evenings and nights are so charming and so warm, one can't avoid 'em.[10]

There was congenial English company with which to share this pleasant easy-going life. John Chute, a forty-year-old bachelor, and his cousin Francis Whithed, eighteen years his junior, moved into Casa Ambrogi with them. The Earl of Lincoln and Spence arrived in October, and dined with them almost every day, although Mann found Spence a bore. 'Spence, I take it, will always be a fellow of a college; that is with all their classical learning extreme tiresome,'[11] he later wrote to Walpole. A very different character, Sir Francis Dashwood, the future leader of the notorious monks of Medmenham Abbey, was also in Florence. Other English visitors were less congenial, such as the eccentric poetess Lady Mary Wortley Montagu. Gray, Walpole and Dashwood tried their hands at the game of searching for suitable descriptions of various people by opening a Virgil at random, and were delighted when for Lady Mary they found the words 'Insanam vatem aspicies' — 'You will see an insane poetess.'

There was congenial Italian company too, and Walpole was drawn into the game of *cicisbeismo*. Marriage among the Florentine aristocracy was a business matter, and husband and wife were expected to beget heirs but not to love each other or even to appear in public together. The wife would have her recognized escort or *cicisbeo*, with whom her relationship might take the form of a mild flirtation or passionate love, and the husband in turn would act as *cicisbeo* to another man's wife. Walpole became the *cicisbeo* of Elisabetta, the beautiful young wife of the Cavaliere Pietro Grifoni, and was generally believed by his friends to be her lover. He sent her letters and presents after leaving Florence, took her portrait to England and kept it in his bedroom, but he was certainly not in love with her. In October 1741 he wrote to Mann, 'How excessively obliging to go to Madam Grifoni's *festino*! but believe me I shall be angry, if for my sake you do things that are out of your character: don't you know that I am infinitely fonder of that than of her?'[12] All the love was on her side, and for some time after his departure she continued to send him pathetic messages through Mann, hoping in vain for some response.

Gray and Walpole also found friends among the Florentine intellectuals. One was Dr Antonio Cocchi, the most distinguished physician in the city. Having spent three years in London, he spoke English fluently, as well as several other languages, and served as medical adviser to Mann and the English colony. In addition to his medical achievements, he was antiquarian, philologist and critic; it was he who discovered and published Cellini's autobiography. Unorthodox in his religious views, he was several times questioned by the Inquisition, which suspected him of circulating banned books, and his posthumously published book on marriage was placed on the Index. In appearance he was a bohemian, with 'free-flowing hair and messy, unbuttoned shirts that made him look like a Lord Byron before the times'.[13] Another intellectual friend was Giuseppe Maria Buondelmonte, who wrote commentaries on *Paradise Lost*, Locke's *Essay concerning Human Understanding* and the *Encyclopédie*. Walpole made a neat English translation of one of his poems, and Gray produced a Latin version of it.

Cocchi and Buondelmonte, like many of the city's liberal and Anglophile intellectuals, were both Freemasons. The Florentine lodge had been founded in 1732 or 1733 by Lord Middlesex, and soon had about sixty members, among them English residents or visitors, Florentine nobles, ecclesiastics and intellectuals, and two Irish Augustinians from the convent of San Spirito. After 1737 it enjoyed the protection of the Grand Duke Francis, who was himself a Freemason. When in 1738 Clement XII issued the bull *In Eminenti*, which condemned Freemasonry as heretical, de Craon forbade its publication in Tuscany, on the ground that as the Freemasons were not a religious organization it encroached on the rights of the Government. The Inquisition retaliated in 1739 by arresting Tommaso Crudeli, a poet and Freemason. Mann and Cocchi used their influence on his behalf, and although found guilty of reading forbidden books and using irreverent language on sacred subjects he was finally released in 1741. Neither Walpole nor Gray was a Freemason, but they must have been aware of these developments.

As their translations of Buondelmonte's poem indicate, both of them wrote a certain amount of verse while in Florence. By July 1740 Walpole had completed 'An Epistle from Florence to T. A. Esq.; Tutor to the Earl of P.', a poem of some 400 lines on the theme 'The greatest curses any Age has known / Have issued from the Temple or the Throne', combining a violent attack on Catholic superstition with a summary of English history written with a strong Whig bias. The only reference to Florence is Walpole's admission that

> fair Florence on her peaceful shore,
> Free from the din of war and battle's roar,
> Has lap'd me trifler in inglorious ease.

Although Gray praised it as 'full of spirit and thought, and a good deal of poetic fire', it is in fact a decidedly flat attempt to imitate Pope.[14] There is more spirit and fire, if not much more thought, in Walpole's 'Inscription for the Neglected Column in the Place of St. Mark at Florence', in which he damns the Medici grand dukes and Francis of Lorraine indiscriminately, and looks forward to the appearance of 'a new Brutus' who will restore liberty to Florence. His revolutionary sentiments need not be taken seriously. Although he could glibly repeat the Whig cant about liberty, Sir Robert Walpole's system of government remained his ideal; he had no compunction about living at the taxpayers' expense on the sinecures which his father had given him, and strongly opposed all projects for parliamentary reform. He hung a copy of Charles I's death-warrant on his wall, with the inscription 'Major Charta', yet when confronted with a real revolution in France he reacted as hysterically as Burke. Nevertheless, Florence's republican traditions could move him sufficiently as a young man to inspire lines which make him a connecting link between the genuine revolutionaries Milton and Shelley.

The poems which Gray wrote in Florence were all in Latin, and of these only the brief farewell to Fiesole, apparently written just before his departure, contains any reference to the district. The fact that he devoted his energies at this time mainly to *De Principiis Cogitandi*, an attempt to expound the philosophy of John Locke in Latin hexameters, suggests that he was less responsive than Walpole to Florence and its traditions. Before 1741–2 his poetic output consisted almost entirely of Latin verse or translations; he wrote far less original English verse than Walpole or West, and possibly less than Ashton, who sent Walpole a fifty-two-line verse letter in 1737. His only original poems dating from this period which have survived are a humorous verse letter to Walpole written in 1734, and four lines in a letter of 1736. Even after English replaced Latin as his verse medium, he produced little — fewer than 1,600 lines in thirty years, of which he published only some 900 lines; his Latin and Greek poems and his translations of Latin, Italian, Norse and Welsh verse in fact surpass in bulk his original English verse.

In his essay on Gray, Matthew Arnold quoted a friend's remark that in his last illness he 'never spoke out' about how ill he was, and commented, '*He never spoke out*. In these four words is contained the whole history of Gray, both as a man and as a poet.' Arnold gave as the reason for his poetic sterility that 'Gray, a born poet, fell upon an age of prose.'[15] This is certainly untrue. Born a century earlier, he would have been merely another minor Metaphysical; a century later, another minor Tennysonian. Fortunately for him, his reputation was established in the 1750s, which produced less verse of high quality than any decade since the 1570s. All the major poets among his contemporaries had died in the 1740s, had ceased to write verse, or had not yet published. Gray had no competitors more serious than Dyer, Shenstone and Akenside, with the result that the flatness of the surrounding country made him look more of an eminence than he really was. There can be little doubt that the reason why 'he never spoke out' was his homosexuality, about which he harboured a deep sense of guilt. Milton had preferred to use Latin for his more intimate personal poems; fearing to reveal the nature of his sexuality, Gray went further, and until he was twenty-five wrote virtually all his original verse in Latin. For him Latin verse was associated with his days at Eton, the happiest of his life; English was the language of a world of which he was afraid.

The months which he and Walpole spent in Florence after returning from Rome had their times of excitement and times of boredom. On 9 October 1740 Gray wrote to his father that the city had been 'gayer than ordinary for this last month, being one round of balls and entertainments, occasioned by the arrival of a great Milanese Lady; for the only thing the Italians shine in, is their reception of strangers'.[16] The death on 20 October of the Emperor Charles VI, the Grand Duke's father-in-law, however, was followed by three months of mourning, during which all entertainments were prohibited. The Emperor's death aroused fears that King Carlos of Naples would seize the opportunity to invade Tuscany, where he would have been welcomed by a large part of the population, and the Austrian garrison was strengthened.

Heavy rain fell throughout most of November, swelling the Arno until Florence was flooded on 3 December. 'The jewellers on the Old Bridge removed their commodities, and in two hours after the bridge was cracked,' Walpole told West.

> The torrent broke down the quays, and drowned several coach-horses, which are kept here in stables under ground. We were moated into our house all day, which is near the Arno, and had the miserable spectacles of the ruins that were washed along with the hurricane. There was a cart with two oxen not quite dead, and four men in it drowned: but what was ridiculous, there came tiding along a fat hay-cock, with a hen and her eggs, and a cat.

To ensure that the floods would not be followed by an epidemic, the miracle-working image of the Virgin known as the Madonna dell 'Impruneta was carried to the cathedral in procession, escorted by the Council of Regency, the Senate, the nobility and the religious orders. Gray 'saw numbers of people possessed with the devil who were brought to be exorcised', and commented, 'The church-doors were always shut before the ceremonies were finished, so that I could not be eye-witness of the event; but that they were all cured is certain, for one never heard any more of them the next morning.' He watched from his window the procession on 12 January 1741 when the image was carried out of the city again, accompanied by thousands of people bearing torches, and found the spectacle impressive. The Emperor's obsequies were publicly celebrated four days later, with Buondelmonte delivering the funeral oration, and the period of mourning finally ended.[17]

Walpole repeatedly postponed their departure day; when the news came that Maria Theresa had given birth to a son, the future Emperor Joseph II, he decided to stay on for the celebrations. 'Eleven months, at different times, have I passed at Florence,' Gray ruefully admitted in a letter to West, 'and yet (God help me) know not either people or language.'[18]

They left Florence at last on 25 April, accompanied by Chute, Whithed and Francesco Suares de la Concha, a young Florentine nobleman affectionately known as 'Cecco'. After a few days in Bologna they went on to Reggio for the annual fair — an event celebrated with operas, masquerades and balls. It was here, on or about 14 May, that Gray and Walpole had a quarrel which ended their friendship for over four years and left a permanent mark on Gray's mind. Afterwards he went on to Venice with Chute and Whithed, while Walpole remained at Reggio. Tensions had been developing ever since the beginning of the tour. Over thirty years later Walpole complained to Gray's biographer William Mason that 'we had not got to Calais before Gray was dissatisfied, for I was a boy, and he, though infinitely more a man, was not enough so to make allowances. Hence am I never mentioned once with kindness in his letters to West.' Gray's incessant note-taking soon began to irritate him. 'By a considerable volume of charts and pyramids, which I saw at Florence, I thought it threatened a publication,' Walpole wrote to Ashton from Rome. 'His travels here really improved him; I wish they may do the same for any one else.' During their long stay in Florence Gray would have liked to visit

Pisa, Lucca and other towns within easy reach; Walpole refused to tear himself away from his pleasures, but offered him the use of his carriage, which Gray was too proud to accept. After Conway sent him an account of the defeat of a motion of no confidence in the Prime Minister, Walpole wrote back, 'Your account of Sir Robert's victory was so extremely well told, that I made Gray translate it into French, and have showed it to all that could taste it, or were inquisitive on the occasion.'[19] The word 'made' suggests that he was apt to treat Gray on occasion as an unpaid secretary.

In correspondence with Mason, Walpole generously took most of the blame for the quarrel upon himself, and gave him permission to include a note to this effect in his book.

> I was too young [he wrote], too fond of my own diversions, nay, I do not doubt, too much intoxicated by indulgence, vanity, and the insolence of my situation, as a Prime Minister's son, not to have been inattentive and insensible to the feelings of one I thought below me; of one, I blush to say it, that I knew was obliged to me; of one whom presumption and folly perhaps made me deem not my superior *then* in parts, though I have since felt my infinite inferiority to him. I treated him insolently: he loved me and I did not think he did. I reproached him with the difference between us, when he acted from conviction of knowing he was my superior; I often disregarded his wishes of seeing places, which I would not quit other amusements to visit, though I offered to send him to them without me. Forgive me, if I say that his temper was not conciliating; at the same time that I will confess to you that he acted a more friendly part, had I the sense to take advantage of it; he freely told me of my faults. I declared I did not desire to hear them, nor would correct them. You will not wonder that with the dignity of his spirit, and the obstinate carelessness of mine, the breach must have grown wider, till we became incompatible.[20]

Although Mason printed almost verbatim the note which Walpole sent him, some people suspected at the time that the full story had not been told. The immediate occasion of the quarrel seems to have been a letter criticizing Walpole which Gray wrote to Ashton, who passed it on to Walpole, but this hardly seems an adequate explanation of so fundamental a breach. The real cause was probably Gray's sexual jealousy, perhaps of Elisabetta Grifoni, but more probably of Horace Mann. The evidence suggests that Walpole had begun a flirtation with Mann early in their acquaintance. He opened some of the letters which he wrote him from Rome 'Dear child' – an unusual way in which to address a diplomat over ten years his senior. On 25 April, the day on which Walpole left Florence, Mann wrote him a letter beginning:

> I am more miserable than I wish you to conceive, therefore I will not attempt to describe it to you; neither would I willingly give you a moment's uneasiness. One thing alone makes me really happy, which is that I am sure you love me and are convinced of my most sincere and tender affection for you. This is all I can say on this subject, though it employs every moment of my thoughts.

Walpole's reply has not survived, which may be significant. Mann wrote back on 2 May, 'I received your dear letter. I knew it must be full of goodness, but not to the excess I found it,' and continued in equally gushing terms.[21] From the following July to 1752 he usually began his letters to Walpole 'My dear child', or on occasion 'My dearest child' or even 'My dearest dear child'. Clearly an emotional relationship between them had been established sufficiently passionate, at least on Mann's side, to provoke Gray's jealousy.

Walpole's letter to Mann describing the quarrel and Mann's reply have both disappeared – probably destroyed by Walpole as too revealing. His embarrassment about the episode is apparent from the fact that he did not mention it to any of his friends in England, except Ashton. In a letter of 23 May, Mann made the curious statement that 'I take the greatest part of the fault on myself',[22] and appealed to Walpole to be reconciled to Gray. The letter also contains a reference to 'the oddness of [Gray's] behaviour with C—', which Walpole later crossed out; 'C—' may have been either Chute or Cecco Suares. At Mann's request Walpole wrote to Gray, who returned to Reggio, but at a meeting between them Gray angrily rejected Walpole's overtures. Whether from a lingering fondness for Gray or a sense of guilt at his own conduct, Walpole secretly arranged for money, supposedly coming from Mann but actually from himself, to be supplied to him for his travelling expenses.

After his return to England in September, Gray sought consolation in his friendship with West, who replaced Walpole in his affections. West had begun a verse tragedy on a classical theme, *Pausanias*, and Gray attempted to rival him with a tragedy of his own, *Agrippina*, of which he sent West the opening scene (his first serious attempt at English verse) early in 1742. In May, West sent him an 'Ode on May', and he replied with his 'Ode on the Spring'. These poems of Gray's illustrate the pernicious effects which years of writing Latin verse had produced – a readiness to borrow phrases and ideas from other poets, so that many of his poems are virtually collages, and a tendency to write English as if it were a dead language rather than one which he daily heard spoken around him. West had perceived these weaknesses in his verse, and in their correspondence about *Agrippina* had attempted unsuccessfully to cure him of them. Despite some serious lapses of taste, notably in the lifeless opening stanza, however, the ode is a success; the last verse in particular gives poignant expression to the sense of isolation and hopelessness which had haunted him since the breach with Walpole. He sent the poem, not knowing that West had died on 1 June. His letter was returned to him unopened, with no explanation, and he learned the reason only when he saw in a newspaper a poem by Ashton on their friend's death.

The loss within little more than a year of both the men whom he had loved came as a traumatic shock, from which he sought relief in poetry. His immediate reaction was to add twenty-nine lines lamenting West's death to *De Principiis Cogitandi*. After a pause, he wrote in August more verse than in any other comparable period of his life.

Of the three poems written at that time, only the sonnet is concerned exclusively with the death of West. It contains some deplorable jargon (when he wishes to say 'the sun rises' he writes 'redning Phoebus lifts his golden Fire'), yet as an expression of his 'lonely anguish' it remains genuinely moving. The fact that he never published it, although its wording is innocent enough, shows how sensitive he was about his emotional relationships with other men. 'Ode on a Distant Prospect of Eton College', ostensibly impersonal in its generalizations, is obviously a very personal poem in its contrast between his happy years at Eton and his present desolation. The list of evils to which adults are subject – 'disdainful Anger', 'pineing Love', 'Jealousy with rankling tooth', 'the stings of Falsehood', 'hard Unkindness' alter'd eye' – suggest that he was even more distressed by the quarrel with Walpole than by West's death. In the third poem, 'Ode to Adversity', he again seems to have Walpole in mind when he speaks with contempt of 'Self-pleasing Folly's idle brood, / Wild Laughter, Noise, and thoughtless Joy', and of 'the summer Friend, the flatt'ring Foe', yet the final appeal to Adversity to 'teach me to love and to forgive' suggests that he was ready for the reconciliation which came three years later.

The writing of these three poems within a month revealed to him that he was destined to write in English, not in Latin. The importance of Gray's stay in Florence consisted not in any inspiration which he derived from the city itself, but in the quarrel with Walpole which immediately followed and the subsequent psychological crisis from which he emerged a poet.

Thomas Gray
TRANSLATION FROM DANTE'S *INFERNO*, CANTO XXXIII

  Thro' a small Crevice opening, what scant light
That grim & antique Tower admitted (since
Of me the Tower of Famine hight & known
To many a Wretch) already 'gan the dawn
To send: the whilst I slumbring lay, A Sleep
Prophetic of my Woes with direful Hand
Oped the dark Veil of fate. I saw methought
Toward Pisa's Mount, that intercepts the view
Of Lucca chas'd by Hell-hounds gaunt & bloody
A Wolf full grown; with fleet & equal speed
His young ones ran beside him, Lanfranc there
And Sigismundo & Gualandi rode
Amain, my deadly foes! headed by this
The deadliest; he their Chief, the foremost he
Flashed to pursue & chear the eager Cry:
Nor long endured the Chase: the panting Sire
Of Strength bereft, his helpless offspring soon
Oerta'en beheld, & in their trembling flanks
The hungry Pack their sharp-set Fangs embrued.

  The Morn had scarce commenced, when I awoke:
My Children (they were with me) Sleep as yet
Gave not to know their Sum of Misery
But yet in low & uncompleated Sounds
I heard 'em wail for bread. oh! thou art cruel
Or thou dost mourn to think, what my poor Heart
Foresaw, foreknew: oh! if thou weep not now,
Where are thy Tears? too soon they had arousd them
Sad with the fears of Sleep, & now the Hour
Of timely food approached: when at the gate
Below I heard the dreadful Clank of bars,
And fastning bolts; then on my Children's eyes
Speechless my Sight I fix'd, nor wept, for all
Within was Stone: they wept, unhappy boys!
They wept, & first my little dear Anselmo
Cried, 'Father, why, why do you gaze so sternly?

What would you have?' yet wept I not, or answerd
All that whole day, or the succeeding Night
Till a new Sun arose with weakly gleam
And wan, such as mought entrance find within
That house of Woe: but oh! when I beheld
My sons & in four faces saw my own
Despair reflected, either hand I gnawed
For Angeuish, which they construed Hunger; straight
Ariseing all they cried, 'far less shall be
Our sufferings, Sir, if you resume your gift;
These miserable limbs with flesh you cloathed;
Take back what once was yours.' I swallowd down
My struggling Sorrow, nor to heighten theirs.
That day & yet another, mute we sate
And motionless: O! Earth! couldst thou not gape
Quick to devour me? yet a fourth day came
When Gaddo at my feet outstretchd, implor'ng
In vain my Help, expire'd: ee'r the sixth Morn
Had dawnd, my other three before my eyes
Died one by one; I saw 'em fall: I heard
Their doleful Cries; for three days more I grop'd
About among their cold remains (for then
Hunger had reft my eyesight) often calling
On their dear Names, that heard me now no more:
The fourth, what Sorrow could not, Famine did.

FAREWELL TO FIESOLE

O Fiesole, hilltop
Pleasantly cooled by the breezes, never too angrily blowing,
You whom gracious Athene chose to be queen of the Tuscan
Apennines, and to flash with the silvery leaves of her olive!
Never again shall I see you from the banks of the Arno
Looming up in the distance, with porticoes for your girdle,
Wearing a crown of white villas, the ridge that you stand upon
    gleaming,
Never again admire your ancient cathedral, the aged

Cypresses growing before it, and rooftops piled upon rooftops.

Translated from the Latin by Charles Hobday

Horace Walpole
SONG
From the Italian of Giuseppe Maria Buondelmonte

Love often in the comely mien
Of friendship fancies to be seen;
Soon again he shifts his dress,
And wears disdain and rancour's face.
To gentle pity then he changes;
Thro' wantonness, thro' piques he ranges;
But in whatever shape he move,
He's still himself, and still is Love.

INSCRIPTION FOR THE NEGLECTED COLUMN
IN THE PLACE OF ST. MARK AT FLORENCE

Escap'd a race, whose vanity ne'er rais'd
A monument, but when themselves it prais'd;
Sacred to truth Oh! let this column rise,
Pure from false trophies and inscriptive lies.

Let no enslavers of their country here
In impudent relievo dare appear:
No pontiff by a ruin'd nation's blood
Lusting to aggrandize his bastard-brood:
Be here no Clement, Alexander seen;
No pois'ning Cardinal, or pois'ning Queen:
No Cosmo, or the Bigot-Duke, or He
Great from the wounds of dying liberty.
No Lorrainer – one lying arch suffice
To tell his virtues and his victories:
Beneath his influence how commerce thriv'd,

And at his smile how dying arts reviv'd:
Let it relate, e'er since his rule begun,
Not what he has, but what he should have done.

Level with Freedom, let this pillar mourn,
Nor rise till the bright blessing shall return;
Then tow'ring boldly to the skies proclaim
Whate'er shall be the happy hero's name,
Who, a new Brutus, shall his country free,
And like a God, shall say, Let there be Liberty.

4

Robert Merry

When the Grand Duke Francis of Tuscany, who since 1745 had also been Emperor, died in 1765 he was succeeded on the imperial throne by his eldest son, Joseph II, and in Tuscany by his second son, Peter Leopold. Whereas Francis had not been near Florence since 1738, Leopold took his duties as Grand Duke very seriously and made Florence his home. Over the next twenty-five years reforms were introduced at breath-taking speed. The administration was reorganized and the system of local government was reformed. Roads were built, marshes drained, new areas brought under cultivation, new and improved crops introduced. Imprisonment for debt was abolished. A new criminal code abolished torture and capital punishment, at a time when in Britain over 200 offences were punishable by death. The tribunal of the Inquisition and the ecclesiastical censorship were abolished, and the civil censorship was relaxed. Religious houses deemed to be of no benefit to society were dissolved. Florence, the population of which had increased by 1780 to about 80,000, benefited considerably from Leopold's reforming zeal. A city council was established in 1781, which repaved the streets and improved the sewers. The hospitals were reformed, a free medical service was provided for the poor and a free public bath was opened. Daily and nightly police patrols were introduced. English visitors highly praised the cleanliness of the streets and the absence of crime.

Leopold ranks high among the benevolent despots of the eighteenth century, but for all his benevolence he remained a despot. A network of spies kept a close watch on the population, and especially on the nobility. This was the more resented because, as a Victorian historian delicately put it, 'his own behaviour offered many vulnerable points for public reprehension'. Mrs Piozzi (formerly Dr Johnson's friend Mrs Thrale), who spent three months in Florence in 1785, commented that the Grand Duke 'tells his subjects when to go to bed, and who to dance with, till the hour he chuses they should retire to rest', adding, 'Much of an English traveller's pleasure is taken off at Florence by the incessant complaints of a government he does not understand, and of oppressions he cannot remedy.'[1]

Despite this drawback, British travellers flocked to Florence in ever-increasing numbers. The weekly *Gazzétta Toscana* reported their arrivals and departures until 1767, when it gave up the task in despair. Tourism was becoming big business. The city council provided a restaurant in the Cascine, and the city's first *gelateria* was opened in 1790. New guide-books with texts in Italian and English were published. Hotel accommodation was expanded and improved until Florentine hotels were regarded as the best in Italy.

Two Englishmen, Charles Hadfield and Meghitt (the name was spelt in many ways), opened hotels catering especially for English guests on the south bank near the Ponte Santa Trinità. Meghitt had a reputation for being fastidious about his guests. When the agriculturist Arthur Young arrived in 1789, 'the great Mr Meggot looked into our cabriolets to examine us before he would give an answer, pretending that his [rooms] were bespoken; and then assured us, as we had no air that promised good plucking, that his were engaged'. Meghitt could afford to pick and choose; when Young dined at his hotel a week later the company included two peers, and George III's brother, the Duke of Cumberland, had stayed there three years before. Mrs Piozzi observed that his guests were prepared to pay through the nose for English food, with the result that 'one eats infinitely worse than one did at Milan, Venice, or Bologna: and infinitely dearer too; but that makes it still more completely *in the English way*'. Thomas Watkins, another English traveller, who stayed there in 1787, did not agree. 'We find everything served up in the English manner, which I am unfashionable enough to prefer to all other. Meggit is not only a good innkeeper, but very moderate in his charges.' A third hotel was run by Mary Vanini, an English widow; Smollett the novelist, a man not easily pleased, who stayed there in 1764, found her 'very obliging', the rooms comfortable and her charges reasonable.[2]

The art-lovers among the tourists profited from Leopold's reforms. He brought to the Uffizi works of art from the Medicis' palaces and villas, the city's lawcourts and the Jesuits' suppressed convents, and had the collections, in which artistic and scientific exhibits had been mingled indiscriminately, rearranged according to genre and period. To improve the lighting the windows were enlarged, and when this reorganization had been completed the gallery was thrown open to the public in 1784 free of charge, the attendants being forbidden to accept tips. Most visitors to the gallery dutifully admired what the critics of the day told them to admire: the classical sculptures and the paintings of the High Renaissance masters and the seventeenth-century Bolognese school. The art of Romanesque, Gothic and quattrocento Florence meant little or nothing to most of them, though there were rare exceptions, such as the painter Thomas Patch, who published engravings of paintings by Masaccio and Giotto in the 1770s. Thomas Watkins thought the Duomo, with the exception of the dome, 'a medley of all the orders, heaped and crowded together in confusion', and visited San Marco, not to admire Fra Angelico's paintings, but to buy the liqueurs and perfumes which the friars manufactured. The Medici Venus, on the other hand, which occupied the place of honour in the Tribuna of the Uffizi, and which a modern critic has dismissed as 'stilted and artificial . . . vapid . . . no more than a large drawing-room ornament', Watkins found 'all beauty and all perfection'. Smollett, however, had the honesty to admit that 'I cannot help thinking that there is no beauty in the features of Venus; and that the attitude is awkward and out of character.'[3]

The British formed the largest foreign colony in Florence, and many of them stayed on for years. The doyen of the colony was Sir Horace Mann (a baronet since 1755), who from 1738 until his death in 1786 remained at his post successively as chargé d'affaires, resident, envoy extraordinary, and finally envoy extraordinary and plenipotentiary. Another long-term resident was George Nassau Clavering-Cowper, third Earl Cowper, who arrived there in 1759 while on the Grand Tour. Having fallen in love with a married woman, the Marchesa Corsi, he stayed on even when his dying father was begging him to return to England, and remained long after his passion for the Marchesa was extinct. In 1775 he married a visiting Englishwoman twenty years younger than himself, but within two years the marriage had broken down; Lady Cowper became the Grand Duke's mistress, while the Earl pursued his own *affaires*. A generous patron of the arts and sciences, he was elected a member of the Accademia della Crusca in 1768, and was popular and respected among the Florentines.

An even more illustrious resident was Prince Charles Edward Stuart, who left Rome for Florence in 1775. His hopes that he would be treated with more respect there were disappointed. The French magistrate Charles Dupaty, who visited Florence in 1785, described him as 'the old man weighed down with infirmities, humiliations and above all with the name of Stuart, who is known as the Count of Albany, and who is completing at Florence, amid all the afflictions of a painful old age, the destiny of a man whose ancestors have been kings, and who has never been able to forget the fact. He will die', Dupaty continued, 'with his eyes fixed on that crown which he has been able to place only on his seal and the panels of his coach.' In 1777 Charles bought the Palazzo Guadagni, in the Via San Sebastiano,* which until comparatively recently was still crowned with a weather-vane pierced with the letters C R. The prince who held his court there was no longer the Bonnie Prince Charlie of 1745, but a prematurely aged alcoholic. His young wife, Princess Louise of Stolberg-Gedern, left him in 1780 to escape from his drunkenness and ill-treatment – as his Scottish mistress Clementina Walkinshaw had done twenty years before – and fled to Rome, where she was joined by her admirer, the poet Vittorio Alfieri. To replace her as head of his household Charles sent in 1784 for Charlotte, his daughter by Clementina, who reluctantly left her lover, the Archbishop of Bordeaux, and the three children she had borne him, to join her father. Charles and Charlotte, whom he had created Duchess of Albany, became a familiar sight in Florence. 'I have been showed, at the horse race, the theatre, &c. the unfortunate grandson of King James the Second,' Mrs Piozzi wrote. 'He goes much into publick still, though old and sickly; gives the English arms and livery, and wears the garter which he has likewise bestowed upon his natural daughter.'[4]

Another Englishman who spent some years in Florence was Robert Merry. Born in 1755, the eldest son of a governor of the Hudson's Bay Company, he was educated at Harrow, where his tutor, Dr Samuel Parr, inculcated in him both a sound knowledge of the classics and radical political views. In 1771 he was admitted to Christ's College, Cambridge, where he devoted more time to enjoying himself than to study, and left without a degree. To please his relations he studied law at Lincoln's Inn, but without enthusiasm. His father died in 1774, and two years later he used his inheritance to purchase a commission in the 1st Troop of the Horse Guards. How seriously he took his military career is hard to say. Although the 1st and 2nd Troops of the Horse Guards, which in 1788 became the 1st and 2nd Life Guards, ranked first in the Army List, they were not highly regarded in military circles; George III's son the Duke of York described them a few years later as 'the most useless and the most

---

* Now the Palazzo San Clemente, in the Via Gino Capponi.

unmilitary troops that ever were seen'. The muster rolls of his troop show that eight weeks after receiving his commission Merry had not yet joined his unit; that he was on duty throughout 1777 and 1778; that in July 1779 and January 1780, and possibly for the months between, he was on leave; and that on 31 May 1780 he left the Army.[5] His pay as a lieutenant of 10s. 6d. a day was insufficient to cater for his expensive tastes, and after dissipating most of his fortune on gambling he sold his commission, presumably at the official price of £1,322, and went abroad. Like Byron's Childe Harold (and Merry often looks like a first rough sketch for Byron), sated with a life of pleasure-seeking he left his native land in quest of new experiences.

Many details of his wanderings are obscure. We do not know for certain whether he left England in 1779 or 1780, which countries he visited, when he settled in Florence, when he left it, or when he finally returned to England. According to one early source, 'he visited most of the principal towns of France, Switzerland, Italy, Germany, and Holland',[6] but this is improbable; there is no evidence in his writings that he was ever in Germany or Holland. In his poem 'Il Viaggio', which is apparently auto-biographical, he mentions Paris, Switzerland, Savoy, Piedmont, Rome, Naples and Pompeii, and this was probably the route he followed. While in Rome he wrote an 'Ode on a Distant Prospect of Rome', a poor imitation of Gray which may be his earliest surviving poem, and it may have been during this visit that he met the French painter Jacques-Louis David. He took up residence in Florence, probably in 1780 and certainly not later than 1782, and it was there that he became a poet.

While in Florence he devoted himself to the study of Italian poetry, and won the friendship of a number of Italian poets and literary men: Alfieri, who presented him with a copy of his tragedies while living in Pisa in 1784–5; Lorenzo Pignotti, whose *Favole* appeared in 1782; Angelo Gianetti, professor of anatomy and *improvvisatore*; Marco Lastri, editor of *Novelle Letterarie*; and Count Angelo D'Elci, verse satirist. Merry was described by his friend Frederick Reynolds as 'a man amiable, and elegant; and possessing a mind stored with talents, and acquirements, far surpassing the usual allotment',[7] and his personal charm no doubt contributed to recommend him to the Florentine literati. His Italian friends, like the friends of Milton and Walpole, were men of liberal views in politics and religion and admirers of English literature and English political institutions. Pignotti, a physician and a Freemason, whose history of Florence was placed on the Index by the Church, wrote poems in praise of Shakespeare and Pope and an imitation of *The Rape of the Lock*; his fables, which satirized the nobility and the clergy, showed the influence of John Gay. Lastri had translated Gray's poems. In one sonnet D'Elci paid tribute to *Paradise Lost*, Pope's Homer, Dryden's Virgil and Shakespeare ('*il Sofocle Britanno*'), and in another to Newton, Captain Cook and the British defence of Gibraltar in 1779–82.

On 7 July 1783 Leopold abolished the Florentine Academy, the Accademia della Crusca and the Accademia degli Apatisti. There was much to be said for this measure, for the academies had ceased to perform any useful function. Even Alfieri, who fiercely protested in a sonnet, was forced to admit that the Accademia della Crusca, 'encumbered by inertia, had long neglected her art; yet in her', he continued, 'the shadow of a great name survived'.[8] As Alfieri and other men of letters saw it, the guardian, however unworthy, of the great traditions of Tuscan literature had been swept away by a despot's fiat. Lastri had been a member of the Accademia della Crusca and Pignotti of the Apatisti, and Merry fully shared his friends' indignation. He was never himself a member of the Accademia della Crusca, as was widely believed in England; the *Catalogo degli Accademici della Fondazione*, published by the academy in 1983 to celebrate its quartercentenary, shows that no new members were elected between 1779 and its dissolution in 1783.

Leopold merged the three academies into one, the Royal Florentine Academy, but it does not seem to have been much more effective than its predecessors. Dupaty wrote of it, 'A few years ago there were four [*sic*] academies in Florence. They did not do anything; they were just four academies . . . The Grand Duke has combined them in one, under the name of the Florentine Academy, but although he created two hundred places, he should at the same time have created two hundred men of talent to fill them.' Merry was elected a member of this body, no doubt through the influence of his literary friends. He proudly described himself on the title-pages of three of his works as 'Member of the Royal Academy of Florence', and on that of his poem *Paulina* as 'Member of the Royal Academy of Florence, late La Crusca'. As Mrs Piozzi makes clear, it was because of his insistence that the academy of which he was a member was the successor to the older and more illustrious body that his English friends nicknamed him 'Della Crusca' – a name which he later used as a pseudonym.[9]

But it was not only literary studies and literary friendships which made him a poet. Soon after his arrival in Florence he met Lady Cowper, of whom Dr John Moore, who was middle-aged and level-headed, had written that she 'is of an amiable character, and affords [the Florentines] a very favourable specimen of English beauty'. Merry, who was still in his twenties, was swept off his feet by her, and the lady, three years younger than himself, was equally attracted by his charm and good looks. So began, in Reynolds's words, 'that attachment for each other which for seven years existed with unabated ardour'. That the Grand Duke himself was his rival, by introducing a spice of danger into the *affaire*, made her all the more attractive in Merry's eyes. As for Earl Cowper, he and his wife had long since agreed to let each other go their own ways. 'Her husband,' to quote Reynolds again, 'having contracted the manner of Italian spouses, and possessing his own little attachments, which monopolized all his time, the domestic arrangements of the 'Home Department' were, at length, entirely surrendered to Merry.'[10] Merry thus found himself officially occupying the position of Lady Cowper's *cavaliere servente* – the term that had replaced *cicisbeo* in general use.

His passion for Lady Cowper found expression in his poetry. *Novelle Letterarie* reported on 10 October 1783 the publication of *Poems by R . . . M . . .* in a limited edition of ten copies. None of these seems to have survived, but the review fortunately gave a list of the ten poems included. It is an indication of the rapid development of Merry's powers of self-criticism that he excluded six of them from *The Florence Miscellany*, published only two years later. Three of the poems which later appeared in the *Miscellany* are undistinguished, but if the fourth, 'Ode on Madness', is identical with the 'Madness' in the later collection Merry had at last found himself as a poet. This wild poem, a madman's lament for his lost love, had a passionate intensity which places Merry with his near-contemporaries Chatterton and Blake among the first generation of English Romantics:

> I've lost my Love, I know not where,
> I ask'd her of the fiend Despair,
> He look'd aghast, and bade me go
> To the dark abode of woe.
> I'll seek her in the glare of day,
> I'll seek her in the milky-way,
> I'll seek her o'er the raging deep;
> Yon wave shall rock her soul to sleep.[11]

The course of true love, it would seem, had not always run as smoothly for Merry as he wished Reynolds to believe. Lady Cowper had been false to her husband and the Grand Duke, and what guarantee had he that she was faithful to him? Merry's other love poems in *The Florence Miscellany*, 'Serenade' and 'Song', which has the refrain 'who never thinks of me', both give voice to a mood of uneasiness. In all three of these poems the strength of his emotion enables him to escape from the stilted diction, derived mainly from Gray, of his more conventional verse; the contrast is apparent in the transition from the lifeless opening lines of 'Serenade' to the song itself.

In addition to his Italian friends, Merry found others among the British residents and visitors, with some of whom he formed a club, the Oziosi or 'Idlers'. A notable addition to this circle was the Scottish painter Allan Ramsay, who arrived in October 1783, a few days before his seventieth birthday, together with his son John. The elder Ramsay, himself the son of a poet, had written verses and pamphlets throughout his life, and in recent years had devoted himself to political pamphleteering. On the day of the Ramsays' arrival at Meghitt's, Merry visited them and established a friendship which remained close until they left Florence several months later. Their circle of friends included another artist, Hugh Hamilton, an Irishman who worked in crayons and painted portraits of Merry and Prince Charles Edward.

Merry sponsored Allan Ramsay's admission to the Oziosi and collaborated with him in a collection of poems. *The Arno Miscellany*, published in the spring of 1784, is notable solely as the first English collection of poems concerned with aviation. The first balloon ascents had taken place in France in 1783, and Florence did not escape the ballooning craze which swept Europe in the following year. A balloon was launched from the Ponte alla Carraia in January, and many other ascents followed, until in April a balloon crashed into the campanile of the cathedral, whereupon the Grand Duke banned further unauthorized experiments. An Abbé C. had produced a Latin epigram on ballooning, and the *Miscellany* contains imitations of it by Merry and Ramsay and two French versions by M. Buignon, the Swiss tutor of a young Englishman making the Grand Tour. Merry also contributed two other poems on the same theme, 'The Air Balloon' and 'Human Greatness', an 'Epistolary Ode' to Ramsay and 'Cruddroddruck', a parody of Gray's 'The Bard'; Ramsay offered a reply to Merry's ode and a pastoral so bad that one hopes it was meant as a burlesque. Horace Walpole's comment in a letter to Mann was to the point: 'You surprise me with the notice that old Ramsay had a hand in that trumpery. I do not mean that I wonder at his being a bad poet; I did not know that he was one at all, though a very great scribbler – but an old dotard! to be sporting and playing at leap frog, with brats!' [12]

Merry found more competent collaborators in 1785. Bertie Greatheed, a young man of liberal views who had inherited from his father sugar plantations in the West Indies and a country house in Warwickshire, was the first to arrive at Meghitt's, together with his wife and their baby son. His unfortunate Christian name he had inherited from his mother's family, the dukes of Ancaster, whose surname it was. The next arrival, William Parsons, like Greatheed was some years younger than Merry. He came from Chichester, and may have derived his income from the flour business. The fact that he had never been to a school or university seems to have given him a sense of inferiority which drove him to make unfounded claims about himself; thus he described himself as 'of the Sussex Militia', although his name nowhere appears on its muster rolls for 1781–3. Greatheed had written some verse, Parsons a great deal.

Finally, late in the evening of 3 June, Gabriele Mario Piozzi arrived with his British wife. Born in 1741, the daughter of a Welsh gentleman with a long pedigree and an empty purse, Hester Lynch Salusbury had made 'a Match of mere Prudence, and common good Liking, without the smallest Pretensions to Passion on either Side', with Henry Thrale, a rich brewer twelve years her senior. She bore him twelve children, of whom only four daughters survived childhood; during her frequent pregnancies he amused himself with prostitutes. The Thrales were introduced in 1765 to Dr Johnson, who afterwards spent much of his time at their home in Southwark or their country house at Streatham, and through him they got to know Reynolds, Goldsmith, Burke, Garrick and Boswell. Thrale died in 1781, and having married once for money his widow three years later married for love. Her choice fell on Piozzi, an Italian singer, instrumentalist and composer of about her own age, who had taught her eldest daughter to sing. Although he was described by one of her friends as 'an handsome man, in middle life, with gentle, pleasing and unaffected manners', and by another as 'a very handsome, gentlemanly, and amiable person', by marrying a singing master, an Italian and a Catholic she outraged the snobbery, insularity and bigotry of many of her circle, including Dr Johnson and her own daughters. [13] The Piozzis remained admirably loyal to each other, however, and in time the marriage became accepted – especially after Piozzi had been naturalized and converted to Anglicanism and had developed into a fair imitation of an English country squire.

Soon after their marriage they left for a prolonged honeymoon tour of Europe. While in Milan, where they spent five months, Mrs Piozzi learned of Johnson's death and began to write her *Anecdotes of the late Samuel Johnson*. In Venice she met the poet Ippolito Pindemonte, another Anglophile and Freemason, and made a verse translation of an ode of his in praise of England. When they reached Florence she was delighted with their 'exceeding handsome' lodgings at Meghitt's, where she found 'the people of the house very attentive, and Cold Baths at next door, & all things cool and comfortable about us'. Florence and its social life she thought equally delightful. 'We lodge on the Banks of the *Arno,*' she wrote to a friend, 'and see the full moon shining over *Fesole* opposite the Window of our common sitting Room: We walk every Evening in a Wood full of Nightingales, where Oaks, and Olives, and Firs of a prodigious Size form an impenetrable Shade; where Pheasants fill the Underwood, and Blackbirds Whistle on the Branches.'

> The People here lie a Bed all Day and sit up all Night – even the Shopkeepers shut up their Windows and go to Rest at Noon. The Ponte della Trinita said to be the most beautiful Bridge in Europe, is our public Walk till twelve o'Clock; and if you are recreant even then, and steal home to Sleep as we did last Night, you are instantly pursued and waked with a Concert under your Window. Mr. Piozzi called me up at about two this Morning to be serenaded, and I assure you that the Moonlight, the River, and the Heat, give charms to their Musick, which ours in England has no Possibility of receiving.[14]

The Piozzis were soon on friendly terms with Merry, Parsons (whom they had already met at Milan), and the Greatheeds, who in turn introduced them to their Italian friends. Although she enjoyed their company, Mrs Piozzi did not take a great liking to any of them except the Greatheeds and Pignotti, 'a quiet inoffensive Companion, with good plain sense, & Taste for elegant Poetry'. Merry, with his volatile temperament and his reputation as a rake, both fascinated and repelled her. What pleased her most in Florence was the respect with which her husband was treated. In accordance with protocol, Sir Horace Mann refused to invite him to functions at which members of the Tuscan nobility were present; she avenged herself in private by joking with Mrs Greatheed about Mann's homosexuality. On 25 July, however, the Piozzis celebrated their wedding anniversary with a dinner and concert, at which the guests included Prince Corsini, his brother Cardinal Corsini, Lord and Lady Cowper, and the Earl of Pembroke, who was also staying at Meghitt's. The Cowpers, she pointedly remarked in a letter to her eldest daughter, 'who are reckon'd difficult to *many*, are kind to *us*', and she later reported that they had been shown Earl Cowper's 'very fine Collection of natural Curiosities', where they saw 'some Experiments in Electricity and Astronomy very well carried through'.[15]

As Mrs Piozzi had written verse since her childhood, it is not surprising that when she found herself daily in the company of a group of English and Italian poets a plan should be formed to produce a collection of poems. 'I have been playing the Baby', she wrote to a friend on 27 July, 'and writing Nonsense to divert our English friends here, who do the same thing themselves; and swear they will print the Collection, and call it an Arno Miscellany.' Obviously she did not take the plan seriously; having heard that nine biographies of Dr Johnson were already in preparation, she was anxious to finish her *Anecdotes* as quickly as possible. Her failure to understand that her friends took what finally became *The Florence Miscellany* very seriously indeed had unfortunate consequences. At their request she supplied the book with a preface which stated 'Why we wrote the verses may be easily explain'd, we wrote them to divert ourselves, and to say kind things of each other.'[16] This sentence has damned the *Miscellany* in the eyes of later critics, especially those who have never read it. It is true that a few of the poems in the book contain an element of mutual back-scratching, but they are very much in the minority.

Two aspects of the *Miscellany* are of particular interest: the political and the metrical. Merry, Greatheed and Parsons were all fiercely critical of what they considered to be Leopold's tyranny, although Merry reserved his attack for a later occasion. Greatheed's poem 'A Dream' describes how the Muse, visiting Florence,

> found her Crusca's triumphs o'er;
> And e'en its name was now no more
> But Ign'rance rear'd her heavy head,
> While ev'ry art and science fled.

In a similar vein Parsons wrote in his 'Epistle to the Marquis Pindemonte at Verona':

> For now no more the blue-eyed Pleasures rove
> Arno's green banks, or Boboli thy grove!
> O'er the change'd scene his baleful pinions spread,
> While the fierce Austrian Eagle rears the head.
> Like tim'rous doves his ravening beak they fly
> To sport and flutter in a kinder sky![17]

To circumvent the censorship a blank was left in the poems where these two passages appeared, and the lines were printed on separate slips that could be pasted in. No such precaution was taken with the most revolutionary poem in the book, Greatheed's 'Ode to Apathy', an impassioned appeal to the Italian people to reclaim their lost liberty. Here, for the first time in the history of English poetry, is heard the voice of the Risorgimento.

Most British visitors to Florence were favourably impressed by Leopold's reforms. Young called him 'the wisest prince in Europe', and Watkins declared that 'there is no country in Europe, in which the prince rules absolutely, that is governed with such policy and moderation'. Merry had his own reasons for disliking his rival in love, but the prejudice against Leopold harboured by Greatheed and Parsons requires explanation. The reason no doubt lies in the company they kept – aristocrats such as D'Elci who disliked all change and were disposed, as Mrs Piozzi observed, to 'lament the Tyranny of the Govt and tremble for fear of Spies', and literary men such as Pignotti and Lastri who objected to Leopold's interference with the academies. Apart from the suppression of the Accademia della Crusca, one recent innovation of Leopold's in particular aroused the indignation of the *Miscellany* group. In 1784, for reasons of hygiene, he had issued strict regulations for the control of funerals, of which even his admirer Young remarked: 'I condemn it as an outrage on the common feelings of mankind; chiefly because it is an unnecessary outrage, from which no use whatever flows.'[18] No comment on this issue appeared in the *Miscellany*, but Parsons in his *Elegy on the Burying Place called Campo Santo* violently denounced Leopold's action and virtually called for his deposition. This poem was published separately as an eight-page pamphlet signed only 'W. P.' and bearing the imprint

'Geneva 1785', although it was no doubt printed in Florence.

The other interesting feature of the *Miscellany* is the contributors' experiments with metre and stanza forms. Whereas most eighteenth-century poets stuck to a few familiar forms, Merry, Greatheed and Parsons tried a wide variety of stanzas rhymed and unrhymed, and showed themselves conscious of the possibilities of combining lines of different length and masculine and feminine endings. Merry's 'Serenade', for example, derives much of its effect from the short final line of each verse, while Greatheed's 'Ode to Duel' is written in a regular unrhymed stanza of his own invention, consisting of six lines varying between three and five stresses, with the third line ending in an unstressed syllable.

Merry contributed nineteen poems to the collection, including 'Serenade', 'Madness' and 'Song'. Among his other contributions, the odes to summer and winter are competent imitations of William Collins's 'Ode to Evening' which reveal his sensitive response to the Tuscan countryside. The 'dithyrambicks' addressed to Bacchus, Diana and Venus are lively and vigorous poems modelled on those of the seventeenth-century poet Francesco Redi; 'To Bacchus' in particular is an admirable imitation of Redi's *Bacco in Toscana*. 'Il Viaggio' and 'La Dimora', modelled on Milton's 'L'Allegro' and 'Il Penseroso', praise respectively travel and a life of retirement. Although all these poems are imitations of admired masters, they are nonetheless profoundly original. Merry's sense of humour, particularly apparent in 'To Bacchus', is again displayed in his neat and pointed 'Fable' and 'To the Criticks', which gives an amusing picture of British visitors to the Uffizi:

> Yes in the Florence Gallery,
> I've often heard your raillery,
> And keenest observation,
> On every statue under contemplation.
> E'en in the TRIBUNE you will say,
> Your judgement to display,
> The famous wrestlers have no merit,
> And no spirit,
> The Arrotino, or the whetter,
> Is nothing better,
> As for the Medicean Venus,
> Extremely bad indeed, and heinous.[19]

But perhaps the most remarkable of Merry's poems in the *Miscellany* is 'Sir Roland, A Fragment', a Gothic romance so horrific that one suspects him of writing it with his tongue in his cheek. It may have originated when he, Greatheed and Mrs Piozzi agreed to see who could invent the most frightening story in the two hours before dinner. Its importance lies in the fact that it provided the starting-point for Coleridge's 'Christabel'; it is impossible to doubt that Coleridge had in mind Merry's lines

> For, as the breeze assailed her gorgeous vest,
> The opening folds disclosed a putrid breast

when he wrote in the original version of his poem:

> Like one that shuddered, she unbound
> The cincture from beneath her breast;
> Her silken robe, and inner vest,
> Dropt to her feet, and full in view,
> Behold! her bosom and half her side
> Are lean and old and foul of hue.[20]

– a passage central to the whole conception of the poem.

Parsons contributed more to the *Miscellany* than any of the others – thirty-one poems in all. His facile verse is rarely powerful or particularly original. Several of his better poems are taken from Italian sources – a translation in heroic couplets of the story of Paolo and Francesca from Dante's *Inferno*, and imitations of a sonnet by Petrarch and passages from Ariosto's *Orlando Furioso*, Tasso's *Aminta* and Metastasio. His 'Story of Francesca' placed him among the pioneer translators from Dante. The first published verse translation from the *Divina Commedia*, a version in heroic couplets of the Ugolino episode by Frederick Howard, Earl of Carlisle, had appeared in 1772, a version in *terza rima* of the first three cantos of the *Inferno* by William Hayley in 1782, and a blank-verse translation of the whole of the *Inferno* by Charles Rogers a few months later, but no complete translation was published until 1802. Parsons's only original poem of any great interest is 'Vallombrosa', the record of a visit to the convent with Greatheed and Piozzi. It is a good example of the prospect poem – a popular eighteenth-century genre in which the poet moralizes on the view from a hilltop and its historical associations, and owes much to John Dyer's *Grongar Hill*. Noteworthy passages are the story of Gualberto, the founder of the monastery, and the reference to the Etruscans, among whom

> the Arts, with dawning ray,
> Gave earnest of a brighter day.[21]

Interest in the Etruscans had been stimulated by the publication in 1726 of *De Etruria Regali*, written a century earlier by a Scottish scholar, Thomas Dempster, and by the 1780s patriotic Tuscans were claiming that the Greeks had derived their civilization from the Etruscans.

Greatheed's main contributions to the collection – 'A Dream', 'Ode to Duel' and 'Ode to Apathy' – have already been mentioned, while Mrs Piozzi's were either light verse or translations. Pignotti was represented by translations of Merry's 'Serenade' and Parsons's 'Ode to the Venus of Medici' and a flattering canzone addressed to his British collaborators, D'Elci by two sonnets and a Latin couplet, and Lastri by a blank-verse poem. The volume ended with a musical setting by Piozzi of Pignotti's 'Serenata'. Most of the English poems are of little value, but the exceptions – at least half of Merry's contributions, and one or two each by Parsons and Greatheed – are of sufficient interest to make *The Florence Miscellany* one of the most remarkable collections published in the 1780s.

The *Miscellany* was enthusiastically welcomed by *Novelle Letterarie*:

> A rare and glorious coincidence for the English nation! Four travellers, or knights errant, among them a lady, leaving the Thames, meet by chance on the Arno, where the same breeze which once echoed the musical voices of Dante and Petrarch, now echoes theirs, all four being poets . . . The Graces appear in company with the Muses, and Reason with Imagination.

This was the third occasion in less than two months when Merry's name had appeared in this journal. His friend Gianetti had delivered a eulogy on Captain Cook at the Royal Florentine Academy on 9 June (Mrs Piozzi, who was present, reported that 'the tender-hearted Italians wiped their Eyes at the Relation of his Death'), and this now appeared with an English translation by Merry.[22] Shortly after, Pignotti's poem *Roberto Manners* (a tribute to the brother of the Duke of Rutland, killed in the Battle of the Saints in 1782) was published in a handsome volume, with Merry's translation into rather too Miltonic blank verse printed on facing pages.

Soon after *The Florence Miscellany* went to press the group responsible for it began to break up. The Piozzis left on 12 September for Lucca and Livorno, where Mrs Piozzi finished her *Anecdotes*, and Parsons moved on to Rome before the end of the year. Greatheed lingered in Florence and made the acquaintance of Prince Charles Edward, who called him his subject and assured him that 'he should soon speak to him in Westminster Hall'. On another occasion, before Charles moved to Rome in December, when Greatheed raised the subject of the '45 rebellion, the Prince was so moved by the memory of his followers' sufferings that he fell to the floor in convulsions. Merry meanwhile was working on a long narrative poem, *Paulina; or, The Russian Daughter*, a story founded on fact which had obsessed him since 1783. Although written in Florence, it contains only two references to the city, in similes drawn from works of art:

> Like Guido's angel beaming on the eye,
> She seemed a meek descendant of the sky
>
> . . . .
> Her form was perfect as the finish'd piece,
> The boast of Florence now, as once of Greece.[23]

The Greatheeds left Florence in the spring of 1786, and by May they were floating down the Brenta to Venice with the Piozzis, while one of the party read *Paulina* aloud.

Before they left, his friends had all tried to persuade Merry to end his liaison with Lady Cowper and return to England, but without success. During 1786 his position in Florence became increasingly uncomfortable. According to one source, scandals were spread about him, and he avenged himself by writing lampoons on those responsible. He himself told Reynolds that the intervention of Lady Cowper's family forced her to break off the *affaire*, although they were still 'tenderly attached to each other', and that after a distressing scene they had parted.[24] He left Florence towards the end of 1786 or early in the new year, and seems to have spent most of 1787 in Brussels, where he found a new lover, a Mrs Hervey. It was presumably to celebrate this transfer of his affections that he wrote his poem 'The Adieu and Recall to Love'.

During the years from 1786 onwards, the authors of *The Florence Miscellany* gradually established literary reputations in England. When

Anecdotes of the late Samuel Johnson was published in March 1786 the 1,000 copies of the first edition sold out in one day, and within six weeks a fourth edition had appeared. After copies of the *Miscellany* reached England many of the poems in it were reprinted in periodicals. *Paulina* was published in Florence in 1786 in an edition of twenty-four copies, and in London early in 1787. Soon after, Parsons brought out his poems from the *Miscellany* and a number of others as *A Poetical Tour, in the Years 1784, 1785 and 1786*. On 29 June 1787 'The Adieu and Recall to Love' was printed in *The World*, with the signature 'Della Crusca'; according to Reynolds, this pseudonym was supplied by the editor, Edward Topham, who was an old friend of Merry. An admiring reply signed 'Anna Matilda' appeared a fortnight later, and for nearly two years 'Della Crusca' and 'Anna Matilda' conducted a poetic flirtation in the columns of *The World*. The pair finally met in March 1789, when Merry discovered that the object of his platonic affections was Hannah Cowley, a married woman over ten years older than himself with three children. Meanwhile several other minor poets had begun contributing verse to *The World* under various pseudonyms, among them Greatheed, who signed himself 'Reuben' or 'Arno'. Most of their verse was characterized by sentimentality, affectation, pretentiousness, rhetoric or bombast, with the result that, rather unfairly to Merry, the term 'Della Cruscan' has come to be applied to verse possessing these qualities.

The British contributors to *The Florence Miscellany* met again for the first time in April 1788, but it was not a happy reunion. Greatheed, whose tragedy *The Regent* had just been produced at Drury Lane, suspected Merry, rightly or wrongly, of being jealous of the success of his play; Parsons made mischief between them, and Mrs Piozzi tried in vain to reconcile them. She still admired Merry's verse ('no Man who has breathed since Thompson* drew his last Sigh can write like Della *Crusca*'), but her feelings about him were more mixed than ever. 'Merry is a dissipated Man become truly wicked; by Accident, rather than by Principle however: of elegant and airy Manners, but of a Melancholy and apparently Conscience-smitten Spirit,' she wrote in her journal after their meeting. Then the memory of his charm returned, and she added, 'his Distresses interest one's Tenderness, his Courage & Learning claim one's true Respect; Merry is a Scholar, a Soldier, a Wit and a Whig, beautiful in

---

* i.e. James Thomson, author of *The Seasons*.

his Person, gay in his Conversation, scornful of a feeble Soul, but full of Reverence for a good one though it be not great'. Merry's Byronic characteristics are very marked in this character sketch. A year later she was writing of him as 'dissolute, wicked, and I fancy wholly worthless'.[25] Three weeks after this was written they met for the last time.

The French Revolution deepened the gulf between them. Mrs Piozzi, who retained the conservative views she had imbibed from Johnson and Burke, was horrified by the Revolution, which she regarded as evidence that the end of the world was imminent. To Merry, who paid a long visit to France in 1789, it gave life a new meaning and purpose, and in the following year he poured his enthusiasm into a long poem, *The Laurel of Liberty*, which, despite a few Della Cruscan absurdities, is an eloquent and dignified statement of his beliefs. Among the tyrants whom he condemned he singled out for a bitter rebuke his old rival Leopold, who on succeeding his brother as Emperor had recently handed over Tuscany to his second son, Ferdinand. This poem won him the friendship of radicals and liberals such as Joseph Priestley, William Godwin, Mary Robinson and Samuel Rogers, and the enmity of the Pittite hack William Gifford, who lampooned him and his friends in a laboured satire, *The Baviad*. Mrs Piozzi was shocked in 1792 to find that the Greatheeds were also infected with 'this Democratic fever',[26] but their friendship survived not only this discovery but even 'Citizen Greatheed's' appearance as the Foxite anti-war candidate for Leicester in the 1796 elections.

In 1791 Merry was married to Ann Brunton, a beautiful and talented actress of twenty-two, who had recently appeared in his tragedy *Lorenzo*. Mrs Piozzi's comments were almost as feline as some of those on her own marriage, but in fact Merry's conduct confirmed the belief that a reformed rake makes the best husband. Although Ann would have liked to continue acting, his family's objections forced her to retire from the stage in 1792. They went to Paris, where they witnessed the overthrow of the monarchy and the September massacres, and Merry renewed his acquaintance with David, who introduced him to some of the revolutionary leaders. After war broke out between Britain and France it was David who obtained them the passport which enabled them to return to England in the summer of 1793.

Three years later Ann was offered the position of leading lady with an American company. She accepted, and sailed with her husband for New York. Life in the United States, which he had regarded as a land of liberty, proved a disappointment, especially after they settled in Baltimore, the capital of the slave state of Maryland. He talked of writing a book on American life and an epic on the French Revolution, but nothing seems to have come of either project. On Christmas Eve 1798 he collapsed while walking in his garden, and died a few hours later, at the age of forty-three. On learning the news even Mrs Piozzi paid the tribute of a sigh to the memory of 'the famous – the celebrated – the hapless Della Crusca'.[27]

Robert Merry
SERENADE

When o'er the Tuscan plain wild Winter threw
Her midnight mantle of a sable hue,
Where far-famed Florence rears her marble pride,
And aged Arno's varying waters glide;
Beneath the terrace of his much-loved fair,
With locks dishevel'd, and his bosom bare,
A fond Italian thus express'd his pain,
Struck the soft lyre, and pour'd the vocal strain.

If she I love be now reposed
In folded arms of downy sleep,
I'm well content to watch, and weep,
My eyes are never closed.

For I adore that angel face,
I love her beauty to despair,
Her azure eye, and auburn hair,
Her bosom's matchless grace.

Alas! no other joy have I,
But near this window's glimm'ring ray,
To breathe in vain the artless lay
Of genuine misery.

Now dreary darkness reigns around,
And nought shall trouble her repose,
Save the sharp wind that rudely blows,
With melancholy sound.

But not the feeble note I raise,
Shall e'er disturb her slumb'ring ear,
Nor do I wish my fair to hear,
Because I sing her praise.

For all the treasures of the East,
For ev'ry monarch's glitt'ring crown,
I would not have my useless moan
Invade her rosy rest.

And O my Passion never heave
That breast the fond abode of joy,
Love would her happiness destroy,
And teach her how to grieve.

She then would feel the rending sigh,
Would mourn perhaps the live-long night,
Unknown to peace, or calm delight,
As sad, as lost as I.

Blow, blow, ye winds, descend ye rains,
I scorn the torrent and the blast,
Ills such as these are quickly past,
Eternal are my pains.

But since my fair one is reposed,
In folded arms of downy sleep,
I'm well content to watch, and weep,
My eyes are never closed.

ODE TO WINTER

O welcome to my soul congenial Pow'r!
Rough Winter hail! I love thy hoary locks,
   Thy tempest-breathing sighs,
   The deluge of thy tears.

The forest shrinks beneath thine iron rod,
And the sad herds a faithless shelter seek,
   Where the time-moulder'd tow'r,
   Hangs tott'ring o'er the plain.

They raise their wistful eyes that seem t' upbraid
The ruthless season; while the raven cries,
    From solitary tree,
    With hoarse, and mournful note.

High Fiesole, of the bright mantle spoil'd
That once he wore with Flora's brede adorn'd,
    In many a low'ring cloud,
    Enwraps his sullen breast.

No longer Arno winds a stealing course
Thro' laughing meads, but on swift eddies borne,
    His rude discordant tide
    Rolls to the western deep.

This is my fav'rite hour of bliss severe,
To me more grateful, than the gaudy time
    When vocal Spring awakes
    Her gaily-painted flowers.

Than when red Summer glares with sultry gaze
On the parch'd hills, or sallow Autumn throws
    His golden treasure round,
    And drains the purple vine.

Amidst the dreary Apennines I hear
The tumbling rocks increase the torrent's roar,
    And the wide-ranging wolf
    Howl on the mountain's side.

While Echo, starting from her icy bed,
Mimicks the uproar wild, and Fancy comes
    In pilgrim robe array'd
    And waves her magic wand.

Lo! at her call the fairy visions rise,
That calm the sense of woe, Remembrance brings
    The mirrour of the past,

And sober Reason reigns.

Where are the jocund hours of wanton Mirth
That late beguil'd my youth, where are the friends
    That join'd the choral lay,
    When life's fair morn began?

Perchance they chase the fleeting pleasures still,
Nor cast one thought on him who listens here
    To the wild storm, and woos
    Grim midnight to his arms.

Then welcome to my soul congenial Pow'r!
Rough Winter hail! I love thy hoary locks,
    Thy tempest-breathing sighs,
    The deluge of thy tears.

from THE LAUREL OF LIBERTY

O SWEET FIRENZE! What are all thy stores,
Thy PARIAN VENUS which the world adores,
What are thy treasur'd gems thy tow'ry domes,
Whilst in thy halls the spectre Slav'ry roams?
Thy rustic palaces that charm the sight,
Thy Gallery's wealth, thy BOBOLI's delight,
Thy Pictures crowding on the raptur'd eye,
Which scarce our living REYNOLDS can outvie,
Thy melting Musick's undulating flow,
That o'er the nerves dilates delicious woe!
These but a poor, a transient comfort give,
To men, without volition doom'd to live.
Oft when the Star of Evening in the West
Sate like a Phoenix on her burning nest,
I've mark'd thy sighing youths, and damsels fair,
Tread the near meads, and whisper their despair,
Seek myrtled FIESOLE's cool bow'rs, to weep,
And pour the bitter curse 'not loud but deep.'

For hard was HE that govern'd; tho' his name,
By Flatt'ry written on the rolls of fame,
Has sometimes lur'd an undiscerning praise,
To swell the trav'ler's page, the poet's lays;
Yet I have view'd him oft on ARNO's side,
In false Humility's dissembled pride,
Have seen him give each abject passion scope,
Scowl at each bliss, and wither ev'ry hope,
Cherish base treach'ry, and to fav'rites yield
That sword, which Justice ought alone to wield,
Force gen'rous social confidence to end,
And tear from each the solace of a friend.
O! since your iron age at length is o'er,
And your stern Duke shall vex your peace no more,
But ris'n to empire, leave the past'ral vale,
To vent his malice on a larger scale;
O may ye now! from such oppression free,
Revive to bliss, and native dignity,
May kinder FERDINAND your ills remove,
And gain your gratitude, and win your love!

Bertie Greatheed

from ODE TO APATHY

O! would the sons of Italy arise,
And shake the leaden slumbers from their eyes,
Gaze on their fertile plains by nature blest,
And rouze the latent fire that warm'd their breast,
That dauntless energy of soul,
Which sav'd the tott'ring Capitol,
When on Tarpeian height, with glory's crown,
Brave Manlius stood,
And hurl'd indignant decads down,
And redden'd Tiber's flood.
To calm the factious rage that tore
Each Guelf, and Ghibbeline of yore,
Must they be lull'd in such repose

As manly vigor never knows;
Retire from martial fame, from glorious strife
And shun the busy scenes of life,
To waste with thee, O Apathy! their days,
Heedless of right, or wrong, of censure, or of praise?

No, let them now the proper medium find;
And prove to all mankind,
That virtue still can charm the present hour,
Nor less admir'd, nor dear,
Than when pale Cataline felt Tully's pow'r,
And violating Appius learn'd to fear;
So radiant Glory's beam divine
Shall once again transcendent shine
On this proud land of old renown'd
Which Apennines divide, and Alps and seas surround.

William Parsons
from VALLOMBROSA

Here the traveller elate
Finds an ever-open gate,
Glad they all his wants supply,
And welcome beams from every eye.
Chief I love to wander wide
With a serious monk my guide,
Who, while each scene he proud displays,
Repeats the pious Founder's praise;
GUALBERTO, who in youthful prime
Forsook Ambition's march sublime,
Neighing steeds, and feats of Arms,
Tournaments, and Beauty's charms
And left the shield and nodding crest,
To be in garb monastic drest;
How Religion's mild controul
Banish'd vengeance from his soul,
When his sword, in anger rais'd,

For a slaughter'd Brother blaz'd;
How his breast, with fury steel'd,
While the prostrate victim kneel'd,
At the Cross's pow'rful sign
Relenting own'd the spark divine,
Learn'd like his Saviour to forgive,
And bade th' appall'd assassin live;
Then his raging passions cease,
Calm'd in the still abode of Peace.

from ELEGY ON THE BURYING PLACE CALLED CAMPO SANTO, MADE LATELY ABOUT THREE MILES FROM FLORENCE, ON THE ROAD TO BOLOGNA

Shall th' unfeeling AUSTRIAN's stern commands
    To quell those sacred sentiments presume,
While with the name of *Prejudice* he brands
    The *Charities* that glow beyond the Tomb?

Thus might rebellious sons be taught to fly
    The long obedience which they owe their sires,
Thus be dissolved chaste wedlock's dearer tie
    And all that *Habit* adds to *Nature's* fires.

But sooner far must cease that slavish awe
    The humbled Vassal to his Tyrant pays,
Crumble that edifice which Pow'r and Law
    On weak Convention's base so proudly raise.

Then tremble Thou, lest th' impatient throng
    Tear the vain crown from thy too impious head;
Ne'er can the LIVING be respected long
    Who teach their subjects to despise the DEAD!

5

Percy Bysshe Shelley

Shelley first saw Florence on 18 August 1818, on his way to visit Byron in Venice. He was overwhelmed by its beauty. After obtaining the Austrian passport which he needed to enter Venetia, he wrote to Mary, his wife, whom he had left behind with their children at Bagni di Lucca:

> Florence itself – that is the Lung Arno (for I have seen no more), I think is the most beautiful city I ever saw. It is surrounded with cultivated hills & from the bridge which crosses the broad channel of the Arno, the view is the most animated and elegant I ever saw. You see three or four bridges – one apparently supported by Corinthian pillars, & the white sails of the boats relieved by the deep green of the forest which comes to the waters edge, & the sloping hills covered with bright villas on every side. Domes & steeples rise on all sides & the cleanliness is remarkably great. – On the other side there are the foldings of the Vale of Arno above, first the hills of olive & vine, then the chesnut woods, & then the blue & misty pine forests which invest the aerial Apennines that fade in the distance. – I have seldom seen a city so lovely at first sight as Florence.

He retained this opinion all his life, and could still speak of 'Florence! beneath the sun, / Of cities fairest one' after he had seen Venice, Rome and Naples.[1]

He had come to Italy in the previous March, when he was twenty-five. He was accompanied by Mary, already at twenty the author of *Frankenstein*; their two babies, William and Clara; Claire Clairmont, Mary's nineteen-year-old stepsister; and Allegra, the infant daughter of Claire and Lord Byron. They had four reasons for leaving England. Shelley's doctors had advised him to move to a warmer climate for the sake of his health. They hoped to solve their financial problems by moving to a country where living costs were lower; as he wrote in 1820, 'a crown here goes as far as a pound note in England'.[2] The Lord Chancellor had denied him custody of his children by his first wife, because of his religious and political views, and he feared that if he stayed his children by Mary would also be taken away from them. As a precaution, he had had

William and Clara christened before he left, lest the omission of this rite should be regarded as evidence that he and Mary were unfit to have custody of them. Finally, Allegra had to be handed over to her father, already permanently settled in Italy.

In Italy as in England, Shelley could never settle in one place for long. During 1818 they stayed for longer or shorter periods at Milan, Livorno, Bagni di Lucca, Este, Venice, Rome and Naples. While they were at Venice Clara died in circumstances which led Mary to regard Shelley as responsible for her death, and for several months relations between them were intensely strained. They returned to Rome in March 1819, and there on 7 June William, a bright little three-year-old, died after a short illness. Both his parents had idolized their 'Willmouse', and they were devastated by his death. 'It seems to me as if, hunted by calamity as I have been, that I should never recover any cheerfulness again,' Shelley wrote on the following day. Mary's misery was even more intense, and lasted longer. Her first child, a girl, had lived only a fortnight; now her two remaining children had died within nine months. 'Everything on earth has lost its interest to me,' she wrote to one friend, and to another, 'I never know one moments ease from the wretchedness and despair that possesses me.'[3] She was pregnant, and was haunted by the fear that this child also would not survive. Three days after William's death his parents fled from Rome, never to return.

They settled in a villa near Livorno, where Shelley's spirits revived as he worked on his tragedy *The Cenci*. They were joined in September by Charles Clairmont, Claire's brother or half-brother (the details of their parentage remain a mystery), who had been travelling in Spain. On 5 September a batch of English newspapers arrived, containing the news that on 16 August a peaceful mass meeting in St Peter's Fields, Manchester, in support of parliamentary reform had been charged by yeomanry and hussars, eleven people being killed and some 400 injured – an event which, with bitter irony, was popularly nicknamed the Battle of Peterloo. Shelley poured his indignation at 'this bloody murderous oppression'[4] into one of the greatest political poems in the language, *The Mask of Anarchy*, which was posted to his friend Leigh Hunt, the editor of *The Examiner*, on 23 September. Hunt had already spent two years in prison for telling the truth about the Prince Regent, and had no desire to repeat the experience, so Shelley's poem remained unpublished until 1832.

Mary's confinement was approaching, and she and Shelley were anxious to secure the services of John Bell, a distinguished Scottish sur-geon who had attended William on his deathbed. Expecting him to be in Florence when Mary's child was born, Shelley booked lodgings at the Palazzo Marini, Via Valfonda 4895, near Santa Maria Novella. The Via Valfonda was described in 1911 at 'a tall, narrow street, sufficiently pic-turesque, but which has now fallen into considerable disrepute', but since then most of it has been swept away to open up the space before the new railway station built in 1935. The Palazzo Marini was a boarding-house kept by Mme Merveilleux du Plantis, the wife of a French naval officer, and their two daughters, Louise and Zoïde. Charles Clairmont, who moved in with the Shelleys at the Palazzo Marini on 2 October, fell in love with Louise, whom Mary described in a letter as 'a good girl clever too but lazy . . . she has lovely hair pretty eyes – nice neck & shoulders for the rest non c'è male'. Shelley noted that Louise was 'in & out of love with Charles as the winds happen to blow', and a month later that he had left for Vienna on 10 November 'not without many lamentations as all true lovers pay on such occasions'. The liaison was disapproved of by Mme du Plantis, who according to Mary 'might go on exceedingly well & gain if she had the brains of a goose but her head is a sive & her temper worse than wildfire it is gunpowder and blows up everything'.[5] After Charles's departure she wrote him an angry letter forbidding him to com-municate with Louise, and the *affaire* came to nothing.

Apart from the city's beauty and the desire that Bell should be present at Mary's confinement, there were two reasons why Shelley was attracted by Florence. In January and February 1819 he and Mary, who planned to write a novel set in medieval Italy, read the *Histoire des républiques italiennes du Moyen Age* by the Genevese historian Jean Charles Léonard Simonde de Sismondi. This sixteen-volume work, published between 1809 and 1818, lays particular emphasis on a few themes: the resistance of the Lombard cities, led by Milan, to Frederick Barbarossa; the later role of Florence as champion of Italian freedom; its policy of maintaining the balance of power in Italy; Pisa's struggle against subjection by Florence; and the con-tribution of the Italian republics, and especially Florence, to the revival of learning and the arts. All these themes recur in Shelley's writings, in 'Marenghi', 'Ode to Liberty', 'Ode to Naples', *Hellas*, *A Philosophical View of Reform* or *A Defence of Poetry*. Under Sismondi's guidance, he learned to think of medieval Florence, like ancient Athens, as the model of a free and healthy society. How profoundly the conception of a decentralized participatory democracy, as embodied in Athens and Florence, influenced his political thought is apparent from a single sentence in the preface to *Prometheus Unbound*, written in 1820: 'If England were divided into forty republics, each equal in population and extent to Athens, there is no reason to suppose but that, under institutions not more perfect than those of Athens, each would produce philosophers and poets equal to those who (if we except Shakespeare) have never been surpassed.'

Florence was a holy city to Shelley also as the birthplace of Dante. Although he already knew Dante's work before he left England, and had published a translation of one of his sonnets, after his arrival in Italy his enthusiasm increased as his knowledge of the language deepened. After describing Milan Cathedral in a letter to Thomas Love Peacock of April 1818 he added, 'There is one solitary spot among these aisles behind the altar where the light of day is dim & yellow under the storied window which I have chosen to visit & read Dante there.' When three years later he visited Ravenna and saw Dante's tomb he 'worshipped the sacred spot'. The gulf between their religious views was for him irrelevant. Dante's Catholicism, he maintained in *A Defence of Poetry*, was not that of the Church: 'The distorted notions of invisible things which Dante and his rival Milton have idealized are merely the mask and the mantle in which these great poets walk through eternity enveloped and disguised.' Dante for him is the supreme poet of love:

> His apotheosis of Beatrice in Paradise, and the gradations of his own love and her loveliness, by which as by steps he feigns himself to have ascended to the throne of the Supreme Cause, is the most glorious imagination of modern poetry. The acutest critics have justly reversed the judgement of the vulgar and the order of the great acts of the *Divina Commedia* in the measure of the admiration which they accord to the Hell, Purgatory, and Paradise. The latter is a perpetual hymn of everlasting love.

A critic has spoken of 'the complete saturation of [Shelley's] mind with the poetry of the great Florentine', and has declared that 'no English poet has so completely assimilated the works of Dante as he'.[6]

During the thirty-two years between Merry's departure and Shelley's arrival Florence had passed through the upheavals of the French Revolutionary, Napoleonic and Restoration periods, from which it had escaped surprisingly lightly. The Grand Duke Ferdinand was a weaker man than his father, but he had the same liberal instincts. He succeeded in keeping Tuscany at peace until March 1799, when the French occupied Florence and ordered him to leave. In July the city was occupied by a gang of religious fanatics led by the British minister William Wyndham, which conducted a pogrom of Jews and alleged Jacobins until the Austrians took control two months later. After Napoleon's victory at Marengo in 1800 the French returned, and Tuscany became a French puppet state. A Kingdom of Etruria was created in 1801 under a son of the Duke of Parma, only to be annexed to the French Empire in 1807. Napoleon's sister Elise was permitted in 1809 to set up her court in Florence, with the title of Grand Duchess of Tuscany. A Scottish visitor, Joseph Forsyth, in 1802 commented on the 'very general change in the exterior manners of the Tuscans' introduced by the French, who had broken down 'the barriers of that dignity, true or false, which once distinguished the politer part of this people' and 'cropped the hair of the powdered fop, hedged his cheeks with the whiskers of a sapeur, and stuck a cigar into his mouth'.[7]

With the fall of Napoleon, Ferdinand was put back on his throne in 1814, and apart from a brief interruption when Murat occupied Florence during the Hundred Days he kept it until his death in 1824. Throughout these changes there was a surprising continuity. Ministers and officials who had supported Leopold's reforms held office alike under the French and under Ferdinand, and ensured that many of the reforms introduced by the French were retained. After the Restoration there was no persecution of 'Jacobins', and political refugees from other Italian states found shelter in Florence. Ferdinand's Tuscany was the most liberal state in Italy, as Shelley recognized when he wrote to Peacock in 1820, 'We live here under a nominal tyranny, administered according to the philosophic laws of Leopold, & the mild opinions which are the fashion here. Tuscany is unlike all the other Italian states, in this respect.'[8] This fact explains why he made his home in Tuscany from June 1819 until his death three years later.

With the Restoration the British were able to return to Florence, from which they had been excluded for twenty years, except for the short period of peace in 1802–3. The novelist Lady Morgan, who was there at the same time as Shelley, recorded that 'we had near fifty Irish names alone on our visiting-book, with as many English, mingled with those of Russians, Prussians, Poles, Swedes, Germans, French, Italians, Greeks, and Americans'. The reason which Byron gave in 1821 for refusing to settle in Florence was 'the prodigious influx of English'.[9] On Saturday evenings many of the British visited the house on the Lungarno Corsini which is now the British consulate but was then the home of the Countess of Albany, Prince Charles Edward's widow. The Shelleys were not among them.

Their social life in Florence was limited because of Mary's delicate state of health. They found some of the other residents at the Palazzo Marini 'tolerably agreeable', among them a Mr and Mrs Meadows, a clergyman named Harding with his wife and children, and an amateur portrait-painter named Tomkins who made a drawing of Shelley, now unfortunately lost. Occasionally they went to the theatre or the opera; Forsyth had remarked with Presbyterian disapproval that 'in a city containing only 84,000 inhabitants there are six theatres'.[10] They had virtually no Italian contacts except Gaspero Pelleschi, a composer who was teaching Claire to sing. Shelley believed that the English residents were avoiding him because of his reputation for atheism. When he mentioned this at the theatre one evening Tomkins suggested that he should take the sacrament at the British embassy to reassure them, but he was not prepared to stoop to such hypocrisy.

Shelley spent much of his time at the Uffizi, studying the exhibits in an attempt to discover 'the degree in which, & the rules according to which, that ideal beauty of which we have so intense yet so obscure an apprehension is realized in external forms'. On the classical sculptures in the gallery he jotted down copious notes in pencil. Influenced by his idealized conception of Athenian civilization and by Winckelmann's *Geschichte der Kunst des Alterthums*, which he had recently read in a French translation, he tended to overrate these works, many of which are inferior Roman copies of Greek originals, but he was not undiscriminating in his admiration. A good test of his artistic judgement is his opinion of the Medici Venus, so long admired as the supreme representation of female beauty. Byron had gushed about it in *Childe Harold*, and when the banker-poet Samuel Rogers was in Florence in 1821 he returned to the Tribuna every day to gaze at it. Even in Merry's day it had had its critics, however, and by 1819 Lady Morgan, who thought it had a silly head, could comment that 'the Medici Venus, like other long-revered antiquities, has felt the blighting breath of revolutionary change'. Shelley made notes on five Venuses, but it seems to have been the Medici Venus which he described as 'a very insipid person in the usual insipid attitude of this lady'. He showed his good taste by praising more highly the sculpture of Venus emerging from her bath, which he declared to be 'perhaps the finest personification of Venus, the Deity of superficial desire, in all antique statuary'. He recognized that the beauty of this work consisted precisely in the sculptor's power to convey 'a breathless yet passive and innocent voluptuousness . . . at once desire and enjoyment and the pleasure arising from both'. Shelley was no prude in his approach to art; on a nude male sculpture he commented, 'Curse these fig leaves; why is a round tin thing more decent than a cylindrical marble one?'[11]

His views on painting were not particularly original; he once wrote that only Raphael, Guido Reni and Salvator Rosa could 'sustain the comparison' with antiquity. His artistic tastes were also influenced, however, by his hatred of institutional Christianity, as distinct from the historical Jesus, for whom he had a deep reverence. His reaction to Ravenna's Byzantine churches, with their glorious mosaics, was the reflection that 'it seems to have been one of the first effects of the Christian religion to destroy the power of producing beauty in art'. He hated above all what he regarded as the morbid obsession of Christian art with cruelty and suffering. The Massacre of the Innocents he thought a 'very horrible' subject; on a painting of the Crucifixion he observed that 'one gets tired indeed whatever may be the conception & execution of it of seeing that monotonous & agonized form forever exhibited in one prescriptive attitude of torture'; and Michelangelo's Last Judgement he dismissed as 'a dull & wicked emblem of a dull & wicked thing'. He was equally prepared to condemn the occasional use of such themes in classical art. The story of the flaying of Marsyas he described as 'one of the few abominations of the Greek religion . . . as bad as the everlasting damnation and hacking and hewing between them of Joshua and Jehovah'.[12]

Ironically enough, the one Florentine painting which fascinated him represented a scene of suffering and death from Greek mythology. There was then in the Uffizi a painting of the severed head of Medusa the Gorgon which was believed to be that 'head of Medusa attired with a coil of serpents, the strangest and most extravagant invention imaginable', which Vasari attributed to Leonardo da Vinci. Lady Morgan described it in *Italy* as 'one of the most precious treasures of the gallery', and devoted more space to it than to any other painting in Florence.[13] Shelley was intrigued by the fact that a work with such a

horrifying subject could be so beautiful, and sought to analyse the para-
dox in a poem which he left unfinished, perhaps because he could find
no satisfactory solution to the problem.

One day early in October he came across the April issue of *The
Quarterly Review* in Delesert's reading room, where foreign periodicals
were available. It contained a venomous review of his *The Revolt of Islam*,
which alleged that he sought to abolish the laws, property, the constitution, religion and marriage, and to encourage promiscuity and incest.
The anonymous writer claimed to possess personal knowledge of his
'disgusting' private life, on the basis of which he accused him of 'low
pride', 'cold selfishness' and 'unmanly cruelty'. The review concluded
with an absurdly pompous climax:

> Like the Egyptian of old, the wheels of his chariot are broken, the path of
> 'mighty waters' closes in upon him behind, and a still deepening ocean is
> before him: – for a short time, are seen his impotent struggles against a
> resistless power, his blasphemous execrations are heard, his despair but
> poorly assumes the tone of triumph and defiance, and he calls ineffectual-
> ly on others to follow him to the same ruin – finally, he sinks 'like lead' to
> the bottom, and is forgotten. So it is now in part, so shortly will it be
> entirely with Mr Shelley.

According to an eyewitness, 'when he came to the end of the paper, to
the irresistibly ludicrous comparison of himself to Pharaoh . . . when he
came to this specimen of bathos, this stick after the explosion of the
rocket, Shelley burst into a convulsive laughter, closed the book with an
hysteric laugh, and hastily left the room, his Ha! ha's ringing down the
stairs'.[14]

Shelley, who had a stronger sense of humour than he is sometimes
credited with, was undoubtedly amused by the passage. In a letter of 15
October to Charles Ollier, his publisher, he referred to 'the droll
remarks of the *Quarterly*', and commented:

> I was amused, too, with the finale; it is like the end of the first act of an
> opera, when that tremendous concordant discord sets up from the orches-
> tra, and everybody talks and sings at once. It describes the result of my
> battle with their Omnipotent God; his pulling me under the sea by the
> hair of my head, like Pharaoh; my calling out like the devil who was game

> to the last; swearing and cursing in all comic and horrid oaths, like a French postillion on Mount Cenis; entreating everybody to drown themselves; pretending not to be drowned myself when I am drowned; and, lastly, *being* drowned.

Two months later he returned to the subject in another letter to Ollier: 'There is one very droll thing in the *Quarterly*. They say that "my chariot-wheels are broken". Heaven forbid! My chariot, you may tell them, was built by one of the best makers in Bond Street, and it has gone several thousand miles in perfect security.'[15]

Despite his attempts to appear indifferent, Shelley was deeply wounded by this attack. It was some consolation that he was defended and the *Quarterly* condemned, not only by Hunt in *The Examiner* but also, more surprisingly, by *Blackwood's Magazine*, which, while condemning his opinions, hailed him as a man of genius and a great poet, and accused the *Quarterly*'s critic of 'deceit, hypocrisy, and falsehood'. Shelley was convinced that the review in the *Quarterly* had been written by Southey, who frequently contributed to it; in fact the real author was John Taylor Coleridge, a relation of the poet, a contemporary of Shelley's at Eton and a future judge. Shelley's mistaken suspicion confirmed him in his belief that all three of the Lake Poets, in abandoning their former democratic principles for support of the Establishment in Church and State, had been guilty of 'delinquency to all public faith & honour'.[16]

When not in the Uffizi he spent much of his time walking alone in the woods of the Cascine 'watching the leaves & the rising & falling of the Arno'. His mood was sombre. Throughout Europe the reactionaries were on the offensive. Peterloo had been followed in September by the Karlsbad Decrees, which suppressed freedom of the press and of assembly throughout Germany. The scurrilous campaign in the Tory press against liberals such as Hunt, Keats and himself formed part of the same offensive, and the Jacobin poets of the 1790s who should have been leading the counter-offensive were fighting on the enemy's side. He passionately desired to strike a blow for freedom through his writings, but these were reviled in the press and found few readers. Mary's *Frankenstein* was selling more copies than all his published works put together. He had heard nothing of the fate of his poems 'Julian and Maddalo' and *The Mask of Anarchy*, both of which he had sent to Hunt some weeks before. As usual, he was in financial difficulties. Mary's father, William Godwin, who considered that he had a moral right to money that he needed and Shelley did not, continued to send her letters demanding funds, in one of which he called his son-in-law 'a disgraceful and flagrant person', although Shelley had already given him £4,700. Mary was still suffering from such deep depression that he was concealing her father's letters from her, and he feared for the consequences if she lost the expected baby. In a letter written in mid-October he had to remind himself that 'it is best that we should think all this for the best even though it be not, because Hope, as Coleridge says, is a solemn duty which we owe alike to ourselves & to the world'.[17]

As he walked in the Cascine, watching the wind sweeping along the dead leaves, he jotted down snatches of verse in one of his notebooks as they occurred to him:

> 'Twas the 20th of October
> And the woods had all grown sober
> As a man does when his hair
> Looks as theirs did grey & spare
> When the dead leaves
> As to mock the stupid
> Like ghosts in . . .

In his melancholy mood the dead leaves recalled to him some lines which he had written over two years before in *The Revolt of Islam*. In that poem which the *Quarterly* found objectionable, amid the reign of terror which follows the crushing of a revolution, one of the revolutionary leaders consoles another in a long speech full of images of seasonal change:

> The blasts of autumn drive the winged seeds
> Over the earth, – next come the snows, and rain,
> And frosts, and storms, which dreary Winter leads
> Out of his Scythian cave, a savage train;
> Behold! Spring sweeps over the world again
>
> . . . .
>
> O Spring, of hope, and love, and youth, and gladness
> Wind-winged emblem! . . .
>
> . . . .

Has not the whirlwind of our spirit driven
Truth's deathless germs to thought's remotest caves?
Lo, Winter comes! . . .

.   .   .   .

The seeds are sleeping in the soil . . .

.   .   .   .

This is the winter of the world; — and here
We die, even as the winds of Autumn fade,
Expiring in the frore and foggy air. —
Behold!   Spring comes, though we must pass, who made
The promise of its birth . . .[18]

The dead leaves had other associations for him. In the previous December
he had visited Pompeii with Mary and Claire, and among the tombs, as he
told Peacock in a letter, he had heard 'the late leaves of autumn shiver &
rustle in the stream of the inconstant wind as it were like the step of
ghosts'. The image lingered in his mind; in 1820 he was to use it again in
the opening lines of his 'Ode to Naples'. As he walked in the Cascine the
review in the *Quarterly* was troubling him. Was he indeed no true poet?
He poured his doubts and fears into a poem in *terza rima* — Dante's stanza, appropriate for a poem written in Dante's city — beginning

And what art thou, presumptuous, who profanest
The wreath to mighty Poets only due?

As he worked on the poem his self-confidence returned, to assert itself in
the proud claim

I shall not creep out of the vital day
To common dust nor wear a common pall
But as my hopes were fire, so my decay
Shall be as ashes covering them. Oh, Earth
Oh friends, if when my — has ebbed away
One spark be unextinguished of that hearth
Kindled in . . .[19]

Here he broke off, leaving the poem uncompleted. Instead he wrote the 'Ode to the West Wind'.

He later recorded in a note to 'Ode to the West Wind' that

> This poem was conceived and chiefly written in a wood that skirts the Arno, near Florence, and on a day when that tempestuous wind, whose temperature is at once mild and animating, was collecting the vapours which pour down the autumnal rains. They began, as I foresaw, at sunset with a violent tempest of hail and rain, attended by that magnificent thunder and lightning peculiar to the Cisalpine regions.

We do not know the exact date when the poem was 'chiefly written', but it was presumably between 20 October and 25 October, when he wrote out a fair copy of the first three stanzas. The rain and storms continued for at least three weeks; Shelley wrote on 28 October 'we have had rains enough to set the Mills going', on 6 November 'we have had lightning & rain here in plenty', and on 16 November 'last night we had a magnificent thunder storm, with claps which shook the house like an earthquake'.[20] Despite the weather he continued his solitary walks in the Cascine; he was indifferent to rain and thoroughly enjoyed thunderstorms.

'Ode to the West Wind' originated in his observation of the autumn weather, in his personal problems, and in his reaction to political developments since Peterloo, both in Britain and beyond. Hence it is at once a poem about a natural phenomenon, like 'The Cloud', a personal poem, and a political poem. The west wind is literally the west wind, but it is also a symbol of freedom. 'From the West swift freedom came'[21] with the American Revolution; it had crossed the Atlantic to France and, Shelley was convinced, was about to sweep through Europe and Asia. For the form of his poem he chose *terza rima*, that of his unfinished 'And what art thou' – but *terza rima* arranged in fourteen-line sections which impose a salutary discipline upon the writer.

The first three sections deal in turn with the impact of the wind upon earth, air and water. In the first, which contains many echoes of the passage of *The Revolt of Islam* quoted above, images of death and rebirth dominate; the 'clarion' of the spring is the trumpet of resurrection, for the coming revolution, symbolized by the west wind, will be a preserver as well as a destroyer. 'Driving sweet buds like flocks to feed in air' suggests a pastoral golden age restored. There are memories of Florence in the second section. When he compared the flying clouds to 'the bright hair uplifted from the head / Of some fierce Maenad' he had in mind an altar carved with four figures of Maenads which he had seen in the Uffizi, and on which he had commented that 'their hair loose and floating seems caught in the tempest of their own tumultuous motion'. 'The dome of a vast sepulchre' to which he compared the coming night was probably suggested by the Chapel of the Princes in San Lorenzo. In the third section he recalled his visit in the previous December to the Bay of Baiae, where he had seen 'the hollow caverns clothed with the glaucous sea-moss, & the leaves & branches of those delicate weeds that pave the unequal bottom of the water', and 'the ruins of its antique grandeur standing like rocks in the transparent sea under our boat'.[22] When he wrote 'Thou / For whose path the Atlantic's level powers / Cleave themselves into chasms', he was again referring to the movement of revolution from America to Europe, but he may also have had in mind the *Quarterly*'s comparison of himself to Pharaoh, upon whom 'the path of "mighty waters" closes in'.

In the last two sections he appeals to the spirit of freedom to liberate him from his depression, impotence and isolation, and to make his verse a political force. As in the first section, images of death and rebirth appear, but now birth is the dominant theme – Shelley, after all, was expecting to become a father in the very near future. His prayer to become 'the trumpet of a prophecy' echoes the reference to spring's clarion, and the idea of resurrection is clearly present. But trumpets have other uses; their primary function, as he was soon to point out in *A Philosophical View of Reform*, is to sing to battle. The first three sections had drawn their imagery from earth, air and water; at the conclusion of the poem, drawing upon the 'And what art thou' fragment, he introduced the fourth element, fire, which throughout history has been a symbol of revolution. He may have had in mind Jesus' saying 'I am come to cast fire on the earth', for we know from Mary's journal that towards the end of 1819 he read the Gospel of Luke aloud in the evenings to Mary and Claire. The first draft of the poem ended with the line 'When Winter comes Spring lags not far behind', but he sensed that the rhythm was wrong; the confidence of the direct statement was belied by the dragging monosyllables. The amendment to 'If Winter comes, can Spring be far behind?' transformed 'the final assertion . . . into a question which was a challenge having behind it all the defiance of Shelley and of the Wind – all the power of man's mind to bring round the cyclic succession of evil by good'.[23]

The writing of 'Ode to the West Wind' overlapped with that of a far longer poem, *Peter Bell the Third*. In the previous April the forthcoming publication of Wordsworth's *Peter Bell* had been announced, whereupon Keats's friend John Hamilton Reynolds had written *Peter Bell: A Lyrical Ballad*, a hilarious parody, which was published a week before Wordsworth's poem. Reviews of Reynolds's poem by Keats and of Wordworth's by Hunt, which appeared in *The Examiner*, reached Shelley in June, but although he was amused he did nothing about them at the time. The attack on himself in the *Quarterly*, which he attributed to Southey, however, again reminded him of the Lake Poets and what he regarded as their apostasy, and he wrote in his notebook some satirical lines beginning

> Proteus Wordsworth who shall bind thee
> Proteus Coleridge who shall find thee
> Hyperprotean Proteus, Southey
> Who shall catch thee who shall know thee . . .

He remembered an ode which Wordsworth had published after Waterloo, in which he had assured 'the God of peace and love' that

> Thy most dreaded instrument,
> In working out a pure intent,
> Is Man – arrayed for mutual slaughter,
> –Yea, Carnage is thy daughter!

This, as Byron later pointed out, was equivalent to saying that Carnage was Christ's sister, and Shelley wrote his own comment in one of his notebooks:

> A poet of the finest water
> Says that Carnage is God's daughter
> This poet lieth as I take
> Under an immense mistake
> As many a man before has done
> Who thinks his spouse's child his own.

On 24 October he finally read Wordsworth's *Peter Bell* at Delesert's. It set his imagination working, and almost immediately he began writing a sequel to it, *Peter Bell the Third*. This poem of 812 lines was completed in six or seven days, and on 2 November Mary finished making a fair copy which Shelley posted to Hunt on the same day, with a request that 'this party squib' should be published immediately without the author's name.[24] It remained unpublished until 1839.

'I think *Peter* not bad in his way; but perhaps no one will believe in anything in the shape of a joke from me,' Shelley wrote to Ollier in December. It is a good joke, but unlike Reynolds's poem it is by no means entirely a joke. Although it is very different from 'Ode to the West Wind', it emerges from the same complex of emotions. Shelley's anger at the *Quarterly*'s attack and at its supposed author, Southey, are there in the characterization of the Devil as sometimes 'a bard bartering rhymes / For sack', and in the slanderous accusations of incest and adultery brought against Peter by the Devil's hired reviewers. His indignation at Peterloo and at those who defended the Government responsible for such an atrocity are there in Peter's 'Ode to the Devil':

> May Carnage and Slaughter,
> Thy niece and thy daughter,
> May Rapine and Famine,
> Thy gorge ever cramming,
> Glut thee with living and dead!
>
> . . . .
>
> Slash them at Manchester . . .

There is nothing of Florence in the poem except the storm, accompanied with thunder, lightning, wind and hail, in which the Devil carries Peter off, and a quotation from Boccaccio, whom Shelley had recently read. Yet since reading Sismondi his mind had been much occupied with the concept of the city. He had depicted the good city in the Florence of 'Marenghi' a few months before, and was to depict it again in the Athens of the 'Ode to Liberty' a few months later. The evil city, Babylon to their Jerusalem, is depicted in the third part of *Peter Bell the Third*, which begins 'Hell is a city much like London'.[25]

'Ode to the West Wind' and *Peter Bell the Third* were not the only poems on which Shelley worked in October 1819. After Peterloo he decided to produce 'a little volume of *popular songs* wholly political, & destined to awaken & direct the imagination of the reformers'.[26] Two of these were 'To Sidmouth and Castlereagh' (later renamed 'Similes for Two Political Characters of 1819' by Mary) and 'A Ballad', both of which were written, at least in part, in October. The latter, in which a beggar woman and her baby die of starvation at the feet of the young clergyman who is the child's father, seems to have been modelled on the poems in *Lyrical Ballads*, as a hint that it is the sort of poem which Wordsworth should be writing, rather than odes to the Devil. Shelley never found a publisher for his book of political songs; 'To Sidmouth and Castlereagh' was first published in 1832, and 'A Ballad' was suppressed by his editors until 1927. Another political poem written in October was 'Ode to the Assertors of Liberty', which after the outbreak of the Spanish Revolution was published in 1820 as 'An Ode written before the Spaniards had recovered their Liberty'. In reality it is concerned not with Spanish but with British politics; the line 'There is blood on the earth that denies ye bread' obviously refers to the blood shed at Peterloo, and the poem, like *The Mask of Anarchy*, is an appeal to the British people to eschew vengeance when they rise in revolt.

'I am about to publish more serious things this winter,' Shelley wrote in the letter which he sent to Hunt with *Peter Bell the Third*.[27] By 'more serious things' he probably meant prose essays on political issues. On the same or the next day he began writing one such work. A republican and freethinking bookseller, Richard Carlile, who had reprinted Thomas Paine's *Age of Reason*, had been found guilty of blasphemous libel on 12 October and sentenced to three years' imprisonment and a £1,500 fine. When Shelley heard the news he recognized in this prosecution another aspect of the Government's offensive that had produced the Peterloo massacre, and began writing a furious protest in the form of a letter to *The Examiner*. Written in three or four days, this 6,000-word statement was posted to Hunt on 6 November. Hunt did not print it, for the same reason that he had not published *The Mask of Anarchy*, but as a defence of freedom of the press and of religion it ranks with Milton's *Areopagitica*.

'I have deserted the odorous gardens of literature to journey across the great sandy desert of Politics,' Shelley wrote on 6 November to his friends John and Maria Gisborne. He was probably referring to the second of his 'more serious things', *A Philosophical View of Reform*, his most ambitious attempt to expound his political ideas in prose. In the aftermath of Peterloo, when either civil war or a military dictatorship appeared to be imminent possibilities, the necessity for such a work seemed urgent. By December, however, the reformers were in disarray, torn between revolutionists and constitutionalists, and the Government was able to rush through the notorious Six Acts against freedom of assembly and of the press. 'I am preparing an octavo on reform – a commonplace kind of book – which, now that I see the passion of party will postpone the great struggle till another year, I shall not trouble myself to finish for this season,' Shelley wrote to Ollier on 15 December. 'I intend it to be an instructive and readable book, appealing from the passions to the reason of men.' [28] Ollier was not interested, and in May Shelley asked Hunt if he could suggest a publisher. Receiving no reply, he left the book unfinished, and it was not published until 1920.

The opening chapter, containing a history of freedom since the fall of the Roman Empire and a political survey of the world in 1819, gives evidence of Shelley's wide reading and his keen interest in the politics, not only of Europe but of North and South America, Asia and the Arab world. Of particular interest is his tribute to Florence and the other medieval Italian republics, in which Sismondi's influence is clearly visible:

> The republics and municipal governments of Italy opposed for some time a systematic and effectual resistance to the all-surrounding tyranny. The Lombard League defeated the armies of the despot in open field, and until Florence was betrayed to those flattered traitors and polished tyrants, the Medici, Freedom had one citadel wherein it could find refuge from a world which was its enemy. Florence long balanced, divided, and weakened the strength of the Empire and the Popedom. To this cause, if to anything, was due the undisputed superiority of Italy in literature and the arts over all its contemporary nations.

After paying tribute to Dante, Raphael and Michelangelo, Shelley continues:

> The father of our own literature, Chaucer, wrought from the simple and powerful language of a nursling of this republic the basis of our own literature. And thus we owe among other causes the exact condition belonging to our own intellectual existence to the generous disdain of submission which burned in the bosoms of men who filled a distant generation and inhabited another land. [29]

Some scholars have seen in *A Philosophical View of Reform* evidence that by

1819 Shelley had ceased to be a revolutionist and had developed into a mild liberal. This argument confuses the short-term political tactics advocated in the book with Shelley's long-term strategy. As an interim measure, he was prepared to accept an extension of the franchise which would be limited to those possessing 'a certain small property' and would exclude women, and even to tolerate the continued existence of the monarchy and the House of Lords. That did not alter his opinion that a king was an 'officer to whom wealth and from whom corruption flows', and the House of Lords an 'order of men privileged to cheat and insult the rest of the members of the state'. To avoid civil war he was ready to accept limited reforms, without abandoning his long-term aims. 'You know my principles incite me to take all the good I can get in politics, for ever aspiring to something more,' he wrote to Hunt in November. 'I am one of those whom nothing will fully satisfy, but who am ready to be partially satisfied by all that is practicable.' Even so, his minimum programme was radical enough. It included triennial parliaments; transfer of parliamentary seats from rotten boroughs to unrepresented cities and districts; extension of the franchise; abolition of the national debt, sinecures and tithes; disbanding of the Army; disestablishment of the Church and equal rights for all religious opinions; cheap, certain and speedy justice; and extension of the use of juries to all legal proceedings. But he looked beyond these measures, as the book makes plain, to his ultimate aim – a republic governed by a single-chamber parliament, elected by universal suffrage from constituencies of equal size; 'the levelling of inordinate wealth, and an agrarian distribution, including the parks and chases of the rich, of the uncultivated districts of the country'; and finally 'that equality in possessions which Jesus Christ so passionately taught', as 'one of the conditions of that system of society towards which, with whatever hope of ultimate success, it is our duty to tend'. [30]

For obtaining reforms he advocated a policy of non-violent resistance, but he never ruled out the use of force if all other means failed. 'I suppose we shall soon have to fight in England,' he wrote to Hunt on 23 December. [31] When in 1821 he heard a report (later found to be false) that a man was to be burned alive for sacrilege at Lucca, he proposed that he and his friends should arm themselves and rescue him by force; it was Byron who ruled out the use of any but diplomatic methods of saving the man. Shelley was a good shot with a pistol, and in defence of his most cherished principles would have been prepared to use one.

119

He wrote to Hunt on 2 November, 'Next Post day you will hear from me again, as I have many things to say, & expect to have to announce Mary's *new work*, now in the press.' Ten days later her child was born, a boy. Although Bell was prevented by his own ill-health from being present, all passed off smoothly; the baby was a healthy one, and Mary made a rapid recovery. The baby's birth relieved her depression, yet she could not rid herself entirely of the fear that he too would die. 'He is my only one,' she wrote on 24 November to Marianne, Hunt's wife, 'and although he is so healthy and promising that for the life of me I cannot fear yet it is a bitter thought that all should be risked on one. Yet how much sweeter than to be childless as I was for 5 hateful months.'[32] Percy Florence, as the baby was named, proved healthy enough to survive to the age of seventy. The son of the Shelleys and the grandson of William Godwin and Mary Wollstonecraft might have been expected to grow into a literary genius with a radical outlook; in fact he proved to be a harmless nonentity, who inherited from his father only a fondness for messing about in boats, and whose only political activity was to stand for Parliament, unsuccessfully, as a Conservative.

Percy Florence's second Christian name was suggested by Sophia Stacey, a young woman who moved into the Palazzo Marini on the day before he was born, together with her older travelling companion, Miss Corbet Parry-Jones. As she was a ward of Shelley's uncle, Robert Parker, Sophia had heard a great deal about him and was eager to meet him. Despite the doubts of Miss Parry-Jones, who had heard that he was 'a very shocking man', friendly relations were soon established. Sophia described him in her diary on 13 November as 'uomo molto interessante', and in a later entry as a 'mysterious yet interesting character'. She noted that he always had a book in his hand, that Greek books were lying about his room, and that he and Mary both had small tables with pen and ink beside their beds. Mary she thought 'sweetly pretty' and 'very delicate and interesting'. In later years she wrote of him, 'I shall never forget his personal appearance. His face was singularly engaging, with strongly marked intellectuality. His eyes were however the most striking portion of his face, blue and large, and of a tenderness of expression unsurpassed. In his manner there was an almost childish simplicity combined with much refinement.'[33]

This friendship inspired Shelley to write some of his best-known lyrics. He enjoyed hearing Sophia sing and play the harp, and on 16

November he promised to write a song for her. He gave her 'I arise from dreams of thee' on the following evening, and on a later occasion 'Thou art fair and few are fairer'. After the Shelleys had dined with Sophia and her friend on Christmas Day, Shelley gave her three days later a copy of Hunt's *Literary Pocket-Book*, in which he had written 'Love's Philosophy', 'Good-Night' and 'Time Long Past'. Despite the amorous tone of most of these poems, there is no reason to believe that he was in love with her; they are merely drawing-room ballads, differing from other songs of the type in quality but not in kind. 'Love's Philosophy' may have been written before he met her, and had been sent in mid-November to Hunt, who published it in *The Indicator* for 22 December.

Although Mary liked Sophia, she took a more detached view of her singing than her husband. 'She is lively & unaffected,' she wrote to Maria Gisborne on 2 December. 'She sings well for an english dilettanti & if she would learn the scales would sing exceedingly well for she has a sweet voice.'[34] Sophia and Miss Parry-Jones left for Rome on 29 December, and Shelley got up early to see them off.

He had recently written other and more important poems than those he had given Sophia. He sent Hunt on 23 December his sonnet 'England in 1819'; realizing that Hunt was not prepared to take unnecessary risks, he told him, 'I do not expect you to publish it, but you may show it to whom you please.' On the same day he wrote to the Gisbornes, 'I have just finished an additional act to Prometheus which Mary is now transcribing.' The first act of *Prometheus Unbound* had been written at Este in October 1818, and the second and third at Rome in March and April 1819. He had intended to end the poem there; the fourth act was an afterthought. In this great hymn of joy, as in the lyrics given to Sophia, we can sense how the birth of his son has dispelled his earlier depression. In Demogorgon's closing speech he squarely confronts the world of Castlereagh, Sidmouth and the *Quarterly* reviewers, Peterloo, blasphemy prosecutions and the Six Acts:

> To defy Power, which seems omnipotent;
> To love, and bear; to hope till Hope creates
> From its own wreck the thing it contemplates;
> Neither to change, nor falter, nor repent . . .[35]

This speech forms a fitting climax to the most poetically productive year of Shelley's life, in which he had written the last three acts of *Prometheus Unbound*, *The Cenci*, *The Mask of Anarchy*, 'Ode to the West Wind', and *Peter Bell the Third*. In the first nine months of the same year Keats had written 'The Eve of St Agnes', 'La Belle Dame Sans Merci', the odes to Psyche, on Indolence, on Melancholy, to a Nightingale and on a Grecian Urn, 'Lamia', 'To Autumn' and the unfinished 'Eve of St Mark' and 'Fall of Hyperion', making 1819 an *annus mirabilis* for English poetry.

The bad weather ushered in by the rain and thunderstorms of late October and early November meanwhile continued. Mary recorded on 29 November that Shelley had described the recent weather as 'an epic of rain with an episode of frost & a few similes concerning fine weather'.[36] In December the weather turned colder, and Shelley suffered badly from a pain in his side. Although their lodgings were warmer than those they had had in Naples in the previous winter, he seems to have taken inadequate precautions to protect himself against the cold out of doors; Tomkins's portrait showed him wearing a fur-collared overcoat but his usual open-necked shirt. Very severe frosts on 9–10 January 1820 were followed by heavy snow, which enabled Claire, the du Plantis girls and the Harding children to play at snowballs. The thaw began on 15 January, but the weather remained extremely cold; Pelleschi told Claire that there had not been so severe a winter at Florence for seventy years. Mary by now was seriously concerned about Shelley's health, and on 24 January they decided to take advantage of a temporary improvement in the weather to move to Pisa, where he would be able to consult a distinguished physician, Dr Andrea Vaccà Berlinghieri. As they had an English clergyman staying in the same house, before they left they had Percy Florence christened by Mr Harding in the evening of 25 January, no doubt for the same reason that William and Clara had been christened. At eight on the following morning they left for Pisa.

Although Shelley afterwards paid only brief visits to Florence, his thoughts often returned there. Before he left it he had formed a plan to accompany 'Julian and Maddalo', which was set in Venice, with 'three other poems, the scenes of which will be laid at Rome, Florence, and Naples, but the subjects of which will all be drawn from dreadful or beautiful realities'.[37] He seemed to have found a subject for his Florentine poem when in April 1821 he and Mary read *L'Osservatore Fiorentino*, by Robert Merry's friend Marco Lastri. This told how in the fifteenth century Ginevra, a Florentine girl of good family, was forced to marry a man whom she did not love. After four years of marriage she fell into a swoon so deep that she was believed to be dead and was taken to the family vault. When she awoke that night she returned to her home, but was refused admission by her husband, her father and her uncle, who thought that she was a ghost. She finally went to the house of the man whom she had loved all along, where she was admitted and nursed back to health. The ecclesiastical court ruled that her marriage had been dissolved by her supposed death, and that she was free to marry again. This story appealed to Shelley, and he began a metrical version of it, 'Ginevra', which he finally abandoned after writing some 200 lines.

After his cousin Thomas Medwin joined the Shelleys at Pisa in October 1821 they read Dante together and discussed the possibility of translating him. According to Medwin,

> [Shelley] lamented that no adequate translation existed of the *Divina Commedia*, and though he thought highly of Cary's work, with which he said he had for the first time studied the original, praising the fidelity of the version – it by no means satisfied him. What he meant by an adequate translation was one in terza rima; for in Shelley's own words, he held it an essential justice to an Author to render him in the same form.[38]

When Medwin asked whether he had attempted this, he showed him 'Matilda gathering flowers', his translation of the first fifty-one lines of the *Purgatorio*, Canto XXVIII. Medwin then tried his hand at a version of the Ugolino episode, to which Shelley made some corrections. Although Shelley seems to have made no further attempts at translating the *Divina Commedia*, Dante's influence on his own verse remained powerful; *La Vita Nuova* was to some extent the model for *Epipsychidion*, and the *Divina Commedia* for his last major work, the unfinished *The Triumph of Life*.

Percy Bysshe Shelley
from MARENGHI

Was Florence the liberticide? that band
    Of free and glorious brothers who had planted,
Like a green isle mid Aethiopian sand,
    A nation amid slaveries, disenchanted
Of many impious faiths – wise, just – do they,
Does Florence, gorge the sated tyrants' prey?

O foster-nurse of man's abandoned glory,
    Since Athens, its great mother, sunk in splendour;
Thou shadowest forth that mighty shape in story,
    As ocean its wrecked fanes, severe yet tender: –
The light-invested angel Poesy
Was drawn from the dim world to welcome thee.

And thou in painting didst transcribe all taught
    By loftiest meditations; marble knew
The sculptor's fearless soul – and as he wrought,
    The grace of his own power and freedom grew.
And more than all, heroic, just, sublime,
Thou wert among the false . . . was this thy crime?

On the Medusa of Leonardo da Vinci in the Florentine Gallery

It lieth, gazing on the midnight sky,
    Upon the cloudy mountain-peak supine;
Below, far lands are seen tremblingly;
    Its horror and its beauty are divine.
Upon its lips and eyelids seems to lie
    Loveliness like a shadow, from which shine
Fiery and lurid, struggling underneath,
The agonies of anguish and of death.

Yet it is less the horror than the grace
    Which turns the gazer's spirit into stone,
Whereon the lineaments of that dead face

Are graven, till the characters be grown
Into itself, and thought no more can trace;
   'Tis the melodious hue of beauty thrown
Athwart the darkness and the glare of pain,
Which humanize and harmonize the strain.

And from its head as from one body grow,
   As — grass out of a watery rock,
Hairs which are vipers, and they curl and flow
   And their long tangles in each other lock,
And with unending involutions show
   Their mailèd radiance, as it were to mock
The torture and the death within, and saw
The solid air with many a ragged jaw.

And, from a stone beside, a poisonous eft
   Peeps idly into those Gorgonian eyes;
Whilst in the air a ghastly bat, bereft
   Of sense, has flitted with a mad surprise
Out of the cave this hideous light had cleft,
   And he comes hastening like a moth that hies
After a taper; and the midnight sky
Flares, a light more dread than obscurity.

'Tis the tempestuous loveliness of terror;
   For from the serpents gleams a brazen glare
Kindled by that inextricable error,
   Which makes a thrilling vapour of the air
Become a — and ever-shifting mirror
   Of all the beauty and the terror there –
A woman's countenance, with serpent-locks,
Gazing in death on Heaven from those wet rocks.

ODE TO THE WEST WIND

I

O wild West Wind, thou breath of Autumn's being,
Thou, from whose unseen presence the leaves dead
Are driven, like ghosts from an enchanter fleeing,

Yellow, and black, and pale, and hectic red,
Pestilence-stricken multitudes: O thou,
Who chariotest to their dark wintry bed

The wingèd seeds, where they lie cold and low,
Each like a corpse within its grave, until
Thine azure sister of the Spring shall blow

Her clarion o'er the dreaming earth, and fill
(Driving sweet buds like flocks to feed in air)
With living hues and odours plain and hill:

Wild Spirit, which art moving everywhere;
Destroyer and preserver; hear, oh, hear!

II

Thou on whose stream, mid the steep sky's commotion,
Loose clouds like earth's decaying leaves are shed,
Shook from the tangled boughs of Heaven and Ocean,

Angels of rain and lightning: there are spread
On the blue surface of thine aëry surge,
Like the bright hair uplifted from the head

Of some fierce Maenad, even from the dim verge
Of the horizon to the zenith's height,
The locks of the approaching storm. Thou dirge

Of the dying year, to which this closing night
Will be the dome of a vast sepulchre,
Vaulted with all thy congregated might

Of vapours, from whose solid atmosphere
Black rain, and fire, and hail will burst: oh, hear!

III

Thou who didst waken from his summer dreams
The blue Mediterranean, where he lay,
Lulled by the coil of his crystalline streams,

Beside a pumice isle in Baiae's bay,
And saw in sleep old palaces and towers
Quivering within the wave's intenser day,

All overgrown with azure moss and flowers
So sweet, the sense faints picturing them! Thou
For whose path the Atlantic's level powers

Cleave themselves into chasms, while far below
The sea-blooms and the oozy woods which wear
The sapless foliage of the ocean, know

Thy voice, and suddenly grow gray with fear,
And tremble and despoil themselves: oh, hear!

IV

If I were a dead leaf thou mightest bear;
If I were a swift cloud to fly with thee;
A wave to pant beneath thy power, and share

The impulse of thy strength, only less free
Than thou, O uncontrollable! If even
I were as in my boyhood, and could be

The comrade of thy wanderings over Heaven,
As then, when to outstrip thy skiey speed
Scarce seemed a vision; I would ne'er have striven

As thus with thee in prayer in my sore need.
Oh, lift me as a wave, a leaf, a cloud!
I fall upon the thorns of life! I bleed!

A heavy weight of hours has chained and bowed
One too like thee: tameless, and swift, and proud.

II

Make me thy lyre, even as the forest is:
What if my leaves are falling like its own!
The tumult of thy mighty harmonies

Will take from both a deep, autumnal tone,
Sweet though in sadness. Be thou, Spirit fierce,
My spirit! Be thou me, impetuous one!

Drive my dead thoughts over the universe
Like withered leaves to quicken a new birth!
And, by the incantation of this verse,

Scatter, as from an unextinguished hearth
Ashes and sparks, my words among mankind!
Be through my lips to unawakened earth

The trumpet of a prophecy! O, Wind,
If Winter comes, can Spring be far behind?

Thomas Medwin
TRANSLATION FROM DANTE'S *INFERNO*, CANTO **XXXIII**
Corrected by Shelley*

Now had the loophole of that dungeon, still
Which bears the name of Famine's Tower from me,
And where 'tis fit that many another will

Be doomed to linger in captivity,
Shown through its narrow opening in my cell
Moon after noon slow waning, when a sleep

That of the future burst the veil, in dream
Visited me. It was a slumber deep
And evil; for I saw, or I did seem

To see, *that* tyrant Lord his revels keep,
The leader of the cruel hunt to them,
Chasing the wolf and wolf-cubs up the steep

Ascent, that from *the Pisan is the screen*
Of *Lucca*; with him Gualandi came,
Sismondi, and Lanfranchi, *bloodhounds lean*,

Trained to the sport and eager for the game
Wide ranging in his front; but soon were seen
Though by so short a course, with *spirits tame*

The father and *his whelps* to flag at once,
And then the sharp fangs gored their bosoms deep.
Ere morn I roused myself, and heard my sons,

For they were with me, moaning in their sleep,
And begging bread. Ah, for those darling ones!
Right cruel art thou, if thou dost not weep

---

* Shelley's corrections are printed in italics.

In thinking of my soul's sad augury;
And if thou weepest not now, weep never more!
They were already waked, as wont drew nigh

The allotted hour for food, and in that hour
Each drew a presage from his dream. When I
Heard locked beneath me of that horrible tower

The outlet; then into their eyes alone
I looked to read myself, without a sign
Or word. I wept not — turned within to stone.

They wept aloud, and little Anselm mine,
Said — 'twas my youngest, dearest little one, —
'What ails thee, father? Why look so at thine?'

In all that day, and all the following night,
I wept not, nor replied; but when to shine
Upon the world, not us, came forth the light

Of the new sun, and thwart my prison thrown
Gleamed through its narrow chink, a doleful sight,
Three faces, each the reflex of my own,

Were imaged by its faint and ghastly ray;
Then I, of either hand unto the bone,
Gnawed, in my agony; and thinking they

'Twas done from sudden pangs, in their excess,
All of a sudden raise themselves, and say,
'Father! our woes, so great, were yet the less

Would you but eat of us, — 'twas *you who clad*
Our bodies in these weeds of wretchedness;
Despoil them.' Not to make their hearts more sad,

I *hushed* myself. That day is at its close, —
Another — still we were all mute. Oh, had

The obdurate earth opened to end our woes!

The fourth day dawned, and when the new sun shone,
Outstretched himself before me as it rose
My Gaddo, saying, 'Help, father! hast thou none

For thine own child — is there no help from thee?'
He died — there at my feet — and one by one,
I saw them fall, plainly as you see me.

Between the fifth and sixth day, ere 'twas dawn,
I found *myself blind-groping o'er the three*.
Three days I called them after they were gone.

Famine of grief can get the mastery.

6

Walter Savage Landor

When Shelley went to Pisa in January 1820 another major English poet was living there: Walter Savage Landor. Shelley greatly admired his poem *Gebir*, and should have liked to meet him. Landor, however, had been prejudiced against Shelley by stories he had heard about his treatment of his first wife, and refused to be introduced, although he knew him well by sight. 'I blush in anguish at my prejudice and injustice,' he wrote only a few years later.[1]

Landor was born at Warwick on 30 January, the anniversary of the execution of Charles I, in 1775, the year in which the American colonists rebelled against George III. It was an appropriate birth-date for a life-long republican. He was the eldest son of Dr Walter Landor and Elizabeth Savage, both of whom belonged to the landed gentry, although Dr Landor practised medicine until he inherited his estates. Landor was sent to Rugby, where he distinguished himself as a classical scholar and writer of Latin verse, and began to write verse in English. Despite his academic attainments, he was far from a model pupil, and in 1791 the headmaster asked his father to remove him, as he 'was rebellious and incited others to rebellion'.[2]

In 1793 he entered Trinity College, Oxford, where he soon acquired a reputation as a 'mad Jacobin', partly because he refused to wear powder on his hair, partly because of the strong terms in which he expressed his sympathy with the French Revolution; his mother had once boxed his ears for saying that he wished the French would invade England and hang George III between the Archbishops of Canterbury and York. Henceforward he was a republican, but he was never a democrat; he regarded no man as his superior, and believed in keeping those whom he considered his social inferiors firmly in their places. He was rusticated for two terms in 1794 for firing a gun at the window-shutters of an unpopular fellow-undergraduate, and never returned to the university. This piece of hooliganism was the result not of his Jacobinism but of his snobbery, for his pretext was that the victim was entertaining a party of 'servitors and other raffs'.[3]

He published in 1795 a promising collection of poems and *A Moral*

132

Epistle to Earl Stanhope, a clever political satire in the style of Pope. During the years after leaving the university he formed a friendship with Bertie Greatheed, who had contributed to *The Florence Miscellany* and whose home, Guy's Cliffe, was near Warwick; when the Piozzis were staying there in 1787 Dr Landor had treated Piozzi for his gout. Another friend living near Warwick was Dr Samuel Parr, the distinguished scholar who had been Robert Merry's tutor at Harrow. Greatheed, Parr and Landor held similar political opinions, and all three cooperated in 1797 in a Foxite campaign against the war with France. In the following year Landor published his masterpiece, *Gebir*, a wild *Arabian Nights* story to which his enthusiasm for the Revolution and his passion for Nancy Jones, a Welsh girl with whom he lived for some years, gave an intensity seldom found elsewhere in his work.

When peace was temporarily restored in 1802 he visited Paris, where he had a close-up view of Bonaparte, then First Consul. He remembered him as a slim young man, 'exceedingly handsome then, with a rich olive complexion and oval face, youthful as a girl's', his expression 'melancholy and reserved, but not morose or proud'. In *Gebir* he had described Bonaparte, in whom he then saw the liberator of Italy and possible liberator of Europe, as 'a mortal man above all mortal praise', but his visit to Paris transformed his ideas.[4] He now saw him as the betrayer of the Revolution and a menace to the peace and liberty of Europe, and acquired a life-long contempt for the French. When in 1808 the French invaded Spain he joined the Spanish forces as a volunteer, and served with them for a few months, although he saw little fighting.

He had previously met Jane Sophia Swift, the 'Ianthe' of his poems. Probably soon after their first meeting, she married her cousin, Godwin Swift, who lived in Ireland, but she and Landor met again at least once in the years that followed. She remained the great love of his life, although there is no evidence that they were ever lovers, as has been suggested. When her husband died in 1814 Landor was already married.

On his father's death in 1805 he inherited an income of about £1,100 a year from the family estates entailed on him as the eldest son — a sufficient amount to make him a desirable catch. At Bath in January 1811 he met and was attracted by Julia Thuillier, a seventeen-year-old girl of Huguenot descent 'without a sixpence, and with very few accomplishments', but 'pretty, graceful, and good-tempered'.[5] Her mother seized the opportunity to press the match, Landor put up little resistance, and in May they were married. It was the greatest mistake of his life. His feelings towards his wife are suggested by the fact that, although he addressed a few poems to Nancy, many to Ianthe and a considerable number to other ladies, the four fat volumes of his *Poetical Works* do not contain a single one addressed to her.

He had previously purchased a 3,000-acre estate in the beautiful Llanthony valley in Monmouthshire, with a ruined Augustinian priory at the centre of it, and there immediately after the honeymoon he took his bride. His ambition was to live the life of a paternalist squire on his own estate, and at Llanthony he attempted to put this plan into practice. Unfortunately he had two disqualifications for this role: he could manage neither money nor men. During the two years which he spent there he quarrelled with his tenants, his workmen, his solicitors and most of his neighbours, became entangled in several lawsuits and libel actions, borrowed money with no clear idea of how he would repay it, and after spending nearly £70,000 on the estate found himself virtually bankrupt. In May 1814 he fled to Jersey, leaving his brother Henry, who was a lawyer, to rescue what could be saved from the financial muddle. His wife joined him there, but when he proposed to live in France she refused to accompany him. A violent quarrel followed, and he left without her.

He settled in Tours, and after a separation of several months was joined by his wife, whose family had persuaded her to change her mind. In October 1815 they moved on to Como, accompanied as far as Milan by Landor's brother Robert, who planned to tour Italy. Robert soon became aware of the tension between them. 'He is seldom out of a passion or a sulky fit excepting at dinner, when he is more boisterous and good-humoured than ever,' he wrote to their mother. 'Then his wife is a darling, a beauty, an angel, or a bird. But for just as little reason the next morning she is a fool. She is certainly gentle, patient, and submissive.'[6] Such a relationship did not augur well for their future happiness.

Landor was ordered to leave Como in September 1818, after he had threatened to beat a government official, and went on to Pisa. Here he remained, except for a few months at Pistoia, until the early summer of 1821, when he finally settled in Florence with his family. He now had two children, Arnold, born at Como in 1818, and Julia, born at Pisa two years later, and two more sons were born at Florence: Walter in 1821 and Charles in 1825. To say that he settled is perhaps misleading, however, for during the eight years he spent in Florence he lived in six houses, in addition to summer residences just outside the town. He began by leasing furnished apartments in the Via della Scala, near Santa Maria Novella, but in September he quarrelled with his landlord, challenged him to a duel and wrote a letter to the Grand Duke's secretary denouncing him. He then moved into the house of the Marchese de' Medici-Tornaquinci in the Borgo degli Albizi, 'an immense palace, with warm and cold baths, and everything desirable'.[7] Here he rented seventeen or eighteen rooms for less than £50 a year, although he claimed to have spent £600 on furnishing them. During the summer months he would rent a villa in the hills outside Florence. He spent the summer of 1822 or 1823 at the Villa Catani, near the Grand Duke's villa of Poggio Imperiale, from which he could hear the music in the evenings. He moved in 1826 to another house owned by the Marchese de' Medici-Tornaquinci in the Via de' Pandolfini, but left it in the following year after he had thrown the Marchese out of his lodgings for keeping his hat on in front of Mrs Landor. For the summer of 1827 he leased the Villa Castiglione, two miles south-east of the city, near the village of Ponte a Ema. His last three homes in Florence were the Casa Cremani, at the Croce al Trebbio; the Casa Castellani, in the Via de' Bianchi; and the Palazzo Giugni, in the Via degli Alfani, near Santissima Annunziata.*

An important source of information on Landor's life in Florence is the city's archives, for he was repeatedly in trouble with the police. Charged with throwing boiling water over a chambermaid, according to the official report he behaved during the preliminary investigation with 'a maximum of scorn, insubordination and irreverence'. Ordered to pay a window-cleaner's bill of sixteen lire, he replied that 'the smallness of the sum does not diminish the iniquity of the decree', and threatened to appeal to the Grand Duke. When he became involved in a dispute with a picture-dealer in 1828 he was warned that if he could not live in peace with his neighbours he would be expelled from Tuscany. A year later an expulsion order actually was issued, after he had threatened to drag an official 'by the throat before the Grand Duke'. Landor immediately wrote to the Grand Duke, as he put it, 'showing him the passion and absurdity of this order', and after his wife and friends had interceded for him the order was cancelled, on the grounds that 'he has already been sufficiently mortified by the measures which were taken against him'. It is not surprising

---

* Now the Palazzo Fraschetti, Via degli Alfani 48.

that a weary police official noted in 1828 that 'Mr Landor, an English gentleman living in this capital for the last seven years, has become notorious for his many eccentricities, and is therefore considered liable to commit any excess in the heat of his temper, which sometimes makes him so furious that he loses control.'[8]

Landor's relations with the British diplomatic representatives in Florence were not much better:

> Before I came to Florence [he wrote], I was obliged to tell our minister here that he had neglected his duty and forgotten his promise, which was to see an injury done me redressed. His secretary, one Dawkins, the most consummate scoundrel in Italy, was afterwards so insolent that I requested him to mention any place in England or France where he might become better acquainted with me in a few minutes.[9]

E. G. Dawkins in fact had a distinguished career in the diplomatic service, becoming minister to Greece, but that did not prevent Landor from lampooning him in his *Imaginary Conversations*. His quarrel with the British minister, together with his reputation for eccentricity, republicanism and atheism, kept him out of favour with the more conventional members of the British colony for several years.

They did not deter visitors from the literary and artistic world, especially after the publication of his *Imaginary Conversations* in 1824. Among the first to visit him was Thomas Lovell Beddoes, author of *Death's Jest Book* and an admirer of Landor's verse. Hazlitt, who was touring Italy, called early in 1825, and introduced Landor to Leigh Hunt, who was living at Maiano, two miles north-east of Florence. Another friend with whom he became acquainted about this time was Charles Armitage Brown, a friend of Keats, a stout and jovial man who was living in a convent at Maiano. Hunt and Brown taught him to appreciate the work of Shelley and Keats, and revealed to him how distorted was his view of Shelley's moral character. Brown introduced him to Seymour Kirkup, a painter, who had known William Blake. As he was thought to be consumptive, Kirkup had been advised to live in Italy; the change of air evidently produced the desired effect, for he survived to be over ninety. He lived in an old palace by the Ponte Vecchio, and there accumulated a large collection of books and manuscripts on Dante and magic — two subjects which fascinated him.

Landor's literary friends were surprised to see how few books he possessed, although he was an exceptionally well-read man. He believed that if he kept a book for reference he would not take the trouble to commit to memory whatever of value it contained, and therefore made a habit of giving books away after he had read them. On the other hand, his friends were often astonished by the size of his collection of paintings, which covered the walls and were even hung upon the doors. Many fine paintings had come upon the market as a result of Peter Leopold's dissolution of some monasteries and the upheavals of the Revolutionary and Napoleonic periods, and Landor was an eager collector. He was a pioneer in his appreciation of the Italian primitives, and was encouraged in this taste by Kirkup, who was responsible for the discovery in 1840 of Giotto's portrait of Dante in the Bargello. Landor's attributions could not always be relied on, however; probably no modern critic would accept his claim that one of the paintings that he owned was by Cimabue. Whatever their views on his collection, his friends learned to be cautious of praising any particular painting, for if they did he would insist on their accepting it as a gift.

On leaving Pisa, Landor had written eight lines summing up his feelings about Florence:

> I leave with unreverted eyes the towers
> Of Pisa pining o'er her desert stream.
> Pleasure (they say) yet lingers in thy bowers,
> Florence, thou patriot's sigh, thou poet's dream!
>
> O could I find thee as thou once wert known,
> Thoughtful and lofty, liberal and free!
> But the pure Spirit from thy wreck has flown,
> And only Pleasure's phantom dwells with thee.[10]

Surprisingly, this is his only poem about Florence, for all his fascination with the city, its history and the works of art within its walls. There is a great deal about Florence, however, in his major prose work, *Imaginary Conversations*.

In these dialogues, which combine characteristics of the drama, the historical novel, the short story and the critical or political essay, he found a useful portmanteau into which he could pack his opinions on any subject which interested him. Four of the first series, published in 1824, are set in Florence, including 'Peter Leopold and President Du Paty', in which some of Landor's characteristic opinions are forcibly expressed – notably his anticlericalism, for his contempt for the Catholic priesthood was equalled only by his dislike of the Anglican hierarchy. Catholicism is described as 'a religion resting on peculation and fattening on vice, with violence on the right hand and falsehood on the left, giving every thing to the slothful and taking every thing from the industrious'. On the Popes he comments, 'If the popes are the servants of God, it must be confessed that God has been very unlucky in the choice of his household. So many, and so atrocious, thieves, liars, and murderers are not to be found in any other trade; much less would you look for them at the head of it.' The Italians in general are said to be 'more addicted to robbery and revenge than other European people; crimes equally proceeding from idleness and effeminacy'. Of the Tuscans we are told, 'In Tuscany there are persons of integrity; few indeed, and therefore the more estimable.' The Florentines are called 'the most loquacious and timid of animals', and the Florentine aristocracy are treated with particular disdain:

> Here counts and marquises are more plentiful than sheep and swine, and there are orders of knighthood where there is not credit for a pound of polenta . . . I have remarked this difference between the gentlemen of Florence and those of other nations. While others reject disdainfully and indignantly from among them any member who has acted publicly and privately with dishonor, those interest themselves warmly in his favor, although they never had visited or known him.

Nor does the English colony in Florence escape censure: 'In Florence, indeed, you see Englishwomen arrogant, presumptuous, suspicious, credulous, and speaking one of another more maliciously than untruly; but Englishwomen in their character as in their clothes contract a great deal of dirt by travelling.' In another dialogue, 'Alfieri and Salomon the Florentine Jew', Landor returns to his attack on the Florentines, declaring that 'certainly no race of men upon earth ever was so unwarlike, so indifferent to national dignity and to personal honor, as the Florentines are now', and contrasts them with his own class, the English gentry, of whom he complacently affirms, 'It is among those who stand between the peerage and the people that there exists a greater mass of virtue and of wisdom than in the rest of Europe.'[11]

More *Imaginary Conversations* followed in 1828 and 1829, in one of which Landor introduced himself conversing with an English visitor and a Florentine on the day in 1824 when the Grand Duke Ferdinand died. Of Ferdinand he writes, 'Equitable, humane, incomparable prince! Whatever you hear good and gracious of him you may well believe.' From such a dedicated republican as Landor this was praise indeed, but he was less complimentary to Ferdinand's subjects. He describes the Florentines as 'a people far indeed from cruel, the least so perhaps of any in Italy, where none deserve the name; but the most selfish, the most ungrateful, the most inconstant'. In a revised version of this dialogue published in 1846 he adds that 'the Italians were always, far exceeding all other nations, parsimonious and avaricious; the Tuscans beyond all other Italians; the Florentines beyond all other Tuscans'. He illustrates this assertion with a scandalous story about the Grand Duke's minister Prince Neri Corsini, who, he alleges, after his wife's death had her clothes sold by auction in his palace. He speaks with high respect, however, of the peasantry of the country round Florence, of whom he says, 'I have found at the distance of twenty miles from Florence some of the best people I have ever yet conversed with. The country people are frank, hospitable, courteous, laborious, disinterested: eager to assist one another, and offended at nothing but the offer of a reward.'[12]

In 1829 Landor at last had the opportunity to live the life of a country squire, as he had always wished. While walking in the hills below Fiesole with a wealthy friend, Joseph Ablett, he pointed out a small cottage with about twelve acres of land which he planned to lease, and suggested that Ablett should take a larger house nearby, the Villa Gherardesca. On making inquiries Ablett found that this villa was for sale with eighty-four acres of land attached, whereupon he bought it for his friend, on the understanding, as Landor wrote to his sisters, that he would 'repay him the money whenever I was rich enough – and if I never was, to leave it for my heirs to settle'.[13] The Villa Gherardesca (now called La Torraccia) lies a quarter of a mile east of San Domenico, at the end of a winding lane. It was a handsome Renaissance building of two storeys (a third has since been added), with a high turret in the centre. There is an old well in front of the house, and two very tame stone lions on either side of the entrance. Cypresses surround it on three sides, and on the fourth, where the ground slopes down towards Florence, there is a formal garden with a fountain in the middle and an ornamental wall on the eastern side with two statues in niches. It has passed through various hands since it ceased to be owned by Landor's descendants; it was at one time an orphanage, and now houses the Fiesole School of Music. Landor would have approved of both uses.

As soon as he moved into the house he began planting and gardening. 'My country now is Italy, where I have a residence for life, and literally may sit under my own vine and my own fig-tree,' he wrote to his sisters on New Year's Day 1830. 'I have some thousands of the one and some scores of the other; with myrtles, pomegranates, oranges, lemons, gagias, and mimosas in great quantity.' A year later he wrote:

> I am putting everything into good order by degrees: in fact, I spend in improvements what I used to spend in house-rent: that is, about £75 a year. I have planted 200 cypresses, 600 vines, 400 roses, 200 arbutuses, and 70 bays, besides laurustinas, &c., &c., and 60 fruit-trees of the best qualities from France. I have not a moment's illness since I resided here, nor have the children. [14]

The days he spent at his villa may well have been the happiest of his life. He had the company of his children, which he found a constant source of delight. He could indulge his love of living things – his dogs, his cats (even though his favourite, Cincirillo, sometimes disgraced himself by killing birds and rabbits), the nightingales, blackbirds and fantail pigeons (or those that escaped the Italians' guns), and his trees and flowers. He was still sought out by literary men, among them Emerson, H. F. Cary, the translator of Dante, who had been his friend at Rugby and Oxford, and Richard Monckton Milnes, later Lord Houghton, Keats's first biographer, who wrote poems on Landor's sons Walter and Charles. He took pleasure in his new home's literary associations; the villa had belonged to the family of Count Ugolino, and the stream which ran through its grounds, the Affrico, figured in Boccaccio's *Ninfale Fiesolano* and *Decamerone*, as he loved to recall. It is not surprising that some of his finest poems were written there, such as the richly sensuous 'Faesulan Idyl' and the Horatian 'To Joseph Ablett'. He would stride the lanes, accompanied by his mastiff Parigi, composing his verses aloud in English or Latin, to the amazement of the peasants, one of whom he heard remark to his companion '*M*atti sono tutti gli Inglesi, ma questo poi . . .' ('All the English are mad, but this one . . . !').[15]

Landor would not have been Landor if he had not found someone to quarrel with. Josèphe Antoir, secretary to the French legation, who lived lower down the hillside, accused him of cutting off his water supply. One of them sent the other a challenge (accounts differ on who it was), and a duel was averted only by the diplomacy of the French minister and Landor's friend Kirkup. The subsequent legal proceedings dragged on for years. In 1834 an official reported:

> For several years now the Civil Tribunals and the Police have had to deal with the lively and ever recurring questions arising between the Englishman W. S. Landor and the Secretary of the French Legation G. Antoir.*The subjects under legal dispute consisting of a few drops of water and a few square yards of land, they buy their victories with gold.[16]

One visit gave Landor particular pleasure. After her first husband's death Mrs Swift had married a French nobleman, the Comte de Molandé, whose death had left her a widow for the second time. In October 1829 she arrived in Florence with her children, to Landor's delight. During her stay he walked into Florence every other day to breakfast with her, and she and her family occasionally dined at his villa. Although he hated such occasions, he accompanied her to the balls given by the Grand Duke at the Pitti Palace, and even to a ball given by the British minister, Lord Burghersh, with whom he had been at daggers drawn ever since his arrival in Florence. Such was his love for his villa that he planned to be buried in its garden, and at his request the Comtesse and her three daughters in January 1830 planted four mimosas to mark the spot which he had selected for his grave. To mark the occasion he wrote his own epitaph:

> Lo! Where the four mimosas blend their shade,
> In calm repose at last is Landor laid;
> For ere he slept he saw them planted here
> By her his soul had ever held most dear,
> And he had lived enough when he had dried her tear.[17]

---

* G stands for Giuseppe, the Italian form of Joseph.

Her visit revived his interest in poetry, which in recent years he had neglected for prose, and in 1831 he published *Gebir, Count Julian, and Other Poems*, which included a number of those addressed to Ianthe.

His idyllic life at the Villa Gherardesca was ended in 1835 by a violent quarrel with his wife, to which the Comtesse's visit seems to have contributed. The roots of this quarrel must be sought in the psychology of both the Landors. The testimony of his friends and acquaintances leaves no doubt that he was a man with many virtues and an attractive personality. Lady Blessington, his friend for many years, listed among his qualities

> the high breeding and urbanity of his manners . . . dignified reserve, when brought in contact with those he disapproves . . . a more than ordinary politeness towards women . . . grave and respectful . . . natural dignity . . . . a fearless and uncompromising expression of his thoughts, incompatible with a mundane policy; the practice of a profuse generosity towards the unfortunate; a simplicity in his own mode of life, in which the indulgence of selfish gratifications is rigidly excluded; and a sternness of mind, and a tenderness of heart, that would lead him to brave a tyrant on his throne, or to soothe a wailing infant with a woman's softness.

Emerson wrote of him:

> I had inferred from his books, or magnified from some anecdotes, an impression of Achillean wrath, – an untamable petulance. I do not know whether the imputation were just or not, but certainly on this May day his courtesy veiled that haughty mind, and he was the most patient and gentle of hosts.

Perhaps the most vivid portrait of him is in Dickens's *Bleak House*, where he appears under the transparent disguise of 'Lawrence Boythorn': 'But it's the inside of the man, the warm heart of the man, the passion of the man, the fresh blood of the man . . . that I speak of . . . His language is as sounding as his voice. He is always in extremes; perpetually in the superlative degree. In his condemnation he is all ferocity. You might suppose him to be an Ogre, from what he says; and I believe he has the reputation of one with some people . . . He was such a true gentleman in his manner, so chivalrously polite, his face was lighted by a smile of so much sweetness and tenderness, and it seemed so plain that he had nothing to hide, but showed himself exactly as he was . . .'[18]

Unfortunately Landor did have something to hide. Inside the courageous, kindly, gentle, generous, courteous, chivalrous gentleman – and he undoubtedly was all these things – lurked a demon. His maniacal fits of rage at the slightest provocation and his habit of hurling his meals out of the window when the food displeased him were notorious, and had earned him the reputation for 'Achillean wrath' to which Emerson alludes. His conviction that his class, the English gentry, represented the fine flower of civilization contributed to make him the ogre which, as Dickens remarked, some people thought him. Edward Landor, a cousin who stayed at the Villa Gherardesca, noticed that 'the smallest unintentional appearance of slight from a superior in rank would at any moment rouse him into a fury of passion'. He was seen at his worst in his dealings with Italian servants and workmen, whom he repeatedly assaulted, as the archives of the Florentine police testify. There was a well-known story that he once threw his cook out of a first-floor window when served with a meal which he considered not up to standard, and immediately exclaimed in contrition, 'Good God! I forgot the violets!' True or false, the story neatly illustrates the two sides of Landor, the man who loved all living things so intensely that he would not even allow flowers to be picked, and the bully who harboured a John Bullish contempt for Italians and in his uncontrollable rages was prepared to risk the lives of those whom he assaulted. He had a schoolboy's irresponsibility, and seems never entirely to have grown up. Leigh Hunt observed that he played with his children 'like a real schoolboy, being, in truth, as ready to complain of an undue knock, as he is to laugh, shout, and scramble'.[19] When angry he often behaved like a small child in a temper tantrum. Dickens's name for him, Boythorn, may be intended to suggest his combination of immaturity and prickliness.

Living with Landor must have resembled life near a volcano which is liable to erupt at any moment, yet Mrs Landor seems to have tried to make a success of their marriage. She had married him when very young, in the expectation of leading a pleasant social life as the wife of a rich landowner. Instead she found herself first carried off to a remote Welsh valley, and then compelled to live in exile, far from her family and friends. Robert Landor's account suggests that after four years of marriage she had learned to endure her husband's whims with patience, and ten years later she favourably impressed Leigh Hunt, who wrote that she 'would

143

have made Ovid's loneliness quite another thing, with her face radiant with good-humour'. When in 1833 Monckton Milnes was taken ill with malaria Mrs Landor nursed him back to health, and, he reported, 'was as attentive and kind to me as if I had been at home'. By this time, however, the marriage had finally broken down. Ianthe's visit and Landor's display of his affection for her seem to have provoked Mrs Landor to end sexual relations with him, with the result that for the next five years they lived in a state of permanent nervous tension. Landor's friend Henry Crabb Robinson, who visited the villa in 1837, wrote in his diary, 'I have no doubt her provocations have been very great indeed. She complains of personal violence, even beating, and I can believe such things'.[20] It is difficult to reconcile wife-beating with Landor's well-known chivalry towards women, but a man who used physical violence against his servants might have attacked his wife in the brief madness of his rage.

Nor was the provocation all on one side. Edward Landor called Mrs Landor 'a foolish talkative woman who used to drive him wild by her gabble', and she could not give her husband the intellectual companionship which he needed. In one of the *Imaginary Conversations* Andrew Marvell defends Milton's views on divorce in terms which unmistakably express Landor's feelings about his own marriage:

> Let it also be remembered that marriage is the metempsychosis of women, – that it turns them into different creatures from what they were before. Liveliness in the girl may have been mistaken for good temper; the little pervicacity which at first is attractively provoking, at last provokes without its attractiveness; negligence of order and propriety, of duties and civilities, long endured, often deprecated, ceases to be tolerable, when children grow up and are in danger of following the example . . . There are women from whom incessant tears of anger swell forth at imaginary wrongs; but, of contrition for their own delinquencies, not one.[21]

The tension between the Landors inevitably affected their children, and especially the two eldest, who in the early 1830s were entering puberty. The archaeologist Sir Austen Henry Layard, who spent his boyhood in Florence and often played with the young Landors, later recalled, 'The only time at which they were subjected to any kind of discipline was when his ungovernable temper was excited by something which they may have done to displease him, when he treated them very harshly. It is not surprising that this mode of bringing up his family should have led to much unhappiness in it.' Edward Landor remembered that 'I have known him at Fiesole carry all the dinner to the window, dish after dish, and throw it out to the dogs, because something had gone wrong. It was ludicrous to see the blank faces of those who sat looking at the empty table – his children hungry and too frightened to say a word.'[22] It is not surprising that when the crisis came Arnold and Julia sided with their mother.

One evening in March 1835 Charles Armitage Brown dined at the villa before leaving for England. During the meal something annoyed Mrs Landor, and she proceeded to abuse her husband for an hour, in front of their guest and their elder children. Landor remained silent until she paused for breath, when he merely said, 'I beg, madam, you will, if you think proper, proceed, as I made up my mind from the first to endure at least twice as much as you have been yet pleased to speak.' He afterwards wrote to Brown, asking whether he thought he had 'acted with propriety in very trying circumstances'. In his reply Brown said:

> For more than eleven years I have been intimate with you, and during that time, frequenting your house, I never once saw you behave towards Mrs Landor otherwise than with the most gentlemanly demeanour, while your love for your children was unbounded . . . When I have elsewhere heard you accused of being a violent man, I have frankly acknowledged it; limiting however your violence to persons guilty of meanness, roguery, or duplicity; by which I meant, and said, that you utterly lost your temper with the Italians.[23]

For three months Landor and his wife kept up the appearance that all was well between them, but early in July he decided that he had had enough. One evening he said, 'Mrs Landor, will you allow me the use of your carriage tomorrow morning to take me the first stage out of Florence?' She agreed, and next day he left for England. 'It was not willingly that I left Tuscany and my children,' he wrote to Southey. 'There was but one spot upon earth on which I had fixed my heart, and four objects on which my affection rested. That they might not hear every day such language as no decent person should ever hear once, nor despise both parents, I left the only delight of my existence'.[24] He made arrangements for the bulk of his income to be settled on his wife and children, and when Arnold came of age the title of the villa and estate were transferred to him.

For the next twenty-three years Landor lived in England, mainly at Bath. He made many new friends in the literary world, among them Browning, Dickens and John Forster, the future biographer of both Dickens and himself. He was not unhappy, but nostalgia for his children and his home never left him. He wrote poems addressed to each of his children, and others voicing his longing for Fiesole: 'Farewell to Italy', 'When the mimosas shall have made . . .', 'The Fig-trees of Gherardesca', 'My Homes' and the following:

> I gaze with fond regret on you,
> My cypresses, so green and tall,
> And sweet acacian avenue,
> Because I nursed and rear'd you all.
>
> On you with fond regret I gaze,
> My hall, with vine-leaves trelliced o'er,
> Because I've seen you many days
> And never am to see you more.
>
> I gaze on you with fond regret,
> My children! for you may be told
> That love (like mine, too!) can forget —
> Only with death does love lie cold.[25]

The same nostalgia for Tuscany breathes through *The Pentameron*, a series of dialogues between Boccaccio and Petrarch which Landor published in 1837, and some of the *Imaginary Conversations* published in 1846. In 'Galileo, Milton, and a Dominican' Milton replies to Galileo's sigh 'Pleasant Arcetri!' with what is obviously a personal reminiscence: 'I often walk along its quiet lanes, somewhat too full of the white eglantine in the narrower parts of them. They are so long and pliant, a little wind is enough to blow them in the face; and they scratch as much as their betters.' In 'Fra Filippo Lippi and Pope Eugenius the Fourth' the friar recalls how, when a captive in Morocco, he had longed for Tuscany: 'Beautiful scenes, on which heaven smiles eternally, how often has my heart ached for you! He who hath lived in this country can enjoy no distant one. He breathes here another air; he lives more life; a brighter sun invigorates his studies, and serener stars influence his repose'.[26]

Landor's memories of Florence were not all happy ones, however. In 1831 he had written *High and Low Life in Italy*, a novel in the form of letters and other documents, and this was published in 1837–8 in Leigh Hunt's magazine *The Monthly Repository*. Into it he had packed all his grievances – his difficulties with the police, the dispute with Antoir, the dishonesty of picture-dealers, etc. It was not a success, for his attempts at humour were decidedly elephantine, and it was never reprinted in full until it appeared in his *CompleteWorks* in 1930. In the dialogue between the Cardinal-Legate Albani and the picture-dealers, which appeared separately in the 1846 edition of his works, the Cardinal warns the dealers against 'this double baptism of pictures, this dipping of old ones in the font again, and substituting a name the original sponsor never dreamed of giving', to which one of them replies, 'I have as much right to call my pictures by what appellation I please as my house-dog.'[27]

Paradoxically, Landor's interest in the Italians' struggle for freedom and unity increased while he was living in England. At the time of the disturbances in 1831 he had written, 'Be assured there is not a patriot in Florence who would have a single pane of glass broken in his window to bring about any change whatever . . . The principle of honour and virtue was extinct in Tuscany long before the Romans appeared.' His attitude gradually changed, under the influence of events and of his reading of Sismondi's *Histoire des républiques italiennes*, which he considered one of the greatest histories ever written. The change is apparent in his imaginary conversation between Machiavelli and Michelangelo, published in 1846, in which they agree that Italy should be a federation of republics, as 'small confederate republics are the most free, the most happy, the most productive of emulation, of learning, of genius, of glory, in every form and aspect'. He followed the reform movements of 1846–7 with increasing excitement, and late in 1847 wrote to Forster, 'O for a Robespierre and a Danton! I have ordered a good handsome sabre and a brace of pistols to be sent forthwith to each of my sons.'[28] The weapons were delivered, but if he expected his sons, then in their twenties, to develop into revolutionists his hopes were disappointed.

When in January 1848 the Italian Revolution began in Palermo he hailed it with an 'Ode to Sicily', as Shelley had welcomed the revolution of 1820 with his 'Ode to Naples'. Other poems on the Italian struggle for freedom followed, and were published under the collective title *Italics*. Landor also published as a pamphlet *King Carlo-Alberto and Princess*

Belgioioso, an imaginary conversation in which he speaks of the Italians with greater respect than in his earlier writings and, evidently under Sismondi's influence, again advocates the formation of a federation of republics. 'The Italians, both in mental and corporal power, are superior to all the nations round about,' the Princess declares:

> They want only good examples and liberal institutions . . . At the present, few nations are prepared for [a republic]; the best prepared is the Italian. Every one of our cities shows the deep traces of its *carroccio*, and many still retain their municipality and their *podestà*.* I see no reason why they should not all be restored to their pristine state and vigor, all equally subject to one strict confederation.

In this dialogue Landor refers to Pope Pius IX, who in his early days in office was regarded as a reformer, as 'the calm, the prudent, the beneficent, the energetic Pio Nono', but his views radically changed after the Pope identified himself with the counter-revolution; in a dialogue published in 1851 one speaker calls him 'the only Pope in modern times who has been caught blowing bubbles to the populace, and exerting his agility at a masquerade'.[29]

With the defeat of the 1848 revolutions Landor's views hardened; in 1851 he published a poem in praise of tyrannicide in a leaflet which declared it 'the duty of all, in every country, to seize and slay, in such manner as raises least commotion, and endangers fewest lives, properties, and comforts, the usurper of that country, or whosoever aids in the subversion of its institutions'.[30] Such statements proved embarrassing when in 1858 the Italian patriot Felice Orsini, who had been his guest at Bath two years before, tried to assassinate Napoleon III, and Landor, whose hatred for the French Emperor was well known, was accused in the press of having instigated the attempt.

His return to Italy was the result of a sordid squabble with a neighbour, Mrs Yescombe, in which he became involved. Threatened with a libel action, he was persuaded in 1857 to apologize and to give an undertaking not to repeat the allegations which he had made. In the following year, however, he published a collection of his writings called *Dry Sticks*, which

---

* In a medieval Italian city-state, the *podestà* was the chief magistrate, and the *carroccio* the cart on which the city's standard was carried into battle.

included three poems repeating the allegations. When he was served with a writ for libel in July 1858 he was persuaded to flee the country and to transfer his estate to his son Arnold. At his family's invitation he returned to the Villa Gherardesca, escorted by his second son, Walter, and arrived there on 27 August. Four days earlier a jury at Bristol assizes had found against him and had awarded Mrs Yescombe £1,000 in damages.

Relations with his children were not easy. Although all four of them were over thirty, none of them was married, and none of them had any occupation. Their education had been neglected by their mother, and they had grown up undisciplined, ignorant and idle. They shared the villa with Mrs Landor, and irritated one another with their presence. 'Charles and Walter are attentive to me; Charles especially,' Landor wrote to his niece in December. 'I have never seen Arnold and Julia exchange a word. Both are equally bad-tempered, fierce and perverse. Even the more placid Charles and Walter seldom speak to their sister.' Arnold, to whom Landor had given almost everything he possessed, had sunk so low as to demand payment for his father's board and other expenses, of which he kept an account. Julia was a soured spinster. Both seem to have absorbed their mother's hatred for their father. Walter, who roamed the hills alone all day, was mentally unstable, and in later years was confined in an asylum for a time. Only Charles was a comparatively normal human being. Arnold and Julia each had a four-year-old illegitimate daughter, and an atmosphere of scandal surrounded the villa. This fact probably explains an incident when an old friend, Lord Normanby, cut Landor and his family in the Cascine, provoking him to protest in a letter ending, 'You, by the favor of a Minister, are Marquis of Normanby; I by the grace of God am Walter Savage Landor.'[31]

He found some consolation in the garden, the three dogs and Julia's little daughter, whom he believed to be an adopted child. He was delighted when on 27 April 1859 mass demonstrations in Florence forced the Grand Duke Leopold II to flee. 'A free government is quietly established here,' he wrote to a friend, 'and gentlemen of the first families are at the head of it.' But even in his beloved garden there were irritants. 'The little platform, in which I hoped to be buried, has, in my absence, been levelled; the mimosas and myrtles have disappeared,' he sadly recorded. He had celebrated in verse the planting of the mimosas by Ianthe and her daughters, now he lamented their disappearance in lines haunted by her memory:

> Never must my bones be laid
> Under the mimosa's shade.
> He to whom I gave my all
> Swept away her guardian wall,
> And her green and level plot
> Green or level now is not. [32]

Increasingly he saw himself as King Lear, the victim of his children's ingratitude; 'I gave my all' is an echo of Lear's words to Regan, 'I gave you all.' The resemblance was closer than he realized; it could be said of him, as of Lear, ''Tis the infirmity of his age; yet he hath ever but slenderly known himself. The best and soundest of his time hath been but rash.' At last, one hot morning in the second week of July, after being 'assailed by Mrs L. in language such as a prostitute could scarcely assail a thief with', this 'very foolish fond old man, / Fourscore and upward, not an hour more nor less', left for ever the home he had so loved 'with eighteen-pence in his pocket', and under the blazing Italian sun walked the two miles into Florence. [33]

By great good fortune, he met Robert Browning in the street. Although they had met only three or four times before, they greatly admired each other's poetry; Landor had described Browning as 'a great poet, a very great poet indeed, as the world will have to agree with us in thinking', and Browning had dedicated *Luria* to Landor in glowing terms. On learning the situation, Browning acted quickly; he found Landor temporary accommodation in a hotel, attempted to mediate between him and his family, and wrote to Forster to ask whether his relations in England would be prepared to assist him. Landor's brothers promised in reply to support him for the rest of his life, and to supply Browning with £200 a year for the purpose. His attempts at mediation were less successful. Julia told him that she would not give her father a glass of water to save his life. When Mrs Landor came to Browning's house and was announced, her husband declared, 'Let her come in and I throw myself out of the window,' to which she retorted, 'The best thing he could do!' [34]

To escape the heat of the Florentine summer the Brownings were about to stay in the hills near Siena. A friend of theirs, the American sculptor William Wetmore Story, was already there, and invited Landor to become his guest. Landor was on his best behaviour, and Browning was able to reassure Forster that according to Story and his wife 'a more considerate, gentle, easily-satisfied guest never entered their house'. Story took a villa for the Brownings and found lodgings in a cottage nearby for Landor, who spent a pleasant summer between the three houses, enjoying the society of the Storys, their young daughter, the Brownings and their guests, the novelist and poet Isa Blagden and Kate Field, a lively American girl. 'The thing he really loves', Browning later wrote, 'is a pretty girl to talk nonsense with; and he finds comfort in American visitors, who hold him in proper respect.' To increase his likeness to King Lear he grew 'a beautiful beard, foam-white and soft'.[35] He amused himself by writing rude poems in Latin about Napoleon III, to the annoyance of Mrs Browning, who hero-worshipped both the Napoleons.

Before the Brownings moved to Rome for the winter they arranged for Landor to stay with Elizabeth Wilson, Mrs Browning's faithful maid, who had accompanied her on her elopement from Wimpole Street and was now married to an Italian called Romagnoli. She lived at Via Nunziatina 2671 (now Via della Chiesa 93), and here Landor took over the first floor. The neighbourhood, which today is rather sordid, was then pleasant enough; the garden of the Carmine convent lay in front of the house, and there was a private garden at the back. It was necessary to arrange for the transfer of some of his belongings from the Villa Gherardesca, and Mrs Landor called on Browning to discuss this. When he told Landor, the following dialogue took place:

BROWNING: Mrs Landor called today.
LANDOR: Ha – why, you did not let her in – never surely let *her* in?
BROWNING: Oh, I should let a dog in, even, bearing your name on the collar.
LANDOR: Oh, ay, a *dog* – good! but a bitch?

Landor loved dogs, and took great pleasure in the company of Giallo, a pretty little Pomeranian which Story had given him, and to which he addressed these lines:

> Giallo! I shall not see thee dead,
> Nor raise a stone above thy head,
> For I shall go some years before,
> Where thou wilt leap at me no more,

Nor bark, as now, to make me mind,
Asking me, am I deaf or blind:
No, Giallo, but I shall be soon,
And thou wilt scratch my turf and moan.[36]

In the spring of 1860, as the weather improved, *il vecchio con quel bel canino* became a familiar sight in the Oltrarno.

There were strains and stresses in his relations with Mrs Romagnoli. On one occasion when his dinner arrived eight minutes late he threw first the soup and then the vegetables out of the window, and only her intervention saved the joint from following them. Usually, however, life was peaceful. He was still writing verse – English and Latin – and imaginary conversations. The unification of Italy pleased him, even if Italy was to be a monarchy and not a federation of republics. When Tuscany's new king, Victor Emmanuel, paid his first visit to Florence in April 1860 Landor watched the fireworks on the river from Kirkup's lodgings. 'No nation upon the earth is so deserving of a good kind ruler,' he wrote to Browning, 'and I believe the Tuscans have found one.' He enjoyed the conversation of Kate Field, who 'looked with wonder upon a person who remembered Napoleon Bonaparte as a slender young man'.[37] Both she and Isa Blagden took him out for carriage rides; during one of these the carriage stopped, at his request, near the Villa Gherardesca, and he gazed at his old home for several minutes with the tears running down his cheeks.

In 1861 Mrs Browning died, and Browning and Kate Field left Florence. Landor's loneliness to some extent was alleviated by visits from his two younger sons, who, he wrote to Browning, 'are very different from Arnold and from their mother and sister'.[38] Walter often took his father out in his carriage, and on one occasion they visited Mrs Browning's grave.

Landor had known poets of five generations from the Della Cruscans to the early Victorians – Greatheed, Southey, Hunt, Beddoes and Browning. On 29 March 1864 he was visited by a representative of a sixth generation, the Pre-Raphaelites, in the person of a tiny young man with a large head and a mop of red hair, who introduced himself as Algernon Charles Swinburne. Although the old man, now in his ninetieth year, was at first overwhelmed by his visitor, on a second visit Swinburne found him 'as alert, brilliant, and altogether delicious as I suppose others may have found him twenty years since . . . He has told me that my presence here has made him happy.' They talked of poetry, politics and religion, finding common ground in their paganism, their republicanism and their enthusiasm for Italian freedom. Landor assured his visitor that he did not believe in the immortality of the soul. When Kirkup, who was now all but stone-deaf, tried to convert him to spiritualism, he had laughed so loudly that even Kirkup heard him. A friend who visited him in June wrote to Landor's niece, 'He is happy, I think, in a quiet gentle way. There is a look of repose in his venerable face, and his folded hands, and a sweetness in his expression, which he never had formerly.'[39]

In his last letter to Browning, Landor said on 22 August, 'I am nearly blind and totally deaf. My son Charles undress [sic] me, and I do not give any trouble. I dine on soup . . .'[40] He died on 17 September in a fit of coughing, and two days later was buried in the evening in the Protestant cemetery, near the graves of two other English poets, Mrs Browning and A. H. Clough, who had died in Florence three years before. The cemetery was then a quiet spot just outside the city wall, but today a busy road runs on the site of the wall, and the pilgrim must risk his life at the hands of Italian motorists. Only Walter and Charles followed him to the grave, but a stone was later erected with the hypocritical claim that it was 'the last sad tribute of his wife and children'. It has since been replaced by a flat slab giving his birth and death dates and the last two verses of a moving tribute written by Swinburne. But he has another monument in Florence, a tablet on the wall of Via della Chiesa 93, which describes him as 'Epico Cuore Poeta Prosatore Eminente Celebratore di Firenze' ('a Heroic Spirit, an Eminent Poet and Prose-writer, a Eulogist of Florence').

'Epico Cuore'. He would have liked that.

Walter Savage Landor

FAESULAN IDYL

Here, where precipitate Spring with one light bound
Into hot Summer's lusty arms expires;
And where go forth at morn, at eve, at night,
Soft airs, that want the lute to play with them,
And softer sighs, that know not what they want;
Under a wall, beneath an orange-tree
Whose tallest flowers could tell the lowlier ones
Of sights in Fiesole right up above,
While I was gazing a few paces off
At what they seemed to show me with their nods,
Their frequent whispers and their pointing shoots,
A gentle maid came down the garden-steps
And gathered the pure treasure in her lap.
I heard the branches rustle, and stept forth
To drive the ox away, or mule, or goat,
(Such I believed it must be); for sweet scents
Are the swift vehicles of still sweeter thoughts,
And nurse and pillow the dull memory
That would let drop without them her best stores.
They bring me tales of youth and tones of love,
And 'tis and ever was my wish and way
To let all flowers live freely, and all die,
Whene'er their Genius bids their souls depart,
Among their kindred in their native place.
I never pluck the rose; the violet's head
Hath shaken with my breath upon its bank
And not reproacht me; the ever-sacred cup
Of the pure lily hath between my hands
Felt safe, unsoil'd, nor lost one grain of gold.
I saw the light that made the glossy leaves
More glossy; the fair arm, the fairer cheek
Warmed by the eye intent on its pursuit;
I saw the foot, that, altho half-erect
From its grey slipper, could not lift her up
To what she wanted: I held down a branch

And gather'd her some blossoms, since their hour
Was come, and bees had wounded them, and flies
Of harder wing were working their way thro
And scattering them in fragments under foot.
So crisp were some, they rattled unevolved,
Others, ere broken off, fell into shells,
For such appear the petals when detacht,
Unbending, brittle, lucid, white like snow,
And like snow not seen thro, by eye or sun:
Yet every one her gown received from me
Was fairer than the first . . . I thought not so,
But so she praised them to reward my care.
I said: *You find the largest.*

> *This indeed,*

Cried she, *is large and sweet.*

> She held one forth,

Whether for me to look at or to take
She knew not, nor did I; but taking it
Would best have solved (and this she felt) her doubts.
I dared not touch it; for it seemed a part
Of her own self; fresh, full, the most mature
Of blossoms, yet a blossom; with a touch
To fall, and yet unfallen.

> She drew back

The boon she tendered, and then, finding not
The ribbon at her waist to fix it in,
Dropt it, as loth to drop it, on the rest.

TO MY CHILD CARLINO

Carlino! what art thou about, my boy?
Often I ask that question, though in vain;
For we are far apart: ah! therefore 'tis
I often ask it; not in such a tone
As wiser fathers do, who know too well.
Were we not children, you and I together?
Stole we not glances from each other's eyes?

Swore we not secrecy in such misdeeds?
Well could we trust each other. Tell me, then,
What thou art doing. Carving out thy name,
Or haply mine, upon my favourite seat,
With the new knife I sent thee over-sea?
Or hast thou broken it, and hid the hilt
Among the myrtles, starr'd with flowers, behind?
Or under that high throne whence fifty lilies
(With sworded tuberoses dense around)
Lift up their heads at once . . . not without fear
That they were looking at thee all the while?
Does Cincirillo follow thee about?
Inverting one swart foot suspensively,
And wagging his dread jaw, at every chirp
Of bird above him on the olive-branch?
Frighten him then away! 'twas he who slew
Our pigeons, our white pigeons, peacock-tailed,
That fear'd not you and me . . . alas, nor him!
I flattened his striped sides along my knee,
And reasoned with him on his bloody mind,
Till he looked blandly, and half-closed his eyes
To ponder on my lecture in the shade.
I doubt his memory much, his heart a little,
And in some minor matters (may I say it?)
Could wish him rather sager. But from thee
God hold back wisdom yet for many years!
Whether in early season or in late
It always comes high priced. For thy pure breast
I have no lesson; it for me has many.
Come, throw it open then! What sports, what cares
(Since there are none too young for these) engage
Thy busy thoughts? Are you again at work,
Walter and you, with those sly labourers,
Geppo, Giovanni, Cecco, and Poeta,
To build more solidly your broken dam
Among the poplars, whence the nightingale
Inquisitively watched you all day long?
I was not of your council in the scheme,

Or might have saved you silver without end,
And sighs too without number. Art thou gone
Below the mulberry, where that cold pool
Urged to devise a warmer, and more fit
For mighty swimmers, swimming three abreast?
Or art thou panting in this summer noon
Upon the lowest step before the hall,
Drawing a slice of watermelon, long
As Cupid's bow, athwart thy wetted lips
(Like one who plays Pan's pipe) and letting drop
The sable seeds from all their separate cells,
And leaving bays profound and rocks abrupt,
Redder than coral round Calypso's cave?

from MY HOMES

From France to Italy my steps I bent
And pitcht at Arno's side my household tent.
Six years the Medicaean palace held
My wandering Lares; then they went afield
Where the hewn rocks of Fiesole impend
O'er Doccia's dell, and fig and olive blend.
There the twin streams in Affrico unite,
One dimly seen, the other out of sight,
But ever playing in his smoothen'd bed
Of polisht stone, and willing to be led
Where clustering vines protect him from the sun,
Never too grave to smile, too tired to run.
Here, by the lake, Boccaccio's *Fair Brigade*
Beguiled the hours and tale for tale repaid.
How happy! O how happy! had I been
With friends and children in this quiet scene!
Its quiet was not destined to be mine;
'Twas hard to keep, 'twas harder to resign.
Now seek I (now Life says, *My gates I close*)
A solitary and a late repose.

Algernon Charles Swinburne
IN MEMORY OF WALTER SAVAGE LANDOR

Back to the flower-town, side by side
    The bright months bring,
New-born, the bridegroom and the bride,
    Freedom and spring.

The sweet land laughs from sea to sea,
    Filled full of sun;
All things come back to her, being free;
    All things but one.

In many a tender wheaten plot
    Flowers that were dead
Live, and old suns revive; but not
    That holier head.

By this white wandering waste of sea,
    Far north, I hear
One face shall never turn to me
    As once this year:

Shall never smile and turn and rest
    On mine as there,
Nor one most sacred hand be prest
    Upon my hair.

I came as one whose thoughts half linger,
    Half run before;
The youngest to the oldest singer
    That England bore.

I found him whom I shall not find
    Till all grief end,
In holiest age our mightiest mind,
    Father and friend.

But thou, if anything endure,
    If hope there be,
O spirit that man's life left pure,
    Man's death set free,

Not with disdain of days that were
    Look earthward now;
Let dreams revive the reverend hair,
    The imperial brow;

Come back in sleep, for in the life
    Where thou art not
We find none like thee. Time and strife
    And the world's lot

Move thee no more; but love at least
    And reverent heart
May move thee, royal and released,
    Soul, as thou art.

And thou, his Florence, to thy trust
    Receive and keep,
Keep safe his dedicated dust,
    His sacred sleep.

So shall thy lovers, come from far,
    Mix with thy name
As morning-star with evening-star
    His faultless fame.

7

Robert Browning and
Elizabeth Barrett Browning

After the most famous elopement in English history, Robert Browning and his bride, Elizabeth Barrett, arrived in Pisa on 14 October 1846, accompanied by Elizabeth Wilson, her maid, and Flush, her spaniel. Browning was a dapper little man of thirty-four, five foot four in height, with black hair and side-whiskers, small eyes constantly blinking, and an aquiline nose, and something of a dandy in his dress. According to his American friend William Wetmore Story, his manner was 'nervous and rapid', and he possessed 'great vivacity, but not the least humour, some sarcasm, considerable critical faculty, and very great frankness and friend-liness of manner and mind'. Elizabeth was frail, a tiny woman of forty, with

> A fiery soul, which working out its way
> Fretted the pigmy body to decay.

Usually dressed in dark blue or black, and quiet in manner, she was some-what overshadowed by her self-assured husband, but Story found her 'very unaffected and pleasant and simple-hearted'.[1]

It was her first visit to Italy, but Browning had been there twice before. His first visit in 1838, in search of background material for *Sordello*, had been confined to the Veneto, but in 1844 he had made a longer tour, cov-ering Naples, Sorrento, Amalfi, Rome, Florence, Pisa and Livorno. The second visit in particular seems to have been something of a pilgrimage to places associated with Shelley, the 'Sun-treader' of *Pauline* and the major influence on his early verse; in Rome he visited the graves of Shelley and Keats, and at Livorno he met Shelley's friend Edward John Trelawney. Italy had provided the setting for five of his longer poems and plays which he wrote before he settled there — *Sordello*, *Pippa Passes*, *King Victor and King Charles*, *Luria* and *A Soul's Tragedy* — as well as such shorter poems as 'My Last Duchess', 'In a Gondola', 'Pictor Ignotus', 'The Italian in England', 'The Englishman in Italy' and 'The Bishop Orders his Tomb at Saint Praxed's Church'. Before 1847 he had no great love for Florence;

we know from his letters that he intensely disliked the English tourists whom he met there. Although he had read Sismondi's history, which provided him with the historical background for *Sordello*, he did not share Sismondi's and Shelley's admiration for the Florentine Republic. In *Luria*, a tragedy which in its austere beauty recalls Racine, the rulers of the medieval republic are depicted as ungrateful, suspicious and treacherous – a view for which ample historical justification could be found.

In the spring of 1847 the Brownings planned to tour northern Italy before returning to Pisa. They arrived in Florence on 20 April, and there their tour ended abruptly, for Elizabeth was so delighted by the city's beauty ('the most beautiful of the cities devised by man', she called it) that they made their home there. Nor did her delight fade with familiarity. Ten years later, in April 1857, she could still write, 'Beautiful, beautiful Florence. How beautiful at this time of year! The trees stand in their "green mist" as if in a trance of joy. Oh, I do hope nothing will drive us out of our Paradise this summer.' Another inducement to stay was the cheapness of life in Florence compared with Pisa, where, Elizabeth admitted, 'we were cheated to the uttermost with all the subtlety of Italy and to the full extent of our ignorance'.[2] This argument would have appealed especially to Robert; unlike Elizabeth, he did not come from a wealthy home, and had a horror of debt and a habit of keeping careful accounts of their expenditure that she found amusing.

Florence in 1847 was a city of some 100,000 people. Its fourteenth-century walls were still standing, and the city gates were closed at 1 a.m. every night. The built-up area was spreading, but there were still many gardens and smallholdings inside the walls. There were signs, however, that Florence was at last moving out of the Middle Ages. Since 1846 the streets had been lit by gas, although the municipal authorities had thriftily ordered that the lamps were to be lit only on nights when there was no moon. Three months after the Brownings' arrival the railway line from Livorno, designed by Robert Stephenson, was officially opened by the Grand Duke, and with the railway came the telegraph.

Equally exciting innovations were taking place in the political field. Leopold II, who had succeeded his father as Grand Duke in 1824, was a kindly, well-meaning man liked but not greatly respected by his subjects, who referred to him as *Babbo* ('Daddy') and twisted his title of *Granduca* to *Granciuco* ('Big Donkey'). He continued his father's comparatively liberal policies; when under pressure from Vienna he suppressed the liberal journal *Antologia* in 1833 he paid the proprietor for the copies seized by the police. By 1847, however, the Tuscans were demanding something more than a tolerant despotism. The new Pope elected in 1846, Pius IX, to the amazement of Europe, had introduced a number of reforms in the Papal States: an amnesty for political prisoners, relaxation of the censorship, the formation of a state council composed of laymen. He thereby stimulated demands for similar reforms in other Italian states. In Tuscany the press censorship was relaxed on 7 May 1847, with the result that new journals appeared which clamoured for more fundamental reforms. Without realizing it, the Brownings had arrived in Florence at a time of mounting political excitement.

After two nights at the Hôtel du Nord, they moved into cheap and very comfortable furnished rooms at Via delle Belle Donne 4222 (now 6). When Elizabeth, who was still recovering from a miscarriage, felt well enough they began sightseeing, and on 26 May she was able to report that 'I have seen the Venus, I have seen the divine Raphaels.' They also went on pilgrimage to the sights associated with Milton: first to Galileo's villa at Arcetri, and then to Vallombrosa, where to escape the heat they planned to spend two months in the monastery. Robert obtained a letter from the Archbishop of Florence requesting the abbot to allow Elizabeth and Wilson to stay, and early in the morning of 14 July they set out. On the last stage of the journey the two women, Flush and their luggage were dragged up the mountainside in two large wine baskets without wheels, each drawn by two white bullocks, while Robert rode beside them on horseback. On their arrival, however, they discovered that there was a new abbot who was 'given to sanctity' and scorned the Archbishop's letter. 'A petticoat stank in his nostrils, said he, and all the beseeching which we could offer him with joined hands was classed with the temptations of St. Anthony,' according to Elizabeth.[3] They were allowed to stay for five days in a guest-house outside the monastery, where they found the bread uneatable, but at the end of that period they were obliged to return to Florence.

The lease of their lodgings was about to expire, but Robert found new and cooler ones at Casa Guidi, a house on the corner of the Via Maggio and the Via Mazzetta, built by the Ridolfi family in the fifteenth century. Because it was the dead season, when there were few visitors in Florence, they were able to lease six luxuriously furnished rooms for two months at a rent which they could afford. San Felice church was immediately opposite, so that they could walk on the terrace without being over-looked, and the rent also allowed them free admission to the Boboli Gardens nearby.

Events moved quickly in the next few weeks. In Rome the Pope had approved the formation of a Civic Guard, and the demand went up for a similar body in Tuscany. Leopold yielded to the popular clamour on 3 September, although to ensure that the radicals did not obtain control of the Civic Guard membership was restricted to property-owners. This concession was greeted with mass demonstrations in the Tuscan cities, culminating in one in Florence on 12 September in which deputations from other cities, said to number 40,000, joined the Florentines in their rejoicings. From their window the Brownings watched as the long pro-cession passed on its way to the Pitti Palace, where the Grand Duke stood in tears at a window with his family to receive his people's thanks. 'The joy and exultation on all sides were most affecting to look upon,' Elizabeth wrote to her friend Miss Mitford.

> Grave men kissed one another, and grateful young women lifted up their children to the level of their own smiles, and the children themselves mixed their shrill little *vivas* with the shouts of the people. At once, a more frenetic gladness and a more innocent manifestation of gladness were never witnessed. During three hours and a half the procession wound on past our windows, and every inch of every house seemed alive with gaz-ers all that time, the white handkerchiefs fluttering like doves, and clouds of flowers and laurel leaves floating down on the heads of those who passed. Banners, too, with inscriptions to suit the popular feeling – 'Liberty' – the 'Union of Italy' – the 'Memory of the Martyrs' – 'Viva Pio Nono' – 'Viva Leopoldo Secundo' – were quite stirred with the breath of the shouters. I am glad to have seen that sight, and to be in Italy at this moment, when such sights are to be seen.[4]

At night the Brownings walked to the Arno to see the illuminations, and were impressed by the orderliness and good humour of the crowd and the absence of drunkenness, fighting or bad language. The only blot on their happiness was that they temporarily lost Flush, but he turned up again next morning.

For the Brownings, and especially for Elizabeth, 12 September 1847 was a date of great significance, for it was the first anniversary of their wedding at St Marylebone church, the event which had liberated her from her father's tyranny. To make her happiness complete, it coincided with this great demonstration of the Tuscan people's happiness at the prospect of freedom. The Tuscan revolution was in its honeymoon stage, when it seemed possible that freedom might be won without bloodshed, by peaceful cooperation between the rulers and the ruled. The atmosphere was similar to that which Wordsworth had found in France in July 1790, when

> Europe at that time was thrilled with joy,
> France standing on the top of golden hours,
> And human nature seeming born again.[5]

It was natural that Elizabeth should identify her own happiness with that of the Tuscans, her liberation with theirs. Despite the radical views which she shared with Robert, unlike him she had taken little interest in the past in the Italians' struggle for independence, unity and freedom. He had already published in 1845 'The Italian in England', his eloquent tribute to the dedication of the Italian patriots, but she had written nothing on the subject. After that memorable 12 September, however, everything was changed. More than any other English poet, she made herself the poet of the Risorgimento and the poet of Florence.

In the aftermath of the revolutions of 1848 three long poems were published which described the experience of living through a revolution. The first to appear was Clough's *Amours de Voyage*, with its vivid picture of Mazzini's Roman Republic and its defence by Garibaldi. The second was Wordsworth's *The Prelude*, written nearly fifty years earlier and published posthumously, which includes his unforgettable account of France in 1790–92. The third was Elizabeth Barrett Browning's *Casa Guidi Windows* – perhaps her greatest poem – Part I of which was written in the winter of 1847–8. It is a political poem, but also an intensely personal one. Although women had been writing political poems at least since the 1770s, for a woman to write on a political theme was still considered vaguely improper; when Elizabeth proposed to write a poem against the Corn Laws her brothers had laughed at her. Defying this prejudice, she took as her subject the demonstration of 12 September, placing it in the perspective of Florence's past and future.

The poem opens magnificently, with a trivial episode that is yet a symbol of hope for the future:

> I heard last night a little child go singing
> 'Neath Casa Guidi windows, by the Church
> 'O bella libertà, o bella.'

For some, the poet muses, Italy means the great artists of the past, but the memory of the great dead should inspire men to great achievements in the future. It is not enough to strew violets on the spot where Savonarola died on the anniversary of his martyrdom; men must continue his work. After paying tribute to Cimabue's Madonna in Santa Maria Novella, Elizabeth recalls that, although Giotto, Fra Angelico and Raphael surpassed Cimabue, it was from him that they derived their inspiration. She describes in detail the procession of 12 September, which honoured Dante by assembling at 'Dante's Stone' by the cathedral. Italy, she declares, needs 'not popular passion . . . but popular conscience', and 'some high soul' able to lead 'the conscious people'. He may be a monk like Luther, a goatherd like William Tell, a fisherman like Masaniello, a peasant or even a Pope; it is hard to believe that a Pope would save Italy, yet

> We fain would grant the possibility
> For *thy* sake, Pio Nono.

If war comes, the peoples of Europe must support Italy against Austria, for they have all, including England, drawn inspiration from Italy:

> England claims, by trump of poetry,
> Verona, Venice, the Ravenna shore,
> And dearer holds John Milton's Fiesole
> Than Langland's Malvern with the stars in flower.

She recalls her visit with Robert to Vallombrosa, the beauty of which 'helped to fill / The cup of Milton's soul', and how,

> standing on the actual blessed sward
> Where Galileo stood at nights to take
> The vision of the stars, we have found it hard

> Gazing upon the earth and heaven, to make
> A choice of beauty.

In conclusion she calls on all, in England or other lands, who have drawn inspiration from Italy to bless

> this great cause of southern men who strive
> In God's name for man's rights, and shall not fail.[6]

The Brownings' lease of Casa Guidi expired on 19 October and, as they were not prepared to pay the double rent which the landlord demanded for the winter, they moved to Via Maggio 1881 (now 21), a few doors away. Although the rooms were comfortable, they found that the sun never reached them, and after ten days they moved again. Their new flat was at Piazza Pitti 1703 (now 3), directly opposite the Pitti Palace, and it not only faced south but also gave them a grandstand view of state occasions. In the next few months they were to find plenty to watch.

The year of revolutions, 1848, opened on 12 January with an uprising in Palermo, which quickly spread to the mainland, and on 29 January King Ferdinand II of Naples and Sicily, who hitherto had resisted all demands for reforms, hastily granted his subjects a constitution. Other Italian rulers, including the Pope, Charles Albert of Piedmont and Leopold II, hurried to follow his example. The Tuscan constitution left the executive power in the hands of the Grand Duke, but provided for a nominated Senate and an Assembly elected by the richer taxpayers. While Catholicism remained the state religion, Protestants and Jews were granted toleration and full civil rights, and freedom of association and the press were guaranteed. These concessions, limited though they were, were greeted with general rejoicings. 'The other evening, the evening after the gift,' Elizabeth wrote to Miss Mitford,

[the Grand Duke] went privately to the opera, was recognised, and in a burst of triumph and a glory of waxen torches was brought back to the Pitti by the people. I was undressing to go to bed, had my hair down over my shoulders under Wilson's ministry, when Robert called me to look out of the window and see. Through the dark night a great flock of stars seemed sweeping up the piazza, but not in silence, nor with very heavenly noises.

The '*Evvivas*' were deafening. So glad I was. *I, too*, stood at the window and clapped my hands.[7]

With the overthrow of King Louis Philippe and the proclamation of the Second French Republic on 24 February the Italian Revolution became a European revolution, which spread in March to nearly all the German states, Austria, Hungary and Bohemia. In Milan the people rose on 18 March, and after five days of street fighting expelled the Austrian garrison. At the same time the Venetians drove out the Austrians and restored the Venetian Republic. In Florence the Austrian legation was set on fire on 24 March, and the Grand Duke ordered his palace to be illuminated to celebrate the expulsion of the Austrians from Milan. 'Every morning as Robert goes to the post and to look at the newspapers I say "Bring me back news of a revolution!"' Elizabeth wrote to her sister Henrietta. 'And generally he brings me back news of *two*!'[8]

On 23 March Piedmontese troops entered Lombardy, launching what patriots regarded as a war of national liberation against Austria. A force of students and other volunteers from Tuscany left for Lombardy, and distinguished themselves by their resistance to a superior Austrian force at Curtatone. Leopold was reluctant to enter the war against his cousin the Austrian Emperor, but under popular pressure he allowed a small force of regulars and volunteers to leave. The Pope dissociated himself from the war on 29 April, however; after a counter-revolution in Naples the Neapolitan contingents were withdrawn from Lombardy; on 25 July Marshal Josef Radetzky defeated the Italian forces at Custozza; and on 9 August an armistice was signed. When the news of Custozza reached Florence popular demonstrations forced the Government to resign.

Many of the English colony had already fled from Florence, but the Brownings refused to yield to panic. 'We are very quiet, politically speaking,' Elizabeth wrote to Miss Mitford on 4 July, 'and though we hear now and then of melancholy mothers who have to part with their sons for Lombardy, and though there are processions for the blessing of flags and an occasional firing of guns for a victory, or a cry in the streets, "Notizie della guerra – leggete, signori", this is all we know of Radetzky in Florence.' Amid all the excitement they continued their usual routine, driving by day through the Cascine, and walking in the evenings 'to sit in the Loggia and look at the Perseus, or, better still, at the divine sunsets on the Arno, turning it all to pure gold under the bridges.'[9]

When their six months' lease of the flat in the Piazza Pitti expired, they were able to lease their former apartment in Casa Guidi unfurnished at a very moderate figure, as the exodus of the English had greatly reduced rents. They moved in on 9 May, and thenceforward Casa Guidi remained their home until Elizabeth's death and Robert's departure from Florence thirteen years later. Hunting for suitable furniture at a reasonable price gave them both a great deal of entertainment. Elizabeth wrote to Henrietta on 24 June:

> I reproach Robert, you know, with a drawer-plague – he was so fond of raining down drawers upon us – but when we came to compare my sofa-plague, and see which evil grew fastest – it was found the other day that we had eight sofas, and only six chests of drawers . . . We have been extravagant enough to place a glass above the drawing room fire place – not very large, but with the most beautiful carved gilt frame I ever saw in my life. Two cupids hold lights at the lower part.[10]

Robert was so proud of their mirror that he mentioned it in *The Ring and the Book* nearly twenty years later.

The same letter to Henrietta contains a remark which gives us a vivid glimpse of life in nineteenth-century London and Florence: 'While I write there's a Punch talking under the windows, just as he would talk in Wimpole Street. You know, or may not know, Punch is Neapolitan by extraction – but I forget this, and unawares fancy myself in London.'[11] How long is it since a Punch and Judy show was last seen in Wimpole Street, or in the Via Mazzetta?

The flat, of course, needed pictures. In their views on painting the Brownings were typical of their time, when artistic tastes were rapidly changing. On the one hand, they still admired the seventeenth-century Bolognese painters; in the summer of 1848 they were shocked to find that Ruskin could 'blaspheme' in *Modern Painters* against Domenichino, and when visiting Fano they returned three times to contemplate Guercino's sentimental, almost Victorian, *Guardian Angel*, about which Robert wrote a poem. On the other, they shared the growing taste for the Florentine Gothic and quattrocento painters, in which, like Landor before them, they were encouraged by Seymour Kirkup. Elizabeth reported in May 1850 that Robert had covered himself with glory by discovering and seizing on (in a corn shop a mile from Florence) five pictures among heaps of trash; and one of the best judges in Florence (Mr Kirkup) throws out such names for them as Cimabue, Ghirlandaio, Giottino, a crucifixion painted on a banner, Giottesque, if not Giotto, but unique, or nearly so, on account of the linen material, and a little Virgin by a Byzantine master.

In *Casa Guidi Windows* Elizabeth paid tribute to the 'bright and brave' Rucellai Madonna in Santa Maria Novella then attributed to Cimabue (now in the Uffizi and attributed to Duccio), which less than thirty years before Lady Morgan had described as 'a horrible Monster!'[12]

While they were busy with their furnishing, a political crisis was developing. Under pressure from the radicals, who had their main stronghold in Livorno, Leopold appointed a new Government on 27 October, with Giuseppe Montanelli, a professor of law who had fought in the Milan uprising and at Curtatone, as Prime Minister and Francesco Domenico Guerrazzi, a lawyer and novelist from Livorno, who claimed to have known Shelley when a student at Pisa, as Minister of the Interior. As a result of differences with his ministers, Leopold left for Siena on 30 January 1849, and during the night of 7–8 February fled secretly to Porto San Stefano, whence he sailed to Gaeta in the Kingdom of Naples. Charles Albert resumed the war with Austria in February, but was defeated at Novara on 23 March and forced to abdicate in favour of his son Victor Emmanuel. In Tuscany a new Assembly was elected by universal suffrage on 12 March, and on learning the news of Novara granted Guerrazzi dictatorial powers. The radicals indulged in childish imitations of the French Revolution, wearing red caps and planting trees of liberty; one such tree, just outside Casa Guidi, was the scene on 12 March of 'a grand festa . . . attended with military music, civic dancing and singing, and the firing of cannons and guns from morning to night'.[13] On 12 April the Florentine municipal authorities seized power, arrested Guerrazzi and invited Leopold to return; he preferred to remain in exile, however, until Austrian troops had overrun Tuscany and crushed all resistance.

The reaction which followed, though milder than in other Italian states, was bad enough by Tuscan standards. Although Leopold had sworn to uphold the constitution, he suspended it in 1850 and abolished it two years later. The press was more strictly censored than it had been before

1847. A Concordat with the Pope was signed in 1851, giving the clergy additional powers, and in the following year two converts to Protestantism, Francesco and Rosa Madiai, were sentenced to terms of imprisonment. The Austrian army of occupation remained on Tuscan soil until 1855, with the Tuscans footing the bill. Henceforward in his sub-jects' eyes Leopold was no longer their Grand Duke, but a ruler imposed upon them by the hated Austrians.

Mrs Browning's letters, which provide a vivid commentary on the events of 1848–9, show her becoming increasingly disillusioned, even cynical. After the armistice of August 1848 she wrote, 'Ah, poor Italy. I am as mortified as an Italian ought to be. They love only the rhetoric of patriots and soldiers, I fear! Tuscany is to be spared forsooth, if she lies still, and here she lies, eating ices and keeping the feast of the Madonna.' Four more extracts complete the story. On 10 October:

> It is painful to feel ourselves growing gradually cooler and cooler on the subject of Italian patriotism, valour, and good sense; but the process is inevitable. The child's play between the Livornese and our Grand Duke provokes a thousand pleasantries. Every now and then a day is fixed for a revolution in Tuscany, but up to the present time a shower has come and put it off.

On 3 December, to a friend who was hesitating whether to go abroad for the winter:

> I would go to Italy and try Florence, where really democratic ministries roar as gently as sucking doves, particularly when they are safe in place. We have listened to dreadful rumours – Florence was to have been sacked several times by the Livornese; the Grand Duke went so far as to send away his fam-ily to Siena, and we had 'Morte a Fiorentini' chalked up on the walls. Still, somehow or other, the peace has been kept in Florentine fashion.

On 30 April 1849:

> We have had two revolutions here at Florence, Grand Duke out, Grand Duke in. The bells in the church opposite rang for both. They first planted a tree of liberty close to our door, and then they pulled it down. The same tune, sung under the windows, did for 'Viva la republica!' and 'Viva Leopoldo!'

And on 14 May:

> Oh heavens! how ignoble it all has been and is! A revolution made by boys
> and *vivas*, and unmade by boys and *vivas* – no, there was blood shed in the
> unmaking – some horror and terror, but not as much patriotism and truth
> as could lift up the blood from the kennel.

The end came on 25 May, when from the terrace of Casa Guidi Elizabeth
watched the Austrians entering Florence, 'the soldiers sitting upon the
cannons, motionless, like dusty statues', watched by a silent crowd. In the
winter of 1852–3 she wrote:

> The state of things here in Tuscany is infamous and cruel. The old serpent,
> the Pope, is wriggling his venom into the heart of all possibilities of free
> thought and action. It is a dreadful state of things. Austria the hand, the
> papal power the brain! and no energy in the victim for resistance – only
> for hatred. They do hate here, I am glad to say'.[14]

Fortunately Elizabeth had other things than politics to think about, for
on 9 March 1849 her first and only child was born: a fat and healthy boy.
He was christened Robert Wiedemann Barrett at the French Protestant
church, 'Wiedemann' being the maiden name of Robert's mother, who
was of mixed German and Scottish descent. When he was two he began
to refer to himself as 'Penini', probably a corruption of the word *piccino*
('little one' or 'child') which he had heard used of himself, and throughout his life he was known to his family and friends as 'Pen'. Like Percy
Florence Shelley, he did not inherit his parents' literary genius; Robert's
attempts to make a classical scholar of him were a failure, but he at least
developed into a competent painter and sculptor.

In the autumn of 1850 Elizabeth recorded her memories of 1848–9 in
Part II of *Casa Guidi Windows*. Whereas the first part had been hopeful and
lyrical in tone, the second was bitter and satirical. She recalled how from
her windows she had watched the Florentines marching to the Pitti Palace
to swear solidarity with the Lombard rebels and how Leopold too had
taken the oath, and she asked forgiveness for ever having 'believed the
man was true'. She remembered with scorn the Florentines' demonstrations of revolutionary fervour:

> How down they pulled the Duki's arms everywhere!
> How up they set new café-signs, to show
>   Where patriots might sip ices in pure air —
> (The fresh paint smelling somewhat)! To and fro
>   How marched the civic guard, and stopped to stare
> When boys broke windows in a civic glow!
>   How rebel songs were sung to loyal tunes,
> And bishops cursed in ecclesiastic metres.

For all their brave words, she noted, few Florentines had shown themselves willing to risk their lives:

> How grown men raged at Austria's wickedness
>   And smoked, – while fifty striplings in a row
> Marched straight to Piedmont for the wrong's redress!
>   . . . .
> We chalked the walls with bloody caveats
>   Against all tyrants. If we did not fight
> Exactly, we fired muskets up the air
>   To show that victory was ours of right.

And so the Florentines betrayed Guerrazzi and recalled the Grand Duke, who did not return until Florence had been occupied by the Austrians. To balance the description of the procession in Part I, Mrs Browning here describes the entry of the Austrians as she had seen it from her windows:

> Then, gazing, I beheld the long-drawn street
>   Live out, from end to end, full in the sun
> With Austria's thousand; sword and bayonet,
>   Horse, foot, artillery, – cannons rolling on
> Like blind slow storm-clouds gestant with the heat
>   Of undeveloped lightnings, each bestrode
> By a single man, dust-white from head to heel,
>   Indifferent as the dreadful thing he rode.

Whatever happens, she reflects, at least we shall not be taken in by Pope Pius again. The Churches must repent, speak the truth and excommunicate their pride, but the people too must learn conviction and courage.

Remembering the child whom she heard singing, she turns to Pen, 'my own young Florentine', and draws hope from his smile.[15]

In addition to *Casa Guidi Windows*, which was published in 1851, Elizabeth wrote several poems during her first years in Italy, including the embarrassingly sentimental 'A Child's Grave at Florence'. Robert, on the other hand, wrote only one poem between 1846 and 1849, 'The Guardian-Angel', which is of more interest as a psychological document than as poetry. Elizabeth had pressed him to abandon the dramatic mono-logue and to speak out on religious and moral issues with his own voice, but that was what he found most difficult to do. A profoundly reserved, even secretive man, he needed a mask behind which he could conceal himself while speaking. Under the influence of Elizabeth and the shock of his mother's death, he tried to write the sort of verse of which both would have approved in *Christmas-Eve and Easter-Day*, published in 1850, but the result was a success neither artistically nor commercially. At the beginning of 1852 he resolved to write a poem a day, and in three days produced 'Women and Roses', the superb 'Childe Roland to the Dark Tower Came' and 'Love Among the Ruins'. It was not until the winter of 1852-3, however, that he recovered his facility and wrote many of the poems which were to appear in *Men and Women*.

Of the fifty-one poems in this book, fourteen are set in Italy – a higher proportion than in any of his other collections – and four in Florence (five if we include 'One Word More' on the strength of its references to Dante and the moon over Fiesole and San Miniato): 'Fra Lippo Lippi', 'The Statue and the Bust', 'Andrea del Sarto' and 'Old Pictures in Florence'. Two of these are concerned with painters – as is his earlier poem with a Florentine setting, 'Pictor Ignotus' – one with paintings, and the fourth with two sculptures. Browning, it would seem, saw Florence primarily in terms of the works of art within its walls; he shows little interest in con-temporary Florence and its inhabitants. A partial exception is the con-cluding verses of 'Old Pictures in Florence', in which he refers to the Civic Guard, 'all plumes and lacquer', as contemptuously as Mrs Browning does in Part II of *Casa Guidi Windows*. It is noteworthy that in this poem, the only one written during his residence in Florence in which he mentions the Italian national movement, he takes it for granted that a liberated Italy will be a republic; in 'The Statue and the Bust' he con-demns the Medicis' 'murder' of the Florentine Republic as a crime.[16]

Among the poems set in Italy we may include 'The Patriot', which tells of a popular leader who takes power amid scenes of frenzied rejoicing but a year later is overthrown and executed, an object of general execration. The word 'patriot' in the title is clearly used in its original sense of a revolutionist: one who defends the interests of his country against those of the ruling class. In its final form the poem contains no indication where the events are taking place, but in the version published in 1855 the last verse began 'Thus I entered Brescia, and thus I go!' When revising the poem Browning removed the place-name, which could be interpreted to suggest that it referred to Arnold of Brescia, the twelfth-century leader of the Roman people against papal misrule. The speaker is intended to be a type rather than any particular individual, as the subtitle 'An Old Story' suggests, and the removal of any reference to place emphasizes the universality of the theme. There are many historical figures to whom the poem could be applied; Robespierre, overthrown exactly a year after he entered the Committee of Public Safety, is an obvious example. Florentine history could supply several others, such as the Duke of Athens, who ruled the city for nearly a year before being overthrown and banished in 1343, or Savonarola. When writing the poem, however, Browning no doubt had in mind more recent events. Between 1847 and 1849 he and his wife had witnessed many outbursts of popular rejoicing similar to that described in the first two verses of the poem, whether to celebrate the formation of the Civic Guard, the promulgation of the constitution, the establishment of the Republic or the restoration of the Grand Duke. If he was thinking of any particular politician when he wrote the poem it was probably Guerrazzi, who had been removed from office and imprisoned shortly after being granted dictatorial powers. 'The Patriot' is Browning's comment on the Tuscan revolution of 1847–9, as *Casa Guidi Windows* is Mrs Browning's.

Browning associated Italy with illicit passion. In *Pippa Passes*, published in 1841, after his visit to the Veneto, two guilty lovers murder the woman's husband. 'In a Gondola', published in the following year, is a rapturous dialogue between two lovers, at the end of which the woman's husband or his hired assassins stab the man. 'The Englishman in Italy', written after Browning's second visit, is addressed by an Englishman to a peasant girl who is evidently his mistress, and dwells lovingly on life's sensual pleasures. 'Fra Lippo Lippi' is the confession of a promiscuous friar. In all these poems except *Pippa Passes* the poet's sympathies are entirely with the lovers; indeed, in 'The Statue and the Bust' he condemns the lovers' failure to consummate their adulterous passion. Even the murderous pair in *Pippa Passes* are given a certain tragic grandeur. Italy represented for Browning a vicarious holiday from the moral teachings of York Street Chapel, Walworth, which as a boy he had attended with his parents, and perhaps also from those of Elizabeth Barrett Browning.

Many of the poems in *Men and Women* deal with love, and especially married love; the title may be intended to suggest not only that the book contains a series of character studies but also that it is concerned with the relationship between the sexes. It is possible to associate many of these poems with a particular time and place: 'A Lovers' Quarrel' with Casa Guidi in March 1853; 'By the Fire-Side' with Bagni di Lucca in the following summer; 'Two in the Campagna' with Rome in May 1854. From these poems, and from others in the collection which are not so openly autobiographical, we can draw inferences about the relationship between Robert and Elizabeth, which was not so consistently idyllic as sentimentalizing biographers have sometimes suggested. In 'Two in the Campagna', for example, Robert muses:

> I would that you were all to me,
> You that are just so much, no more.
> Nor yours, nor mine, — nor slave nor free!
> Where does the fault lie? What the core
> Of the wound, since wound must be?[17]

Even more disturbing is 'Andrea del Sarto', in which the painter reflects that but for his wife's influence he might have rivalled Raphael, and that neither Leonardo, Raphael nor Michelangelo has a wife. If asked, Browning would have angrily denied that there was any autobiographical element in this poem, but it is difficult not to associate it with the failure of his poetic powers in 1846–9. This was only one aspect of their relationship, however; to complete the picture we must take into account the tenderness and intimacy of 'By the Fire-Side'. In *Men and Women* his poetic achievement reached its height, and for this Elizabeth could fairly have claimed a large share of the credit.

There were three questions on which she and Robert consistently disagreed. The first was Pen's clothing. Elizabeth longed to have a daughter, but after four miscarriages she was forced to abandon the hope. She consoled herself by refusing to allow Pen's hair to be cut, and dressing him in extraordinary costumes of her own devising adorned with feathers, ribbons, lace and embroidery, which were neither masculine nor feminine. The result was that in the streets strangers stared and asked whether the child was a boy or a girl. It is difficult to imagine any greater humiliation for a self-respecting boy. Pen, who even at twelve was still being paraded in shoulder-length ringlets, embroidered jackets, baggy shorts reaching below his knees and white ankle socks, begged to be allowed to wear normal clothes, but Elizabeth was adamant. Although Robert sympathized with his son, he was too weak-willed to insist on his son's right to be treated as a boy and not as his mother's doll.

A second cause of disagreement was their views on Louis Napoleon Bonaparte, President of the French Republic from 1848 to 1852 and subsequently the Emperor Napoleon III. At first there was no great difference on the subject between them. After his election Elizabeth described as 'childish' 'those French patriots and republicans, who crown their great deeds by electing to the presidency such a man as Prince Louis Napoleon, simply because "C'est le neveu de son oncle"!' Her references to him in her correspondence gradually became more favourable, however, even after he sent troops to suppress the Roman Republic and reinstate the Pope. As it happened, the Brownings were in Paris on 2 December 1851 when President Bonaparte carried out the coup by which he made himself dictator, and Elizabeth's reaction can only be described as ecstatic. She saw in the coup 'a grand thing, dramatically and poetically speaking', and callously dismissed the 400 people shot down by the troops as 'nothing but a little popular scum'. Robert, who, as he declared, hated 'all Buonapartes, past, present or to come', took a very different view. The situation was all the more paradoxical because Elizabeth prided herself on being more radical politically than her husband. In 1848 she had written, 'Robert and I think just alike on most points – but if one of us goes further than the other, I conscientiously believe it is I,' and when eleven years later he was invited to dine with the Prince of Wales in Rome she advised him not to say 'Though I don't go as far in politics as my wife, yet I call myself a republican.'[18] Although she attempted to justify her support for Louis Napoleon by specious arguments – that as his opponents were reactionaries and the people were behind him his actions were democratic in spirit – there is little doubt that it had an emotional basis. Despite her father's tyranny over his children and his cruelty towards her after her marriage, she still retained her admiration for his strength of will. If

Robert had manifested a similar quality he might have ousted her father from her regard, but he insisted on leaving decisions to her. Hence in her search for a substitute for the father who had rejected her, possibly under the influence of Carlyle's cult of the hero-king, she found what she sought in the sordid political adventurer who by a combination of force and fraud had imposed his dictatorship on the French people.

The third point at issue between Robert and Elizabeth was her addiction to spiritualism. As the craze swept through the United States and western Europe, 'spirits rapped, tables tipped, invisible hands wrote, guitars played by themselves, humans levitated, furniture floated, and uneducated mediums spoke Greek', and by the autumn of 1852 it had reached Florence. Many of the Brownings' friends in the Anglo-American colony – Kirkup, the American sculptor Hiram Powers, the English poets Frederick Tennyson and Robert Lytton – were believers or sympathizers. Elizabeth was honest enough to admit that the messages supposedly received from the other world were 'abundantly foolish', but this did not affect her insistence on finding a deep spiritual significance in such conjuring tricks as moving tables. Robert meanwhile remained immovably sceptical, and he took a particular dislike to the notorious medium Daniel Douglas Home (or Hume). After they attended a séance conducted by Home in London in 1855 Elizabeth wrote to Henrietta that spiritualism was 'a *tabooed* subject in this house – Robert and I taking completely different views, and he being a good deal irritated by any discussion of it'. Robert, she continued, 'cries out against Hume's *humbugging*. Oh! It is difficult to convince any man (even my Robert) against his will. I think that what chiefly went against the exhibition, in Robert's mind, was the trance at the conclusion during which the medium talked a great deal of much such twaddle as may be heard in any fifth rate conventicle.' Even after Home's moral conduct during a visit to Florence in the following year caused a scandal, Elizabeth emphasized that 'his *mediumship* is undisproved, as far as I can understand'.[19]

While Robert was writing *Men and Women*, Elizabeth was busy with her most ambitious work, *Aurora Leigh*. Poets in the 1840s and 1850s, faced with the challenge from Dickens, Thackeray, Disraeli, Mrs Gaskell, the Brontës, Trollope and George Eliot, had to face the fact that the novel was surpassing poetry in popularity and prestige. Their reaction was to write novels in verse dealing with contemporary society. Byron had set the example in *Don Juan*, but he had had few successors until the late 1840s and early 1850s, when Clough's *The Bothie of Tober-na-Vuolich* and *Amours de Voyage*, Tennyson's *Maud* and Patmore's *The Angel in the House* appeared within a few years. As early as 1844 Elizabeth had toyed with the idea of writing 'a true poetical novel' which 'might be as good a poem as any other, and much more popular besides', but she did not begin to write it until that same winter of 1852–3 when Robert produced most of the poems in *Men and Women*. Completed in London in the summer of 1856 and published in the autumn, it received rapturous reviews and quickly ran through three editions, in contrast to the unenthusiastic response to the publication of *Men and Women* a year earlier. Like Shelley, Browning had the mortifying experience of knowing that the income from his wife's writings was far greater than that from his own. Their friend John Kenyon, to whom *Aurora Leigh* was dedicated, died shortly after its publication, and helped to put the Brownings in a sound financial position for the first time by leaving Robert £6,500 and Elizabeth £4,500. It is not surprising that they celebrated the 1857 carnival enthusiastically, attending a masked ball at which the Grand Duke mixed with his subjects 'as if he were innocent'.[20]

Florence plays a large part in *Aurora Leigh*, in which Italy represents an alternative society to England's repressive religion, hypocrisy, snobbery and exploitation. The heroine is born in Florence, the daughter of an Englishman and a Florentine girl whom he first saw walking in a religious procession to Santissima Annunziata. Her mother dies when she is four, and her father settles in the mountains above Pelago. When she is thirteen he too dies, and she is taken to relations in England. In Book VII she returns to Florence as a woman and takes a house at Bellosguardo, the view from which over the city is beautifully described. In this book Mrs Browning pays her tribute to the city which she loved. Although Aurora boasts that

> This Florence sits upon me easily,
> With native air and tongue,

she finds trying the noonday heat in summer, when the town

> seems to seethe
> In this Medaean boil-pot of the sun,
> And all the patient hills are bubbling round
> As if a prick would leave them flat.

She dwells lovingly upon the Tuscan flowers, the 'grandiose red tulips', 'purple lilies' and 'tall flowering reeds', and the animal life: the moths, butterflies and fireflies, the

> melodious owls,
> (If music had but one note and was sad,
> 'Twould sound just so), and all the silent swirl
> Of bats, that seem to follow in the air
> Some grand circumference of a shadowy dome
> To which we are blind: and then, the nightingales,
> Which pluck our heart across a garden-wall.

Even the reptiles and amphibians are described with affection:

> The harmless opal snakes, and large-mouthed frogs,
> (Those noisy vaunters of their shallow streams)
> And lizards, the green lightnings of the wall,
> Which, if you sit down still, nor sigh too loud,
> Will flatter you and take you for a stone,
> And flash familiarly about your feet
> With such prodigious eyes in such small heads!

The city itself is described:

> the narrow unrecognising streets,
> Where many a palace-front peers gloomily
> Through stony vizors iron-barred
>
> . . . .
>
> the churches with mild open doors
> And plaintive wail of vespers, where a few,
> Those chiefly women, sprinkled round in blots
> Upon the dusky pavement, knelt and prayed
> Toward the altar's silver glory,

and even the Italians eating ice-cream at Doney's in the Via Tornabuoni, where the Brownings and many British, French and American writers were among the customers:

Each lovely lady close to a cavalier
Who holds her dear fan while she feeds her smile
On meditative spoonfuls of vanille,
He breathing hot protesting vows of love,
Enough to thaw her cream, and scorch his beard.[21]

Such descriptive passages come as welcome oases among the poem's arid wastes of moralizing.

The Brownings were in Rome when the decisive struggle for Italian unity and independence began on 26 April 1859 with the outbreak of war between Austria and Piedmont, and so missed the opportunity of witnessing the Tuscan revolution. On 27 April mass demonstrations in Florence demanded the Grand Duke's abdication; Leopold refused to comply, but instead left Florence for Vienna, confident that, as in 1849, he would soon be recalled. The 'rose-water revolution' passed off in complete order, thanks to the strict discipline imposed by the radical leaders; as Leopold's carriage left through the Porta San Gallo many of the crowd politely raised their hats. The Municipality on the following day formed a Provisional Government, which invited the King of Piedmont to assume a temporary dictatorship. He declined it, but accepted a protectorate over Tuscany, with the Piedmontese ambassador, Carlo Boncompagni, as his representative. France entered the war as Piedmont's ally, and similar revolutions to that in Tuscany took place in the duchies of Parma and Modena and the Papal Legations.

The Brownings were naturally delighted at these developments. 'Things have ripened since 48 and 49,' Elizabeth wrote to Henrietta. 'Tuscany, for instance, has conducted itself with a "superhuman virtue" say certain of our friends who witnessed the late movements there, and I am going back in joy to the tricolour, and a "government united to Piedmont". Oh, it seems to me like a beautiful dream.'[22] She and Robert returned at the beginning of June to find a French force occupying Florence, and hung out an Italian and a French flag from the terrace of Casa Guidi. Elizabeth rapturously celebrated the Franco-Piedmontese alliance in two poems, 'Napoleon III in Italy', a long-winded panegyric of her hero, and 'The Dance', describing an incident when French officers danced with Italian ladies in the Cascine. Although the summer was unusually hot, the temperature sometimes reaching 102 in the shade, the Brownings remained in Florence so that they could read the war bulletins as soon as they came in.

Then came disillusionment. Napoleon III met the Austrian Emperor at Villafranca and concluded a truce. Austria, they agreed, would cede Lombardy to Piedmont but would retain Venetia; the Grand Duke of Tuscany and the Duke of Modena would be reinstated; and Italy would become a confederation under the presidency of the Pope. The news, which reached Florence on 13 July, as Elizabeth put it, 'fell like a bomb on us all'. Portraits and busts of Napoleon III disappeared from the shop windows, and in some were replaced by portraits of Orsini, his would-be assassin. The effect of the news on Elizabeth is not difficult to imagine. She had two political loyalties, to Italy and to Napoleon III, and now one had betrayed the other. She even, 'to Penini's extreme disgust (who insisted on it that his dear Napoleon couldn't do anything wrong, and that the fault was in the telegraph), wouldn't let him wear his Napoleon medal'.[23] Under the double impact of Villafranca and the heat, she collapsed with the worst attack of illness she had had since she came to Italy. For three weeks Robert nursed her night and day, and when she was well enough to be moved he took her to Siena, where they enjoyed the company of the Storys and Landor.

During their absence Boncompagni handed over his powers to a Government headed by Baron Bettino Ricasoli, which organized elections on a narrowly restricted franchise; Guerrazzi's candidature was disqualified. The new Assembly unanimously voted on 16 August that the house of Lorraine was deposed, and four days later adopted a resolution declaring 'the firm intention of Tuscany to make part of a strong Italian kingdom under the constitutional sceptre of Victor Emmanuel'. Elizabeth meanwhile had had time to reconsider the Villafranca agreement. Having decided that Napoleon III had been forced to accept it by the pressure of the great powers, she expounded this view in a poem, 'A Tale of Villafranca'. She dealt with the clause in the agreement providing for the reinstatement of the Grand Duke in 'An August Voice', a masterpiece of irony put into Napoleon III's mouth:

> You'll take back your Grand-duke?
>> There are some things to object to.
> He cheated, betrayed, and forsook,
>> Then called in the foe to protect you.
> He taxed you for wines and for meats

> Throughout that eight years' pastime
> Of Austria's drum in your streets —
>   Of course you remember the last time
> You called back your Grand-duke?[24]

Her new political poems were published in March 1860 under the title *Poems before Congress* (the name referred to a European congress which was to have been held to settle the Italian question, but which never took place), and were violently abused in the British press.

While the Brownings were spending the winter of 1859–60 in Rome, the fate of Tuscany was decided. Although Napoleon III disliked the idea of the annexation of the central-Italian duchies by Piedmont, he was prepared to accept it if Piedmont ceded Savoy and Nice to France. Plebiscites held in March 1860 offered the voters a choice between 'annexation to the constitutional monarchy of King Victor Emmanuel' or 'a separate kingdom'. Leopold had abdicated in favour of his son Ferdinand, but as the latter had fought for the Austrians in the war with Piedmont he had no hope of being restored. The plebiscites produced overwhelming majorities in favour of union with Piedmont, and on 16 April Victor Emmanuel entered Florence in triumph. The Brownings were not there to see it, but Elizabeth wrote a poem to celebrate the occasion:

> Flowers, flowers, from the flowery city!
>   Such innocent thanks for a deed so pure,
>   As, melting away for joy into flowers,
> The nation invites him to enter his Pitti
>   And evermore reign in this Florence of ours.[25]

Italy's struggle was still much on her mind; of the twenty-eight poems in her last collection, eleven dealt with the Risorgimento.

Not that she was entirely concerned with politics. She wrote a very different poem, 'Bianca among the Nightingales', a tragic love-story which later suggested a title to T. S. Eliot, and wove into it happy memories of Florentine festivals:

> My native Florence! dear, forgone!
>   I see across the Alpine ridge

How the last feast-day of Saint John
    Shot rockets from Carraia bridge.
The luminous city, tall with fire,
    Trod deep down in that river of ours,
While many a boat with lamp and choir
    Skimmed birdlike over glittering towers.
I will not hear these nightingales.[26]

Robert too was busily writing in Rome in the winter of 1859–60, 'working at a long poem which I have not seen a line of', Elizabeth told a friend, 'and producing short lyrics which I *have* seen'. The long poem was 'Mr Sludge, "The Medium"', a venomous pen-portrait of Home; as Elizabeth still believed in him, it is not surprising that Robert did not allow her to see it. At about the same time he began drafting a satire on her hero Napoleon III, which appeared eleven years later under the title *Prince Hohenstiel-Schwangau, Saviour of Society*. When the French Emperor went to war for Italy's freedom Browning had temporarily modified his low opinion of him, but after Villafranca had been followed by the annexation of Savoy and Nice he had summed up the whole sequence of events in the phrase 'It was a great action; but he has taken eighteenpence for it, which is a pity' – a judgement which Elizabeth thought unfair. It is significant that a reference to 'friend Home's stilts and tongs and medium-ware' occurs near the beginning of *Prince Hohenstiel-Schwangau*, suggesting that Napoleon III and Home were permanently associated in his mind as two charlatans by whom Elizabeth had been taken in.[27]

The Brownings returned to Florence on 9 June 1860, and stayed for four weeks before moving on to Siena. One day while turning over the books on a junk stall in the Piazza San Lorenzo, Robert noticed one, partly printed, partly manuscript, with an intriguing title: *Position of the Whole Criminal Case against Guido Franceschini, a Nobleman of Arezzo, and his Cutthroats, Executed in Rome on 22 February 1698, the First by Beheading and the Others by Hanging. A Roman Murder Case. In which is Disputed Whether and When a Husband may Kill an Adulterous Wife without Suffering the Usual Penalty*. Always fascinated by crime, he bought the book for a lira and read it all the way home, along the Via Tornabuoni, over the Ponte Santa Trinità and up the Via Maggio to Casa Guidi, where he finished it, as he later described in *The Ring and the Book*:

> The book was shut and done with and laid by
> On the cream-coloured massive agate, broad
> 'Neath the twin cherubs in the tarnished frame
> O' the mirror, tall thence to the ceiling-top.
> And from the reading, and that slab I leant
> My elbow on, the while I read and read,
> I turned, to free myself and find the world,
> And stepped out on the narrow terrace, built
> Over the street and opposite the church,
> And paced its lozenge-brickwork sprinkled cool:
> Because Felice-church-side stretched, a-glow
> Through each square window fringed for festival,
> Whence came the clear voice of the cloistered ones
> Chanting a chant made for midsummer nights –
> I know not what particular praise of God,
> It always came and went with June.[28]

Elizabeth, who did not share her husband's obsession with the infinite potentialities of human wickedness, took no interest in the book and would not even look at it. For the time being he put it aside.

The year from July 1860 to June 1861 followed much the same pattern as the previous twelve months. The Brownings spent the summer at Siena with the Storys and Landor, returned to Casa Guidi for a month in October, and went on to Rome for the winter and spring. Elizabeth's health was giving cause for anxiety. During their first five years in Italy it had greatly improved – so much so that in June 1851 she had been strong enough to climb to the top of Milan Cathedral. Visits to damp, smoky London in 1851, 1852, 1855 and 1856 brought back the bronchitis from which she suffered, however; by 1857 she was again an invalid, and her serious illness in the summer of 1859 further weakened her. Ten days after the Brownings' arrival in Rome in November 1860 she suffered the shock of learning that her dearly loved sister Henrietta had died of cancer. Throughout the winter she remained indoors, although she insisted that Robert must play a full part in the city's social life. When the spring of 1861 came she felt well enough to go out in a carriage. On one such outing she was introduced to Hans Christian Andersen, and the meeting inspired 'The North and the South', a graceful tribute to Andersen that was to be her last poem.

When the Brownings returned to Casa Guidi on 5 June she seemed to be in reasonably good health. Then came another shock: the unexpected news that Count Cavour, the architect of Italian unity, had died. Elizabeth, who reverenced him, was prostrated by grief. 'If tears or blood could have saved him to us, he should have had mine,' she wrote to Robert's sister Sarianna. She never left Casa Guidi again, too weak even to walk on the terrace, yet no one, not even Robert, guessed that death was near. As Story afterwards wrote:

> Though she had always been so frail that one only wondered what kept body and soul together at all, we had become so accustomed to thinking of her as different from all others in the matter of health that we began to think she might even outlast us. Fifteen years ago her physicians told her that life was impossible, yet she had lived and borne a child and written immortal verses and shown an amazing energy of spirit and intellect.[29]

On 20 June Elizabeth caught a chill from sitting in the draught from an open window, and bronchial complications set in. During the night of 28–9 June Robert sat by her, as he had done throughout her illness. 'At four o'clock', he later wrote to a friend,

> there were symptoms that alarmed me; I called the maid and sent for the doctor. She smiled as I proposed to bathe her feet, 'Well you *are* determined to make an exaggerated case of it!' Then came what my heart will keep till I see her again and longer – the most perfect expression of her love to me within my whole knowledge of her. Always smilingly, happily, and with a face like a girl's, in a few minutes she died in my arms, her head on my cheek.

He told Story that after death she looked 'like a young girl; all the outlines rounded and filled up, all traces of disease effaced, and a smile on her face so living that they could not for hours persuade themselves she was really dead'.[30]

She was buried in the evening of 1 July in the Protestant cemetery outside the walls. Many of her friends and admirers – Italian as well as British and American – followed the coffin, on which Story had laid two large wreaths, of white roses and of laurel. The shops in the Via Maggio were closed as a gesture of respect while the procession passed. Although the Brownings were Dissenters, by Robert's wish the Anglican service was used and, according to Story, was 'blundered through by a fat English parson in a brutally careless way'.[31] The monument erected over the grave in 1865 was designed by Frederic Leighton, whom the Brownings had met in Rome and whom Robert subsequently introduced to Ruskin.

It was not Elizabeth's only monument in Florence. The municipal authorities placed a tablet on the Via Maggio wall of Casa Guidi with the following inscription, composed by the poet Niccolò Tommaseo: 'Here wrote and died Elizabeth Barrett Browning, who in her woman's heart united the learning of a scholar with the spirit of a poet, and made of her verse a golden ring between Italy and England. Grateful Florence erected this memorial in 1861.' Moved by this tribute, Browning dedicated *Last Poems*, the posthumous collection of her poems which he published in 1862, 'To "Grateful Florence", to the Municipality, her Representative, and to Tommaseo, its Spokesman, most gratefully'. In 1916, when Britain and Italy were allies in the First World War, a second tablet, bearing the opening lines of *Casa Guidi Windows* in English and Italian, was placed on the Via Mazzetta side of Casa Guidi.

'Life must now be begun anew – all the old cast off and the new put on,' Browning told Story. 'I shall go away, break up everything, go to England and live and work and write.' Four days after Elizabeth's death he made one break with the past by doing what he should have done years before – he had Pen's hair cut short and bought him a boy's suit with long trousers. When a prominent Florentine visited him on 12 July to ask him to stay in Florence and bring up Pen as a Florentine he politely refused. He left Florence with Pen on 1 August, never to return. Over twenty years later he told Story's daughter, 'In no case should I – probably – trust myself again in Florence.'[32]

For many years he avoided Italy, both in life and in his poetry. His next collection, *Dramatis Personae*, published in 1864, largely consisted of the poems which he had written in Rome in the winter of 1859–60, including 'Mr Sludge, "The Medium"', yet only one of them, 'A Face', contains any Italian references. Poems with an Italian setting are comparatively rare in his later books, and only two, 'Filippo Baldinucci on the Privilege of Burial' and 'Francis Furini', are set in Florence and its neighbourhood. The great exception is of course *The Ring and the Book*, the enormous poem based on the book which he had picked up in the Piazza San

Lorenzo. He hesitated for four years before beginning to write it, perhaps deterred by the memory of Elizabeth's dislike of the subject, and even suggested it to some of his friends as a possible theme for a poem or a novel. He finally decided to go ahead in 1864, and the poem appeared in 1868–9. The Florentine references in it are confined to Book I, most of the story being set in Rome and Arezzo, but they include the description of the discovery of the 'square old yellow Book', the fullest treatment of contemporary Florentine life in any of his poems. He returns to the neighbourhood of Florence at the beginning of Book XI, with Franceschini's description of the Certosa di Val d'Ema, the Carthusian monastery a few miles south of the city:

> Acciaiuoli – ah, your ancestor it was
> Built the huge battlemented convent-block
> Over the little forky flashing Greve
> That takes the quick turn at the foot o' the hill
> Just as one first sees Florence: oh, those days!
> 'Tis Ema, though, the other rivulet,
> The one-arched brown brick bridge yawns over, – yes,
> Gallop and go five minutes, and you gain
> The Roman Gate from where the Ema's bridged:
> Kingfishers fly there: how I see the bend
> O'erturreted by Certosa which he built.

Without a doubt, this is Browning's reminiscence of an excursion from Florence – the kingfishers would be enough to prove that. At the end of the poem, addressing Elizabeth, he recalls Tommaseo's inscription on Casa Guidi:

> Thy rare gold ring of verse (the poet praised)
> Linking our England to his Italy![33]

Browning returned to Italy for the first time since Elizabeth's death in 1878; not to Florence, but to Asolo and Venice, which he had seen during his first visit forty years before. Pen bought the Palazzo Rezzonico in Venice in 1887, and it was there that Browning died on 12 December 1889. At Sarianna's suggestion Pen applied for permission for him to be buried next to Elizabeth, but was informed that the old Protestant cemetery was closed and could not be reopened. 'I now hear from Venice that Browning is to be buried in London, in the Abbey,' Emelyn Story, the sculptor's widow, wrote to her daughter. 'I am sorry; one feels it so much more suitable that he should be in Florence and beside *her*. But I suppose the stupid authorities would not, after what they have done, permit the intramural burial. What a mistake to have forfeited such an honour and glory to Florence!'[34]

Elizabeth Barrett Browning
from CASA GUIDI WINDOWS, PART I

[The procession of 12 September 1847]

The people, with accumulated heats
    And faces turned one way, as if one fire
Both drew and flushed them, left their ancient beats
    And went up toward the palace-Pitti wall
To thank their Grand-duke who, not quite of course,
    Had graciously permitted, at their call,
The citizens to use their civic force
    To guard their civic homes. So, one and all,
The Tuscan cities streamed up to the source
    Of this new good at Florence, taking it
As good so far, presageful of more good, –
    The first torch of Italian freedom, lit
To toss in the next tiger's face who should
    Approach too near them in a greedy fit, –
The first pulse of an even flow of blood
    To prove the level of Italian veins
Towards rights perceived and granted. How we gazed
    From Casa Guidi windows while, in trains
Of orderly procession – banners raised,
    And intermittent bursts of martial strains
Which died upon the shout, as if amazed
    By gladness beyond music – they passed on!
The Magistracy, with insignia, passed, –
    And all the people shouted in the sun
And all the thousand windows which had cast
    A ripple of silks in blue and scarlet down
(As if the houses overflowed at last),
    Seemed growing larger with fair heads and eyes.
The Lawyers passed, – and still arose the shout,
    And hands broke from the windows to surprise
Those grave calm brows with bay-tree leaves thrown out.
    The Priesthood passed, – the friars with worldly-wise
Keen sidelong glances from their beards about

189

The street to see who shouted; many a monk
Who takes a long rope in the waist, was there:
　　Whereat the popular exultation drunk
With indrawn 'vivas' the whole sunny air,
　　While through the murmuring windows rose and sunk
A cloud of kerchiefed hands, – 'The church makes fair
　　Her welcome in the new Pope's name.' Ensued
The black sign of the 'Martyrs' – (name no name,
　　But count the graves in silence). Next were viewed
The Artists; next, the Trades; and after came
　　The People, – flag and sign, and rights as good –
And very loud the shout was for that same
　　Motto, 'Il popolo.' IL POPOLO, –
The word means dukedom, empire, majesty,
　　And kings in such an hour might read it so.
And next, with banners, each in his degree,
　　Deputed representatives a-row
Of every separate state of Tuscany:
　　Siena's she-wolf, bristling on the fold
Of the first flag, preceded Pisa's hare,
　　And Massa's lion floated calm in gold,
Pienza's following with his silver stare,
　　Arezzo's steed pranced clear from bridle-hold, –
And well might shout our Florence, greeting there
　　These, and more brethren. Last, the world had sent
The various children of her teeming flanks –
　　Greek, English, French – as if to a parliament
Of lovers of her Italy in ranks,
　　Each bearing its land's symbol reverent;
At which the stones seemed breaking into thanks
　　And rattling up the sky, such sounds in proof
Arose; the very house-walls seemed to bend;
　　The very windows, up from door to roof,
Flashed out a rapture of bright heads, to mend
　　With passionate looks the gesture's whirling off
A hurricane of leaves. Three hours did end
　　While all these passed; and ever in the crowd,
Rude men, unconscious of the tears that kept

Their beards moist, shouted; some few laughed aloud,
And none asked any why they laughed and wept:
    Friends kissed each other's cheeks, and foes long vowed
More warmly did it; two-months' babies leapt
    Right upward in their mothers' arms, whose black
Wide glittering eyes looked elsewhere; lovers pressed
    Each before either, neither glancing back;
And peasant maidens smoothly 'tired and tressed
    Forgot to finger on their throats the slack
Great pearl-strings; while old blind men would not rest,
    But pattered with their staves and slid their shoes
Along the stones, and smiled as if they saw.
    O heaven, I think that day had noble use
Among God's days!

[Vallombrosa]

And Vallombrosa, we two went to see
    Last June, beloved companion, – where sublime
The mountains live in holy families,
    And the slow pinewoods ever climb and climb
Half up their breasts, just stagger as they seize
    Some grey crag, drop back with it many a time,
And straggle blindly down the precipice.
    The Vallombrosan brooks were strewn as thick
That June-day, knee-deep with dead beechen leaves,
    As Milton saw them ere his heart grew sick
And his eyes blind. I think the monks and beeves
    Are all the same too: scarce have they changed the wick
On good Saint Gualbert's altar which receives
    The convent's pilgrims; and the pool in front
(Wherein the hill-stream trout are cast, to wait
    The beatific visit and the grunt
Used at refectory) keeps its weedy state,
    To baffle saintly abbots who would count
The fish across their breviary nor 'bate
    The measure of their steps. O waterfalls
And forests! sound and silence! mountains bare

That leap up peak by peak and catch the palls
Of purple and silver mist to rend and share
  With one another, at electric calls
Of life in the sunbeams, – till we cannot dare
  Fix your shapes, count your number! we must think
Your beauty and your glory helped to fill
  The cup of Milton's soul so to the brink,
He never more was thirsty when God's will
  Had shattered to his sense the last chain-link
By which he had drawn from Nature's visible
  The fresh well-water. Satisfied by this,
He sang of Adam's paradise and smiled,
  Remembering Vallombrosa. Therefore is
The place divine to English man and child,
  And pilgrims leave their souls here in a kiss.

from AURORA LEIGH, SEVENTH BOOK

I found a house, at Florence, on the hill
Of Bellosguardo. 'Tis a tower that keeps
A post of double-observation o'er
The valley of Arno (holding as a hand
The outspread city) straight toward Fiesole
And Mount Morello and the setting sun, –
The Vallombrosan mountains to the right,
Which sunrise fills as full as crystal cups
Wine-filled, and red to the brim because it's red.
No sun could die, nor yet be born, unseen
By dwellers at my villa: morn and eve
Were magnified before us in the pure
Illimitable space and pause of sky,
Intense as angels, garments blanched with God,
Less blue than radiant. From the outer wall
Of the garden, dropped the mystic floating grey
Of olive-trees, (with interruptions green
From maize and vine) until 'twas caught and torn
On that abrupt black line of cypresses

Which signed the way to Florence. Beautiful
The city lay along the ample vale,
Cathedral, tower and palace, piazza and street;
The river trailing like a silver cord
Through all, and curling loosely, both before
And after, over the whole stretch of land
Sown whitely up and down its opposite slopes
With farms and villas.

THE DANCE

You remember down at Florence our Cascine,
    Where the people on the feast-days walk and drive,
And, through the trees, long-drawn in many a green way
    O'er-roofing hum and murmur like a hive,
    The river and the mountains look alive?

You remember the piazzone there, the stand-place
    Of carriages a-brim with Florence Beauties,
Who lean and melt to music as the band plays,
    Or smile and chat with someone who a-foot is,
    Or on horseback, in observance of male duties?

'Tis so pretty, in the afternoons of summer,
    So many gracious faces brought together!
Call it rout, or call it concert, they have come here,
    In the floating of the fan and of the feather,
    To reciprocate with beauty the fine weather.

While the flower-girls offer nosegays (because *they* too
    Go with other sweets) at every carriage-door;
Here, by shake of a white finger, signed away to
    Some next buyer, who sits buying score on score,
    Piling roses upon roses evermore.

And last season, when the French camp had its station
    In the meadow-ground, things quickened and grew gayer

Through the mingling of the liberating nation
    With this people; groups of Frenchmen everywhere,
    Strolling, gazing, judging lightly – 'who was fair.'

Then the noblest lady present took upon her
    To speak nobly from her carriage for the rest:
'Pray these officers from France to do us honour
    By dancing with us straightway.' The request
    Was gravely apprehended as addressed.

And the men of France, bareheaded, bowing lowly,
    Led out each a proud signora to the space
Which the startled crowd had rounded for them – slowly,
    Just a touch of still emotion in his face,
    Not presuming, through the symbol, on the grace.

There was silence in the people: some lips trembled,
    But none jested. Broke the music, at a glance:
And the daughters of our princes, thus assembled,
    Stepped the measure with the gallant sons of France,
    Hush! it might have been a Mass, and not a dance.

And they danced there till the blue that overskied us
    Swooned with passion, though the footing seemed sedate;
And the mountains, heaving mighty hearts beside us,
    Sighed a rapture in a shadow, to dilate,
    And touch the holy stone where Dante sate.

Then the sons of France, bareheaded, lowly bowing,
    Led the ladies back where kinsmen of the south
Stood, received them; till, with burst of overflowing
    Feeling – husbands, brothers, Florence's male youth,
    Turned, and kissed the martial strangers mouth to mouth.

And a cry went up, a cry from all that people!
    – You have heard a people cheering, you suppose,
For the Member, mayor . . . with chorus from the steeple?
    This was different: scarce as loud, perhaps (who knows?),

For we saw wet eyes around us ere the close.

And we felt as if a nation, too long borne in
> By hard wrongers, – comprehending in such attitude
That God had spoken somewhere since the morning,
> That men were somehow brothers, by no platitude, –
> Cried exultant in great wonder and free gratitude.

Robert Browning

from THE RING AND THE BOOK, BOOK I

Do you see this square old yellow Book, I toss
I' the air, and catch again, and twirl about
By the crumpled vellum covers, – pure crude fact
Secreted from man's life when hearts beat hard,
And brains, high-blooded, ticked two centuries since?
Examine it yourselves! I found this book,
Gave a *lira* for it, eightpence English just,
(Mark the predestination!) when a Hand,
Always above my shoulder, pushed me once,
One day still fierce 'mid many a day struck calm,
Across a Square in Florence, crammed with booths,
Buzzing and blaze, noontide and market-time,
Toward Baccio's marble, – ay, the basement-ledge
O' the pedestal where sits and menaces
John of the Black Bands with the upright spear,
'Twixt palace and church, – Riccardi where they lived,
His race, and San Lorenzo where they lie.
This book, – precisely on that palace-step
Which, meant for lounging knaves o' the Medici,
Now serves re-venders to display their ware, –
'Mongst odds and ends of ravage, picture-frames
White through the worn gilt, mirror-sconces chipped,
Bronze angel-heads once knobs attached to chests,
(Handled when ancient dames chose forth brocade)
Modern chalk drawings, studies from the nude,
Samples of stone, jet, breccia, porphyry

Polished and rough, sundry amazing busts
In baked earth, (broken, Providence be praised!)
A wreck of tapestry, proudly-purposed web
When reds and blues were indeed red and blue,
Now offered as a mat to save bare feet
(Since carpets constitute a cruel cost)
Treading the chill scagliola bedward: then
A pile of brown-etched prints, two *crazie* each,
Stopped by a conch a-top from fluttering forth
– Sowing the Square with works of one and the same
Master, the imaginative Sienese
Great in the scenic backgrounds – (name and fame
None of you know, nor does he fare the worse:)
From these . . . Oh, with a Lionard going cheap
If it should prove, as promised, that Joconde
Whereof a copy contents the Louvre! – these
I picked this book from. Five compeers in flank
Stood left and right of it as tempting more –
A dogseared Spicilegium, the fond tale
O' the Frail One of the Flower, by young Dumas,
Vulgarized Horace for the use of schools,
The Life, Death, Miracles of Saint Somebody,
Saint Somebody Else, his Miracles, Death and Life, –
With this, one glance at the lettered back of which,
And 'Stall!' cried I: a *lira* made it mine.

Here it is, this I toss and take again;
Small-quarto size, part print part manuscript:
A book in shape but, really, pure crude fact
Secreted from man's life when hearts beat hard,
And brains, high-blooded, ticked two centuries since.
Give it me back! The thing's restorative
I' the touch and sight.

          That memorable day,
(June was the month, Lorenzo named the Square)
I leaned a little and overlooked my prize
By the low railing round the fountain-source

Close to the statue, where a step descends:
While clinked the cans of copper, as stooped and rose
Thick-ankled girls who brimmed them, and made place
For marketmen glad to pitch basket down,
Dip a broad melon-leaf that holds the wet,
And whisk their faded fresh. And on I read
Presently, though my path grew perilous
Between the outspread straw-work, piles of plait
Soon to be flapping, each o'er two black eyes
And swathe of Tuscan hair, on festas fine:
Through fire-irons, tribes of tongs, shovels in sheaves,
Skeleton bedsteads, wardrobe-drawers agape,
Rows of tall slim brass lamps with dangling gear, –
And worse, cast clothes a-sweetening in the sun:
None of them took my eye from off my prize.
Still read I on, from written title-page
To written index, on, through street and street,
At the Strozzi, at the Pillar, at the Bridge;
Till, by the time I stood at home again
In Casa Guidi by Felice Church,
Under the doorway where the black begins
With the first stone-slab of the staircase cold,
I had mastered the contents, knew the whole truth
Gathered together, bound up in this book,
Print three-fifths, written supplement the rest.

8

The Brownings' Circle

There were probably more British poets and novelists living in Florence in the 1850s than at any other time in the city's history. Among the novelists were Mrs Frances Trollope, the mother of Anthony Trollope; her eldest son, Thomas Adolphus Trollope; Charles Lever, an Irishman; and Isabella Blagden. In addition to the Brownings and Landor, the poets included Joseph Garrow; his daughter Theodosia, who married Thomas Trollope; Frederick Tennyson, the Poet Laureate's elder brother; Robert Lytton, son of a once famous novelist; and, again, Isabella Blagden. Although Frederick Tennyson had his home in Florence for some years and published his first collection, *Days and Hours*, while living there, no trace of the city or indeed of Italy can be found in his verse, which (except in some admirable satirical fragments which he never published) inhabits a rarefied atmosphere remote from this earth. This leaves us with four poets — Joseph Garrow, Theodosia Trollope, Robert Lytton and Isabella Blagden — each of whom wrote poems on which Florence has left its imprint. All four were friends of the Brownings, of Landor or of both, and, by a curious coincidence, all four had some connection with India.

Joseph Garrow, the eldest of the four, had an unusual career which falls into three distinct periods, each spent in a different country. He was born in Madras on 29 October 1789, the illegitimate son of Joseph Garrow, an East India Company official of Scottish descent, and Sultaun, a Muslim woman. The elder Joseph died in 1792, leaving £5,000 (then a considerable sum) in trust for his son and a house and an income for life to Sultaun. She died soon after, and the boy was sent to England, where he was brought up by his father's family. As, in the words of his son-in-law, he 'carried about with him very unmistakable evidence of his eastern origin in his yellow skin, and the tinge of the white of his eyes, which was almost that of an Indian',[1] it became necessary to invent an explanation of his mixed blood more respectable than the facts warranted. The story was spread that his parents had been married, and that his mother had come of a high-caste Brahmin family, thereby qualifying as a lady. As Muslims did not recognize the caste system, she was posthumously converted to Hinduism.

With his removal to England Garrow began his career as an English gentleman. He received the education of his class, taking his degree at St John's College, Cambridge, in 1812. He had already been admitted to Lincoln's Inn, where he studied for the bar, but he never practised. On 17 March 1812, when he was only twenty-two, he married Theodosia Fisher, the widow of a naval officer who had died a year or two earlier. Mrs Fisher, who although a Christian was of Jewish descent, was considerably older than himself and had two children, a boy, who was later converted to Catholicism and became a priest, and a baby girl named Harriet Theodosia. According to Thomas Trollope, who may well have been prejudiced, Garrow's wife was neither clever nor amiable, and 'did not, I fear, contribute to the happiness of any member of her family'. Her great beauty was 'a pair of what must once have been magnificent, and were still brilliant and fierce black eyes', and her main accomplishment her skill in music.[2] Why Garrow married her we can only conjecture. An orphan since early childhood, he may have been attracted to an older woman by his longing for a substitute mother, and she may have accepted him because of her need for a father for her children. If his family raised any objections to the match, the fact that she was comfortably off may have reconciled them to it.

They settled in Torquay, where Mrs Garrow was already living, and there Garrow entered fully into the public life of the district. After his death *The Gentleman's Magazine* wrote of him:

> Mr Garrow was for many years a magistrate for the co. of Devon, and took an active part in all the public business of that neighbourhood, having been Chairman of the Newton Abbot Board of Guardians, Vice-President of the Torquay Mechanics' Institute, and an earnest supporter of every local institution which tended to relieve the distresses or elevate the condition of the industrious classes.[3]

A useful and benevolent career, but hardly a poetic one. We have no evidence that he wrote a line of verse in the first fifty years of his life, although he included among his friends at least two poets, Landor and Elizabeth Barrett's relation John Kenyon.

Several years after her marriage, in 1820 or a year or two later,[4] Mrs Garrow had a daughter who was christened Theodosia, a name which she shared with her mother and her half-sister. By the time she was in her middle teens she had developed into a bright and lively girl with a talent for languages and music, and was turning out a great deal of sentimental verse. Her intellectual interests produced a close companionship between her and her father, which excited her mother's jealousy. Harriet, on the other hand, although not at all intellectual, greatly admired her younger sister, and the two were united by a deep affection.

Through Kenyon Theodosia was brought into contact with Elizabeth Barrett, who came to Torquay in 1838 to recuperate after a severe illness, but the friendship between them was not particularly close. A more stimulating friendship was that with Landor, who spent several months in Torquay in 1837 and again in 1840. When Garrow sent him some of Theodosia's poems in 1838 Landor allowed his loyalty to his friends to run away with his critical sense, and declared that Elizabeth Barrett's poems 'bear no proportion to Miss Garrow's'.[5] While in London he showed the poems to his friend the Countess of Blessington, who edited *Heath's Book of Beauty*, and suggested that she should make room for them by omitting two poems of his own which she had accepted. Lady Blessington replied that she would insert both, and two excruciatingly sentimental poems by Theodosia, 'The Gazelles' and 'On Presenting a Young Invalid with a Bunch of Early Violets', accordingly appeared in the *Book of Beauty* for 1839, together with two dramatic scenes by Landor and poems by Sir Lytton Bulwer, Disraeli, Monckton Milnes and various members of the aristocracy.

Landor's enthusiasm did not stop there. Theodosia, he insisted, must publish a collection of her poems. 'Milman* has written the two best volumes of poetry we have seen lately,' he wrote to Garrow, 'but when Miss Garrow publishes hers I am certain there will be a total eclipse of them.'[6] When he returned to Torquay in the spring of 1840 he helped her to revise her poems in preparation for publication, and promised to review them when they appeared. The plan was held up for various reasons, however, and was finally abandoned when the Garrow family went abroad. Poems and verse translations by Theodosia continued to appear in various periodicals for the rest of her life, but no collection of them has ever been published, even in these days when the work of neglected women poets is receiving sympathetic consideration. It might repay some postgraduate student in search of a subject for a thesis to seek them out.

---

*Henry Hart Milman (1791–1868), poet, dramatist and ecclesiastical historian, who in 1849 became Dean of St Paul's.

In the early 1840s the Garrows left England, whether for health or financial reasons. They lived for a year or two in Tours, perhaps on Landor's recommendation, and then moved in 1844 to Florence, where they took lodgings in the Piazza di Santa Maria Novella. Soon after their arrival they called on Frances Trollope and her son Thomas, then living in the Via dei Malcontenti, with a letter of introduction from a friend. Theodosia and Harriet, Thomas remembered, 'were dressed exactly alike and very dowdily . . . and everything about them from top to toe was provincial, not to say shabby'. He was nevertheless attracted by Theodosia's appearance, for although by no means beautiful she had three striking features: 'the perfect gracefulness of a very slender and elastic figure', a wealth of very dark brown hair with copper glints in it, and clear grey eyes, 'among the largest I ever saw'.[7] As it was a Friday – Mrs Trollope's at-home day – the room soon filled, but Thomas and Theodosia, who had got into conversation, remained so oblivious of the crowd around them that Garrow had to call his daughter several times before she tore herself away.

Florence made a poet of Garrow and diverted Theodosia's poetic activities into a new direction. Garrow made the first English translation of Dante's *La Vita Nuova*, which was published in Florence in 1846, with the Italian and English texts on facing pages, under the title *The Early Life of Dante Alighieri*. It seems to have attracted little attention, and only fifteen years later was replaced as the standard version by Rossetti's translation, yet Garrow's renderings of the verse interludes, his only known attempts at poetry, stand up surprisingly well to comparison with Rossetti's. Translating Italian love poetry, however, was not the sort of conduct expected of a magistrate and a Chairman of the Newton Abbot Board of Guardians, and Garrow's obituarist in *The Gentleman's Magazine* charitably omitted all mention of it.

Theodosia found a new theme for her verse in the Italian struggle for freedom. Her uncritical admirer Landor wrote to Browning in 1845, 'This very year there is in the *Book of Beauty* a poem by my friend Theodosia Garrow on Italy, far surpassing those of M. Angelo and Filicaia. Sappho is far less intense; Pindar is far less animated.' In the following year she published a translation of Giovanni Battista Niccolini's tragedy *Arnaldo da Brescia*, which she dedicated to Landor. The play, which deals with an anti-papal political and religious reformer martyred in 1154, no doubt appealed to her because of its revolutionary and anticlerical sentiments; in her preface she praised Niccolini as 'a stout champion of civil and religious liberty', and in an article on him written nearly twenty years later described him as 'the dauntless defender of political freedom, the special terror and abhorrence of the Church of Rome'. According to Thomas Trollope, although Niccolini was 'a somewhat crabbed old man, not at all disposed to make new acquaintances', her translation won her his 'cordial admiration and friendship'.[8] In the outburst of enthusiasm aroused by the reforms in the Papal States and Tuscany, a group of English residents in Florence began publishing on 30 October 1847 a weekly called *The Tuscan Athenaeum*, thirteen issues of which appeared. Thomas Trollope probably wrote the political articles, and Theodosia contributed translations of Italian patriotic poems.

The friendship between them, which had begun at their first meeting, was probably strengthened by their work on the paper and their similar political views. There was some opposition to their marriage from their families, as he had nothing but what he could earn with his pen, and she 'possessed just one thousand pounds in her own right, and little or no prospect of ever possessing any more'.[9] They finally succeeded in obtaining their families' consent, however, and were married on 3 April 1848 at the British minister's chapel. They took a house on the corner of the Piazza Maria Antonia, which became known as the Villino Trollope, and shared it with his mother. When Harriet Fisher died of smallpox on 12 November she bequeathed all she had to her half-sister, considerably improving the Trollopes' financial position. Garrow and his wife subsequently returned to Torquay, but after her death on 4 November 1849 he came back to Florence and moved into the Villino Trollope. A daughter, Beatrice, was born to the Trollopes in 1853.

The Villino Trollope was a hive of industry, for both Frances Trollope and Tom, as he was generally known among the English colony, were voluminous novelists, like their son and brother Anthony. In addition, Tom turned out historical works and a great deal of miscellaneous journalism. Theodosia was less productive, yet she too contributed articles on Italian politics and literature and translations of Italian verse to *The Athenaeum* and *The Cornhill Magazine*. Work was suspended on their at-home days, when the house was overrun with British, American and Italian intellectuals. The Trollopes were on friendly terms with the Brownings, but the relationship was by no means close. Mrs Browning disliked Frances Trollope, of whom she had written in 1832, long before

she met her, 'she has neither the delicacy nor the candour which constitute true nobility of mind, and her extent of talent forms but a scanty veil
to shadow her other defects', and she also disapproved of the very mixed
company to be found at the Villino Trollope. Relations between the
Trollopes and the Brownings were not formally established until January
1851, when Mrs Browning wrote to a friend:

Mrs Trollope and her daughter-in-law called on us, and it is settled that we
are to know them . . . We mean to be quite friends, and to lend each other
books, and to forget one another's offences, in print or otherwise. Also,
she admits us on her private days; for she has public days (dreadful to
relate!), and is in the full flood and flow of Florentine society.

During the winter of 1852–3 she told Isa Blagden, 'We have seen the
Trollopes once, the younger ones, but the elder Mrs Trollope was visible
neither at that time nor since.' To Miss Mitford she wrote in 1854, 'Mrs
Trollope . . . "receives" every Saturday morning in the most heterogeneous
way possible. It must be amusing to anybody not overwhelmed by it, and
people say she snatches up "characters" for her "so many volumes a year"
out of the diversities of masks presented to her on these occasions.'[10]

Unlike Mrs Browning, whose political enthusiasms she shared,
Theodosia was fortunate enough to be an eyewitness to the overthrow of
the house of Lorraine. In the first of a series of articles on political developments in Florence, which she contributed to *The Athenaeum* and later published as *Social Aspects of the Italian Revolution*, she wrote on 27 April 1859:

I saw our great new square (whilom Piazza Maria Antonia, henceforth
Piazza della Indipendenza) thronged this morning with near twelve thousand people, all a-bloom with red, green, and white banners (the old
beloved Italian tricolour), ringing with shouts of 'Viva la *nostra* Italia!' and
with the liberty hymn of '48, yet so orderly, so righteously peaceable in
its whole aspect, that timid women came out to join the throng, and little
children climbed upon the stone benches and shouted and clapped their
weak hands at the glorious show.[11]

Social Aspects of the Italian Revolution, the only original work that
Theodosia published in book form, is of great interest both as an eyewitness account of one aspect of the Risorgimento and for the light which it

throws upon its author's mind. It is clear that during her fifteen years in Florence she had learned to think of herself as an Italian, and especially a Tuscan. Even her use of language is sometimes Italian rather than English, as when she writes of 'a bill for the declaration of the decadence of the Austro-Lorenese dynasty', using 'decadence' as if, like the Italian *decadenza*, it could mean 'deposition'. Her identification with the Tuscans is particularly evident in her report on the elections of August 1859, which begins: 'We are a proud little nation to-day, we of the old Etruscan stock, who built the mighty Cyclopean walls which yet look down from Fiesole on Florence, and who sit so stolidly, I had almost said aldermanically, on their alabaster sarcophagi as at a banquet, with goblet in hand and great massive gold chains round their portly necks.'[12] 'We of the old Etruscan stock' comes oddly from a writer who by descent was a quarter Scottish, a quarter Indian and half Jewish.

British interest in Etruscan civilization was something comparatively new. All educated Englishmen, having read Livy, had long been aware of the Etruscans as neighbours and sometimes enemies of the early Romans, as Milton had shown when he referred to Lucca as 'Lucumonis urbs', but it was not until the nineteenth century that they became aware that the culture of the Etruscans was not unworthy of comparison with that of the Greeks. The book which, more than any other, revealed Etruscan civilization to British readers was George Dennis's *The Cities and Cemeteries of Etruria*, published in 1848. There were aspects of Etruscan society as depicted by Dennis of which Theodosia would have strongly disapproved. He regarded it as a society ruled by a priestly aristocracy, in which the mass of the people were politically powerless serfs and freedom of thought did not exist, and explicitly compared it to her *bête noire*, the Papal States. On the other hand, he demonstrated the Etruscans' mastery of the arts and sciences, saw in them 'the great civilizers of Italy', and suggested that it was no coincidence that it was in Tuscany that the arts and sciences revived in the Renaissance.[13] In particular he emphasized that women enjoyed a far higher status in Etruria than among the Greeks, and were not excluded from education or from religious functions.

Theodosia's description of the Tuscan elections continues:

> We have a Parliament at last! a Parliament to our mind, too, and what will seem more astonishing to ultramontane ears, a Parliament elected without riots, without broken windows or broken heads, innocent of gin or other

Above: Dante and medieval Florence, from a fifteenth-century painting by Domenico di Michelino in Florence Cathedral

Left: Galileo in old age, by Giusto Sustermans

Above: The Cascine, Florence, in which Shelley wrote 'Ode to the West Wind', from a lithograph of 1848 by Lindemann Frommel

Left: The Piazza della Signoria, Florence, in the mid-eighteenth century, by Bernardo Bellotto

By permission of Giusti di Becocci, Florence

Above: The demonstration of 12 September 1847, which the Brownings witnessed and Mrs Browning described in *Casa Guidi Windows*, crossing the Ponte Santa Trinità, from a contemporary print

By permission of Soprintendenza ai beni storici e artistici di Firenze

Left: The Villa Gherardesca, Landor's home near Fiesole, from John Forster's *Walter Savage Landor: A Biography* (1869)

Above: Elizabeth Barrett Browning's tomb in the Protestant cemetery, Florence, from a photograph by Helen Hobday

Below: An Etruscan bronze sculpture of a chimera in the Museo Archeologico, Florence, which D. H. Lawrence admired

By permission of Giusti di Becocci, Florence

> potent incentives to patriotism, utterly unconscious of the virtue of rotten eggs, as of still more rotten hustings-professions; above all, free from any warning fear of petitions against returns, inasmuch as we have not yet arrived at bribery heat in our rising scale of civilization.

Mrs Browning had contrasted the orderliness of Florentine crowds with the drunken rowdyism of the English, but only in private letters; Theodosia was not afraid to point out publicly that a Tuscan election had been free from the drunkenness, disorder and corruption which characterized elections in the England of Eatanswill. In her political statements she sometimes indulged in a romantic republicanism, as when she contrasts 'the days of the evil Medicean rule' with 'the stalwart days of the old Republic', but in her approach to the politics of 1859–60 she strongly supported Victor Emmanuel and Cavour against 'men committed to the wildest schemes of the Mazzinian creed'.[14] As her book had begun with the expulsion of the Grand Duke from Florence, it ends with Victor Emmanuel's entry into the city.

In one respect she never lost her radicalism. She remained as hostile to the papacy and the Catholic clergy in the 1860s as she had been when she translated *Arnaldo da Brescia*. In her book she applauds the new regime's abolition of the Concordat and its return to the Leopoldine Code, records with approval the growing influence of the Evangelical Church in Florence, and optimistically suggests that 'that lust of sway and spirit of insolent aggression which has lost Rome the spiritual dominion over other States . . . will sooner or later separate Central Italy from its religious allegiance to the Pope'. Her husband recorded that 'many of her verses written during her latter years are fiercely denunciatory or humorously satirical of the Italian priesthood, and especially of the Pontifical Government'.[15] Even her poem 'In the noon-day's golden pleasance', which begins as a delightful picture of her little daughter Beatrice tormenting her old nurse, ends as a passionate denunciation of the Church's use of superstitious fears to enslave the minds of women.

Her marriage was a happy one, and she seems to have maintained good relations with the mother-in-law who shared her house. In 1861 she had the pleasure of seeing Italian unity achieved, except for Venetia and Rome. Her later years were overshadowed with sorrows, however. Joseph Garrow suffered a paralytic stroke on 10 November 1857, dying a few hours later, and Frances Trollope died on 6 October 1863.

Theodosia regularly visited her old friend Landor during his last years, until his death in 1864. Finally she herself died, after a long illness, on 13 April 1865. After her death a plaque was placed on the Villino Trollope, which stated (in Italian), 'On the 13th day of April 1865 there died in this house Theodosia Garrow Trollope, who wrote in English, with an Italian heart, of the struggles and triumphs of Liberty.'

A closer friend of the Brownings was Robert Lytton. He was born Edward Robert Lytton Bulwer on 8 November 1831, the only son of Edward George Earle Lytton Bulwer, famous in his day as the author of such novels as *The Last Days of Pompeii*. After his mother's death in 1843 the elder Bulwer adopted her maiden name of Lytton, and in 1866 he was raised to the peerage as Baron Lytton. To distinguish him from his father, the son was known from 1850 onwards as Robert Lytton, rather to his regret, for he disliked the name Robert. He was educated at Harrow, and after further study in Germany sailed to America in 1850 to take up a post as unpaid attaché to his uncle Sir Henry Bulwer, the British ambassador in Washington. Having written verse since childhood, he would have liked to make literature his career, but his father, perhaps fearing competition, insisted that he must devote himself to diplomacy.

Sir Henry Bulwer was transferred to Florence in 1852 as minister to Tuscany, and Lytton joined him in the autumn, again as an unpaid attaché. Soon after his arrival he called on the Brownings with a letter of introduction from John Forster, whom he had known since childhood. They were favourably impressed; Mrs Browning described him in a letter as 'refined and gentle in manners', and in another as 'very young, as you may suppose, with all sorts of high aspirations – and visionary enough to suit *me*, which is saying much – and affectionate, with an apparent liking to us both, which is engaging to us, of course'. One recommendation was that he shared Mrs Browning's interest in spiritualism, although he was never entirely converted; after his eldest child died in 1871 he wrote to his father, 'I do greatly hope that the dead continue to live somehow and somewhere . . . But I see no fact in life or in death to confirm this hope.' He rented a villa at Bellosguardo, where he was able to entertain the Brownings and Frederick Tennyson. While staying at Bagni di Lucca in July 1853 Mrs Browning wrote to Isa Blagden:

> Mr Lytton had a reception on the terrace of his villa at Bellosguardo the

evening before our last in Florence, and we were all bachelors together there, and I made tea, and we ate strawberries and cream and talked spiritualism through one of the pleasantest two hours that I remember. Such a view! Florence dissolving in the purple of the hills; and the stars looking on.[16]

Lytton's nearest neighbours at Bellosguardo were Captain Fleetwood Wilson of the 8th Hussars and Harriet his wife, who lived at the Villa Ombrellino. They had married in 1849, and had come to Italy for a prolonged honeymoon. While at Florence they learned that Wilson's brother, to whom he had entrusted his fortune, had gone bankrupt, whereupon they decided to settle there. Harriet Wilson, who in 1852 was twenty-six or twenty-seven, was a pretty woman with a lissom figure, what a contemporary described as 'grave, starlike eyes', and 'a low broad forehead overshadowed by waves of brown hair' with golden tints in it. Lytton formed a close friendship with both of them, dining at the Villa Ombrellino at least once every week. For Harriet Wilson his feelings soon became stronger than friendship; he fell passionately in love with her, and there are indications that she returned his love. Their attachment soon became sufficiently obvious to give rise to gossip among the English colony in Florence, and in time reports of it reached the elder Lytton in England. Writing to his father in March 1854, Lytton described the Wilsons as 'my most intimate friends since I have been in Florence', but denied that there was any truth in the rumours about Mrs Wilson and himself.[17] If Captain Wilson heard the gossip he evidently did not believe it, for he and Lytton remained good friends.

Lytton meanwhile was busily writing verse, including a drama, *Clytemnestra*, which Mrs Browning described as 'too ambitious because after Aeschylus, but full of promise'. Much of his verse dealt with his love for Harriet Wilson, and succeeded in conveying an intense passion, as in the conclusion of 'At her Casement':

> I would that there in her chamber I stood,
> Full-face to her terrible beauty: I would
> I were laid on her queenly breast, at her lips,
> With her warm hair wound thro' my finger-tips,
> Draining her soul at one deep-drawn kiss.
> And I would be humbly content, for this,

> To die, as is due, before the morn,
> Kill'd by her slowly-returning scorn.[18]

There is passion too in 'An Evening in Tuscany', though here it is expressed not through dwelling on the physical but through an identification with the warm pulsing life of nature. This is the one poem in which he places his love story in its Florentine setting; elsewhere he avoids Florence in his verse, as if anxious to avoid making the autobiographical element in it too obvious.

He left for England in the early summer of 1854 to arrange for the publication of a collection of his poems. His father reluctantly agreed to its appearance, on condition that he used a pseudonym and did not write any more verse for two years after its publication. *Clytemnestra, The Earl's Return, The Artist and Other Poems* accordingly appeared in the spring of 1855 as the work of 'Owen Meredith', although its authorship seems to have been an open secret. It is a substantial collection, containing six longer and forty-four shorter poems, some of which went back to his Harrow days. Mrs Browning had detected his weakness as a poet when she wrote of him in 1853, 'I expect much from him one day, when he shakes himself clear of the poetical influences of the age, which he will have strength to do presently.' In fact he did not; throughout his career echoes of other poets continued to be heard in his work so often that a critic has described him as 'imitative to the point of plagiarism'.[19] Many of the poems in his first collection read like watered-down Tennyson, and others, including 'An Evening in Tuscany', suffer from his fondness for imitating Browning's silly-clever double rhymes.

He was appointed unpaid attaché in Paris in August 1854, and was transferred to a similar post in The Hague in March 1856. After his appointment to Paris he wrote to the Brownings asking them to make friends with the Wilsons.

> Mrs Wilson is a very dear friend of mine [he wrote], and I have a sincere interest in all that concerns her welfare; for during two years of 'that beautiful life-in-death among the Cypresses' at Florence, she shared all my studies and thinkings . . . She is not a demonstrative Person, and is very shy and diffident, and wants drawing out; but I feel quite sure that you wd not know her long without loving and esteeming her . . . Wilson you will find, if you penetrate his outward manner, an honourable, thorough gen-

tleman, I think; and full of sound good sense — though not aspirations'.

He also sent Browning from Paris a light-hearted verse letter that he never published but which is better poetry than much of his serious writing.

Before he could obtain a paid post in the diplomatic service Lytton was required to submit reports on commercial and social conditions in the countries where he had served, and he therefore returned to Florence in July 1857 to prepare his report on Tuscany. He was heartily welcomed by the Brownings, who although they had rented a house in Bagni di Lucca for the summer lingered on in Florence to enjoy his company. Mrs Browning explained in a letter to her sister that 'we didn't like to leave directly, since he was in Florence chiefly for us', suggesting that his need to study social conditions in Tuscany was merely a pretext for revisiting his friends there. The two years during which he was forbidden to write verse had ended in the spring, and since then he had made up for lost time. Mrs Browning recalled 'several delightful evenings' on the terrace of Isa Blagden's house at Bellosguardo, the Villa Brichieri, 'listening to new poems of Lytton's which he read musically'. He joined them in August at Bagni di Lucca, but having been, in Mrs Browning's words, 'entirely *dis*-acclimatized by four years (nearly) in the north', he became gravely ill with gastric fever.[21] Isa Blagden sat up with him night after night, until Browning insisted on taking her place at his bedside. When he was sufficiently recovered to be moved, she carried him off to the Villa Brichieri to convalesce.

Before the end of September he was well enough to work on his report and also on his second collection of poems, *The Wanderer*. The first of the six books into which is divided, 'In Italy', and the long prologue with which it opens are largely concerned with his love for Harriet Wilson, who is referred to as 'Irene'. The tone and style of the prologue are decidedly Byronic:

> Midnight, and love, and youth, and Italy!
>   Love in the land where love most lovely seems!
> Land of my love, tho' I be far from thee,
>   Lend, for love's sake, the light of thy moonbeams,
> The spirit of thy cypress-grove, and all
>   Thy dark-eyed beauty, for a little while

> To my desire. Yet once more let her smile
> Fall o'er me: o'er me let her long hair fall
>
> . . . .
>
> Under the blessed darkness unreproved
>   We were alone, in that best hour of time,
> Which first reveal'd to us how much we loved.
>   'Neath the thick starlight. The young night sublime
> Hung trembling o'er us. At her feet I knelt,
>   And gazed up from her feet into her eyes.
>   Her face was bow'd: we breath'd each other's sighs:
> We did not speak: not move: we look'd: we felt.

After all this passion, it comes very much as an anticlimax to be repeatedly assured that their relationship was entirely innocent:

> It was enough for me to clasp her hand:
>   To blend with her love-looks my own: no more.
>
> . . . .
>
> How little know they life's divinest bliss,
>   That know not to possess and yet refrain![22]

The landscape in which the poems on 'Irene' are set is that of the Florentine countryside, but Florence itself is never named. To put the reader off the scent, two of the poems are set in Venice, which Lytton had never visited. The later books – 'In France', 'In England', 'In Switzerland', 'In Holland' and 'Palingenesis' – are semi-autobiographical, tracing his movements since 1854; the 'Palingenesis' section consists of religious poems, apparently written after his illness at Bagni di Lucca. Throughout the book the influence of many poets is discernible, among them Byron, Shelley, Tennyson, Browning and Heine. One poem, 'Indian Love-Song', reads as if Shelley had collaborated with the author of the Song of Songs.

Lytton returned to England in March 1858 to take the entrance examination for the diplomatic corps, and also to arrange for the publication of *The Wanderer*. Having been officially placed on the diplomatic list, he held appointments in the next few years at The Hague, Vienna, Copenhagen and Athens, but he still kept up his correspondence with the

Brownings. In a long letter to Mrs Browning he discussed the issues raised by her *Poems before Congress*. 'I start with a strong doubt', he wrote, 'as to how far politics are a fair and fitting subject for poetry . . . I cannot yet give up the consideration of politics as a science – a science . . . to be approached by the reason, and that somewhat humbly, since we know so little. If so, it is clearly not the *best* subject for poetry which deals with passion and sentiment.' On the Italian question he said, 'I never was, and I think I never shall be, a lover of the Austrian or the Bourbon in that land of lands. I shall be heartily glad to see Italy permanently free and pure Italian from end to end. All I dread is the substitution of French for Austrian supremacy there.' His judgements on political figures are also of interest. On Napoleon III he observed, 'When the whole world mistrusts a man, the whole world is rarely very far wrong . . . perhaps I am over-mistrustful of hero-worship – lest it shd unconsciously degenerate into devil-worship, or the substitution of personality for principle.' Mazzini he dismissed as 'a poor monomaniac', and Garibaldi he described as 'the only hero to whom I am ready to do homage without mistrust'. 'As for Cavour,' he added, 'I can't swallow him without spoonfuls of salt. I esteem him a shifty, tricksy fellow, but I suppose he who goes to work in earnest must not mind about dirtying his hands a little.'[23] The letter, with its implied rebuke to Mrs Browning's emotional approach to politics and her uncritical hero-worship of Napoleon III and Cavour, raises one's respect for Lytton, even if his conception of politics purely as a science and his failure to appreciate the moral grandeur of Mazzini suggest that he had serious limitations.

He returned to Florence for the last time in June 1861, and renewed his friendship with the Brownings, the Wilsons and Landor, whom he had met in London in 1855. He visited Casa Guidi in the morning of 28 June, a few hours before Mrs Browning died, and afterwards did all he could to comfort Browning, who wrote to Forster in August, 'I have never told you how affectionately and unremittingly Lytton devoted himself to me in those last days at Florence.' In the years that followed he rose steadily in the diplomatic corps, while keeping up a steady output of volumes of verse. His father's friend Disraeli appointed him Viceroy of India in 1875, although he admitted that he knew nothing of that country. In this capacity he launched a British invasion of Afghanistan – a decision which aroused much controversy. Already a baron since his father's death in 1873, on his resignation in 1880 he was created Earl of Lytton. His last appointment was as ambassador to Paris, where he died in 1891. When he died he had not seen Italy for thirty years, yet late in life he could still write: 'How I long for Italy once more – Oh Florence, Florence!'[24]

According to her gravestone in Florence's Protestant cemetery, Isabella Blagden was born on 30 June 1816. That is all we know with any certainty of her life before she came to Florence. The cemetery's register gives her father's name as Thomas Blagden, her nationality as Swiss and her age at death (incorrectly) as fifty-five. A woman who had met her when a girl wrote sixty years later, 'The impression that remains is that she was small, slight, delicate, with very black eyes and jet black hair, olive complexion, she might have passed for an Italian.'[25] Among the English colony it was widely believed that she was, like Joseph Garrow, the child of an English father and an Indian mother, but no one was sure whether they had been married or whether she was born in England or in India. No record of a Thomas Blagden has been found among the East India Company's papers, yet in her last novel, *The Crown of a Life*, she seems to show first-hand knowledge of India. One possible explanation of her Swiss nationality and dark eyes, hair and skin would be that she was born in Switzerland, the daughter of an English father and an Italian mother, but in the absence of further evidence any certainty is impossible.

Isabella, or 'Isa' as everyone called her, came to Florence in 1849. She spent most of the years 1851–4 in Rome or in England, but from 1854 onwards she made Florence her home, with the exception of two long visits to England and France in 1855–6 and 1861–2. By 1850 she already knew the Brownings, and she soon became their closest friend in Florence. As Mrs Browning's health grew worse and she felt that she was no longer stimulating company for Robert, at her insistence he spent many of his evenings at Isa's villa, sometimes visiting her four times a week. She was also 'the intimate and very specially highly-valued friend' of Tom and Theodosia Trollope. Tom described her as 'a very bright, very warm-hearted, very clever little woman, who knew everybody, and was, I think, more universally beloved than any other individual among us'. Mrs Browning called her 'a very affectionate friend of mine and very loveable on her own account', and Lytton wrote, 'A dozen or more good and dear women must have gone to the making of that one little body. I know of none so essentially loveable and absolutely to be loved, through and through.'[26]

While everybody praised her for her kind heart, nobody seems to have praised her poetry. Mrs Browning's letters, which often speak highly of Lytton's and Frederick Tennyson's verse, never mention hers, yet a case could be made for claiming that she was the best poet of the three. She may have been shy of showing her poems to her friends because of the atmosphere of pagan sensuousness which permeates some of them, such as 'A Love Rhapsody', apparently a record of a love affair in Rome in 1852, or her masterpiece 'L'Ariccia. Death in Life'. It is noteworthy that in this poem she identifies 'the Pagan glory' with the Etruscans, antici-pating D. H. Lawrence's conception of them as a people with a profound joy in life, so that even their underworld was a gay place. The same sen-suousness is present in 'Invitation', an expression of her intense joy in the sights and sounds of the Tuscan countryside, and 'Wild Flowers', which sings of 'the glory of our Tuscan spring'. In politics she was as passion-ately devoted to the cause of Italian unity as her friends Elizabeth Barrett Browning and Theodosia Trollope, and welcomed the victories of the Risorgimento in verse, such as 'On the Italian Colours being Replaced on the Palazzo Vecchio', which celebrated the Tuscan revolution of 1859. Inspired by the success of *Aurora Leigh*, she published her first novel, *Agnes Tremorne*, in 1861. Publishers were reluctant to accept her work, so she persuaded her friends Robert Browning and Anthony Trollope to use their influence on her behalf. Four other novels appeared anonymously at two-year intervals between 1863 and 1869, but only *Agnes Tremorne* and its immediate successor, *The Cost of a Secret*, enjoyed a limited success.

Her years at the Villa Brichieri, from 1856 to 1861, were perhaps the happiest of her life. Through her friendships with the Brownings and the Trollopes she came into contact with most of the literary figures who lived in or passed through Florence, and she delighted to entertain them at her luncheons or her Saturday at-homes, when tea was served on the terrace. This happy period ended abruptly on 29 June 1861 with the death of Mrs Browning, whom she had visited and thought to be improv-ing only a few hours before. Heart-broken though she was, she took charge of Pen while Browning recovered from the shock of Elizabeth's death, and abandoned her own plans for the summer to accompany them to England. Another cause of grief was her parting from Lytton, whom she had nursed during his illness four years before and for whom she probably harboured a secret passion.

During the years after her return in 1862 Florence underwent many changes. Now a city of some 118,000 people, it was proclaimed the capital of the new Kingdom of Italy in 1864, and the king and the government installed themselves there in the following year. The Pitti Palace, until 1859 the home of the grand dukes, became the royal residence, Parliament met in the Palazzo Vecchio, and the various ministries took over the city's palaces and monasteries. Much of the historic centre and most of the city walls were demolished in the name of town planning, and even after the capital was transferred to Rome in 1871 the work of modernization went on. Meanwhile at Bellosguardo Isa continued to turn out a novel every two years and to write poems. Although Browning never returned to Florence, she kept in touch with him by letter; they had agreed that she should write on the twelfth of each month, and he would reply on the nineteenth.

Her longest and most ambitious poem, 'The Story of Two Lives', was published anonymously in *Fraser's Magazine* in April 1864. It tells the story of a woman who has been seduced and then deserted by a man, and sinks into poverty and prostitution – a bold theme for a woman to handle in mid-Victorian England. It is told in two dramatic monologues in freely handled couplets: the first spoken by the repentant seducer after hearing of the woman's death, the other by the woman herself. The poem contains some powerful social satire, as when the man recalls his regular attendance at church:

> When from the church pealed loud the hour of prayer,
> I entered with a self-applauding air;
> Observance of these rites to God is due,
> My station claims my presence in my pew;
> I doubt the dogma, but respect the form,
> Nor yawn unless the tedious day be warm.
> I gravely hear of life, of sin, of death.
> And sanction give to Him of Nazareth:
> Religion is a social state machine;
> A fence to keep the untutored herd within.
> I listen, and I hear unmoved the doom —
> 'Woe, woe to him through whom offences come!'[27]

Apart from its intrinsic merits, the poem has a biographical interest. Browning had picked up his 'old yellow Book' in Florence in June 1860, but although fascinated by the story which it contained he had made no use of it. Then in August 1864, while on holiday in the Pyrenees, he suddenly had the idea of telling the story from the different points of view of those concerned in it. 'The Story of Two Lives', in which a story is told from the different viewpoints of the two main actors, had been published four months earlier, and Browning had almost certainly read it. Did Isa Blagden's poem suggest to him the plan of *The Ring and the Book*?

As more of her old friends died – Landor in 1864 and Theodosia Trollope, whom she nursed in her last illness, in 1865 – so new ones entered her life. Visiting intellectuals still came to her new home at Bellosguardo, the Villa Castellani, which she had turned into a refuge for ill-treated dogs, such as Venezia, a white French poodle which she had rescued from boys who proposed to drown it in a Venetian canal. Among her new friends was Henry James, who remembered her thirty years later as having written 'the inevitable nice novel or two of the wandering English spinster' and also 'befriended the lonely, cheered the exile and nursed the sick'. He continued:

> These friendships and generosities, in a setting of Florentine villas and views, of overhanging terraces and arched *pianterreni*, of Italian loyalties and English longings, of shy literary yearning and confessed literary starvation – these things formed her kindly little legend, and they still, after long years, melt together, for my personal reminiscence, into the springtime air of a garden at Bellosguardo. I feel again the sun of Florence in the morning walk out of the Porta Romana and up the long winding hill; I catch again, in the great softness, the 'accent' of the straight, black cypresses; I lose myself again in the sense of the large, cool villa, already then a centre of histories, memories, echoes, all generations deep; I face the Val d'Arno, vast and delicate, as if it were a painted picture; in special I talk with an eager little lady who has gentle, gay black eyes and whose type gives, visibly enough, the hint of East-Indian blood.[28]

Another new friend was Alfred Austin, whom she first met in 1865. Austin, then a man of thirty, was a bumptious, conceited barrister-turned-journalist who produced large quantities of bad verse, and avenged himself for the world's failure to appreciate his efforts by violently attacking better poets than himself. Among his victims was Browning, who described him in a letter to Isa as 'a filthy little snob', and satirized him in *Pacchiarotto and how he worked in Distemper* as 'Banjo

Byron'. Apart from Browning's resentment of Austin's attacks on himself, there were political differences between them: Austin wrote a long poem called 'Why England is Conservative'; Browning wrote a sonnet called 'Why I am a Liberal'. When after Isa's death Browning learned that Austin was to edit her poems, he was furious at 'the association of a dearly-loved name with that of Mr Alfred Austin'.[29] Fortunately he did not live to see Austin's appointment as Poet Laureate – partly because of his politics, partly because, as Lord Salisbury (then Prime Minister) explained, no one else had asked for the job – or he would probably have exploded. In fact he had his revenge, for Austin's elevation to this post made him a national laughing-stock.

Isa kept up her interest in politics to the last. When the unification of Italy was completed in 1870 by the entry of Italian troops into Rome she wrote a poem to commemorate the event, in which she spoke of Italy as 'my country'.[30] She shared Mrs Browning's admiration of Napoleon III, and had a portrait of him hanging in her villa; if she was out when Tom Trollope called he would turn the face of the picture to the wall to show that he had been there. When Napoleon died on 9 January 1873 she began to write a poem to his memory, which was left incomplete when she herself died suddenly eleven days later. She was buried in the Protestant cemetery, where Harriet Fisher, Joseph Garrow, Elizabeth Barrett Browning, Frances Trollope, Walter Savage Landor and Theodosia Trollope already lay.

Joseph Garrow
TRANSLATION OF A SONNET FROM DANTE'S *VITA NUOVA*

> I pray you Pilgrims, musing as ye go
>   On things which are perchance no more at hand,
>   Say if ye come from such a distant Land
>   As by your outward mien you seem to show?
> For as ye pass along, no tears o'erflow,
>   Though in the grieving City's heart ye stand,
>   Like unto men who do not understand
>   Aught of the heavy pressure of her woe.
> If ye, to hear me, will awhile defer
>   Your going, you shall after wend your way
>   (So says my sighing heart) dissolved in tears.
> Her own sweet Beatrice is lost to her —
>   And what men's tongues can of that Lady say
>   Has power to move to weeping him who hears.

Theodosia Trollope

> In the noon-day's golden pleasance,
>   Little Bice, baby fair,
> With a fresh and flowery presence
>   Dances round her nurse's chair,
> In the old grey loggia dances, haloed by her shining hair.
>
> Pretty pearl in sober setting,
>   Where the arches garner shade!
> Cones of maize like golden netting
>   Fringe the sturdy colonnade,
> And the lizards pertly pausing glance across the balustrade.
>
> Brown cicala drily proses,
>   Creaking the hot air to sleep.
> Bounteous orange flowers and roses
>   Yield the wealth of love they keep
> To the sun's imperious ardour in a dream of fragrance deep.
> And a cypress, mystic-hearted,

217

Cleaves the quiet dome of light
   With its black green masses parted
     But by gaps of blacker night,
Which the giddy moth and beetle circle round in dubious flight.

Here the well chain's pleasant clanging
    Sings of coolness deep below;
There the vine leaves breathless hanging
    Shine transfigured in the glow,
And the pillars stare in silence at the shadows which they throw.

Portly nurse, black-browed, red-vested,
    Knits and dozes, drowsed with heat;
Bice, like a wren gold-crested,
    Chirps and teases round her seat,
Hides the needles, plucks the stocking, rolls the cotton o'er her feet.

Nurse must fetch a draught of water
    In the glass with painted wings,
Nurse must show her little daughter
    All her tale of silver rings,
Dear sweet nurse must sing a couplet – solemn nurse, who *never* sings!

Blest Madonna! what a clamour!
    Now the little torment tries,
Perched on tiptoe, all the glamour
    Of her coaxing hands and eyes!
May she hold the glass she drinks from – just one moment, Bice cries.

Nurse lifts high the Venice beaker,
    Bossed with masks, and flecked with gold,
Scarce in time to 'scape the quicker
    Little fingers over-bold,
Craving tendril – like to grasp it, with the will of four years old.

Pretty wood bird, pecking, flitting
    Round the cherries on the tree,
Ware the scarecrow, grimly sitting

Crouched for silly things like thee!
Nurse hath plenty such in ambush. 'Touch not, for it burns,' quoth she.

And thine eyes' blue mirror widens
    With an awestroke of belief;
Meekly following that blind guidance,
    On thy finger's rosy sheaf
Blow'st thou softly, fancy wounded, soothing down a painless grief.

Nurse and nursling, learner, teacher,
    Thus foreshadow things to come,
When the girl shall grow the creature
    Of false terrors vain and dumb
And entrust their baleful fetish with her being's scope and sum.

Then her heart shall shrink and wither,
    Custom-straitened like her waist,
All her thoughts to cower together,
    Huddling sheep-like with the rest,
With the flock of soulless bodies on a pattern schooled and laced,

Till the stream of years encrust her
    With a numbing mail of stone,
Till her laugh lose half its lustre
    And her truth forswear its tone
And she see God's might and mercy darkly through a glass alone!

While our childhood fair and sacred
    Sapless doctrines doth rehearse.
And the milk of falsehoods acrid
    Burns our babe-lips like a curse,
Cling we must to godless prophets, as the suckling to the nurse.

As the seed time, so the reaping.
    Shame on us who overreach,
While our eyes yet smart with weeping,
    Hearts so all our own to teach!
Better they and we lay sleeping where the darkness hath no speech!

219

THE LAST WILL AND TESTAMENT OF THE ROYAL AND IMPERIAL HOUSE
OF LORRAINE*
From the Italian of Francesco Dall'Ongaro

Our Dad one morning woke and rubbed his eyes
    And saw the town all tricolours and crosses.
His knees grew weak with fear, and in surprise
    He rang for all his footmen . . . and his forces.
'Who set those banners floating from the towers?'
'Your Highness, they are but the first spring flowers.'
'Those crosses, too, which daze such sight as mine is?'
'Only the cross of Piedmont, please your Highness.'

'Ferrari! pray what guns have you within
    The forts of Belvedere and San Giovanni?
Open that paper . . . *you* know what I mean . . .
    And cure my griefs. By Jove, they're one too many!
Paint me all Florence decent black and yellow!
To graveyards with those crosses, my good fellow!

'The Lord, for His wise ends and means of grace,
    Chastens the sons He loves the best, they say.
I to the Tuscans hold the selfsame place;
    I'll treat my children in the selfsame way.
Rare way! – friend Bomba had the sense to see it.
They'll nickname me Bombarda, and so be it!'

O our own Dad! O love that cannot fail!
    O lucid mirror of Grand-Ducal *nous*!
He claps his children in his model jail
    And sends the whitecoats to his country house.
He gives the whitecoats pocketfuls of pelf
    And on his Tuscans . . . points the guns himself!

---

* This poem refers to sealed orders for the bombardment of Florence in the event of a popular uprising said to have been found in the Fortezza da Basso and Forte Belvedere after the expulsion of the Grand Duke in 1859. 'Dad' = *Babbo,* the popular nickname for the Grand Duke. General Ferrari, the Commander-in-Chief, was said to have written the orders. King Ferdinand II of Naples was nicknamed Bomba after he ordered the bombardment of Messina during the Sicilian uprising of 1848–9. 'Whitecoats' = Austrian troops.

Dad! your example shan't be lost the while.
    If you'd come back after your late quandary,
We'll give you a salute in proper style
    From forts of San Giovanni and Belvederè;
We'll prove our love by an unerring test:
As the Lord chastens whom He loves the best,
We'll prove our tenderness, whene'er you come,
By lots of grape, by musket-ball and bomb!

Robert Lytton
An Evening in Tuscany

Look! the sun sets. Now's the rarest
    Hour of all the blessèd day.
(Just the hour, love, you look fairest!)
    Even the snails are out to play.

Cool the breeze mounts, like this Chianti
    Which I drain down to the sun.
—There! shut up that old green Dante —
    Turn the page, where we begun,

At the last news of Ulysses —
    A grand image, fit to close
Just such grand gold eves as this is,
    Full of splendour and repose!

So loop up those long bright tresses —
    Only, one or two must fall
Down your warm neck, Evening kisses
    Through the soft curls spite of all.

And look down now, o'er the city
    Sleeping soft among the hills —
Our dear Florence! That great Pitti
    With its steady shadow fills

Half the town up: its unwinking
    Cold white windows, as they glare
Down the long street, set one thinking
    Of the old Dukes who lived there;

For one knows them, those strange men, so —
    Subtle brains, and iron thews!
There, the gardens of Lorenzo —
    The long cypress avenues —

Creep up slow the stately hill side
    Where the merry loungers are.
But far more I love this still side —
    The blue plain you see so far!

Where the shore of bright white villas
    Leaves off faint: the purple breadths
Of the olives and the willows:
    And the gold-rimm'd mountain-widths:

All transfused in slumbrous glory
    To one burning point — the sun!
But up here — slow, cold, and hoary
    Reach the olives, one by one:

And the land looks fresh: the yellow
    Arbute-berries, here and there,
Growing slowly ripe and mellow
    Through a flush of rosy hair.

For the Tramontana last week
    Was about: 'Tis scarce three weeks
Since the snow lay, one white vast streak,
    Upon those old purple peaks.

So to-day among the grasses
    One may pick up tens and twelves
Of young olives, as one passes,

Blown about, and by themselves

Blackening sullen-ripe. The corn too
    Grows each day from green to golden.
The large-eyed wildflowers forlorn too
    Blow among it, unbeholden:

Some are white, some crimson, others
    Purple blackening to the heart.
From the deep wheat-sea, which smothers
    Their bright globes up, how they start!

And the small wild pinks from tender
    Feather-grasses peep at us:
While above them burns, on slender
    Stems, the red gladiolus:

Are the grapes yet green? this season
    They'll be round and sound and true,
If no after-blight should seize on
    Those young bunches turning blue.

O that night of purple weather!
    (Just before the moon had set)
You remember how together
    We walk'd home? – the grass was wet –

The long grass in the Poderé –
    With the balmy dew among it:
And that Nightingale – his airy
    Song – how fairy-like he sung it!

All the fig-trees had grown heavy
    With the young figs white and woolly:
And the fireflies, bevy on bevy
    Of soft sparkles, pouring fully

Their warm life through trance on trances

Of thick citron-shades behind,
Rose, like swarms of loving fancies
    Through some rich and pensive mind.

So we reach'd the Loggia. Leaning
    Faint, we sat there in the shade.
Neither spoke. The night's deep meaning
    Fill'd the silence up unsaid.

Hoarsely through the Cypress-alley
    A Civetta out of tune
Tried his voice by fits. The valley
    Lay all dark below the moon.

Until into song you burst out –
    That old song I made for you
When we found our rose – the first out
    Last sweet Spring-time in the dew.

Well! . . . if things had gone less wildly –
    Had I settled down before
There, in England – labour'd mildly –
    And been patient – and learn'd more

Of how men should live in London –
    Been less happy – or more wise –
Left no great works tried and undone –
    Never look'd in your soft eyes –

I . . . but what's the use of thinking?
    Hark! our Nightingale – he sings –
Now a rising note – now sinking
    Back in little broken rings

Of warm song, that spread and eddy –
    Now he picks up heart – and draws
His great music, slow and steady,
    To a silver-centred pause!

A LETTER TO ROBERT BROWNING

Paris
Wednesday, 13 Sept., 1854

My dear Browning,

All day I've been writing Dispatches
(You should see them!) . . . blue paper in batches
As huge as those piles of the Druid
At Stonehenge! . . . the ink is yet fluid.
And, tired of red tape and scratches,
And labelling, sealing, and docketing,
I sit here at last, dull and heavy,
Like a stick that went up with a rocket in,
Which, while the blue sparks in a bevy
Die off through the dark midnight skies there,
Falls down quite good for nothing, and lies there.
I am out of my wits with deciphering
The day's news, come so fast (telegraphic)
That the sense of it's left quite behind it all.
As a man who, in choosing his wife a ring,
Spends the day, finding none to her mind at all,
May wish all the goldsmiths to hell (a graphic
and adequate figure of speech?); so I
Wish (could my sides but reach so high!)
Admiral Dundas and Marshal St. Arnaud
Neck and crop into the Seine or the Arno.

2

Till I fall half-asleep – having nothing to do better –
Stretch my legs, light my pipe, close my eyes . . . and, by Jupiter,
No end to the horrible visions and fancies
That flit over my brain! . . . Turk-encampments, strange dances

---

Dundas, St. Arnaud: commanders respectively of the British naval forces and the French land forces in the opening stages of the Crimean War

Of wild Bashi-bazouks round the walls of Sebastopol,
Ships burning by hundreds, and oceans that cast up whole
Shoals of green cholera-corpses and skeletons,
Till the whole world seems driving posthaste into hell at once!
Just such damnable notions as choke the last trances
Of opium, or which one conceives that a man sees
In a glare of green water, as down he goes, drowning,
Through cold water lilies and marsh weeds Ophelia-wise;
When the water sings loud in the ears, and you feel your eyes
Closed with a clammy and comfortless pressure.
Then, at last, I start up . . . some new thought, full of pleasure!
And, 'I wonder now what he's about – Robert Browning?'

3

No doubt somewhere in the Pitti
(There's no place that's half so fit!) he
Lingers thrall'd beneath the eyes
Of Titian's Flora: artist-wise,
Does he praise that level colour
Whence even Rubens' self grows duller,
All the warmth in that white side?
Or does he (seldom comes so pat a line!)
Choose, perhaps, Salvator's Cataline
For his musing, wonder-eyed?

Nay, 'tis night, and in the Pitti
All is dark. Well, Florence city
Draws him through her glimmering streets,
Where, at every turn, he meets
That which shall his steps arrest –
Some grim Fresco half-effaced,
Date and Artist to be guessed:
Or some green tablet, dimly placed
In dark Borgo, to attest
'Here so-and-so lived long ago,

Bashi-bazouks: Turkish irregular troops

Where the Tower stood . . .'; or to say
'There such a fray on such a day
Took place'; or 'Pater Patriae'
(If the letters one could see)
'Cosmus Dux' – he does you it
From the barbarous, half-illegible
Latin lines into intelligible
English doubtless – 'antiquorum
Dilectus ille Fiorentorum
Hoc monumentum posuit.'

No, the moon shines: the lamps quiver
Warmly down the shallow river,
Shining o'er each white Divinity
On the old bridge of the Trinity.
No doubt he wanders now, *adagio*
Adagio, down that Via Maggio
(For the nights are rich and warm)
Somewhere slowly, arm in arm
With some friend who'd gladly walk
Ten miles more to hear him talk,
And then go supperless to bed
Feeling feasted-full, and fed
With the grand things he hath said.

Or, perhaps, he lounges home
(Where, alas, I shall not meet him!)
With odd scraps of news from Rome . . .
(Has Gibson daub'd with paint some statue?
How he flings great angers at you!)
Past the doorway he hath come;
In that Tapestried Room he'll seat him –
And straight some Muse is there to greet him!

Gibson: the sculptor John Gibson (1790–1866), who lived in Rome and frequently added colour to his statues

4

For one feels the subtle Presence
Of some spirit fair and wise,
Not mere mortal – the quintessence
Of divinest sympathies,
Whose divineness is most human.
If not Clio from calm skies,
'Tis the noblest, sweetest woman
This world's womanhood supplies.
Search the world through you'll find none such,
None with such deep-minded powers
Crown'd 'to spin her own free hours.'
Nature can but furnish one such,
Labouring fondly to perfect
That imperial intellect!

5

She hath walked in Grecian bowers;
She hath heard Apollo sing;
Crown'd with parsley leaves and flowers
Seen Anacreon revelling.
She hath traversed o'er and o'er
The old mazy Hebrew lore:
Knows what tunes the Psalmist sung
To his harp when he was young
The white sheepfolds all among.
Plato is her friend: all others
Great and wise are her soul's brothers.
With Vanini in his Prison,
And with Bruno at the stake,
Her fine spirit hath soared and risen:
Yet, for human nature's sake,
Stays on earth, lest hearts should break.
Gently, she hath often come

Vanini, Bruno: sixteenth-century Italian philosophers burned at the stake for heresy

From Tully left at Tusculum,
(Or from commune with some Rabbin)
To smile into Earth's lowliest cabin.
And the little children drooping
In hot English Factories
Love her. She hath pled for these.
A healing spirit, stored with sanities
Of all warm and wise humanities!

I have time to write no more –
Not a word to add to what I've written
But that which you well knew before
How I'm your true friend,

Robert Lytton.

Isabella Blagden
L'Ariccia. Death in Life

I gaze upon a scene of Arcady.
'Tis noon, and o'er the vales and through the woods
The myriad voices of the summer's hymn
Ring out 'tis noon throughout their solitudes!
Such glittering radiance in the air, that dim
And distant seems the blue and cloudless sky,
As if a space for visioned dreams were given,
The veil withdrawn midway 'twixt earth and heaven,
That, bathed in golden light, the painter's eye
Seraphic glories in its depths might trace,
Or, leaning down o'er earth, a tender face
(Its sweetness mortal, but its calm divine),
Fair Nature smiling o'er her chosen shrine!
Ay – Time for once calls back fair Arcady;
And as I gaze, in rapture deep and still,
Before me winding pass through vale and hill
And through the arches of the wooded glades
The herds as slow they seek the forest shades,

While wears the sun his noontide majesty;
And first, with watchful eye and steadfast tread,
The broad disparted crescents on their brows
Austerely borne, the grey-hued steers have led
The rustic path; and then with antic play
And many a sidelong bound, grotesquely wreathing
Their wild fantastic horns amid the boughs,
The milk-white goats across the steep banks stray.
It seems as 'twere some sculptured pageant breathing,
A chiselled record of the Pagan Past —
A fair procession bound for sacrifice!
And nought we miss — for even the choral song
And dance is here: where yonder pines have cast
A thicker shade, a joyous laughing throng
Of brown-cheeked girls with large and flashing eyes
And ebony locks vine-garlanded are grouped;
And one who, fairer than the rest, has looped
Those scarlet blossoms 'mid the tendrils, flings
High o'er her head her tambourine, and sings
A measured chant, which through the greenwood rings: —

> 'Our vineyard toils today are done,
>   Sisters, let us rest,
> Each beside her chosen one,
>   I on my mother's breast.

> 'For me, no lover's smiles e'er shone,
>   Beguiling where it charms;
> I seek it not, I envy none,
>   Clasped in my mother's arms.

> 'My love is hers, and hers alone,
>   Each pulse of hers a part;
> My very life to hers has grown,
>   Linked to my mother's heart.

> 'Ye smile: "No mother hast thou known,
>   An orphan from thy birth."

Her tender love ye all may own
Our loving mother – Earth.

'But most am I her cherished one,
She calls me to my rest,
To lay all toil and sorrow down
Asleep upon her breast!'

I heard a cadence in this simple song
Which echoed of the Etruscan age, most sweet
And yet most sad: such ever did belong
To these, the early children of the earth,
Who from her affluent breasts derived their birth
And knew no other source or end; complete
In them the sensuous life, and oh! how fair
The clime which poured its sunshine through their veins
And with a passionate and raptured heart
Of Beauty filled all earth, and sky, and air!
Beats that quick fiery pulse no more? remains
Of that intoxicating charm no part?
Ah! yes, there lives by mount and vale and stream
The Pagan glory, and its soul throbs there
Voluptuous still – lo! where we catch the gleam
Of yon Bacchante's dark far-floating hair,
Inebriate with joy and life and youth,
Yet with divine yet half-unconscious sense
Of Nature's deep pathetic influence
In her wild song; the instinct of the south,
This Life luxuriant, fervent and supreme,
The type and rose and crown of all beneath
The gorgeous mask, the hollow brows of Death!

ON THE ITALIAN COLOURS BEING REPLACED ON THE PALAZZO VECCHIO

O'er the old tower, like bright flame curled
　　Which leapeth sudden to the sky,
Its emblem hues all wide unfurled,
　　Upsprings the flag of Italy.

Its emblem hues! the brave blood shed,
　　The true life-blood by heroes given,
The green palms of the martyred dead,
　　The snowy robes they wear in heaven!

These colours all high hearts must bear;
　　They tell of courage, truth and faith,
The heart to know, to will, to dare,
　　The threefold life which o'ercomes death.

The death which tyrants deemed held fast
　　The lands o'er which their armies trod
Hath no more power, the grave is past.
　　A living people bless Thee, God.

Freed from the yoke of alien kings,
　　The nations wake to life and breath;
Th'immortal from the mortal springs,
　　'Out of the body of that death.'

No sepulchres can freedom hold.
　　'Tis life; and life o'er death must rise.
Glad bells ring out in triumph bold;
　　Wave, flag of freedom, to the skies!

My Florence, which so fair doth lie,
　　A dream of beauty, at my feet,
While smiles above that dappled sky,
　　While glows around that ripening wheat,

As fair, as shining, and as bright
    Art thou as she we hear came down
From heaven in bridal robes of white,
    Thy New Jerusalem, St. John.

And like hers too a promise stands
    In this great victory won by thee,
A hope to all the yearning lands,
    Witness and pledge to Italy.

9

Eugene Lee-Hamilton

Eugene Jacob Lee-Hamilton, the only child of James and Matilda Lee-Hamilton, was born in London on 6 January 1845. Little is known of his father, who is said to have married Matilda Adams, the daughter of a Welsh landowner, solely for her money. They soon separated, and Mrs Lee-Hamilton joined her brother William in France. After the deaths of her husband and her brother she married Eugene's tutor, Henry Ferguson Paget, in 1855, and in the following year their daughter, Violet, was born. The family spent their time between one Continental watering-place and another, only occasionally visiting England. This wandering way of life had at least one advantage, in that both Eugene and his half-sister grew up speaking fluent French, German and Italian.

The most powerful influence on Lee-Hamilton's life was that of his mother. Matilda Paget was a paradoxical personality, a gentle and sensitive woman with a will of iron. Her emotional life centred on her son, to whom she had turned for comfort after the failure of her first marriage, and who meant far more to her than either her second husband or her daughter. Her reluctance to be separated from him no doubt explains why he was never sent to school but received his education at home, from his mother and from tutors. The system evidently worked, for in addition to his linguistic attainments his writings show him to have been exceptionally widely read, with an intimate knowledge of some of the more obscure aspects of European history. In his thinking on religious matters his mother's influence was particularly strong. Her father had been 'an ardent Voltairian, who spent much of his time disputing with the local parsons and refusing to pay tithes', and she had inherited his views. According to Violet Paget, she 'clung, even in the 'seventies . . . to the heresies which I later identified as Voltairian or derived from Rousseau and Tom Paine; and her politics were those of Charles James Fox'.[1] She declared that she lived abroad in order to escape the English Sunday. Her son and her daughter in their turn maintained the family tradition of rejection of religious orthodoxy.

Mother and son were separated for the first time in 1864, when Lee-Hamilton entered Oriel College, Oxford. His mother wrote to him every day, showering him with good advice and anxious enquiries about his health, and expected him to reply equally frequently. Judging by his poem 'Oxford', written some ten years after he went down, he seems to have been happy enough at the university; he won the Taylorian scholarship in modern languages and literature, he enjoyed good health, he wrote verse, he became an expert skater. The vacations he spent on the Xontinent with his family. In 1866, however, despite his mother's pleas, he left the university without taking his degree, 'the first of a series of steps which well may be interpreted as an unconscious evasion of life'.[2] His need of his mother, it seems, was even greater than his mother's need of him.

For the next three years he was content to drift round France, Switzerland and Italy with his family, but in 1869 he entered the diplomatic service. After some months in the Foreign Office he was appointed to the embassy in Paris in February 1870. The Franco-Prussian War broke out five months later, and the British embassy followed the French Government as it moved first to Tours, then to Bordeaux and finally to Versailles. In 1872 Lee-Hamilton was sent to Geneva, as secretary to the British delegation negotiating on compensation for the damage to American shipping caused by the British-built Confederate commerce-raider *Alabama* during the Civil War. His work was highly praised, and a diplomatic career as distinguished as Robert Lytton's seemed to lie before him. In January 1873, however, he was offered the post of third secretary to the British embassy in Buenos Aires. The prospect of being banished, as he saw it, to a barbarous country thousands of miles from European civilization infuriated him. 'I am inclined to see them damned before I accept one of the worst posts in the world after services such as I am pretty sure no other attaché has ever rendered,'[3] he wrote to his mother, and he found an obliging doctor who testified that his alarming state of health necessitated immediate sick leave. The Buenos Aires plan was dropped, and instead he was offered a post at Lisbon, but by then it was too late. He had succeeded in making himself really ill.

The exact nature of his illness is a mystery, which is deepened by his having given several different explanations of it to his relations and friends. His widow attributed it after his death to 'anaemia and an alarming disturbance of the circulation'. William Sharp, editor of the selection from his poems published in 1903, described it as 'a cerebro-spinal disease . . . the same dread and agonising disease which had kept Heine on his mattress-grave for so many weary years', though presumably he did not intend to suggest that the complaint, like Heine's, was of syphilitic origin. The American novelist Edith Wharton believed that 'the long period of over-strain and over-work [during the Franco-Prussian War], followed by the privations and horrors of the siege of Paris, had brought about a bad nervous break-down, of a kind which the doctors of that day had not learned to deal with'. As Lee-Hamilton was not in Paris during the siege, this account suggests that he enjoyed romancing about his experiences. There can be little doubt that his illness was essentially psychosomatic, and had its roots in his relationship with his mother. His half-sister was a precocious young woman who at sixteen already showed signs of developing into a more successful writer than himself. Fear of being exiled from his mother to a remote capital, jealousy of his sister, perhaps an Oedipal jealousy of Henry Paget, all contributed to produce a psychological crisis which resulted in a physical collapse. 'It is difficult', Violet Paget's biographer wrote, 'not to see Eugene's illness as a desperate attempt to protect himself from the world by returning to the warmth of his mother's love, and to seek in illness and maternal devotion a refuge from her or others' critical comparison of his abilities with those of his brilliant half-sister.' There are indications in his verse that he was conscious of being the cause of his own sufferings, as in the poignant conclusion of the sonnet 'The Wreck-Rock Bell':

> Too late, too late. Man sails, by foul or fine,
>   One voyage only in his life's frail bark;
>   One and no more. What made thee shipwreck thine?'[4]

A sense of guilt at having wasted his life may account for his tendency to evade his responsibility by inventing fantastic explanations for his illness.

Although he did not resign from the diplomatic service until 1875, from the spring of 1873 onwards he was a helpless invalid. He returned to his family, and they abandoned their wanderings to settle in Florence. After a period in hotels or lodgings, they lived first at Via Solferino 12, near the Cascine; from 1881 or early in 1882 at Via Garibaldi 5, in the same area; and finally from 1889 at the Villa Il Palmerino, a large farmhouse in a valley between Florence and Fiesole. For over twenty years Lee-Hamilton lay on a wheeled sofa in a darkened room, unable to move, or at times even to speak more than a few words. He could neither read nor write, and an amanuensis was hired to read to him and to take down his poems from his faltering dictation. In the mornings his mother and sister would accompany him on drives into the country in a carriage built to contain his sofa. When his health would permit, visitors were admitted in the evening, and his room became a meeting-place for British, American, French, Italian and Russian intellectuals. The summer would be spent at Bagni di Lucca or Siena.

His circle of friends included Henry James, who on 12 January 1887 paid him a particularly memorable visit. The Countess Maria Gamba, whose husband was a nephew of Byron's mistress the Countess Teresa Guiccioli, was also present, and it emerged in conversation that the Gambas owned Byron's letters to the Countess Guiccioli. When Lee-Hamilton suggested that they should publish them, or at least allow English scholars to see them, the Countess angrily refused, declaring that the letters were discreditable to Byron, and admitted that she had herself burned one of them. This conversation reminded Lee-Hamilton of a story about Claire Clairmont which he had heard from another American friend, the painter John Singer Sargent. After Shelley's death Claire had supported herself by working as a governess in Austria, Russia, Germany and England, and finally settled in Florence. Perhaps remembering happier days in 1819–20, she lived from 1868 to 1871 in the Via Valfonda. In the following year she rented an apartment in the Palazzo Cruciato, at Via Romana 43 (now 73), where she lived with her niece Paula until her death in 1879. In October 1872 Edward Silsbee, an American sea captain and a fanatical admirer of Shelley, who longed to lay hands on the Shelley papers which Claire was known to possess, moved into the apartment as a lodger. He became Paula's lover for a time, but as he was unable to afford the high price which Claire asked for the papers he went back to America. After Claire's death he returned to Florence, and the sequel can be told as James recorded it in his notebook: 'The old woman *did* die – and then he approached the younger one – the old maid of 50 – on the subject of his desires. Her answer was – "I will give you all the letters if you marry me!" H. says that Silsbee *court encore*. Certainly there is a little subject there.'[5] This conversation supplied James with the plot of *The Aspern Papers*, which appeared a year later in *The Atlantic Monthly*.

Lee-Hamilton had written verse at least since his Oxford days, and during his illness he found both an occupation and consolation in composing poems, of which he was sometimes too weak to dictate more than a line or two at a time. His first collection, *Poems and Transcripts*, which was

237

published in 1878, largely consisted of revised versions of poems written several years earlier. The most interesting poems in the book contain reminiscences of France in 1870–71, and probably date from that period. There are poems in blank verse, a metre which encouraged his tendency to prolixity, experiments with classical elegiac couplets, poems in lyrical metres, historical ballads, and translations from Italian and German poets. *Gods, Saints, and Men*, published in 1880, contains twelve stories, most of them of his own invention, written in blank verse, octosyllabic couplets or various stanza forms. Violet Paget published her first book, *Studies of the Eighteenth Century in Italy,* in the same year under the pseudonym Vernon Lee, and followed this with many other works of fiction and criticism. The rivalry between the brother and sister was thereby intensified, but for the present their relations remained apparently amicable.

The New Medusa and Other Poems, Lee-Hamilton's third collection, which appeared in 1882, largely consisted of narrative poems, but it made two important innovations. It ended with ten sonnets, a form which he had not previously used, but which he was to cultivate for the rest of his life. It was also his first book to contain poems on Florentine or Tuscan themes, among them 'A Ballad of the Plague of Florence', telling the same story which Shelley had planned to use in his unfinished 'Ginevra', 'A Ballad of the Sack of Prato' and 'On a Tuscan Road', a moving description of a peasant's funeral. Two more personal poems contain vivid descriptive passages. 'An Elegy on the Death of a Lady who died at Florence Feb. 29, 1880' opens with a picture of Tuscany in spring, and closes as follows:

> But now the sun is low: before it leaves
> It sends a slanting ray to kiss the stone.
> Then pearly twilight settles over all;
> The cypresses grow black, the air grows chill,
> The mighty dome of Florence stands distinct,
> With Giotto's belfry near it, on the sky.
> Then by degrees they mingle with the night,
> Like fading ghosts. The city's hum is hushed,
> And through the dusk there comes the mellow boom
> Of a great bell, tolled slowly, which brings home
> A sense of peace in mutability.

'A Letter to Miss A. Mary F. Robinson' skilfully evokes the atmosphere of summer and autumn in Tuscany:

> Come when no more the endless noontide creeps,
> And each hot tile-roof tremulously streams;
> Come when no more the shrill cicala keeps
> Sawing the empty air, and he who sleeps
>   Abhors it through his dreams.
>
> Come when no more the vesper bell shall rouse
> The inmates of each sun-entranced abode;
> And when no more the peasant shades with boughs
> His slow white oxen's fly-tormented brows
>   Upon the glaring road.[6]

The poem is addressed, and the book is dedicated, to a close friend of Violet Paget, who was herself a skilful lyric poet, and to whom both Lee-Hamilton and his sister seem to have been sexually attracted. When in 1888 she married a French professor Violet Paget suffered a nervous breakdown, and was encouraged by Lee-Hamilton to break off all relations with her friend.

Apollo and Marsyas and Other Poems, published in 1884, follows a similar pattern to *The New Medusa*. It contains several stories in narrative or dialogue form, two poems on Tuscan themes ('An Ode of the Tuscan Shore', on the death of Shelley, and 'A Pageant of Siena', on the *palio*) and twenty-one sonnets. His next collection, *Imaginary Sonnets*, which appeared in 1888, is more original. It consists of an introductory sonnet and 100 dramatic monologues in sonnet form, spoken by figures from European history. Arranged in chronological order, they range from Henry I of England lamenting his son's death in the White Ship to Napoleon on St Helena seven centuries later. Several of them are spoken by men or women suffering a long imprisonment (Raleigh and Lady Arabella Stuart in the Tower, Alexander Selkirk on his island, Latude in the Bastille) who give voice to Lee-Hamilton's own frustrations. No less than eleven of the sonnets are put into the mouths of figures from Florentine history: Farinata degli Uberti, the leader of the Florentine Ghibellines; Donna Bella, the mother of Dante; Leonardo da Vinci; Lorenzo de Medici; Savonarola; the painter Luca Signorelli; Michelangelo; the diehard republican Filippo Strozzi; Benvenuto Cellini; Galileo; and Prince Charles Edward in his old age. Some of these are characterized with remarkable skill. In the speech of Farinata degli Uberti, for example, who is depicted at the moment when, after the disastrous Guelf defeat at Montaperti, he alone resisted the Tuscan Ghibellines' proposal to destroy Florence, Lee-Hamilton suggests both the pride and the magnanimity of the great feudal nobleman who, according to Dante, even in hell seemed 'to hold hell in great contempt'.[7]

Imaginary Sonnets was the first of Lee-Hamilton's books which attained any great success, in contrast to the complete failure of its successor. Two of the *Imaginary Sonnets* deal with the Spanish explorer Juan Ponce de León and his legendary quest for a miraculous fountain possessing the power to restore the youth of whoever drank from it. The theme seems to have fascinated Lee-Hamilton, who made it the subject of his next book, *The Fountain of Youth. A Fantastic Tragedy*, which was published in 1891. Although written in dramatic form, this work was presumably not intended for the stage, for the author shows himself to be completely devoid of any dramatic instinct whatsoever. Its one point of interest is the choruses spoken at intervals by spirits of youth, spirits of age, dawn spirits and the like; these are merely feeble imitations of Swinburne, but they may have given Hardy a hint for the choruses of spirits in *The Dynasts*.

His next book, *Sonnets of the Wingless Hours*, which appeared in 1894, was perhaps his best. It consists entirely of sonnets, including a number which had appeared in his previous collections. The first of the five sections into which the book is divided, 'A Wheeled Bed 1873–1893', contains sonnets on his illness, which in tone are understandably bitter but are generally free from self-pity. The remaining sections include sonnets suggested by paintings or sculptures and reflections on life and the concept of an afterlife. Lee-Hamilton is seen at his best in his sonnets, because the limits of the form imposed restraints upon him. When he was free to write at whatever length he pleased he often went on far too long; 'Prince Charlie's Weather-Vane', for example, would be a good poem if it stopped after the first forty lines, but instead it continues for another 115 to deal with the '45, the French Revolution, the Napoleonic Wars and the growth of the British Empire. The sonnets, on the other hand, display an admirable economy; his normal method is to present a picture or tell a story in the octave, and to make whatever comment is needed in the sestet.

The section of *Sonnets of the Wingless Hours* headed 'Life And Fate' is remarkable for the variety of symbols which he uses: Faustus's ring which renewed the wearer's youth, treasures sunk in the sea, a game of chess, a ruined tower among sand-dunes, a sledge pursued by wolves, a reveller who sees his own hanged body. A curious feature of the book is the number of sonnets on fairy themes, examples of the type of whimsy which apparently delighted our forefathers (Arthur Quiller-Couch in 1912 included no less than four of Lee-Hamilton's fairy sonnets in *The Oxford Book of Victorian Verse*) but has little appeal today. Only a handful of sonnets deal with Florentine themes: 'Corso de' Fiori', on a battle of flowers, 'Fading Glories II' (later renamed 'On some Fourteenth-Century Saints'), 'On a Group of Fra Angelico's Angels', 'On Leonardo's Head of Medusa' and 'On the Fly-leaf of Dante's *Vita Nuova*'.

If Lee-Hamilton is judged by the five collections which he published between 1880 and 1894 he must be ranked high among the many minor Victorian poets. As with most minor poets, influences are easily identified: primarily Browning, Rossetti and Swinburne, but also Coleridge, Shelley, Keats, Tennyson, Poe, Baudelaire, Goethe and *The Ingoldsby Legends*. Browning's influence is immediately apparent in such poems as 'The Mandolin', which owes its form, the deathbed mutterings of a worldly sixteenth-century ecclesiastic, to 'The Bishop Orders his Tomb at Saint Praxed's Church', or in 'A Rival of Fallopius' and 'Abraham Carew', in each of which the speaker seeks to justify a crime. Rossetti was Lee-Hamilton's model as a sonneteer, and tribute is twice paid to him in *Sonnets of the Wingless Hours* in 'In Memoriam' and in the conclusion of 'What the Sonnet is', where as a master of the form he is classed with Dante, Petrarch and Shakespeare. As for Swinburne, in the 1880s and 1890s 'every warbler had his tune by heart',[8] with results that were usually unfortunate, as in the choruses in *The Fountain of Youth*. Lee-Hamilton, however, is often at his most powerful when he is writing under a greater poet's influence, as in the sonnet 'Promethean Fancies', which seems to owe something to Shelley, or in the admirable sonnet 'Baudelaire'.

In his views on religion he was very much his mother's son, and this is clearly apparent in his verse. In an early poem, 'A Dwarf', the sight of a crippled dwarf inspires a lengthy diatribe on the evils of the Catholic Middle Ages which is very eighteenth-century in spirit. Religious asceticism is attacked in 'The Idyl of the Anchorite', which tells how a hermit drives away a woman who has taken refuge in his cell, believing her to be a demon, with the result that she is killed by wolves, and in 'The Bride of Porphyrion', a dialogue between an early Christian, who has deserted his bride on their wedding day in order to become a hermit, and his wife, who has sunk into prostitution. His attacks on religious fanaticism are not directed exclusively against the Catholic Church; 'Abraham Carew' is the defence of a zealous Nonconformist who has killed his only child, believing that, like Abraham, he has been commanded by God to do so. It is not surprising that Lee-Hamilton 'used to find pleasure in arguing with catholic and protestant alike, writing to his sister descriptions of visitors' discomfort under his relentless, albeit somewhat adolescent rationalizing of their most cherished beliefs'. As an alternative to Christianity he presents a sentimental picture of days

> When Gods as men in every myrtle grove
> Of Hellas trod;
> And man, though proud of being man, yet strove
> To be a God,

in a passage that bears a suspiciously close resemblance to Swinburne's

> In the fair days when God
> By man as godlike trod,
> And each alike was Greek, alike was free.

More impressive are the sonnets, such as 'Sea-shell Murmurs' and 'The Wreck of Heaven', in which he rejects the idea of personal immortality. Against it he sets the concept of service to humanity in this life, as in the conclusion of 'Wine of Omar Khayyam':

> Lo – Just because we have no life but this,
> Turn it to use; be noble while you can:
> Search, help, create; then pass into the night,

or that of a beneficent influence exercised through his poems, as in 'My Own Hereafter'.[9]

Yet there is an interesting inconsistency in his attitude towards Catholicism. Living in a Catholic country, he could not escape the strong fascination which Catholicism can exercise upon the imagination, and three of the poems in *Gods, Saints, and Men* are Catholic in tone. In 'The Fiddle and the Slipper' a musician unjustly sentenced to be burned for sacrilege is saved by the miraculous intervention of the Virgin Mary, whose mercy is contrasted with the cruelty and injustice of the clergy. 'The Keys of the Convent' tells the well-known story of a nun who has run away with her lover but on repenting and returning to her convent finds that her absence has gone undetected because the Virgin has taken her place. In 'The Witness' a youth swears before a crucifix to marry a girl, who remains faithful to him; when years later he returns from overseas he denies that he ever made such a promise, but the figure of Christ on the crucifix confirms her story. Catholicism, it seems, could appeal to Lee-Hamilton's imagination while failing to convince his reason.

In 'The Fiddle and the Slipper' and 'The Keys of the Convent' Mary appears as a benevolent mother-figure, but a more typical role for the female figures in his poems is that of sinister enchantress. 'The Last Love of Venus' in *Gods, Saints, and Men,* a variant on the Tannhäuser story, tells of a German knight who falls in love with a statue of Venus. The goddess herself appears to him and carries him off through the air, but during the flight changes to a hideous witch. 'Sister Mary of the Plague' in *Apollo and Marsyas* is the story of a saintly nun, apparently a ministering angel, who in her sleep turns into a vampire, killing her patients by sucking their lifeblood. It is difficult to avoid the suspicion that Sister Mary (the choice of name is significant) represents the mother who, by making Lee-Hamilton totally dependent upon herself, as he saw it, had deprived him of his individuality.

One of the salient characteristics of his poetry is an obsession with cruelty and pain. This first becomes apparent in 'A Rival of Fallopius' in *Gods, Saints, and Men*, in which an anatomist kidnaps a youth in order to vivisect him, and justifies his action as necessary to the advancement of science. This obsession largely dominates *Imaginary Sonnets*, and Lee-Hamilton finds it necessary in an introductory note to justify his choice of subjects with the plea that 'if in this Masque of Sonnets the darker and stormier passions play too prominent a part it is not his fault, but that of the dark and stormy centuries themselves'.[10] This special pleading is not convincing, for no necessity compelled him to select those particular themes from the whole extent of European history. Two especially revolting sonnets develop the theme of 'A Rival of Fallopius'. In one the anatomist Fallopius gloats over the prospect of being allowed to dissect living convicts; in the other an artist, Domingo Lopez, plans to crucify a Jew whom he has kidnapped and imprisoned, in order to use him as a model for a painting of the Passion of Christ. One form of cruelty which particularly fascinated Lee-Hamilton was beheading. In his poems on the French Revolution – for example, 'Hunting the King' in *Apollo and Marsyas* and 'Cazotte to a Supper Party' in *Imaginary Sonnets* – it is on the heads dropping into the basket that he dwells, rather than the Revolution's ideals and achievements.

The two themes of woman as an evil power and beheading are combined in a group of poems which deal with the story of Medusa. 'The New Medusa' tells of an Englishman travelling in Italy who falls in love with a beautiful woman who has been picked up at sea; he discovers that at night her hair turns to snakes, and promptly cuts her head off. In 'Benvenuto Cellini to his Mistress' in *Imaginary Sonnets* Cellini, planning his statue of Perseus, dwells lovingly on the blood pouring from Medusa's severed head and neck, and recalls how they had seen a girl beheaded a few days before. The association in Lee-Hamilton's mind between cruelty and sexual pleasure is clear in this poem, with its references to Perseus' nakedness, Cellini's use of his mistress as his model for Medusa and her 'convulsive writhes'. The painting of Medusa's head attributed to Leonardo, on which Shelley had written a poem, so fascinated Lee-Hamilton that he wrote two sonnets on it, which appear in *Imaginary Sonnets* and *Sonnets of the Wingless Hours*. A variation on the Medusa theme in his verse is the Judith theme, in which a woman beheads a man. 'A Ballad of the Sack of Prato' tells how a married woman, who had been carried off by a Spanish captain when her town was sacked, after seven years cut off his head and took it back to her husband as proof that she had not deserted him willingly. The same theme reappears in two sonnets 'On Mantegna's Sepia Drawing of Judith' in *Apollo and Marsyas*.

Lee-Hamilton's obsession with cruelty reaches its climax in *The Fountain of Youth*, in which the Indian High Priest maintains that cruelty is the law of nature:

> He is the great and all-pervading god
> Of Cosmic Cruelty, named Ataflis;

> And it is owing to his boundless power
> That Nature preys for ever on herself,
> And that the earth and air and sea are filled with millions
> Who feed on others and themselves are eaten
>
> .   .   .   .
>
> The two great ruling principles of Nature
> Are Cruelty and Beauty.

The same philosophy is expounded by the Indian arrow-poisoners, who sing as they work:

> The juice of creation
>   Is venom and blood,
> And torture is master
>   Of earth and of flood.
>
> All nature is teeming
>   With claw and with fang:
> Above is the beauty,
>   Beneath is the pang.[11]

In the last act of the play Ponce de León's daughter, Rosita, is sacrificed by the Indians by being offered to a monstrous man-eating flower (surely the most bizarre fate ever suffered by a tragic heroine), and Ponce is shot with a poisoned arrow when, as he believes, he is just about to taste the Fountain of Youth. The philosophy of the High Priest and the arrow-poisoners is closely akin to that of the Marquis de Sade, as expounded in his novels *Justine* and *Juliette*, which Lee-Hamilton had probably read while living in France.

In his well-known critical study *The Romantic Agony* Mario Praz identified Sade as a major influence and sado-masochism, Medusa, vampirism and the *femme fatale* as recurrent themes in the work of the Romantics and their successors, the Decadents of the later nineteenth century. He might have been writing about Lee-Hamilton, yet he never mentioned him and probably had never heard of him. We are faced with the question whether, in dealing with these themes, Lee-Hamilton was merely following a literary fashion. This is unlikely; it is difficult to read

Imaginary Sonnets without reaching the conclusion that he was obsessed with the infliction of pain. We cannot ignore the sexual repression to which his illness condemned him, nor the leisure which it gave him to indulge in sexual fantasies. At an earlier period, however, he would probably have been far more discreet in allowing these fantasies to provide subject-matter for his verse. In Praz's words, 'one is forced to the conclusion that perhaps the unlimited licence to deal with subjects of vice and cruelty, which was introduced into literature together with Romanticism, created an atmosphere favourable to the expression of individual feeling, which, in different circumstances, would have remained latent and repressed'.[12]

Throughout Lee-Hamilton's illness his family had consulted various specialists in the hope of finding a cure, but without success. In 1893 they approached Dr Erb of Heidelberg, who diagnosed his complaint as 'a purely *functional* one, produced by a very high degree of auto-suggestion'.[13] He was persuaded to follow the regimen which Dr Erb prescribed, and by 1895 was well enough to walk. It is possible that one contributory factor in his recovery was Henry Paget's death in 1894, which removed one potential source of friction in his relations with his mother. Matilda Paget herself died in 1896, and was buried in the new Protestant cemetery outside the Porta Romana. When Violet Paget returned from the funeral, which her brother had not attended, he informed her that he was leaving the Villa Il Palmerino.

Freed from his family relationships, Lee-Hamilton began a new life, 'eager for new experiences, new scenes and countries'. He visited Canada and the United States in 1897, and stayed with Edith Wharton, who had been among his visitors at Il Palmerino, at Land's End, her home in Rhode Island. She remembered him as 'rejoicing in his recovered vigour, and keeping us and our guests in shouts of laughter by his high spirits and inimitable stories'.[14] Soon after his return to Florence he was introduced to Annie Holdsworth, a popular novelist of the day, and on 21 July 1898, less than a year after their meeting, they were married at Lyndhurst, in Hampshire. They spent their honeymoon in the New Forest, and there collaborated in writing a collection of pretty but insipid lyrics, *Forest Notes*, which was published in the following year.

He published in the year of his marriage a version of Dante's *Inferno*, which was intended to be the first volume of a complete translation of the

Divina Commedia. In his introduction he singled out as the salient characteristics of Dante's versification the eleven-syllable line, ending in an
unstressed syllable, the arrangement of the lines in triplets, and the
rhyme-scheme. As it is impossible to reproduce all three in English, he
retained the hendecasyllabic line and the division into triplets, while
abandoning rhyme. A few lines from his rendering of the story of Count
Ugolino will give the effect:

> When I awoke, before the break of morning,
>> I heard my children wailing in their slumber,
>> Who were beside me, and entreating bread there.
> Cruel indeed art thou, if thou lament not
>> At the mere thought of what my heart foretold me;
>> And if thou weep'st not, what art wont to weep at?
> Now they had wak'd; and th' hour was approaching
>> At which the food had hitherto been brought us;
>> And from his vision, each of us was doubting.
> And then I heard them locking, down below us,
>> The frightful tower's door; at which I fastened
>> My eyes on my sons' faces without speaking.
> I did not weep, inside I grew so stony;
>> But they were weeping; and my sweet small Anselm
>> Said, 'Father, thou art staring so; what is it?'
> Yet still I shed no tear, nor did I answer
>> All through that day, nor yet the night that followed,
>> Till the next sun came forth upon the world there.

The translation was not well received, and has been described as 'one of
the poorest attempts in English'.[15] This is surely too harsh, as a comparison with Gray's and Medwin's versions of the passage will confirm.
The great virtue of Lee-Hamilton's translation is the faithfulness to the
original which it owes to his rejection of rhyme; its weakness is the
padding that his consistent use of an eleven-syllable line forced him to
introduce. Of the eighteen lines quoted, two end with a 'there' which
is not in the original; of the twenty-one following, three more end with
'there' and another with 'then'. Lee-Hamilton continued to work at his
translation after his marriage, but although he completed the *Purgatorio*
it did not find a publisher.

Lee-Hamilton and his wife settled in 1900 at the Villa Benedettini, at San Gervasio, between Florence and Fiesole. Probably with her encouragement, he there wrote a historical novel, *The Lord of the Dark Red Star: Being the Story of the Supernatural Influences in the Life of an Italian Despot of the Thirteenth Century*, which was published in 1903. The career of Ezzelino da Romano, the Ghibelline war-lord of the Veneto, on which the novel is based, was lurid enough, but Lee-Hamilton makes it even more so. Ezzelino murders Gisla, his wife, in order that he may marry Selvaggia, the natural daughter of the Emperor Frederick II. Adalhita, his mother, who is a witch, reveals to him that he is the son of Satan, and has a magic shirt of mail made for him. In a vision he descends into hell, where Satan promises him that he will become king of all Northern Italy if he sacrifices to him unbaptized his first male child by Selvaggia. After the marriage a boy is born, but when Ezzelino repeatedly postpones his christening Selvaggia secretly takes him to a hermit, Fra Luca, who baptizes him. Adalhita kidnaps and sacrifices the baby, then herself drops dead. Fra Luca preaches a crusade against Ezzelino, and the cities under his control rebel against him. Before he goes into battle against them, Selvaggia, who suspects the truth about her child's death, steals his magic shirt of mail, and at her instigation one of his captains stabs him in the back. He is taken prisoner by his enemies, and dies raving in a dungeon. The sensationalism of the book reminds one of Harrison Ainsworth, but a more sophisticated Ainsworth who has read Poe.

Although Lee-Hamilton's sadism is abundantly apparent in this novel, it is displayed more subtly than in some of the poems. The historical Ezzelino was a monster of cruelty, but his atrocities are suggested rather than described. He is given an exposition of his sadistic philosophy in conversation with Fra Luca, which is far more convincing that the High Priest's in *The Fountain of Youth*: 'I look on nature and see but pain – successful violence, and the strong that prey upon the weak, the great that prey upon the small: beast, bird, fish, reptile, through the livelong day – and man, the Slaughterer, preying upon them all.' From this statement of general principles he proceeds to his own experience:

> When I was a mere child, long before I dreamed of racks and dungeons,
> I loved to torture the small things that I caught – the fly whose wings I

tore, the bird I blinded, the beast I maimed. Oh, then my pulses thrilled with a new rapture, and I longed to find new torments, till I strained the limbs of men, and longed to design new engines for their use. To me the sight of pain is like strong wine; and when it means revenge for human hate and human treasons, or when it means the spread of fear, on which my power rests, it flushes and intoxicates my soul.[16]

The emphasis on the physical pleasure derived from the infliction of pain, which is paralleled in the sonnet 'Benvenuto Cellini to his Mistress', suggests that Lee-Hamilton is speaking from personal experience.

The year 1903, in which his novel was published, was probably one of the happiest of his adult life. In the same year *Dramatic Sonnets, Poems, and Ballads*, a selection from his poems made by himself, including a few previously unpublished, was issued in the Canterbury Poets. As this series consisted almost entirely of the work of established poets, his inclusion was a high compliment.

Even more important to him was the birth of his only child, Persis Margaret, which seemed to mark the climax of his restoration to life which had begun ten years before. Every morning he would sit beside her cot, working on his translation of the *Purgatorio* or *Ezelin*, an attempt to adapt his novel into a verse tragedy. What seems to be the opening scene of this, in which Adalhita is impregnated by Satan, is included in the 1903 selection, and in its laboured attempts to make the reader's flesh creep becomes unintentionally hilarious. No detail that might add to the effect is omitted: a pitch-black night, thunder, lightning, howling wolves, birds of evil augury, water-snakes (borrowed from *The Ancient Mariner*), a werewolf, a shrieking vampire, prowling ghouls, fleshless souls, and a chorus of nine witches who sing:

> In the deep black moat,
> Where the rank weeds float,
>   And the snakes with a dumb speed glide,
> We swim nine times
> Round thy walls, and the crimes
>   That thy towers in the darkness hide.
> And we sing, as we swim,

> Thy nuptial hymn,
> To the tune that the tempest hums:
> For, riding a wind
> Of souls that sinned,
> Thy wonderful Bridegroom comes.

This epithalamum ushers in Satan, who is represented only by a voice, and the scene closes with Adalhita's cry:

> Ha, the first
> Unutterable clasp! . . . My scorched limbs hiss
> In an embrace that nature cannot burst.
> Has the live lightning quivered through my frame
> To make me big with fire, or God's Accurst
> Filled me with hell? . . . I swoon in night and flame.

This is the only fragment of *Ezelin* that has certainly survived in print, but a chorus of archangels included in *Dramatic Sonnets*, an imitation of Goethe in the style of Swinburne, may also have been written for it; the archangels' phrase 'a great woman-soul gathered to grace' may refer to Ezzelino's saintly wife, Gisla.[17] If so, it suggests that the action of the play, as in *Faust*, was to have been set within the framework of a cosmic conflict between heaven and hell.

Lee-Hamilton's happiness was shattered when on 2 October 1904 the baby Persis died. 'Life had dealt him too hard a blow,' his widow afterwards wrote, 'and his strength was spent. Weakness and depression culminated in a stroke of paralysis; and after months of tragic suffering death came. He died at Bagni di Lucca on September 7, 1907; and was brought to Florence to lie beside his mother and his child.'[18] Although he and Violet Paget had been estranged for some years before his death, when she died in 1935 her remains, by her own wish, were cremated and the casket placed in his grave.

His only literary work in the last three years of his life was a sequence of twenty-nine sonnets on his child's death and two 'Last Sonnets', which were published in 1909 under the title *Mimma Bella*. From these poems, which are among the finest he ever wrote, all the affectations which marred some of his earlier works seem to have been purged away by his grief. The frequent references to Florence and the surrounding countryside which they contain are evidence of his deep affection for the city where so much of his life had been spent. In 'Purple Shadows', the second of the 'Last Sonnets' and presumably the last poem which he ever wrote, night falling over Florence and the tolling of a bell, as in 'An Elegy on the Death of a Lady', are used as symbols of the inevitability of death:

> We stand upon the terrace, looking down
> On Florence, that the sunset rays have kissed,
> And that is robing in her purple mist
> As the slow daylight wanes upon the town;
> While her great dome, in deeper purple shown,
> Seems, for a moment, built of amethyst,
> Ere blending with the shadows that insist,
> And with the hills that evening makes his own.
> Then out of the still city, as it looms
> Dreamy and restful, suddenly there booms
> The deep reverberation of a bell;
> Recalling what the unrelenting year
> Has swept away, of lives that were too dear,
> And sounding their illimitable knell.

Eugene Lee-Hamilton
FARINATA DEGLI UBERTI TO CONQUERED FLORENCE

(1260)

Now shall the ploughshare over thee be passed,
 And wiped away each crowded square and street;
 And seed shall sprinkle thee, and wholesome wheat
Replace thy crops of human hate at last;

And, through the empty valley where thou wast,
 Arno shall seek thee wondering, and repeat
 To land and sea the news that on the seat
Of stately Florence cornfields ripen fast!

And yet, thou evil city, I was born
 Within thee, and I hesitating stand:
Enough that I should scorch thee with my scorn:

Live on, thou nest of scorpions! Not my hand
 Shall pull thee down to sow the yellow corn.
Live, and repent thee – spared at my command.

BENVENUTO CELLINI TO HIS MISTRESS

(1545)

Now will I make my Perseus – first of wax –
 Slim, naked, young, exulting. In his left
 He shall hold high thy vipered head fresh cleft,
Whence clotted blood shall pour, as, 'neath the axe,

That girl's last week. His foot upon thy back's
 Convulsive writhes shall rest; while, in his right,
 He'll hold a short fantastic falchion tight.
Thy neck shall pour, just like the head it lacks.

Then to his heels and helmet I will tie
    Wings that o'er wondrous fairy lands have flown;
And he shall breathe such triumphs as did I

When my good harquebuss hurled Bourbon down
    Rome's wall; or when I wiped my dagger dry
In my first brawl, and thrilled from toe to crown.

Corso de' Fiori

This is the Fight of Roses; and to-day
    Florence does credit to its flow'ry name;
    And every carriage, rose-wreathed wheel and frame,
Panel and trappings, seeks the dewy fray

To fling its yellow rosebuds, or display
    Bright silk-clad human blossoms; till the flame
    Of sunset dwindles, and the fair hands aim
Their last wet rose as daylight wanes away.

And all are gone to see it, and to breathe
    Great April's breath, who marshals his approach
With such a pomp and pageantry of hue,

That even I have half a mind to wreathe
    The wheels of my uncomfortable coach
With rosebuds, too, to give great Spring his due.

On the Fly-leaf of Dante's *Vita Nuova*

There was a tall stern Exile once of old,
    Who paced Verona's streets as dusk shades fell,
    With step as measured as the vesper bell,
And face half-hidden by his hood's dark fold;

One whom the children, as he grimly stroll'd,

Would shrink from in the fear of a vague spell,
    Crying, 'The man who has been down to Hell,'
Or hanging in his footsteps, if more bold.

This little book is not by that stern man,
    But by his younger self, such as he seems
In Giotto's fresco, holding up the flower,

Thinking of her whose hand, by Fate's strange plan,
    He never touched on earth, but who, in dreams
Oft led him into Heaven for an hour.

from PRINCE CHARLIE'S WEATHER-VANE

At Florence, in a listless street,
    A dull old palace stands,
Where many gardens lone and sweet
Grow odorous in the waning heat,
    As evening's shade expands.

Stone shepherdesses quaint and grey
    Stand round it, and clipped trees;
And half-neglect and faint decay
Bring gently home a by-gone day
    In twilight's blunt degrees.

Upon the roof, against the sky,
    There stands a weather-vane, –
A metal flag that with each sigh
Of breeze that passes fitfully,
    Shifts like a thing in pain.

And if you be not over far,
    Against the pearly light,
You see two letters stamped, – C. R.,
Upon it, near some clear white star,
    Just twinkling into sight.

Few are the passers-by who know
　　Whose those initials be;
Or who, in empty regal show,
Saw here his ungrasped kingdom grow
　　Each year more shadowy.

Who thinks, out here, of that stiff race
　　Of Stuarts, who ne'er could find
The heart to veer or change their face,
And left here, as their only trace,
　　A weather-cock behind?

Thou rusty Jacobitish vane,
　　Does thy faint creak still tell
The sparrows, that, spite sun and rain,
The King shall have his own again,
　　And all shall yet be well?

Or dost thou tell the breeze that fans
　　The tree-tops near thee there,
An endless tale of Prestonpans,
Of Falkirk and the conquering clans,
　　Culloden and despair?

SONNET FROM *MIMMA BELLA*

'Tis March; and on the hills that stretch away
In misty furrows on the growing night
The peasants keep their old Etruscan rite,
And wave strange fires, like will-o'-wisps at play;

Chanting an incantation that shall lay
The spirits that bring drought and hail and blight,
And keeping with the sheaves of straw they light
In the green wheat all demon spite at bay.

Ah me! this spring we have no seed to shield

From life's dark possibilities of ill;
Nor look we on the hills where wave the fires;

Nor, hopeful as the tillers of the field,
Repeat the words of magic that they still
Intone in March, as did their antique sires.

10

D. H. Lawrence 1919–1921

When D. H. Lawrence left England on 14 November 1919 he had a little over ten more years of life before him. During those years he made only four visits to England, totalling less than five months. As Alvina, the heroine of *The Lost Girl*, written early in 1920, sails away from England she sees it as 'like a long, ash-grey coffin slowly submerging', which 'seemed to repudiate the sunshine, to remain unilluminated, long and ash-grey and dead, with streaks of snow like cerements'. Here Lawrence, embittered by the vicious persecution which he had suffered during the war years, was clearly expressing his own feelings. Although he was to spend longer or shorter terms in France, Germany, Austria, Switzerland, Ceylon, Australia, the United States and Mexico, the greater part of his time was passed in Italy, which he saw, like Alvina, as a land of light, with a golden sun over a 'glowing antique landscape', in contrast to the darkness of England.[1] He travelled widely in Italy, but it was in Florence or its immediate neighbourhood that he chose to live longer than in any other place.

He had been fascinated by Florence long before he went there. Between July 1918 and April 1919 he had written a school textbook for the Oxford University Press, *Movements in European History*, in which he sought to depict alternatives to twentieth-century industrial society. On the one hand, he brought to life with astonishing success the primitive societies of the Germans, Huns, Goths, Gauls and Franks; on the other, he depicted with equal sympathy the very different society of medieval Florence, which he called 'the queen of Tuscany, the flower of Italy'. 'At home, the merchants lived in a stately manner,' he wrote:

> They built noble palaces. And yet, in Florence at least, they were careful not to pretend to be princes. They were friendly and familiar with the citizens. All the splendour they made they professed to make for the city, not for their own persons. And the citizens were glad. They were passionately proud of their city. They wished their greatest burghers to have the handsomest palaces in the world, the finest fame. For the city – all was for the fame of the city.[2]

This civic pride, Lawrence clearly implied, was something from which modern society could profit. Elsewhere in his book he gave a detailed but unsympathetic account of Savonarola's career, and devoted his chapter on the Renaissance almost entirely to Florentines – Dante, Boccaccio, the Medici, Leonardo, Michelangelo and Galileo. No schoolboy taught from *Movements in European History* would be in danger of underestimating the Florentine contribution to European civilization.

It is not surprising, therefore, that when Lawrence left England he went straight to Florence, which apart from other considerations was recommended to him by its reputation for cheapness. He had one acquaintance there, the novelist Norman Douglas, whom he had known before the war. He had previously written to Douglas asking him to find him a cheap room and to leave a note at Thomas Cook's office in the Via Tornabuoni. When he arrived in Florence, on the cold and rainy evening of 19 November, the city struck him at first view as 'grim and dark and rather awful'. Leaving his luggage at the station, he walked to Cook's and picked up a note from Douglas recommending the Pensione Balestra, at Piazza Mentana 5, where Douglas himself was staying. On the way there he met Douglas, who was accompanied by another lodger at the pensione, Maurice Magnus, and they went on together. In the Piazza Mentana he noticed 'the over-dramatic group of statuary . . . the over-pathetic dead soldier on the arm of his over-heroic pistol-firing comrade'.[3]

He found the pensione 'very good and cheap', the food 'good and plenty', and 'everything a bit haphazard and untidy, but pleasant, kind, easy-going'. His room he described as 'charming' and 'really sunny', with a good view over the Arno. That at least is what he said in his letters. In his introduction to Magnus's *Memoirs of the Foreign Legion*, written two years later, he waits in 'an awful plush and gilt drawing-room', where he is given 'a cup of weird muddy brown slush called tea, and a bit of weird brown mush called jam on some bits of bread', and is then taken to 'a big and lonely, stone-comfortless room'.[4] It is a salutary reminder of his tendency to embroider facts for artistic effect.

His two fellow-lodgers, Douglas and Magnus, both belonged to Florence's colony of homosexual exiles. They had two other features in common: both gave such imaginative accounts of their past that it is difficult to arrive at the truth about them, and both appear in Lawrence's novels, Douglas as James Argyle in *Aaron's Rod* and Magnus as Mr May in *The Lost Girl*.

Douglas, the son of a Scottish father and a German mother, was born in Austria in 1868 and received most of his education in Germany. Perhaps as a result, he acquired a wide knowledge in many fields of scholarship; his earliest published works were zoological studies. He entered the Foreign Office in 1893, and in the following year was sent to St Petersburg. His diplomatic career, however, was brought to an abrupt end by his sexual exploits, which the *Dictionary of National Biography* tactfully sums up as follows: 'He was, at different times of his life, an ardent lover of both sexes. His adventures involved exile and sudden departures, but he avoided serious trouble.'[5] According to his own account, he had an *affaire* with a Russian lady of such high rank that he had to flee the country with the secret police at his heels, and voluntarily resigned from the diplomatic service. He was married in 1898 and became the father of two sons, but in 1904 the marriage ended in divorce. Between 1911 and 1915 he published three travel books, *Siren Land*, *Fountains in the Sand* and *Old Calabria*, which won him a high reputation.

After the failure of his marriage he seems to have sought sexual satisfaction in indulging a taste for adolescent boys, with the result that in 1916 the authorities gave him the choice between leaving England immediately and facing prosecution. He went to Capri, and there wrote *South Wind*, a brilliant novel advocating an amoral hedonism. It was an immediate success, and went through twenty-one impressions in the thirty years after it was published.

His *affaires* with boys led to periodic scandals which forced him to flee, on one occasion from Austria into Italy, leaving all his luggage behind him, on another from Italy into France. Lawrence describes him in *Aaron's Rod* as having

a certain wicked whimsicality that was very attractive, when levelled against someone else, and not against oneself. He must have been very handsome in his day, with his natural dignity, and his clean-shaven strong square face. But now his face was all red and softened and inflamed, his eyes had gone small and wicked under his bushy grey brows. Still he had a presence. And his grey hair, almost gone white, was still handsome.

Richard Aldington, who knew Douglas well, described this portrait as 'of a most authentic reality'.[6]

Magnus was born in New York in 1876, the son of German parents; his mother claimed to be the daughter of a German emperor, though whether Wilhelm I or his son Friedrich III no one seemed to know. He had lived a wandering life (according to Lawrence, 'he knew all the short cuts in all the big towns of Europe'), now acting as manager to the dancer Isadora Duncan, now editing the short-lived *Roman Review*. In his travels he had acquired a wide knowledge of languages, and had translated German, Norwegian and Russian plays into English. Like Douglas, he had been married, but his marriage had failed; unlike Douglas, who disliked all forms of Christianity, he was a Catholic convert and toyed with the idea of becoming a monk. This was hard to reconcile with his taste for luxury; he liked to travel first class and to stay in the best hotels, whether he could pay the bill or not. In his room at the pensione, Lawrence noticed, 'all he had was expensive and finicking'. In 1916 he had joined the French Foreign Legion, according to his own account because of his sympathy for the Allied cause; his German origin makes this improbable, and it is more likely that he had done so in order to evade the Italian police. Finding the life intolerable, he soon deserted and escaped across the French frontier into Italy, whence he sailed for Spain. In appearance he was 'a tubby, fresh-faced little man in a suit of grey, faced cloth bound at the edges with grey silk braid', with 'light blue eyes, tired underneath, and crisp, curly, dark brown hair just grey at the temples'. There was something bird-like about him, 'like a sparrow painted to resemble a tom-tit'; in the brilliantly lifelike portrait of him as Mr May in *The Lost Girl*, Lawrence more than once described him as 'perky'and 'jaunty'.[7] He left for Rome two or three days after their first meeting, but Lawrence had not seen the last of him.

A third homosexual whom Lawrence met was Reginald Turner, an ageing, well-to-do Jewish novelist who was almost the last survivor of Oscar Wilde's circle. Despite the mediocrity of his writing, he was respected in the literary world for his wit and his loyalty to Wilde in his disgrace, when many of his friends deserted him. Turner appears in *Aaron's Rod* as 'little Algy Constable', who 'had a very pleasant flat indeed, kept more scrupulously neat and finicking than ever any woman's flat was kept. So today, with its bowls of flowers and its pictures and books and old furniture, and Algy, very nicely dressed, fluttering and blinking and making really a charming host, it was all very delightful.' Argyle (i.e. Douglas) comments that Algy 'can be most entertaining, most witty, and amusing. But he's out of place here. He should be in Kensington, dandling round the ladies' drawing-rooms and making his *mots*.'[8]

Florence did not disappoint Lawrence's expectations. How intensely he reacted to the city's beauty, and especially to the Piazza della Signoria and Michelangelo's David, is apparent from his essay 'David', written at the time. He sees in Michelangelo's sculpture the product of one 'moment of perfection' before the coming of 'equality, democracy, the masses, like drops of water in one sea, overwhelming all outstanding loveliness of the individual soul'. And yet 'David, with his knitted brow and full limbs, is unvanquished. Livid, maybe, corpse-coloured, quenched with innumerable rains of morality and democracy. Yet deep fountains of fire lurk within him.'[9]

Lawrence develops this theme at greater length in the Florentine chapters of *Aaron's Rod*. In the Piazza della Signoria

[Aaron] looked at the three great naked men, David so much whiter, and standing forward, self-conscious: then at the great splendid front of the Palazzo Vecchio: and at the fountain splashing water upon its wet, wet figures; and the distant equestrian statue; and the stone-flagged space of the grim square. And he felt that here he was in one of the world's living centres . . . Here men had been at their intensest, most naked pitch, here, at the end of the old world and the beginning of the new.

From Argyle's attic, level with the roof of the Baptistery, Aaron sees the sunlight that

caught the façade of the cathedral sideways, like the tips of a flower, and sideways lit up the stem of Giotto's tower, like a lily stem, or a long, lovely pale pink and white and green pistil of the lily of the cathedral. Florence, the flowery town. Firenze-fiorenze – the flowery town: the red lilies. The Fiorentini, the flower-souled. Flowers with good roots in the mud and muck, as should be: and fearless blossoms in air, like the cathedral and the tower and the David.

Aaron's friend Lilly comments:

I reckon here men for a moment were themselves, as a plant in flower is for the moment completely itself. Then it goes off. As Florence has gone off. No flowers now. But it has flowered. And I don't see why a race should be like an aloe tree, flower once and die. Why should it? Why not flower again? Why not?'[10]

It was not only the city's buildings and works of art that fascinated Lawrence, but also the people – especially the peasants who came in on market days. 'Here I still sit in my room over the river, which is swollen with heavy rain, and yellow,' he wrote to a friend. 'The horses and mules, as they cross the bridge, have nice grey bonnets on their heads, and the carters are hidden under big green umbrellas. On they trot in the rain, busy as ever. Here they always cover the horse's *head*, to keep him warm.' He developed this picture in *Aaron's Rod*:

> There was a noise and clatter of traffic: boys pushing handbarrows over the cobble-stones, slow bullocks stepping side by side, and shouldering one another affectionately, drawing a load of country produce, then horses in great brilliant scarlet cloths, like vivid palls, slowly pulling the long narrow carts of the district and men hu-huing! – and people calling: all the sharp, clattering morning noise of Florence.

And in the Piazza della Signoria were

> the curious, fine-nosed Tuscan farmers, with their half-sardonic, amber-coloured eyes. Their curious individuality, their clothes worn so easy and reckless, their hats with the personal twist. Their curious full oval cheeks, their tendency to be too fat, to have a belly and heavy limbs. Their close-sitting dark hair. And above all, their sharp, almost acrid, mocking expression, the silent curl of the nose, the eternal challenge, the rock-bottom unbelief, and the subtle fearlessness.[11]

There was an atmosphere of political crisis when Lawrence arrived in Italy. The elections of November 1919 resulted in the return of 156 Socialists, who formed the largest group in the Chamber, and 101 candidates of the Popular Party, a Catholic organization which sought to attract peasant support away from the Socialists by a programme of agrarian reform. Lawrence was not worried. 'Italy is still gay – does all her weeping in her press – takes her politics with her wine, and enjoys them,' he wrote. 'Great excitement over the elections – but lively and amused excitement, nothing tragic or serious.' On a general strike in the first week of December which led to disturbances in Florence his only comment was 'Florence has had a strike – over now – some rows.' When his wife, Frieda, who had been visiting her mother in Germany, arrived in Florence at four o'clock in the morning of 3 December, he took her for a drive in an open carriage to see the city by moonlight. His final verdict on his stay was 'Florence was so nice: its genuine culture still creating a certain perfection in the town.'[12]

They left on 10 December, and travelled via Rome, which compared with Florence he found 'tawdry',[13] to Capri. There he wrote to Magnus, and on receiving a reply from an expensive hotel at Anzio, the tone of which suggested that he was in money difficulties, sent him £5. In his reply Magnus asked him to meet him at the Benedictine monastery at Monte Cassino. When he did so, Magnus explained that he had made out a cheque at Anzio with no money in the bank to meet it and had taken sanctuary in the monastery. Lawrence and Frieda rented a house at Taormina, in Sicily, in March 1920, but they had not escaped from Magnus, who turned up there in April, explaining that he had fled from Monte Cassino on learning that the police were looking for him. Besides paying his hotel bill, Lawrence attempted to persuade editors and publishers to take an interest in Magnus's writings, with little success.

The Lawrences visited Malta in May, sailing second class, only to find that Magnus was travelling first class on the same ship. 'Magnus is a jewel,' Lawrence wrote to a friend. 'He was in Malta, in a white suit, floating in whiskies and soda and "come to lunch tomorrow. . . He has taken a small house at Città Vecchia, and is going to sit elegantly on Malta till he bursts again.'[14] In fact he stayed there, living on money borrowed from two young Maltese, until 4 November, when on learning that he was to be extradited to Italy to face a charge of fraud he poisoned himself. To pay his debts to the two Maltese Lawrence arranged for the publication of his *Memoirs of the Foreign Legion*, to which he contributed a long introduction. Annoyed at Lawrence's portrayal of himself as Argyle in *Aaron's Rod*, which appeared in 1922, Douglas published in 1925 *D. H. Lawrence and Maurice Magnus*, a pamphlet containing a distorted account of the episode, to which Lawrence crushingly replied in a long letter to *The New Statesman*.

The summer of 1920 was exceptionally hot, especially in Sicily, and the Lawrences decided to travel in search of what Lawrence called 'a bit of northerliness, greenness and comparative cool'. While Frieda paid another visit to her mother, he joined two friends in a walking tour during which they visited Lake Como, Lake Garda, Verona and Venice. After leaving them he returned on 2 September to Florence, where he spent the night at a boarding-house on the Lungarno Guicciardini run by two English sisters. He found the company there uncongenial, but fortunately he received the offer of the Villa Canovaia at San Gervasio from his friend Rosalind Baynes. Having left a husband ten years older than herself, who later divorced her, she had settled in Florence with her three little girls at Lawrence's recommendation. All the windows of the villa which she had rented had been blown out by an explosion at an ammunition depot on the Campo di Marte on 10 August ('powder factories always explode in Italy', Lawrence commented in a letter), and she had moved to Fiesole with her children. The Villa Canovaia was

> a beautiful, decaying old house of great character, not only in its appear-
> ance but in the population of cats, puppies, goats, chickens and children
> which wandered in and out of its large rooms. The exterior had a court-
> yard where a fountain played; there was a turret overlooking Florence,
> a shaded balcony decked with vines, and a terraced garden with persim-
> mon trees and a fascinating world of animal and insect life – lizards, tor-
> toises, cicadas and fireflies.

As the weather remained hot and dry the broken windows did not worry Lawrence in the least. 'I've got no glass in the windows,' he wrote to a friend, 'but a garden and a lovely view and air and peace and the gar-dener's family behind. But I cook and clean for myself; my old style.' This tranquil life was disturbed only by an earthquake shock on 8 September, which he found 'horrid frightening'.[15]

He enjoyed a busy social life during this period. 'I give luncheon and tea parties to elegant people, mostly American,' he wrote on the day of the earthquake. 'We picnicked out behind Settignano today – my word, such a gorgeous rich tea.' Douglas was in Mentone with his *amico*, a boy of about fifteen, but Lawrence sometimes met Reggie Turner, who was looking 'rather shaky'. He also renewed his friendship with the antiquar-ian bookseller Giuseppe Orioli, whom he had met in Cornwall during the war. Orioli, known to his friends as 'Pino' (an abbreviation of 'Giuseppino'), had received little education and had been apprenticed to a barber at twelve. After doing his military service he went to London, where he earned a living by singing in the streets, becoming a claqueur at the Alhambra and giving Italian lessons; one of his pupils, he claimed, was the notorious Crippen. In partnership with another of his former pupils, he opened in 1910 a bookshop in Florence, which was transferred to London three years later. Called up when Italy entered the war, he was kept out of the trenches through a friend's influence and in 1916 was sent back to London for service with the Italian military mission there. He returned to Florence in April 1920 and opened a bookshop on the Lungarno Acciaioli. Like Douglas, with whom he later formed a close friendship, he was a homosexual with a lively imagination, which made his accounts of his past colourful but unreliable. Aldington described him as 'inexhaustibly cheerful' and 'a natural actor, doubled by a natural story-teller of genius', who 'took a scene from life or from something he had imagined and re-acted it for you with all the embellishments of a vivid fancy'.[16] His English friends' pleasure in his performances was increased by the peculiarities of his English pronunciation, notably a tendency to transpose the letters *v* and *w*.

Lawrence's second stay in Florence coincided with the occupation of the factories, the climax of the intense political and social unrest of the postwar years. After wage negotiations between the engineering work-ers' union and the employers had broken down, the employers' confed-eration on 31 August ordered a national lockout. In the next few days engineering works and shipbuilding plants from Turin to Palermo were taken over by their employees; the red flag flew over some factories, and to resist any attempts to expel the workers 'red guard' units were orga-nized and weapons and bombs were manufactured. Although Socialists hoped and non-Socialists feared that a revolution had begun, the occupa-tion nearly everywhere passed off without violence; there were fewer political murders in Italy in September 1920 than in the preceding and the following months. The wily old Prime Minister, Giovanni Giolitti, finally negotiated a settlement which provided for wage increases and the establishment of a joint commission of employers and union representa-tives to draw up a plan for workers' participation in the management of industry. A majority of the engineering workers voted in favour of accept-ing these terms, and by the end of September the occupation was over.

Although by 1920 Florence had grown to an industrial city of over 250,000 people, as a centre of light industries such as clothing and footwear it was little affected by the occupation of the engineering works. In the Epilogue which he wrote in 1924 for the second edition of

Movements in European History, however, Lawrence painted a lurid picture of life in Florence during those weeks. 'In Italy, in Florence, there was the same lingering ease and goodwill in 1919 as before the war,' he wrote.

> By 1920 prices had gone up three times, and socialism was rampant. Now we began to be bullied in every way. Servants were rude, cabmen insulted one and demanded treble fare, railway porters demanded large sums for carrying a bag from the train to the street, and threatened to attack one if the money were not paid . . . In the summer of 1920 I went north, and Florence was in a state of continual socialistic riot: sudden shots, sudden stones smashing into the restaurants where one was drinking coffee, all the shops suddenly barred and closed.

There was undoubtedly some truth in this account. There had been an ugly incident on 30 August, three days before Lawrence arrived, when a police officer was shot dead during a political demonstration, whereupon the police opened fire, killing two people and wounding seven others. It is difficult, however, to reconcile his description of 'continual socialistic riot' with the twenty-two surviving letters which he wrote while in Florence. The only suggestion in them of any unrest in the city is the humorous phrase 'the Italians cry out that they are persecuted like Job: what with earthquakes and manquakes'. It is equally difficult to reconcile his description of the conduct of the railway porters with what he wrote on 16 July to a friend who was coming to Italy: 'In Turin you must say to any porter "Milano" – and he'll take you to your train at once – say prima classe or seconda classe – and there you are. They are perfectly sensible . . . One tips a porter about 1 franc for each bag: not more: one Lira in Italy.'[17]

The contradiction can be explained only when Lawrence's psychology is taken into account. Throughout his life he was torn between the influences of his miner father and his mother, who, because as a girl she had been a pupil teacher until she was dismissed for incompetence, regarded herself as her husband's social superior. At times he could identify with his father and with the working class in general; at others he despised him, as his mother had taught him to do. Long after his death he was remembered with disapproval in his native Eastwood because he had been unfair to his father, a man highly respected in the mining community. With his mother's encouragement, he had risen by his own efforts out of the working class into the middle class. Yet he was never at ease in his new environment, and offended many of his intellectual friends by spitefully caricaturing them in his novels. He was fully conscious of his dilemma, which he summed up in the lines

> My father was a working man
>> and a collier was he,
> at six in the morning they turned him down
>> and they turned him up for tea.
>
> My mother was a superior soul
>> a superior soul was she,
> cut out to play a superior rôle
>> in the god-damn bourgeoisie.
>
> We children were the in-betweens
>> little non-descripts were we,
> indoors we called each other *you*,
>> outside, it was *tha* and *thee*.
>
> But time has fled, our parents are dead
>> we've risen in the world all three;
> but still we are in-betweens, we tread
>> between the devil and the deep cold sea.[18]

This internal conflict was reflected in his politics. At times he thought of himself as a socialist, even a revolutionary; at others he despised the mass of humanity as he had despised his father, and loudly demanded an authoritarian system run by natural aristocrats such as himself. In this mood he denounced democracy, which he identified with the demagogy of Lloyd George and Horatio Bottomley, and could often sound surprisingly like Colonel Blimp. This mood is dominant in much of his writing of the early 1920s, such as the 'novels of power'(*Aaron's Rod*, *Kangaroo* and *The Plumed Serpent*) and the Epilogue to *Movements in European History*, which the Oxford University Press wisely refused to print. His description of Florence in 1920 in the Epilogue is propaganda, not history.

For his reaction to the 'manquakes' of September 1920 we must turn to his poems 'The Revolutionary'and 'St Luke', both probably written in the first half of the month, when hope still lingered of an imminent revolution. In response to a request from *The New Republic* for poems, he sent a batch to his American agent, Robert Mountsier, on 15 September; these evidently included 'The Revolutionary', which appeared in the magazine in January 1921. The first to be written of 'The Evangelistic Beasts', the group of poems which includes 'St Luke', was apparently 'St Mark'; this abounds in references to Venice, and may have been written after his visit there at the end of August.

In 'The Revolutionary' he sees the engineers then occupying the factories as Samson 'blind, at the round-turning mill'; it is significant that many of the images in the poem are drawn from metals. He clearly has *Samson Agonistes* in mind, but his Samson, unlike Milton's, is destined to survive the destruction of the old society. Some critics have interpreted the poem in purely personal terms, assuming that 'Lawrence sees himself as the Samson who will pull down the pillars of "pale-face authority".' [19] This analysis contains an element of truth, in that Lawrence identifies himself with the revolutionary workers, but to regard the poem merely as a personal manifesto impoverishes it. Like 'Ode to the West Wind', it is both a personal and a political poem. His sympathy with the Italian workers was probably increased by the fact that the English miners, his father's workmates, were threatening to strike.

The political element in 'St Luke' is even more obvious. Luke is the leveller among the evangelists; he prophesies that the mighty will be put down from their seats and every mountain and hill brought low, and calls down blessings on the poor and woes on the rich. Hence it is appropriate that Lawrence should use the bull, Luke's symbol in religious art, to symbolize the working class. In ancient Rome the poor were called *proletarii* because they were considered to serve the state only by producing offspring (*proles*), like a stud bull. But the bull is also a fighting beast, and the poem ends with the ringing declaration:

> And so it is war.
> The bull of the proletariat has got his head down. [20]

Here the reference to the situation in September 1920 is inescapable.

The four weeks which Lawrence spent at San Gervasio were an exceptionally fertile period for his poetry. In addition to 'The Revolutionary' and the four poems on the Evangelistic Beasts, he wrote five on fruits, six on a family of tortoises which lived in the garden of the

Villa Canovaia, 'Cypresses' and 'Turkey-Cock' – eighteen poems in all. These formed the nucleus of what he considered his best collection, *Birds, Beasts and Flowers*. Several factors contributed to produce this outburst of productivity, after a period in which he had written little verse: privacy, leisure, the natural beauty of his surroundings, a Tuscan vintage season, hope and excitement at the political situation. The fruit poems have the same sensuous joy in the Tuscan countryside as Landor's 'Faesulan Idyl', Lytton's 'An Evening in Tuscany'and Isa Blagden's 'L'Ariccia. Death in Life'. The San Gervasio poems also make use of myths of destruction and renewal, death and resurrection: Orpheus in 'Medlars and Sorb-Apples', Osiris in 'Lui et Elle', the Deluge in 'Grapes', the phoenix in 'St John'. The last poem, which follows 'St Luke' in the Evangelistic Beasts sequence, ends with a vision of the new phoenix rising from the flaming nest – an appropriate symbol of the new society which Lawrence hoped was about to emerge from a revolution.

'Cypresses' is remarkable as Lawrence's first work dealing with the Etruscans, a people who were to become of importance to him. His interest in them may have been stimulated by seeing the remains of Fiesole's Etruscan walls, or by visiting Florence's Archaeological Museum. In the opening chapter of *Movements in European History* he had presented a highly idealized picture of the Romans, but after his discovery of the Etruscans the Romans became for him a symbol of materialism and brute force. In *Fantasia of the Unconscious*, written a little later, he put forward a grotesque theory that in the glacial period men had moved freely over the earth, sharing a common wisdom. With the melting of the glaciers, which created the existing oceans, some had degenerated into cavemen, while others, such as the Druids, Etruscans, Chaldeans, Amerindians and Chinese, 'refused to forget, but taught the old wisdom; only in its half-forgotten, symbolic forms'.[21] Here, as in 'Cypresses', the Etruscans and the Amerindians are bracketed together as alternative societies to the life-denying materialism of the ancient Romans and the modern Americans.

Lawrence saw as the true Etruscan quality 'ease, naturalness, and an abundance of life', so that even death was 'just a natural continuance of the fullness of life'. And for him the fullness of life included sexual freedom, typified by the phallic stones at the doors of Etruscan tombs. The original text of 'Cypresses', published in the *Adelphi* of October 1923, contains six lines which Lawrence later suppressed. After his reference to 'the rare and orchid-like / Evil-yclept Etruscan' we read:

> Among the cypresses
> To sit with pure, slim, long-nosed,
> Evil-called, sensitive Etruscans, naked except for their boots;
> To be able to smile back at them
> And exchange the lost kiss
> And come to dark connection.

Lawrence obviously omitted these lines from later editions because in them he betrayed the homosexuality that he tried to conceal from the world and even from himself. The friend who wrote 'Lawrence was a homosexual gone wrong, repressed in childhood by a puritan environment' had grasped part of the truth about him.[22]

He left Florence on 28 September for Venice, where he met Frieda, and returned with her to Taormina. For some months he continued to expect a revolution, half hopefully, half fearfully. As late as 20 January 1921 he wrote to a friend:

> If I knew how to, I'd really join myself to the revolutionary socialists now. I think the time has come for a real struggle. That's the only thing I care for: the death struggle. I don't care for politics. But I know there *must* and *should* be a deadly revolution very soon, and I would take part in it if I knew how.

In November 1920, however, the fascist squads, armed and equipped by the army, financed by industrialists and landowners, and with the collusion and often the assistance of the police and magistrates, launched a violent offensive against the socialists, trade unions and cooperatives, and also against the peasant unions organized by the Popular Party. For the next two years Italy was in a condition of virtual civil war. In these circumstances Lawrence lost hope. In March 1921 he wrote, 'Italy begins to tire me. I hear the official opinion now is that there will be no definite revolution or bolshing at all: that it is going to resolve itself into continual faction fights between socialists and fascisti – genuine Italian Guelph and Ghibelline business, and let the world wag elsewhere. Rather dull.' From this mood it was a short step to the authoritarianism of the novels of power. In April 1922 he wrote, 'I don't believe either in liberty or democracy. I believe in actual, sacred, inspired authority: divine right of natural kings: I believe in the divine right of natural aristocracy, the right, the sacred duty to wield undisputed authority.'[23]

In May 1921 the Oxford University Press suggested that Lawrence should write a history of painting for children, with illustrations supplied by the Medici Society. He was attracted by the idea, and decided that the obvious place to write the book was Florence. At this point a friend, Nellie Morrison, offered him the use of her flat in Florence while she was away. The offer was too good to be refused. Although the plan for the book was abandoned, as Lawrence was not satisfied with the Medici Society's choice of illustrations, he and Frieda moved into Via de' Bardi 32 on 25 August, and stayed there until 20 September. The house, which was supposed to be the original of Romola's home in George Eliot's novel, was a tall one with a terrace overlooking the Arno, where in fine weather the Lawrences had their meals. His feelings about the flat varied. On 1 September he assured Miss Morrison, 'We like your flat more every day,' yet in his poem 'Man and Bat' his room is 'a crash-box over that great stone rattle / The Via de' Bardi'. He found the flat noisy and complained to Mountsier on 9 September, 'Even Florence wearies me – I feel I just want to get away from its infernal noise . . . I can't work here.'[24]

In a letter written (in German) on the following day to Frieda's mother, Baroness Anna von Richthofen, he gave a very different picture of life in the Via de' Bardi:

Always very beautiful here. Day before yesterday was a holiday – yesterday Mary's birthday. On the Arno many boats with great lovely lanterns – and lanterns through the streets. It was pretty – the evening so warm. The sun is still hot, but the air fresh. We were on the height in Fiesole – one sees far, far, the Apennines and the great valley, with the Arno, the river, which comes down from the distance just like steps – down exactly like steps. – The grapes still hang black, mysteriously black beneath the leaves, and peaches so red and gold. It's so lovely, when one can see far, far, and on the plain the city so alone, so feminine, and on the hills the villas, white or pink, and again and again the cypresses, like black shadowflames crowding together. This is Tuscany, and nowhere are the cypresses so beautiful and proud, like black-flames from primeval times, before the Romans had come, when the Etruscans were still here, slender and fine and still and with naked elegance, black-haired, with narrow feet. We are sitting on the terrace. It is evening, the sun sinks behind the Carrara mountains, the hills grow dark. On the Ponte Vecchio the windows of the little houses shine yellow, and make golden points on the water. Now I must light the electric table-lamp to write. We are eating supper out here.'[25]

Cypresses evidently were still associated in Lawrence's mind with the Etruscans, as when he wrote his poem a year before.

Florence was commemorating the six-hundredth anniversary of Dante's death, and Lawrence's varying moods are amusingly reflected in his references to the event. In his letter to the Baroness he continued:

> On the 15th the Dante festa begins here. They're doing something lovely – a procession is coming from the country, and is supposed to be exactly as when the Florentines with Dante returned home from the Battle of Campoldino – in about 1260. They'll all have the old local costume and old weapons and armour, and come in a throng through the Porta Romana, knights, grooms, and all.

This enthusiasm is in marked contrast to his reference to the event in a letter written on 16 September: 'Florence wildly festivating Dante – such a row.'[26]

Despite his complaint to Mountsier that he could not work, he wrote two poems between 9 and 17 September, 'Bat' and 'Man and Bat'. These are his only poems which are set in Florence itself; those written in the previous year, such as 'Cypresses' and the tortoise poems, belong to San Gervasio or Fiesole. Whereas in the other *Birds, Beasts and Flowers* poems he can empathize with the most varied creatures, from a snake to an elephant, he displays a horror of bats, which he calls 'disgusting', 'unclean' and 'obscene'. He seems to have been one of those people who harbour an irrational fear that the claws of bats flying overhead may become tangled in their hair. Yet in 'Man and Bat', obviously a record of a real incident, in which he drove out, with considerable difficulty, a bat that had flown into his room, he overcomes his horror sufficiently to appreciate the bat's fear of the daylight. It is perhaps the most remarkable example of his ability to enter sympathetically into the minds of living creatures – even those which he found most repulsive.

D. H. Lawrence
THE REVOLUTIONARY

Look at them standing there in authority,
The pale-faces,
As if it could have any effect any more.

Pale-face authority,
Caryatids,
Pillars of white bronze standing rigid, lest the skies fall.

What a job they've got to keep it up.
Their poor, idealist foreheads naked capitals
To the entablature of clouded heaven.

When the skies are going to fall, fall they will
In a great chute and rush of débâcle downwards.

Oh and I wish the high and super-gothic heavens would come down now,
The heavens above, that we yearn to and aspire to.

I do not yearn, nor aspire, for I am a blind Samson.
And what is daylight to me that I would look skyward?
Only I grope among you, pale-faces, caryatids, as among a forest
    of pillars that hold up the dome of high ideal heaven
Which is my prison,
And all these human pillars of loftiness, going stiff, metallic-stunned
    with the weight of their responsibility
I stumble against them.
Stumbling-blocks, painful ones.

To keep on holding up this ideal civilisation
Must be excruciating: unless you stiffen into metal, when it is easier
    to stand stock rigid than to move.

That is why I tug at them, individually, with my arm round their waist,
The human pillars.
    They are not stronger than I am, blind Samson.

The house sways.

I shall be so glad when it comes down.
I am so tired of the limitations of their infinite.
I am so sick of the pretensions of the Spirit.
I am so weary of pale-face importance.

Am I not blind, at the round-turning mill?
Then why should I fear their pale faces?
Or love the effulgence of their holy light,
The sun of their righteousness?

To me, all faces are dark,
All lips are dusky and valved.

Save your lips, O pale-faces,
Which are slips of metal,
Like slits in an automatic-machine, you columns of give-and-take.

To me, the earth rolls ponderously, superbly
Coming my way without forethought or afterthought.
To me, men's footfalls fall with a dull, soft rumble, ominous and
    lovely,
Coming my way.

But not your foot-falls, pale-faces,
They are a clicketing of bits of disjointed metal
Working in motion.

To me, men are palpable, invisible nearnesses in the dark
Sending out magnetic vibrations of warning, pitch-dark throbs of
    invitation.
But you, pale-faces,
You are painful, harsh-surfaced pillars that give off nothing except
    rigidity,
And I jut against you if I try to move, for you are everywhere,
    and I am blind,
Sightless among all your visuality,

You staring caryatids.
See if I don't bring you down, and all your high opinion
And all your ponderous roofed-in erection of right and wrong,
Your particular heavens,
With a smash.

See if your skies aren't falling!
And my head, at least, is thick enough to stand it, the smash.

See if I don't move under a dark and nude, vast heaven
When your world is in ruins, under your fallen skies.
Caryatids, pale-faces.
See if I am not Lord of the dark and moving hosts
Before I die.

Florence.

CYPRESSES

Tuscan cypresses,
What is it?

Folded in like a dark thought
For which the language is lost,
Tuscan cypresses,
Is there a great secret?
Are our words no good?

The undeliverable secret,
Dead with a dead face and a dead speech, and yet
Darkly monumental in you,
Etruscan cypresses.

Ah, how I admire your fidelity,
Dark cypresses!

Is it the secret of the long-nosed Etruscans?
The long-nosed, sensitive-footed, subtly-smiling Etruscans,

Who made so little noise outside the cypress groves?

Among the sinuous, flame-tall cypresses
That swayed their length of darkness all around
Etruscan-dusky, waver ing men of old Etruria:
Naked except for fanciful long shoes,
Going with insidious, half-smiling quietness
And some of Africa's imperturbable sang-froid
About a forgotten business.

What business, then?
Nay, tongues are dead, and words are hollow as hollow seed-pods,
Having shed their sound and finished all their echoing
Etruscan syllables,
That had the telling.

Yet more I see you darkly concentrate,
Tuscan cypresses,
On one old thought:
On one old slim imperishable thought, while you remain
Etruscan cypresses;
Dusky, slim marrow-thought of slender, flickering men of Etruria,
Whom Rome called vicious.

Vicious, dark cypresses:
Vicious, you supple, brooding, softly-swaying pillars of dark flame.
Monumental to a dead, dead race
Embalmed in you!

Were they then vicious, the slender, tender-footed,
Long-nosed men of Etruria?
Or was their way only evasive and different, dark, like cypress-trees
    in a wind?

They are all dead, with all their vices,
And all that is left
Is the shadowy monomania of some cypresses
And tombs.

The smile, the subtle Etruscan smile still lurking
Within the tombs,
Etruscan cypresses.
He laughs longest who laughs last;
Nay, Leonardo only bungled the pure Etruscan smile.

What would I not give
To bring back the rare and orchid-like
Evil-yclept Etruscan?

For as to the evil
We have only Roman word for it,
Which I, being a little weary of Roman virtue,
Don't hang much weight on.

For oh, I know, in the dust where we have buried
The silenced races and all their abominations,
We have buried so much of the delicate magic of life.

There in the deeps
That churn the frankincense and ooze the myrrh,
Cypress shadowy,
Such an aroma of lost human life!

They say the fit survive,
But I invoke the spirits of the lost,
Those that have not survived, the darkly lost,
To bring their meaning back into life again,
Which they have taken away
And wrapt inviolable in soft cypress-trees,
Etruscan cypresses.

Evil, what is evil?
There is only one evil, to deny life
As Rome denied Etruria
And mechanical America Montezuma still.

                                        Fiesole

277

BAT

At evening, sitting on this terrace,
When the sun from the west, beyond Pisa, beyond the mountains
    of Carrara
Departs, and the world is taken by surprise . . .

When the tired flower of Florence is in gloom beneath the glowing
Brown hills surrounding . . .

When under the arches of the Ponte Vecchio
A green light enters against stream, flush from the west,
Against the current of obscure Arno . . .

Look up, and you see things flying
Between the day and the night;
Swallows with spools of dark thread sewing the shadows together.

A circle swoop, and a quick parabola under the bridge arches
Where light pushes through;
A sudden turning upon itself of a thing in the air.
A dip to the water.

And you think:
'The swallows are flying so late!'

Swallows?

Dark air-life looping
Yet missing the pure loop . . .
A twitch, a twitter, an elastic shudder in flight
And serrated wings against the sky,
Like a glove, a black glove thrown up at the light,
And falling back.

Never swallows!
Bats!
The swallows are gone.

At a wavering instant the swallows give way to bats
By the Ponte Vecchio . . .
Changing guard.

Bats, and an uneasy creeping in one's scalp
As the bats swoop overhead!
Flying madly.

Pipistrello!
Black piper on an infinitesimal pipe.
Little lumps that fly in air and have voices indefinite, wildly
    vindictive;

Wings like bits of umbrella.

Bats!
Creatures that hang themselves up like an old rag, to sleep;
And disgustingly upside down.
Hanging upside down like rows of disgusting old rags
And grinning in their sleep.
Bats!

In China the bat is symbol of happiness.

Not for me!

11

D. H. Lawrence 1926–1929

Between 1922 and 1925 Lawrence and Frieda visited Ceylon, Australia, the United States, Mexico, England, France and Germany. The lure of Italy could not be resisted, however, and in November 1925 they rented a villa at Spotorno, on the Italian Riviera. After a visit to the museum at Perugia in March 1926 had reawakened his interest in the Etruscans, he suggested to his English publisher, Martin Secker, that he should write 'a book on Umbria and the Etruscan remains . . . half a travel book – of the region round Perugia, Assisi, Spoleto, Cortona, and the Maremma – and half a book about the Etruscan things, which interest me very much'. To Richard Aldington he wrote, 'The Etruscan things appeal *very much* to my imagination. They are so curiously natural – somebody said bourgeois, but that's a lie, considering all the phallic monuments.'[1] At first he thought of going to Perugia to write his book, but in the end he settled for Florence, where he had first become conscious of the Etruscans. On 20 April he and Frieda moved into the Pensione Lucchesi, on the Lungarno Zecca.

Since they were last in Florence the political situation had been transformed by the establishment of the fascist regime. In Florence, where the socialists enjoyed strong support, the fascists had displayed particular brutality. On the last day of 1924 thousands of them occupied the city, wrecking the premises of an opposition newspaper, an ex-servicemen's club, Masonic lodges and the offices of prominent socialists, republicans and liberals, until 'Florence looked like a city in the hands of enemy troops'.[2] Between 25 September and 3 October 1925 the fascists conducted a manhunt of Freemasons, many of whom were beaten up, and after a Freemason had shot a fascist in self-defence they attacked, looted and burned the houses, shops and offices of known anti-fascists. At least six people were murdered; a former socialist deputy, who had lost an arm in the war and been decorated for bravery, was dragged from his bed and shot in front of his wife. On another occasion Lawrence's friend Orioli was beaten up by four Blackshirts, who knocked him down, stamped on him and ground his broken spectacles into his face in an attempt to blind him.

Although Lawrence had already described the fascists' brutalities in the Epilogue to *Movements in European History* as 'only another kind of bul-lying', his first reaction to fascism after his return to Florence was one of detached curiosity. 'It's the *Natale Romana* here,' he wrote on 21 April, 'Fascist substitute for 1 May, and a great buzzing and playing of "Giovanezza! Giovanezza!" in the Piazza della Signoria . . . It is queer, this Fascist movement: one wonders what the end will be. – Interesting, in its way.' He soon realized that Florence was 'irritable to a degree with Fascism', and came to the conclusion that it was not natural to the Italians. As time passed his references to fascism became mocking ('Mussolino says *Vivi pericolosamente!* and then makes millions of laws against anybody who takes a pot shot at him') or hostile. 'Yes, one can ignore Fascism in Italy for a time,' he wrote to a friend in March 1928. 'But after a while, the sense of false power forced against life is very depressing. And one can't escape – except by the trick of abstraction, which is no good.'[3]

By good fortune, a few days after their arrival in Florence the Lawrences met Arthur Gair Wilkinson, an English landscape painter, who knew of a villa which, he thought, might suit them. Lawrence found Wilkinson's eccentricities amusing (he was a socialist, vegetarian and anti-vivisectionist, and had been a conscientious objector during the war), but appreciated his cheerful kindness. He wrote to his niece:

> He's got the wildest red beard, sticking out all round, and wife and daugh-ter and son, all with sandals and knapsacks. But they're jolly and very clever: paint, and play the guitar and things. They used to have a very fine puppet show, puppets they made themselves, and play plays they wrote themselves, going with a caravan and giving shows in all the villages in England. Rather fun! I want them to bring the caravan and puppets here,[4] and I'll go with them and bang the drum, in the Italian villages'.

The Wilkinsons lived near Scandicci, seven miles south-west of Florence, then a village, now 'one of the grislier and glummer suburbs of the city'. Scandicci had an honourable anti-fascist record; when in February and March 1921 the fascists, supported by the police and troops, attacked the Florentine trade unions and peasant unions and mur-dered at least seven people, the people of Scandicci barricaded a bridge at the entrance to their village and kept the *carabinieri* at bay with bombs, until artillery was called in. About a mile and a half from the village was the fifteenth-century Villa Mirenda, which Lawrence described as an

> old square whitish villa on a little hill all of its own, with the peasant hous-
> es and cypresses behind, and the vines and olives and corn on all the
> slopes. It's very picturesque, and many a paintable bit. Away in front lies
> the Arno valley, and mountains beyond. Behind are pine woods. The
> rooms inside are big and rather bare – with red-brick floors: spacious,
> rather nice, and very still.

The villa was owned by a cavalry officer who occasionally spent a night
there and came for about a month at the wine harvest. He offered the
Lawrences the use of the first floor and the garden for 4,000 lire a year
(about £25 at the 1926 exchange rate), and they jumped at the bargain.
The house had its drawbacks; neither electricity nor running water was
laid on, and cooking had to be done on a charcoal fire. There were only
'about five sticks of furniture', as Lawrence put it, in the big rooms, and
he had to buy linen and cooking utensils, but the surroundings and the
view alone were enough to compensate for such inconveniences.[5]

The villa was within easy reach of Florence, but not too easy. It was half
an hour's walk to the tram terminus at Scandicci, and then another half-
hour's ride to the Duomo. Lawrence and Frieda would go in once or twice
a week to do their shopping and hear the news from Orioli. Occasionally
they made a special visit, as on 24 June, St John's Day, when they went to
see the firework display and illuminations in honour of the city's patron
saint. Lawrence wrote an account of the festivities, which concludes:

> The cathedral dome, the top of Giotto's tower, like a lily-stem, and the
> straight lines of the top of the Baptistery are outlined with rather sparse
> electric bulbs. It looks very unfinished. Yet, with that light above illumi-
> nating the pale and coloured marbles ghostly, and the red tiles of the dome
> in the night-sky, and the abrupt end of the lily-stem without a flower, and
> the old hard lines of the Baptistery's top, there is a lovely ethereal quality
> to the great cathedral group; and you think again of the Lily of Florence.[6]

Clearly, for Lawrence familiarity had not staled the city's beauty.

'Florence isn't a bad place to live outside of,' was his opinion. He had
no desire for the company of the British colony, with their never-ending
gossip. 'Of Florence we see little. I am bored with spite and that's all you

get,' Frieda explained to a friend. There were exceptions, of course. They kept up their friendship with Reggie Turner, even though, as Lawrence put it, 'like most of the people there, he's going rather rapidly to pieces. Really, he's getting quite gaga.' Norman Douglas he pointedly ignored. 'I saw Douglas in a café and didn't speak to him: felt I couldn't stand him,' he told Secker.[7]

Apart from the Wilkinsons, the British colony generally left Lawrence in peace, to enjoy the beauty of the Tuscan countryside and the company of the peasants. He had grown up in a village, even though Eastwood was a mining village, and he remained a countryman at heart. There is a lyrical quality in the letters and essays which he wrote at the Villa Mirenda. 'I continue to like Tuscany,' he wrote to an American friend in July 1926. 'The cicalas are rattling away in the sun, the bells of all the little churches are ringing midday, the big white oxen are walking slowly home from under the olives. There is something eternal about it.' Four days later he wrote to another friend:

Here it is full summer: hot, quiet, the cicalas sing all day long like so many little sewing-machines in the leafy trees. The peasant girls and men are all cutting the wheat, with sickles, among the olive trees, and binding it into small, long sheaves. In some places they have already made the wheat stacks, and I hear the thresher away at a big farm. Fruit is in: big apricots, great big figs that they call fiori, peaches, plums, the first sweet little pears. But the grapes are green and hard yet.[8]

And then there were the flowers. Lawrence had a detailed knowledge of botany; walking in the hills near Florence with a friend, he identified at least thirty flowers by name. His long essay 'Flowery Tuscany' is among the most beautiful things he ever wrote. Frieda shared his enthusiasm; there is the same lyrical note in her description of the Tuscan flowers:

The spring that first year was a revelation in flowers, from the first violets in the woods . . . Carpets of them we found, and as usual in our walks we took joyful possession of the unspoiled, almost medieval country around us. By the stream in the valley were tufts of enormous primroses, where the willow trees had been blood red through the winter. On the edge of the umbrella-pine woods, in the fields, were red and purple big anemones, strange, narrow-pointed, red and yellow wild tulips, bee orchids and purple orchids, tufts of tight-scented lavender . . . flowers thick like velvety carpets, like the ground in a Fra Angelico picture'.[9]

As a true countryman, Lawrence loved the earth. In 'Flowery Tuscany' he described how Italian agriculture, while intensively cultivating the earth, had still respected it:

> For centuries upon centuries man has been patiently modelling the surface of the Mediterranean countries, gently rounding the hills, and graduating the big slopes and the little slopes into the almost invisible levels of terraces. Thousands of square miles of Italy have been lifted in human hands, piled and laid back in tiny little flats, held up by the drystone walls, whose stones come from the lifted earth. It is a work of many, many centuries. It is the gentle sensitive sculpture of all the landscape. And it is the achieving of the peculiar Italian beauty which is so exquisitely natural, because man, feeling his way sensitively to the fruitfulness of the earth, has moulded the earth to his necessity without violating it.[10]

Another essay rich in poetry which was written at Villa Mirenda is 'The Nightingale'. 'Tuscany is full of nightingales,' it begins, 'and in spring and summer they sing all the time, save in the middle of the night and the middle of the day.' Lawrence dismisses with scorn the idea that there is anything melancholy in the nightingale's song:

> He is the noisiest, most inconsiderate, most obstreperous and jaunty bird in the whole kingdom of birds . . . The nightingale sings with a ringing, punching vividness and a pristine assertiveness that makes a mere man stand still. A kind of brilliant calling and interweaving of glittering exclamation such as must have been heard on the first day of creation, when the angels suddenly found themselves created, and shouting aloud before they knew it.[11]

But from nature we receive but what we give; as the melancholy which Milton and Keats found in the nightingale's song was in themselves, so Lawrence heard the overflowing joy which he derived from the Tuscan countryside.

He is seen at his best in his relations with the peasants who cultivated the estate attached to the villa. There were three families of them, the

Orsini, Bandelli and Pinis, twenty-seven people in all, sharecroppers living in a poverty that horrified him. 'They're very much poorer than even the really poor, in England,' he told a friend:

> You see, there's no money. They just live on the wine and oil and corn and vegetables of the earth, and have no wages, no cash, unless they manage to sell a barrel of wine. But this year there wasn't much. – Here, the peasants are supposed to do all the work on the land, and then they take half the produce: the landlord taking the other half. But when it's a little hilly estate like this, no pasture, no cattle, all just the hard labour of wine and a bit of wheat, a few vegetables, and the olives, they don't come off very well. This bit of land round the villa has to support twenty-seven peasants, counting children. In England, it wouldn't support seven. But we've no idea how poorly they live – like cattle. Still, they are nice, and when we give them things, they always send us back a few dried grapes, or figs, or olives.

To Lawrence and Frieda the Orsini, Bandelli and Pinis were not merely the poor, deserving or undeserving objects of pity; they could appreciate the pride and dignity with which they refused to accept charity. Their relations with their maid, the 'gay and amusing and wise' Giulia Pini, and her brother Pietro were particularly close. Aldington, who stayed with them for a few days in October 1926, left an amusing account of Lawrence's generosity to the peasants' children. While he and Lawrence were sitting under the trees outside the villa, every now and then a child would bring a bunch of grapes, in return for which Lawrence would give him a piece of chocolate, or some sugar when the chocolate was gone. 'And each time he apologised to me for the seeming generosity (for at Vendemmia grapes are worth nothing, and chocolate and sugar are always luxuries) by telling me how poor the peasants were, and how the children ought to have sugar for the sake of their health.'[12] When she learned that ten-year-old Dino Bandello was suffering from a rupture, Frieda called in the best doctor in Florence, Dr Giglioli, and arranged for him to be operated on.

Lawrence took life easily in the spring and early summer of 1926. He read all the books he could find on the Etruscans – English, Italian or German – and came to the conclusion that 'there really is next to nothing to be said, *scientifically*, about the Etruscans', and that his own book 'must take the imaginative line'. He revisited the Archaeological Museum, and sent his friend S. S. Koteliansky a postcard of the famous bronze chimera in its collection, but made no attempt to visit the Etruscan tombs. Part of the Etruscans' attraction for him was that they represented an alternative to the Romans, then glorified by the fascist regime. He wrote to Frieda's sister:

> Italy is so wildly nationalistic that I think Tuscany feels she may as well go one further back than Rome, and derive herself from Etruria. But they all feel scared, because Etruria was so luxurious and 'merely physical'. Let's hope the other parts of Italy will go and derive themselves from Samnites, Sabellians, Tapygians, and so forth. The 'fascia' would then be a variegated one, and perhaps more fun.[13]

As Lawrence's residence at San Gervasio had coincided with the occupation of the factories, so his settlement in the Villa Mirenda took place while the British general strike was in progress. Italian press reports about the strike he found deeply disturbing. 'I feel bad about that strike,' he wrote to a friend in England. 'Italian papers say "The government will maintain an iron resistance." Since the war, I've no belief in iron resistances.' When he paid his last visit to England in August and September 1926, the general strike was over, but the long agony of the miners' lockout still dragged on. As he toured the mining areas of Derbyshire and his native Nottinghamshire he saw 'families living on bread and margarine and potatoes – nothing more', and was conscious of a bitter class hatred as 'the quiet volcano over which the English life is built'. The sight, he wrote three months later, 'was like a spear through one's heart'. Yet during this visit he recovered his love of England, which he had lost in the war years, and especially of the working class from which he came:

> I like England again, now I am up in my own regions. It braces me up: and there seems a queer, odd sort of potentiality in the people, especially the common people. One feels in them some odd, unaccustomed sort of plasm twinkling and nascent. They are not finished. And they have a funny sort of purity and gentleness, and at the same time, unbreakableness, that attracts me.[14]

This rediscovery of England and new identification with his father's people, together with his dislike of Italian fascism and his close contact with the local peasants, profoundly affected his political thinking. In letters to his friends he repudiated the cult of the Leader which he had preached in his political novels. To Rolf Gardiner, whose political leanings were to the extreme right, he wrote, 'I'm afraid the whole business of leaders and followers is somehow wrong, now. When leadership has died, then it will be born again, perhaps, new and changed, and based on reciprocity of tenderness.' To the American poet Witter Bynner, who had criticized *The Plumed Serpent*, he replied: 'I think you're right. The hero is obsolete, and the leader of men is a back number.' His new ideal was 'something quite different: neither capitalism nor bolshevism, but men'.[15]

But, whatever his feelings for England, it was good to be back in the Virgilian atmosphere of a warm Tuscan October. The Orsini, Bandelli and Pinis were bringing in the grapes in a wagon drawn by two white oxen, to be stored in vats on the ground floor, so that the Villa Mirenda was filled with their sour smell. Grapes hung in festoons in the rooms, and if not eaten fast enough turned to raisins. The only feature of life that infuriated Lawrence was the behaviour of the Italian sportsmen, who were firing at every little bird they saw. 'To see a middle-aged man stalking a sparrow with as much intensity as if it were a male rhinoceros, and letting bang at it with a great gun, is too much for my patience. They will offer you a string of little birds for a shilling, robins, finches, larks, even nightingales. Makes one tired!'[16]

After his return he began to see more of the English literary world than he had done previously. Aldington, like Lawrence both a novelist and a poet, came for a short stay in October. Aldous Huxley, another novelist and poet, was in Florence in the last week of October with his Belgian wife, Maria, and met the Lawrences several times. On one occasion they introduced Lawrence to Violet Paget, Eugene Lee-Hamilton's half-sister. Despite the profound difference of temperament between them, Huxley became Lawrence's closest friend in the few years of life that remained to him. During that same October, perhaps stimulated by the company of Aldington and the Huxleys, Lawrence made two important new beginnings: he turned his hand to painting, and he started to write *Lady Chatterley's Lover*.

He had always been interested in painting, as his willingness to undertake a book on the subject suggests, and in the past he had occasionally produced landscapes or copies from old masters. His painting in October was purely utilitarian, intended to brighten up their rooms. 'I have painted windowframes by the mile, doors by the acre, painted a chest of

287

drawers till it turned into a bureau, and am not through, by a long chalk,' he wrote to Frieda's son on 31 October. Four days earlier Maria Huxley had given him four large canvases that her brother had painted on but abandoned. As he now had a stock of paints, brushes and canvases, Frieda suggested that he should paint some pictures to hang on the bare walls. He met her challenge enthusiastically. Propping up a canvas against a chair, he sat on the floor and slapped on paint with his brushes, a rag, his fingers and the palms of his hands, until Frieda suggested that he should try using his toes as well. Within an hour he had roughly outlined his first picture, which he called 'A Holy Family'. On 11 November he was able to report to the Huxleys that he had finished and hung up his first painting, in which 'the *bambino* – with a *nimbus* – is just watching anxiously to see the young man give the semi-nude young woman *un gros baiser. Molto moderno!*' When the Wilkinsons called, bohemians though they were, they thought it 'most unpleasant' and 'a revolting blot on the wall'. 'Why do vegetarians always behave as if the world were vegetably propagated, even?' Lawrence wondered. By 20 December he had completed two more paintings, 'all with their shirt off': one of men bathing, which was hung in Frieda's room, and 'a picture of Boccaccio's story of the nuns who find their gardener asleep in the garden on a hot afternoon, with his shirt blown back from what other people are pleased to call his *pudenda*, and which the nuns named his *glorietta*'.[17] So, like Chaucer before him, Lawrence found a source of inspiration in Boccaccio.

By the New Year he had reached the conclusion that 'painting is a much more amusing art than writing, and much less to it, costs are less, amuses one more'. On the strength of his limited experience he set up as an art critic. When his American friend Earl Brewster, himself an artist, introduced him to the Florentine abstract painter Alberto Magnelli he admired his colour and design, and yet found 'inside it all, nothing – emptiness, ashes, an old bone'. At an exhibition of contemporary Florentine painting he admired the work of two artists, Giovanni Colacicchi and Ottone Rosai, and dismissed the rest as 'piffle, oodles, slop'.[18]

In the third or fourth week of October Lawrence began writing the first draft of *Lady Chatterley's Lover*, which was published after his death as *The First Lady Chatterley*. It was his normal practice to begin a novel with a rough draft and to rewrite it twice, although *Lady Chatterley's Lover* is the only novel of his of which all three versions have survived. He wrote the first version very quickly, probably completing it early in December. Each morning he would sit on the ground in the woods near the Villa Mirenda, with his back against a large umbrella pine and an exercise book on his knees, and write for several hours, so motionless except for his swiftly moving hand that birds hopped around him unafraid and lizards ran over him. At lunch-time he would return to the villa and submit the morning's work to Frieda for her approval before they settled down for their siesta.

She preferred the first draft to its two successors, and there can be little doubt that she was right. It has a freshness and spontaneity that they lack, and is comparatively free from their windy philosophizing, puerile ecstasies over the phallus and childish exhibitionism in the use of four-letter words. Lawrence originally intended his story to be a novella rather than a full-length novel, and many of the additions that he made to the later versions to bring them up to the length of the standard novel are little better than padding.

The manuscript of the first draft was headed *Lady Chatterley's Lover*, and after considering such alternative titles as *Tenderness*, *My Lady's Keeper* and *John Thomas and Lady Jane* he returned to his original idea. In so doing he was playing a trick on his readers. The 'nice and old-fashioned sounding' title, as he called it in a letter to Secker, was intended to recall such Victorian favourites as *Lady Audley's Secret* and *Lady Windermere's Fan*, and to suggest that the story was about a scandal in high society. In fact the book, begun little more than a month after his visit to the areas affected by the miners' lockout, largely deals with the English class system and the effects of industrialism. It is as much concerned with relations between classes, and between individuals of different classes, as it is with relations between men and women. Lawrence's reactions to the England of 1926 are revealed in two of the finest passages of the book: Lady Chatterley's drive to Uthwaite, which presents a panoramic view of a changing England where the collieries are driving out the gentry's country mansions, and the scene, at once comic and moving, in which she is the Tewsons' guest at high tea. Her feelings during the drive are obviously Lawrence's: 'It was the hopeless, dismal ugliness that so depressed her . . . She could never get used to this awful colliery region of the north Midlands. And yet she liked it too: it gave her a certain feeling of blind virility, a certain blind, pathetic forcefulness of life'.[19] The repeated 'blind' recalls the blind Samson of 'The Revolutionary', another work inspired by a social conflict. *Lady Chatterley's Lover* is in one aspect a parable, in which the love of Constance and Oliver Parkin (the Mellors of the

289

final version), who in the first draft becomes an active communist, sym-bolizes the new relationship between classes which Lawrence advocated. That is not to say that the sexual element in the book is unimportant. It was certainly important to Lawrence – all the more so because in 1926 he seems to have become permanently impotent. He put a great deal of himself into both the main male characters, Sir Clifford Chatterley, the impotent, semi-invalid husband whose wife was unfaithful, as Lawrence knew that Frieda sometimes was, and Oliver Parkin, the man from a mining village who won the love of a married woman belonging to the aristocracy. It was both the problems of industrial England and his own personal problems to which Lawrence was seeking a solution.

Wragby Hall and Tevershall may seem remote from Florence and the Villa Mirenda, yet at times the two worlds are one in all three versions of *Lady Chatterley's Lover*. In his descriptions of the woods in which Constance and Parkin meet, Lawrence is expressing his joy both in the Tuscan coun-tryside in which he was writing and in the Nottinghamshire woods – once haunted by Robin Hood, as he reminds us in each version of the novel – where he had wandered as a boy and which he had recently revisited. When he wrote 'Constance sat down with her back to a young pine tree that swayed against her like an animate creature' he was describing the tree against which he was himself seated. In the second draft of the novel Constance recalls 'the sight of Florence in the sunshine' as one of the experiences from which she has derived a 'curious rapture and fulfil-ment', and elsewhere she exclaims, 'How I love Italy when the almond and peach-blossom is all pink clouds under a blue sky!'[20]

There is a more remarkable reminiscence of Florence in the final ver-sion of the book, when Mellors wishes that 'men walked with legs close bright scarlet, an' buttocks nice and showing scarlet under a little white jacket'. References in two essays written shortly after confirm that the colourful figures whom Lawrence had in mind were the quattrocento Florentine gallants whom he had seen on paintings in the Uffizi and else-where. In 'Red Trousers' he regrets 'the really great periods like the Renaissance', when 'the young men swaggered down the street with one leg bright red, one leg bright yellow, doublet of puce velvet and yellow feather in silk cap', and in 'Making Pictures' he recalls 'that "Wedding" with the scarlet legs, in the Uffizi' as one of the Italian paintings which have given him a 'deep thrill'. He was probably referring to the wedding scene on the fifteenth-century painted chest, known as the Adimari cassone, in the Accademia. In his letter at the end of *Lady Chatterley's Lover* Mellors returns to this theme:

> If the men wore scarlet trousers as I said, they wouldn't think so much of money: if they could dance and hop and skip, and sing and swagger and be handsome, they could do with very little cash. And amuse the women themselves, and be amused by the women. They ought to learn to be naked and handsome, and to sing in a mass and dance the old group dances, and carve the stools they sit on, and embroider their own emblems. Then they wouldn't need money.[21]

Here Lawrence is passing in review some of his favourite alternative societies; from the Renaissance Florentines he moves on to the naked Etruscans, who had also lived in Tuscany, and the Amerindians whose dances he described in *Mornings in Mexico* and who were frequently associated in his mind with the Etruscans.

At Christmas Lawrence attempted to put into practice the plea for a closer and more human relationship between classes which he had made in *The First Lady Chatterley* by organizing a party for the local peasants. When Frieda proposed to buy a Christmas tree Pietro assured her that that was unnecessary, and in the small hours of 24 December he brought her a young pine tree which he had cut in the priest's wood. The Lawrences, Giulia and Pietro enjoyed decorating the tree with candles and 'glittery things' and covering the pine-cones on it with gold and silver paper, while Pietro shouted at intervals, 'Guarda, guarda, signora, che bellezza!' All the twenty-seven members of the Orsino, Bandello and Pini families came in later in the day for the party, 'with the children washed beyond recognition, the rascal Filiberto, who as a rule doesn't have much but dirt and his shirt to cover him, looking like a diminutive chauffeur'.[22] There were presents for all on the tree: cheap wooden toys and bags of sweets for the children, cigars for the men, and biscuits for the women. The adults drank Marsala, three teenage girls, Tosca, Lilla and Teresina, sang and danced to entertain the company, and everyone had such a good time that in the end the exhausted Lawrences had difficulty in persuading them all to go home.

During the first two months of 1927 Lawrence was busy painting and writing the second draft of his novel, which he had begun before Christmas. It is a pity that when this remarkable book was finally published in 1972 it was given the title *John Thomas and Lady Jane*; these phrases, which do not appear in this draft, give the impression that it is obscene, although it is far less so than the final version. In the freshness of its descriptions of natural beauty it sometimes surpasses even the first version, and this mood was carried forward from the novel into the essay 'Flowery Tuscany', most of which was written in March. Passages in *The First Lady Chatterley* are sometimes effectively expanded or developed, as in Constance's reflections during her drive to Uthwaite:

> But transplanted into these Midlands, she seemed to have left England altogether, to have entered some weird and unnatural country where everything came from underground. It was no country. It was another no-man's-land. Yet, gradually, it came to have a certain hold over her. It was sad country, with a grey, almost gruesome sadness. Yet it was not dead. It was alive, labouring under a queer, savage weight of dismalness and acquiescence. It was not cowed or broken, either. No, the very ugliness seemed to have preserved a manly restlessness in the men, a sort of slow, smouldering courage of death and desperation. But no hope. No immediate hope. There was a grim sort of acceptance of hopelessness, something underground and uncanny. And, when the disillusion was complete, a capacity for a ruthless destruction.[23]

Above all, *John Thomas and Lady Jane* is the only version of the novel that has a satisfying conclusion. Lawrence had ended the first draft abruptly, having no clear idea of how to round it off. Now he found his solution. The scene at the Tewsons', the climax of the social theme of the book, had come well before the end of *The First Lady Chatterley*; here it forms the penultimate chapter, and is immediately followed by the scene between Constance and Parkin in Hucknell Torkard church, the climax of the love story.

Lawrence had come to Florence with the intention of writing a book on the Etruscans. He had read a good deal on the subject, and while in London in September 1926 had studied the Etruscan exhibits in the British Museum, but since his return to the Villa Mirenda his energies had been diverted to his painting and the first two drafts of *Lady Chatterley's Lover*. Once he had completed his second version, however, he found himself in a quandary. 'I've done my novel – I like it – but it's so improper, according to the poor conventional fools, that it'll never be printed,' he wrote to a friend on 8 March, adding defiantly, 'And I will *not* cut it.' Progress in this direction apparently blocked, he turned back to the Etruscans. In the first half of April he made a tour with Earl Brewster, during which they visited the Etruscan museum in the Villa Giulia in Rome, the tombs at Cerveteri, the museum and the painted tombs at Tarquinia, the tombs at Volci, and the city walls and the museum at Volterra. The tour gave him intense pleasure. 'I was really happy', he wrote to another American friend, 'looking at Etruscan tombs by the coast north of Rome – Cerveteri, Tarquinia etc. No rush there! Even the ass brays slowly and leisurely, and the tombs are far more twinkling and alive than the houses of men.' To Baroness von Richthofen he wrote, 'I had a very lovely week . . . They were a lively, fresh, jolly people, lived their own life, without wanting to dominate the life of others. I am fond of my Etruscans.'[24] It was in this spirit that he wrote in June the six essays later published as *Etruscan Places* – perhaps the most delightful of his travel books. He planned to visit the Etruscan cities of Arezzo, Cortona, Chiusi, Orvieto and Perugia and to write essays on them and the Etruscan relics in Florence and Fiesole. With these and what he had already written he proposed to make up a book of twelve or fourteen essays, and to follow it with a second volume on the smaller Etruscan cities. But nothing was to come of these grandiose projects.

While at Volterra he saw an Easter toy in a shop window, a model of a man chasing a runaway cock, which gave him an idea for a story. Before the end of April he had written the long short story published in America as 'The Escaped Cock' and in England as 'The Man Who Died', in which Jesus, having been taken down from the cross while still alive, escapes from the sepulchre, flees to Phoenicia, and becomes the lover of a priestess of Isis, who believes him to be Osiris restored to life. Lawrence introduced into the story the same ideas which he expressed in *Lady Chatterley's Lover* and *Etruscan Places* and which inspired several of his paintings: the triumph of the flesh over the spirit and of pagan over Christian values. When 'The Escaped Cock' was published in an American magazine in 1928 it provoked violent protests; fortunately for Lawrence, it did not appear in England until 1931, when he was safely dead.

In the evening of 29 April he noticed in the streets of Florence two German youths with heavy rucksacks on their backs. While in Germany three years before he had seen the bands of *Wandervögel*, and had reflected, 'These queer gangs of *Young Socialists*, youths and girls, with their non-materialistic professions, their half-mystic assertions, they strike one as strange. Something primitive, like loose, roving gangs of broken, scattered tribes, so they affect one.' Now the sight of the two young Germans filled him with the same uneasiness. 'When I see the *Wandervögel* pushing at evening out of the Por Santa Maria, across the blaze of sun and into the Ponte Vecchio,' he wrote, 'then Germany becomes again to me what it was to the Romans: the mysterious, half-dark land of the north, bristling with gloomy forests, resounding to the cry of wild geese and of swans, the land of the stork and the bear and the *drachen* and the *greifen*.'[25] Lawrence was totally free from anti-German prejudice – he was married to a German wife, and during the war he had been suspected of pro-German sympathies – but his antennae were sensitive enough to detect something sinister and dangerous stirring in Germany.

At about this time Orioli persuaded him to be reconciled to Douglas; he agreed the more willingly because on re-reading some of Douglas's travel essays he was impressed by the quality of the writing. When three weeks later they met in Orioli's shop Douglas offered Lawrence his snuff-box and he accepted a pinch as a gesture of reconciliation, remarking, 'Isn't it curious, only Norman and my father ever give me snuff?'[26] Although thereafter they remained nominally friends, neither seems to have forgiven the other. When after Lawrence's death Douglas edited the English text of Orioli's *Adventures of a Bookseller*, he removed or altered all Orioli's friendly references to Lawrence.

On 23 May Osbert and Edith Sitwell came to tea at the Villa Mirenda. 'They were very nice, and we liked them much better than we had thought,' Lawrence wrote to Aldington. 'But he all the same makes me feel sort of upset and worried. Of him I want to ask: But what ails thee, then? Tha's got nowt amiss as much as a' that.' In a letter to another friend he described them as 'not a bit affected or bouncing: only absorbed in themselves and their parents. I never in my life saw such a strong, strange *family* complex: as if they were marooned on a desert island, and nobody in the world but their lost selves. Queer!' Lawrence had already met their parents, Sir George and Lady Ida Sitwell, with whom he had had lunch a year before at their Italian home, the Castello Montegufoni, about fourteen miles from Florence. He had been surprised to find that Sir George collected beds, 'those four-poster golden Venetian monsters that look like Mexican high-altars', and also 'gilt and wiggly-carved chairs' that one was not allowed to sit on.[27]

Although the summer of 1927 was exceptionally hot, Lawrence insisted on working as usual. One afternoon early in July he gathered a basket of peaches in the sun, and then went to his room to rest. When shortly after Frieda heard him call her in 'a strange, gurgling voice'[28] she ran to his room and found him lying on his bed while a stream of blood flowed from his mouth. It was the worst of three haemorrhages that he had had in a little over two years, and although he insisted that they were bronchial in origin he must have known that they were in fact tubercular. Frieda immediately sent for Dr Giglioli, and nursed Lawrence for a month through heat so intense that milk, even after being boiled, was sour by midday. When he was well enough he was moved to the Austrian Alps, where he spent most of August before moving on to stay with Frieda's relations in Bavaria.

He and Frieda returned to the Villa Mirenda on 19 October, and were warmly welcomed by the Wilkinsons, Giulia and the peasants. Frieda was blissfully happy, but since his illness Florence and Italy had lost their charm for Lawrence. He remained depressed and lethargic, with little desire either to write or to paint. Unlike his month at San Gervasio, life at the Villa Mirenda had not inspired him to write verse; his poetry in 1926–7 went into the first two versions of *Lady Chatterley's Lover*, his essays and his paintings. He wrote to an American friend in November, 'I've not written a poem, hardly these last three years and more – not a jingle in me. Instead I paint pictures, here – which seems the right thing to do, in Tuscany of the painters.'[29] In the same month, however, he began revising his poems for a collected edition, which, as it turned out, meant that he rewrote many of them so thoroughly that they came to bear little resemblance to those which he had originally written.

It was nearly a month after his return before he could summon up the energy to go to Florence, but he gradually picked up the threads of his literary friendships. Turner and Orioli came to tea, together with C. K. Scott Moncrieff, the translator of Proust and minor poet, and the young Harold Acton. On 16 November, a sunny day, Lawrence looked down on Florence, 'so clear and beautiful in the sun, the Lily town', and looked forward with pleasure to accepting Turner's invitation to lunch on the following day, yet when he went he found that 'towns mean nothing to me, only noise and nuisance'. The visit nevertheless produced an important result, for over lunch his friends – Turner, Orioli and perhaps Douglas – suggested that, since no British or American publisher was likely to bring out an unexpurgated *Lady Chatterley's Lover,* he should publish it himself privately in Florence, as Douglas did with his books. The more he considered the idea, the better he liked it. It meant that he could bring out his book as he wanted it, and not in a version cut by some publisher terrified of prosecution for obscenity. Production was cheap: he might make a profit of several hundred pounds, and could evade a tax of 20 per cent which the British Government had recently imposed on the royalties of authors living overseas. With these considerations in mind, he began another complete rewriting of his novel a week or so later, and when he broke off for Christmas the first half was finished. Once again the peasants had their tree on Christmas Eve. On Christmas Day the Huxleys drove Lawrence and Frieda to a friend's house in Florence, where they had turkey, crackers and a Christmas tree ('not so big and grand as ours, only finer'), and two days later the Huxleys came to the Villa Mirenda for lunch, when they ate a plum pudding presented by the Wilkinsons.[30] The festivities over, Lawrence returned to his novel, which was completed by 8 January 1928.

In accordance with his usual custom, he introduced some of his literary friends into the book. Huxley made a brief appearance as Hammond, 'a tall thin fellow with a wife and two children, but much more closely connected with a typewriter'.[31] This was merely a private joke between friends, and Huxley was not offended. More questionable was the introduction of the novelist Michael Arlen, an old acquaintance of Lawrence whom he had recently met in Florence, as Michaelis, Lady Chatterley's first lover. Clifford Chatterley in this version of the novel was given some resemblance to Osbert Sitwell, and was provided with a brother and sister who played no part in the story. The trio were described in terms that made it impossible not to recognize them as portraits of the Sitwells, who never forgave Lawrence. He gave to the main male characters more of his own qualities; Sir Clifford, who was very much a composite figure, became a writer of fiction, and Mellors (the new name given to Parkin) a boy from a mining village with a grammar-school education and a knowledge of French and German.

Artistically the final version of the novel was a disaster. The book was written during a period of 'physical invalidity, anxiety, insecurity, depression, irrational instability, diminished judgment, acute feelings of isolation, and paranoia', and these feelings left their mark upon it. The delicate balance between the social and the sexual themes of the two earlier versions was lost as increased stress was laid upon the latter. In the first two drafts Constance's drive to Uthwaite had produced an objective picture of the condition of England, but the final version has nothing to offer but a black despair: 'She felt again in a wave of terror the grey, gritty hopelessness of it all. With such creatures for the industrial masses, and the upper classes as she knew them, there was no hope, no hope any more.'[32] The changes introduced into the story were almost all for the worse. The admirable conclusion of the second version was ruthlessly scrapped and replaced by a new ending that at times, as in the scene between Mellors and Constance's father, is embarrassingly bad. On the other hand, the ugliest element in the second version, the notorious episode of anal intercourse, was not only retained but expanded. Four-letter words were used so freely as to suggest a dirty-minded schoolboy chalking on a wall. It is a tragedy that *Lady Chatterley's Lover* should be most widely known in this version, by far the worst of the three.

Getting his manuscript typed caused some difficulties. Nellie Morrison agreed to do it, but after finishing five chapters refused to go any further. In the end the remainder of the first half of the book was typed in London and Maria Huxley dealt with the second half, which contained the objectionable language. On 9 March Lawrence had lunch with Orioli and then delivered the manuscript at the Tipografia Giuntina, at Via del Sole 4. This was, as Lawrence told his agent, 'a nice little printing shop all working away by hand – cosy and bit by bit, real Florentine manner – and the printer doesn't know a word of English – nobody in the place knows a word – where ignorance is bliss!' He insisted on explaining to the master-printer, Franceschini, a little man with a white moustache who had just married for the second time, that the book dealt with certain subjects and contained certain words in English, and advised him not to print it if he thought it would get him into trouble with the authorities. When the nature of the book was explained to him Franceschini nonchalantly replied, 'Oh! *ma*! but we do it every day.'[33] And so, as there was nothing political in the book, and the printer was working in fascist Italy and not in free England, he was able to proceed without fear of prosecution.

There were still difficulties ahead. As the printers had only enough type for half of the book, the first half had to be printed and the type distributed before the second half could be set up. Then the printer's ignorance of English made proof-reading a nightmare. 'The printer would do fairly well for a few pages,' Lawrence later recalled, 'then he would go drunk, or something. And then the words danced weird and macabre, but not English.'[34] The paper-makers' failure to deliver on time caused further delays, but in the end, on 7 June, the very last proofs were corrected. Three days later Lawrence and Frieda left Florence.

They never returned, except for one or two short visits. When the lease of the Villa Mirenda expired at the beginning of May Lawrence had decided not to renew it. He took down his pictures and began to pack, but Frieda was so unhappy about leaving the house that he hung the pictures up again and paid another six months' rent. By September he had definitely decided to give up the house, which he believed to be bad for his health, and on 4 October Frieda came there alone and packed their belongings. Yet he continued to talk of returning to Florence to finish his book on the Etruscans, and on 9 May 1929 he wrote to Orioli, 'If you hear of a nice place in the hills round Florence, let me know. I want to find a place, if possible, which we can keep.'[35]

On 14 June 1929 an exhibition of his paintings opened in London, and at about the same time a volume of reproductions of the paintings was published. He considered going to London but decided against it, fearing that he would be arrested; copies of *Lady Chatterley's Lover* sent to England and two manuscripts of his collection of satirical poems, *Pansies*, had been seized by the police in the previous January. Instead Frieda went to London, while Lawrence joined the Huxleys at Forte dei Marmi, the Tuscan seaside resort. On 6 July he went on to Florence for what was to be his last visit. When he arrived he looked so ill that Orioli took him to his own flat at Lungarno Corsini 6, put him to bed and telegraphed Frieda. Lawrence was suffering from a severe chill, and his condition was not improved by the news that on 5 July the police had raided the exhibition and carried off thirteen paintings, which the inspector in charge considered to be obscene because they depicted nudes with pubic hair. When Frieda's telegram arrived to say that she was on her way Orioli asked: 'What will Frieda say when she arrives?' Lawrence replied, 'Do you see those peaches in the bowl? She will say "What lovely peaches", and she will devour them.'[36] Which is exactly what did happen, as Frieda was thirsty after her journey.

By 16 July he was well enough to travel, and he and Frieda left for Baden-Baden. From there they moved on to Rottach, in Bavaria, where they spent the first half of September. In his letters he spoke of returning to Florence to look for a house, but his doctors advised against it. By this time he was so weak that he was forced to face the fact that he was dying, and out of that consciousness came some of his loveliest poems. When Frieda placed a huge bunch of gentians on the floor beside his bed their shape reminded him of torches, and of his descent with Brewster into the darkness of the Etruscan tombs, which in turn recalled the myth of Persephone's descent into the underworld. From this combination of ideas emerged 'Bavarian Gentians':

> Reach me a gentian, give me a torch!
> let me guide myself with the blue, forked torch of a flower
> down the darker and darker stairs, where blue is darkened on blueness
> down the way Persephone goes, just now, in first-frosted September . . .

He remembered too the tomb at Cerveteri inside which he had seen, together with the dead man's armour, weapons, jewels, tools and little dishes, the bronze model ship which would carry him over to the other world. These memories provided the central image for 'The Ship of Death', on which he worked during the last weeks of his life:

> Now launch the small ship, now as the body dies
> and life departs, launch out, the fragile soul
> in the fragile ship of courage, the ark of faith
> with its store of food and little cooking pans
> and change of clothes,
> upon the flood's vast waste
> upon the waters of the end
> upon the sea of death, where still we sail
> darkly, for we cannot steer, and have no port.[37]

On medical advice he moved to Bandol, near Toulon, where he had spent the previous winter. He still dreamed of Florence; on 1 December he wrote to an English friend who lived on the Lungarno Acciaioli, 'And we will meet in spring in Florence, when your terrace is full of flowers, and it will be lovely.'[38] But he was never to return there. He left Bandol only for a sanatorium at Vence, whence on 2 March 1930 his ship of death put out to sea.

D. H. Lawrence
from TO PINO

O Pino
What a bean-o!
when we printed Lady C.!

Little Giuntina
couldn't have been a
better little bee!

When you told him
perhaps they'd scold him
for printing those naughty words

All he could say:
'But we do it every day!
like the pigeons and the other little birds!'

12

Natives, Residents and Visitors

We have not exhausted the list of English poets who lived in Florence or its immediate neighbourhood for a longer or shorter period. Leigh Hunt, for example, lived there from 1823 to 1825. He had come to Italy in 1822, with his wife and his seven children, at the invitation of Byron and Shelley, who proposed that the three of them should collaborate in producing a periodical. A week after they arrived Shelley was drowned, but Hunt and Byron went ahead with the publication, now named *The Liberal*. Byron lost interest, however, and after four issues *The Liberal* expired. In July 1823 Byron sailed for Greece on the journey that was to end at Missolonghi, and a few days later Mary Shelley left for England. Without the company of his English friends Hunt tired of Genoa, where they had been living, and on 22 August left with his family for Florence, hoping to find there 'more conveniences for us, more books, more fine arts, more illustrious memories, and a greater concourse of Englishmen'. Although travelling in the heat of an Italian summer made the whole family ill, his first impressions of Florence were favourable, as he later recalled:

In Genoa you heard nothing in the streets but the talk of money. I hailed it as a good omen in Florence that the first two words which caught my ears were 'flowers' and 'women' (*fiori* and *donne*). The night of our arrival we put up at a hotel in a very public street, and were kept awake (as agreeably as illness would let us be) by songs and guitars. It was one of our pleasantest experiences of the south; and, for the moment, we lived in the Italy of books. One performer to a jovial accompaniment sang a song about somebody's fair wife, which set the street in roars of laughter. From the hotel we went to a lodging in the Street of Beautiful Women — *Via delle Belle Donne* — a name which it is a sort of tune to pronounce. We there heard one night a concert in the street; and looking out, saw music-stands, books, etc. in regular order, and amateurs performing as in a room. Opposite our lodgings was an inscription on a house, purporting that it was the hospital of the monks of Vallombrosa. Wherever you turned was music or a graceful memory.[1]

The Hunts' next lodging was a corner house on the left side of the Piazza Santa Croce, near the church; their landlord was a Greek appropriately named Dionysius, who was always drunk. But Hunt, though very much a townsman, liked to live in rural surroundings, and he soon moved on to Maiano, a village about two miles north-east of Florence. There he rented the first floor of the Villa Morandi; the ground floor was occupied by a cultured Jewish family, who held concerts in the garden in the evening. 'The manners of this hamlet were very pleasant and cheerful,' he afterwards wrote:

> The priest used to come of an evening, and take a Christian game at cards with his Hebrew friends. A young Abate would dance round a well with the daughters of the vine-growers, the whole party singing as they footed . . . One evening all the young peasantry in the neighbourhood assembled in the hall of the village, by leave of the proprietor (an old custom), and had the most energetic ball I ever beheld. The walls of the room seem to spin round with the waltz, as though it would never leave off -- the whirling faces all looking grave, hot, and astonished at one another.[2]

Although homesick for England and his friends, Hunt found many pleasures at Maiano. He loved the beauty of the countryside, and revelled in his walks to Fiesole and the panorama of Florence which he could contemplate at leisure from the terrace before his villa. He liked to recall the district's associations with Boccaccio, and was amused to hear a neighbour scolding Dante, her little boy, for getting dirty and tearing his clothes. He had one English friend in the neighbourhood, Charles Armitage Brown; Hazlitt arrived in February 1825; and he was introduced to Landor, with whom he formed a close friendship, and to Seymour Kirkup. Hunt also derived a great deal of pleasure from Florence's works of art, within the limits of what was fashionable at the time; thus he considered the interior of Santa Croce, with its frescos by Giotto, as disappointing as its unfinished exterior. On one point, however, he defied fashion; although he found the body of the Medici Venus 'perfection', he thought 'neither the gesture of the figure modest, nor the face worthy even of the gesture'.[3] Hazlitt agreed with him.

While at Maiano, Hunt was busily engaged in writing essays for *The Examiner* and *The New Monthly*, as well as a book on his religious views. He also proposed to a Florentine bookseller that he should bring out a monthly magazine for British residents and visitors, which would reprint the best articles from English periodicals. The bookseller was enthusiastic, but the difficulties raised by the Tuscan authorities, who insisted that the contents must be submitted to the censors to ensure that nothing touching on religion or politics was included, prevented the scheme from going ahead. The most important literary product of Hunt's years in Florence was his translation of Francesco Redi's *Bacco in Toscana*, a poem which Robert Merry had already imitated. Hunt had a thorough knowledge of Italian literature, and a deep fondness for it; one of his most treasured possessions was the *Parnaso Italiano*, an anthology of Italian poetry in fifty-six volumes, which he had bought while he was in prison for libelling the Prince Regent and had brought to Italy with him. He made many translations from Italian poets of all periods from Dante to Alfieri, but none more lively and vigorous than his version of Redi's great dithyramb in praise of wine. It was published in 1825 with a dedication to Hunt's brother John, in which he said, 'I cannot send you, as I could wish, a pipe of Tuscan wine, or a hamper of Tuscan sunshine, which is much the same thing; so in default of being able to do this, I do what I can, and send you, for a new year's present, a translation of a Tuscan bacchanal.'[4]

Amid all these activities Hunt still longed to be back in England, but he could never find the money for the journey. At last Henry Colburn, publisher of *The New Monthly*, sent him a cheque on the understanding that he would write a number of books for him. Hunt accepted this condition, and after a cheerful evening with Brown and Kirkup left Maiano with his family at six a.m. on 10 September 1825. He retained happy memories of Florence, of which he later wrote:

> I loved Florence, and saw nothing in it but cheerfulness and elegance. I loved the name; I loved the fine arts and the old palaces; I loved the memories of Pulci and Lorenzo de' Medici, the latter of whom I could never consider in any other light than that of a high-minded patron of genius, himself a poet; I loved the good-natured, intelligent inhabitants, who saw fair play between industry and amusement; nay, I loved the Government itself, however afraid it was of English periodicals; for at that time it was good-natured also, and could 'live and let live', after a certain quiet fashion, in that beautiful by-corner of Europe.[5]

Although Hunt never returned to Florence, the city supplied him with the plot for the most successful of his many attempts to write for the stage, *A Legend of Florence*. The story was that which Shelley had begun to tell in 'Ginevra', and which Lee-Hamilton was later to use in 'A Ballad of the Plague of Florence', and Hunt acknowledged his debt to Shelley by printing four lines from his poem on the title-page of the play.

Many British poets have lived and several have died in Florence, but only two have been born there. The first of these, George Arthur Greene, who was born in 1853, was the son of an Anglo-Irish clergyman. After receiving much of his education in Florence, he took his degree at Trinity College, Dublin, and had a successful career as a university lecturer and examiner. In the 1890s he was a member of the Rhymers' Club, the society of poets meeting at the Cheshire Cheese in Fleet Street which also included his fellow Irishman W. B. Yeats, John Davidson, Ernest Dowson, Lionel Johnson and Arthur Symons. The fact that Yeats nowhere mentions Greene in *Autobiographies*, which contains the best-known description of the club, suggests that he made little impression on the other members.[6]

His first book, *Italian Lyrists of To-day*, published in 1893, was a collection of competent verse translations, and must have been among the earliest sources from which English readers could derive some knowledge of D'Annunzio's poems. His next book, *Dantesques*, which appeared ten years later, is something of a curiosity. Described as 'a sonnet companion to the Inferno', it consists of thirty-five sonnets which, according to the foreword, 'seek to reproduce what is left most clearly and permanently imprinted upon the mind after the perusal of each canto of the Inferno'.[6] Greene selects the most striking episodes in Dante's poem, such as the stories of Francesca da Rimini, Ulysses and Count Ugolino, and paraphrases them in sonnet form, usually sticking closely to the wording of the original. It is difficult to see what useful purpose is served by this exercise. Greene brought together his original verse in his last and largest collection, *Songs of the Open Air*, published in 1912. This contains sixty-one poems, of which some date from his Rhymers' Club period and others may be even earlier, but only two, 'The Return' and 'Southern Memories', deal with Italian themes. In the latter his tribute to the past greatness of Florence achieves a genuine eloquence. He died in 1921.

Another member of the Rhymers' Club, Herbert Percy Horne, lived in Florence in later life. Born in 1864, Horne was an art historian and architect as well as a poet. His only collection, *Diversi Colores*, which appeared anonymously in 1891, was a slim volume of polished, rather precious lyrics designed and published by himself. In 1905 he settled in Florence, where he bought and restored the fifteenth-century Palazzo Gondi, in the Via de' Benci. Here he lived in austere conditions, denying himself every comfort in order that he might amass a priceless collection of works of art, and wrote a standard biography of Botticelli. On his death in 1916 he left the palazzo, now known as the Museo Horne, to the city to house his collection.

There were almost as many British poets and novelists in Florence in the 1920s as there had been in the 1850s. Lawrence, Huxley, Aldington and Harold Acton were both poets and novelists. Other poets were the long-forgotten Herbert Trench, 'burly and beetle-browed, a country squire seduced from his shooting by the Muses', to whom his admirers attributed 'gifts of the first order',[7] and C. K. Scott Moncrieff, who had addressed a sequence of love sonnets to Wilfred Owen. Among the novelists were Norman Douglas, Ronald Firbank and Reggie Turner. Any of these, Acton recalled in his memoirs, could be met shopping in the Via Tornabuoni or gossiping in Orioli's bookshop.

Harold Mario Mitchell Acton was unique as the only English poet who was born, lived most of his life and died in Florence. He was born on 5 July 1904 at the Villa La Pietra, a fifteenth-century house largely rebuilt in the seventeenth, standing a mile north of the Porta San Gallo. His ancestors, English Catholic exiles, for generations had served the Bourbon kings of Naples. His father had three great interests in life: his villa, his garden and his collection of paintings. Growing up in an atmosphere where the arts were of paramount importance, in his school days Acton was undecided whether to make painting or writing his career. During his last year at Eton he collaborated with his friend Brian Howard in producing a magazine, *The Eton Candle*, the single issue of which attracted considerable attention. The poems which he contributed to it made obvious his admiration for T. S. Eliot, the Sitwells and the Diaghilev ballet, and paraded the author's world-weary sophistication; one began

> I often wish to cut my veins,
> Inside a comfortable bath . . .

His first two collections, *Aquarium* (1923) and *An Indian Ass* (1925), both appeared while he was at Oxford. He still practised his cult of Eliot and the Sitwells (he read *The Waste Land* at a Conservative Party fête, and was present at the first performance of *Façade*), but other influences are discernible in his verse – not only Aldous Huxley, Rimbaud, Hopkins and the poets of the 1890s, but also the Georgians, whom he claimed to despise. The most striking feature of his early work is his fondness for exotic and sonorous words: *farandole*, *nenuphar*, *mephitic*, *nacreous*, *girandoles*, *manticor*. He was so pleased with the phrase 'hispid stars' (an obvious imitation of Edith Sitwell's 'furred night') that he used it twice in *An Indian Ass*. His best collection, *Five Saints and an Appendix*, published in 1927, opens with narrative poems on Sts Catherine of Alexandria, Nicholas of Myra, Elizabeth of Hungary, and Cosmo and Damian, written with an ironic humour reminiscent of Huxley's early work. His last book of verse, *This Chaos*, which was published in Paris in a limited edition in 1930, went almost unnoticed.

In its brittle sophistication, most of his verse could have been written only in the 1920s. Like other poets active in that decade – Edith Sitwell, Huxley, Edgell Rickword – he abandoned verse about 1930 as if conscious that his poetic technique was inadequate to deal with the new world situation created by the great slump. His poems have one surprising feature: although he spent a greater part of his life in Florence than any other English poet, they do not contain a single reference to that city or to any of the works of art within its walls. At Eton he voiced his homesickness in a poem called 'My Home', but without giving any indication where his home was.

Acton found his true métier in history, as was appropriate for a distant relation of the Victorian historian Lord Acton. His first venture into that field, *The Last Medici*, appeared in 1932. From 1932 to 1939 he lived mainly in Peking, where he acquired a profound knowledge of Chinese poetry and drama. After serving in the RAF during the war he returned to Florence, and there produced several volumes on Neapolitan and Tuscan history – *The Bourbons of Naples* (1956), *The Last Bourbons of Naples* (1961), *Florence* (1961), *Tuscan Villas* (1973), and *The Pazzi Conspiracy* (1979) – as well as two volumes of memoirs. He was knighted in 1974 and, which probably pleased him more, was created an honorary citizen of Florence in 1976. He died on 27 February 1994, and in his will bequeathed his villa and its contents to the University of New York for use as a study centre.

Among the thousands of British tourists visiting Florence in the nineteenth century were several poets, who usually wrote a verse or two as a souvenir of the occasion. The first to come was the poetic banker Samuel Rogers, who arrived with his unmarried sister Sarah on 31 October 1814, six months after Napoleon's abdication had again made it possible for British tourists to travel on the Continent. Although almost forgotten today, in his lifetime he enjoyed a high reputation and even popularity; his *Pleasures of Memory*, published in 1792, sold over 22,000 copies in fourteen years. He stayed at Schneider's hotel, on the Lungarno near the Ponte alla Carraia, which catered for well-to-do British clients. It was expensive, charging ten shillings a day for bed, breakfast, dinner and as much wine as one could drink — more than twice as much as other Florentine hotels, but less than what the dinner alone would have cost in England. The food must have been excellent, or Rogers, who was something of an epicure, would not have stayed there; he noted in his journal on 5 November that at dinner he had ortolans, 'white as snow & wonderfully rich & delicate'.[8] He concluded his first day in Florence, however, by dining with Lord Holland, the Whig politician and patron of the arts, and attending the Countess of Albany's salon.

Rogers was better qualified than most tourists to be a judge of Florence's works of art. He possessed a valuable collection of paintings, four of which are now in the National Gallery, and could appreciate the work of periods which were not then in fashion, such as Italian Gothic buildings and fourteenth- and early fifteenth-century paintings. Unlike Leigh Hunt, he admired the paintings by Cimabue and Giotto in Santa Croce, and he was so impressed by Masaccio's frescos in the Brancacci Chapel in Santa Maria del Carmine that he paid them three visits. He was also prepared to praise the work of little-known artists; after seeing for the second time the painting of the martyrdom of St Catherine by Giuliano Bugiardini in Santa Maria Novella he wrote in his journal, 'Is not this the best in Florence?'[9]

On 2 November, the Day of the Dead, he attended mass in San Lorenzo and joined the procession, headed by a black banner showing a flower and a crowned skull, which visited Michelangelo's New Sacristy and the vaults where the Medici princes are buried. 'It was finely imagined', he commented, 'once a year with light & choral music & frankincense & holy water to descend, if I may say so, into the dwelling-places of the dead.' He became fascinated by the statue in the New

Sacristy of Lorenzo, Duke of Urbino, returning day after day to gaze at it. 'The visage of Lorenzo under the shade of that scowling & helmet-like bonnet is scarcely visible,' he noted in his journal:

> You can just discern the likeness of human features; but whether alive or dead, whether a face or a scull, that of a mortal man or a Spirit from heaven or hell, you cannot say. His figure is gigantic & noble, not such as to shock belief, or remind you that it is but a statue. It is the most real & unreal thing in stone that ever came from the chissel.

On 15 November he could write, 'I am released. The demon loses his influence. The beautiful forms in the Tribune & the Gallery have won me back to truth and nature'.[10] Yet on the same day, and again on 16 November, after visiting the Tribuna he could not resist returning to the New Sacristy.

Another memory haunted him: that of Milton. During his stay the weather was exceptionally mild for November, and as he walked by the river he saw baskets of violets offered for sale everywhere. Reminded of the 'Epitaphium Damonis', he wrote in his journal, 'Well might Milton speak with delight of his gathering violets on the banks of the Arno.' He made the customary pilgrimage to Vallombrosa with his sister and spent two nights there; as the monks had been expelled in 1810 and did not return until 1817, the priest in charge, 'a very gentlemanlike man', raised no such objection to her sleeping on the premises as the Brownings were later to meet.[11]

They drove up to Fiesole on 14 November and walked back, enjoying a view of Florence that inspired a lyrical passage in his journal:

> An evening mist, like the bloom of a plum, had overspread the mountains & the distant parts of the valley. Fiesole behind us, with its tower, & in front seen over cypresses, the towers & dome of Florence! A heavenly dream. In the sky a red streak so often in Italian paintings; & which I used to think unnatural. What a life was a life passed in such a city – in such a valley – in such a country – with such people in the golden days of Florence! Here came in succession Dante, Petrarch, Boccaccio, Machiavel, Galileo, M Angelo, Raphael, Milton – The dome against the bright sky noble; &, being less elevated than that of St Pauls is what makes it perhaps appear less. As we crossed the Arno, the glow on the water & in the sky; & the soft scenery in the West.[12]

As Rogers and his sister left Florence at sunrise on 18 November they saw something of that busy traffic that was to fascinate Lawrence: 'at the gates found country-people with carts & mules & horses & asses, a long train that had assembled without, before the opening of the Gates'.[13] They went on to Rome, where they stayed over Christmas and until the carnival, and then to Naples. On 6 March 1815 the news came that Napoleon had escaped from Elba. Not greatly disturbed, Rogers stayed on until 18 March before beginning his return journey. He arrived in Florence on 31 March, and again visited his favourite sights, such as the New Sacristy and the Brancacci Chapel. On the same day the King of Naples, Joachim Murat, issued a proclamation calling on the Italians to fight for their independence and unity, and Italy was plunged into war. Warned that the Neapolitan army would soon be in Florence, Rogers hurriedly left in the afternoon of 2 April, though he found time to write a farewell to the city in his journal:

> After all Florence strikes me most. I acknowledge the Grandeur of Rome, the Beauty of Naples; but Florence has won my heart, & in Florence I should wish to live beyond all the Cities in the World. Rome is sad, Naples is gay; but in Florence there is a cheerfulness, a classic elegance that at once fills & gladdens the heart.[14]

Avoiding France, now controlled by Napoleon, he returned home via Austria, Germany, Holland and Belgium, and sailed from Ostend six weeks before Waterloo.

When he next visited Florence it was in Lord Byron's company. Byron usually avoided Florence, as he disliked the English colony there. 'You may easily suppose that the English don't seek me, and I avoid them,' he had written to Tom Moore from Venice in April 1817. 'To be sure, there are but few or none here, save passengers. Florence and Naples are their Margate and Ramsgate, and much the same sort of company too, by all accounts – which hurts us among the Italians . . . I have not the least curiosity about Florence, though I must see it for the sake of the Venus, &c., &c.'[15] He spent a day there in the same month while on his way to Rome, and recorded his impression in Canto IV of *Childe Harold's Pilgrimage*. The Medici Venus, recently brought back from Paris, to which it had been taken by Napoleon, received forty-five lines of conventionally ecstatic praise; Michelangelo, Machiavelli, Galileo and Alfieri, the great dead of Santa Croce, eighteen lines; Dante, Petrarch and Boccaccio thirty-six; and the Chapel of the Princes nine.

Rogers returned to Italy in the autumn of 1821, and wrote to Byron, whom he had known for many years but had not seen since 1816, proposing that they should meet. Byron replied that he was about to move from Ravenna to Pisa, and suggested they should rendezvous at Bologna and cross the Apennines together. Rogers agreed, and they travelled to Florence in company. Rogers did not greatly enjoy the journey; Byron was accompanied by 'a dog, a cat, a hawk, an old gondolier from Venice, and other sundries',[16] and had a habit of rising so late in the morning that they missed much of the finest scenery on their route. On the last day of their journey together he did not get up until after lunch, with the result that they had to enter Florence in the dark. As on his previous visit, he spent only one day there, and Rogers declined his invitation to accompany him to Pisa, as he wished to go on to Rome.

Rogers stayed in Florence for three weeks, from 29 October to 18 November, during which he attempted to recapture some of the experiences of his previous visit; on the Day of the Dead, for example, he attended mass in San Lorenzo. He had many disappointments. Schneider's hotel was full, and he had to put up in a little inn which Schneider had bought ('that leviathan swallows up everything, and is said to be worth half a million'), with the result that his dinner, which had to be brought over the bridge, was cold when he got it. This was hard on a gourmet like Rogers, and to make things worse the ortolan season was over, the figs were tasteless and frost-bitten, and the grapes were beginning to shrivel. The weather, though dry and sunny, was very chilly, and he caught a bad cold by driving to see Galileo's house in an open carriage. There were no violets for sale in the streets this time. His disappointments left him feeling disgruntled. The Tuscans, he decided, were 'the least handsome people I have seen', and they had a bad habit of singing under his window at night very loudly and very badly. But there were compensations. He enjoyed lounging in the Boboli Gardens, and the beauty of the moonlit nights. Above all, he fell in love with the Medici Venus, which at the time of his previous visit had still been in the Louvre. Every morning he went to admire it, until a young Englishman wrote a verse epistle from Venus to Rogers begging him not to ogle her, and left it between the fingers of the statue where he could not help seeing it. 'Florence is to me as beautiful as ever,' he wrote to his sister, 'the Tribune and the Pitti as glorious;

but somehow or other I should not be sorry to find myself home again.'[17] Yet whatever his disappointments, his Italian tours had inspired by far the best of his books, *Italy*.

Wordsworth made a Continental tour with his friend Henry Crabb Robinson in 1837, during which they stayed in Florence from 29 May to 6 June. Like Rogers, and for the same reason, he was disappointed in his companion. As the weakness of his eyes prevented him from reading or writing by candlelight, he rose at dawn and went to bed at sunset, whereas Robinson preferred to get up at a reasonable hour and to enjoy his social life in the evenings.

Wordsworth was conscientious in his sightseeing. He made the pilgrimage to Vallombrosa while on his way from Rome to Florence, although it involved setting out at five in the morning and a long ride up a steep hillside, during which his guide managed to lose them in a wood. He was shown over the convent by a monk, who delighted him by pointing out where Milton had allegedly stayed, and then explored the surrounding woods under the guidance of a boy of about fourteen. To celebrate the occasion he produced a poem in galumphing anapaests. He visited the Tribuna of the Uffizi, where he turned his back on the Medici Venus and fell asleep; he preferred Raphael's painting of John the Baptist, on which he wrote a sonnet. He sat on 'Dante's Stone' opposite the Duomo and wrote another. When he published these poems in 1842 as *Memorials of a Tour in Italy, 1837* he included two translations of sonnets by Michelangelo which he headed 'At Florence', suggesting that they were written there; in fact at least one of them dates from 1839.

His guide in Florence was Enrico Mayer, a fervent Italian patriot, although he was the son of a German father and a French mother. He had known Byron when a young man, and later became a friend of Mazzini and fought in the war of 1848. He and Wordsworth had some disappointments, for in one day they found three places shut which they expected to be open. Many of us have had similar experiences in Italy.

While they were in Florence, Robinson visited Mrs Landor, in the hope of bringing about a reconciliation between her and her husband, and she afterwards, as Wordsworth told his daughter, 'called in her carriage to give us an airing or rather as it proved a damping in the Cascina'. Wordsworth was struck with the low cost of living in the city, and reckoned that 'with 300 a year a man at Florence might live quite in style! and with 800 like a prince'.[18]

Wordsworth's successor as Poet Laureate, Alfred Tennyson, came to Florence in September 1851, and stayed with his brother Frederick. As he was unable to obtain English pipe tobacco, however, he soon returned to England, without going on to Rome as he had intended. He put his memories of Italy into a charming poem, 'The Daisy', in which Florence receives honourable mention:

> At Florence too what golden hours,
> In those long galleries, were ours;
> What drives about the fresh Cascine,
> Or walks in Boboli's ducal bowers.
>
> In bright vignettes, and each complete,
> Of tower or duomo, sunny-sweet,
> Or palace, how the city glitter'd,
> Thro' cypress avenues, at our feet.[19]

The young Oscar Wilde spent several days in Florence in June 1875, and was particularly impressed by the Etruscan exhibits in the Archaeological Museum. 'They must have been a people among whom artistic feeling and power was most widely spread,' he remarked in a letter.[20] There is no mention of the Etruscans in the three poems which he wrote in Florence, however. 'By the Arno' is a skilful pastiche of the style and stanza of *In Memoriam*; 'San Miniato' and 'Ave Maria Gratia Plena' have an unctuous religiosity which reminds us that he was flirting with Catholicism at this time. This did not prevent him from writing poems in praise of revolution and an amoral aestheticism; philosophies to Wilde were like hats, which he liked to try on for size.

It was common for literary-minded visitors to Florence in the 1880s and early 1890s to pay a call on Eugene Lee-Hamilton and Violet Paget. One frequent visitor before 1889 was their friend Agnes Mary Frances Robinson, who by her two marriages became successively Mary Darmesteter and Mary Duclaux. Though not particularly original, her verse displays a command of verbal music learned, at least in part, from Italian poets. Some of her best poems – 'Florentine May', 'The Feast of St John', 'Tuscan Cypress', 'Tuscan Olive', 'Etruscan Tombs' – are on Florentine or Tuscan themes, and she makes skilful use of Italian verse forms. Another of Lee-Hamilton's visitors was Thomas Hardy, who came to Florence in April 1887. None of the 'Poems of Pilgrimage' which he wrote during this tour deals with Florence, however, although the Roman theatre at Fiesole inspired a sonnet. Wilde returned to Florence in May 1895, just before his trial, and called on Lee-Hamilton, whose verse he admired. 'It was a great success,' a friend wrote. 'Oscar talked like an angel, and they all fell in love with him, even Vernon Lee, who had hated him almost as much as he had hated her. He, for his part, was charmed with her.'[21]

Leigh Hunt

from BACCHUS IN TUSCANY
Translated from the Italian of Francesco Redi

This well of a goblet, so round and so long,
So full of wine, so gallant and strong,
That it draws one's teeth in its frolics and freaks,
And squeezes the tears from the sides of one's cheeks,
Like a torrent it comes, all swollen and swift,
And fills one's throat like a mountain rift,
And dashes so headlong, and plays such pranks,
It almost theatens to burst the banks.
No wonder; for down from the heights it came,
Where the Fiesolan Atlas, of hoary fame,
Basks his strength in the blaze of noon,
And warms his old sides with the toasting sun.
Long live Fiesole, green old name!
And with this long life to thy sylvan fame,
Lovely Maiano, lord of dells,
Where my gentle Salviati dwells.
Many a time and oft doth he
Crown me with bumpers full fervently,
And I, in return, preserve him still
From every crude and importunate ill.
I keep by my side,
For my joy and my pride,
That gallant in chief of his royal cellar,
Val di Marina, the blithe care-killer;
But with the wine yclept Val di Botte,
Day and night I could flout me the gouty.
Precious it is, I know, in the eyes
Of the masters, the masters, of those who are wise.
A glass of it brimming, a full-flowing cup,
Goes to my heart, and so it lays it up,
That not my Salvini, that book o' the south,
Could tell it, for all the tongues in his mouth.

G. A. Greene
UGOLINO

A little ray of light, unearthly pale,
　　Into that Tower of Famine fell and sank
　　Without a glow; and there, upon the blank
Of sleep, ill visions rose and rent the veil.

I saw mine adversary on the trail
　　Of wolf and young, with hounds in serried rank,
　　Gualandi and Sismondi and Lanfranc,
On hills which Lucca hide from Pisan vale.

And when both sire and cubs exhausted fell
　　Beneath the assailing tusks, while yet I slept
　　I heard my sons that called for bread and wept.

Then, through the throbbing stillness audible,
　　Men nailing up the locked door of the keep –
　　If now thou weepest not, when can'st thou weep?

I wept not, but my heart within me froze.
　　Yet Anselm could not from his tears refrain:
　　'Father, why look'st thou so?' he asked in vain;
I wept not, neither answered, till the close

Of that long night; but when the sun arose,
　　By the scant gleam that makes the darkness plain
　　I saw in their four faces my own pain.
Ah solid earth, why did'st thou not unclose?

And when the fourth day dawned uncertain-slow,
　　Gaddo my son fell at my feet and cried
　　'Father, why dost not help me?'
　　　　　　　　　　Then he died.

So sank they all, and I with sightless eyes
　　Sought them three days with vain unanswered cries,

Till famine did its work, more sure than woe.

from SOUTHERN MEMORIES

O city fragrant with sweet memories,
 Where Giotto's voice bade sleeping Art awake,
Where he who viewed the veiled eternities
 Breathed the love-passionate air, ere he could take
  That solemn sacred path;
Is not thy past a victory o'er Time?
 Fame is a halo round thy lilied locks;
 Thine is the key whose turning gold unlocks
The treasury of song, immortal rhyme,
  And love, and tragic wrath.

Florence! the world hath heard thy name with awe,
 Thine old and stern republican renown;
Thou held'st the scales of victory and of law;
 Kings, popes and kaisers trembled at thy frown;
  Out of thy cloistered glooms
Fierce voices shook the triple crowns of Rome;
 When Faith and Freedom manned thy citadels,
 The felon despots, crouching in their cells,
Saw the dead Liberties beneath thy dome
  Rise living from their tombs.

O mighty of mankind! whose lives of light
 Are beacons on waste waters of Earth's hours,
Soon cease your rays to flash athwart the night,
 Saturnian children, whom old Time devours!
  Ye lived, and are no more:
The record-rolls of Song, the sovereign Arts
 Are blazoned with your fame; but we must pass
 To where the cypress-shadowed emerald grass
Grows o'er those graves illustrious in our hearts,
  Girt with a city's roar.

There they who lived for thoughts more high than Fame,
    And who shall live when Fame shall be no more,
Lie in the solemn sleep that hath no name,
      Waiting till death shall die and time be o'er.
        There till the heavens unclose
They sleep their sleep, the men whom we have known;
    Around their feet the ancient city lies;
    The wondrous dome that lifts into the skies
Its airy lantern, dreams all night alone
      Above their long repose.

The silences of night, intense, divine,
    Brood o'er the unawakened valleys dim;
The distant, clear, star-glorious Apennine
    Rises far north, a many-mountained rim;
      And west, where died the day,
Carrara's violet peaks beneath the moon
    Lift their rough ridges cleft with quarried white
    Far-gleaming in the arrowy star-shine bright,
While southward San Miniato will be soon
      Touched by the morning ray.

Samuel Rogers
from FLORENCE

Nor then forget that Chamber of the Dead,
Where the gigantic shapes of Night and Day,
Turned into stone, rest everlastingly;
Yet still are breathing, and shed round at noon
A two-fold influence — only to be felt —
A light, a darkness, mingling each with each;
Both and yet neither. There, from age to age,
Two Ghosts are sitting on their sepulchres.
That is the Duke Lorenzo. Mark him well.
He meditates, his head upon his hand.
What from beneath his helm-like bonnet scowls?
Is it a face, or but an eyeless skull?

'Tis lost in shade; yet, like the basilisk,
It fascinates, and is intolerable.
His mien is noble, most majestical!
Then most so, when the distant choir is heard
At morn or eve – nor fail thou to attend
On that thrice-hallowed day, when all are there:
When all, propitiating with holy songs,
Visit the Dead. Then wilt thou feel his Power!

from THE CAMPAGNA OF FLORENCE

Nearer we hail
Thy sunny slope, Arcetri, sung of old
For its green wine; dearer to me, to most
As dwelt on by that great Astronomer,
Seven years a prisoner at the city-gate,
Let in but in his grave-clothes. Sacred be
His villa (justly was it called The Gem!)
Sacred the lawn, where many a cypress threw
Its length of shadow, while he watched the stars!
Sacred the vineyard, where, while yet his sight
Glimmered, at blush of morn he dressed his vines,
Chanting aloud in gaiety of heart
Some verse of Ariosto. There, unseen,
In manly beauty Milton stood before him,
Gazing with reverent awe – Milton, his guest,
Just then come forth, all life and enterprize;
He in his old age and extremity,
Blind, at noon-day exploring with his staff;
His eyes upturned as to the golden sun,
His eye-balls idly rolling. Little then
Did Galileo think whom he received;
That in his hand he held the hand of one
Who could requite him – who could spread his name
O'er lands and seas – great as himself, nay greater;
Milton as little thought in him he saw,
As in a glass, what he himself should be,

Destined so soon to fall on evil days
And evil tongues – so soon, alas, to live
In darkness, and with dangers compassed round,
And solitude.

William Wordsworth
AT FLORENCE

Under the shadow of a stately Pile,
The dome of Florence, pensive and alone,
Nor giving heed to aught that passed the while,
I stood, and gazed upon a marble stone,
The laurelled Dante's favourite seat. A throne,
In just esteem, it rivals; though no style
Be there of decoration to beguile
The mind, depressed by thought of greatness flown.
As a true man, who long had served the lyre,
I gazed with earnestness, and dared no more.
But in his breast the mighty Poet bore
A Patriot's heart, warm with undying fire.
Bold with the thought, in reverence I sate down,
And, for a moment, filled that empty Throne.

Oscar Wilde
BY THE ARNO

The oleander on the wall
    Grows crimson in the dawning light,
    Though the grey shadows of the night
Lie yet on Florence like a pall.

The dew is bright upon the hill,
    And bright the blossoms overhead,
    But ah! the grasshoppers have fled,
The little Attic song is still.

Only the leaves are gently stirred
   By the soft breathing of the gale,
   And in the almond-scented vale
The lonely nightingale is heard.

The day will make thee silent soon,
   O nightingale sing on for love!
   While yet upon the shadowy grove
Splinter the arrows of the moon.

Before across the silent lawn
   In sea-green vest the morning steals
   And to love's frightened eyes reveals
The long white fingers of the dawn

Fast climbing up the eastern sky
   To grasp and slay the shuddering night,
   All careless of the heart's delight,
Or if the nightingale should die.

Epilogue

More English poets, it is probably safe to say, have lived in Florence or its immediate neighbourhood than in any other city or town outside the United Kingdom. What is it about Florence that has attracted them, and what sort of poets have felt the attraction? To the first question there are several obvious answers: the beauty of the city and its surrounding countryside; the artistic masterpieces that it contains; its literary and historical associations; and, in the nineteenth century at least, its reputation for cheapness. These considerations attracted Shelley and the Brownings, for example, and all the poets whom we have considered (apart from Chaucer, who came for reasons beyond his control) were certainly influenced by some of them.

Except during the French Revolutionary, Napoleonic and Second World Wars, there has been an English colony in Florence since the eighteenth century. Leigh Hunt estimated in 1825 that there were 200 English families living there. Their presence may have deterred some English poets, such as Byron, from visiting the city, but the knowledge that they would find people speaking their own language, with a similar background and similar interests to their own, attracted far more. To these we may add the American colony that has existed since the early nineteenth century and the many British and American writers and artists who have visited the city for longer or shorter periods. Hence we have the Anglo-American colony of poets, novelists, painters and sculptors that existed in the 1850s and the situation whereby Lee-Hamilton could meet Henry James, Mary Robinson, Hardy and Wilde without leaving his bed.

The results of the growth of the English-speaking colony were not entirely beneficial. The fact that Milton does not seem to have met any Englishmen in Florence apparently did not disturb him, for his command of languages enabled him to mingle with the Florentine intelligentsia on equal terms. Although there were more English people in Florence in the eighteenth century, that did not prevent Gray and Walpole, and later Merry and his circle, from establishing friendly relations with Florentine writers. Shelley, Landor and the Brownings, on the other hand, seem to have had comparatively few contacts with any Italians except servants, and what contacts Landor did have were usually stormy. The fruitful intercourse between two cultures exemplified by Milton's friendship with Carlo Dati and other members of the Florentine academies and the collaboration of English and Italian poets in producing *The Florence Miscellany* was largely lost in the nineteenth and early twentieth centuries. There were exceptions, such as Lawrence's relationship with the peasants at the Villa Mirenda and Orioli's friendships with British writers, but these did not alter the general trend.

Florence's associations with Dante and Boccaccio helped to attract English visitors with literary interests. Milton, Gray, Parsons, Shelley, Hunt, the Brownings, Garrow and Lee-Hamilton all had an intimate knowledge of Dante's work, and most of them tried their hand at translating him. Boccaccio inspired English writers from Chaucer to Lawrence. With the passing of time, the city's associations with the English poets also contributed to attract other English poets. Milton recalled in his 'Mansus' that 'Tityrus' (Chaucer) had visited Italy. The memory of Milton sent Greatheed and Parsons, Rogers, Wordsworth and the Brownings on pilgrimages to Vallombrosa. Browning had previously visited Florence during a tour of places where Shelley had been before him. Lee-Hamilton wrote on Shelley's death in 'An Ode of the Tuscan Shore'; Greene devoted the most moving passage of 'Southern Memories' to the same theme; and two of the eight 'Poems of Pilgrimage' that Hardy wrote in Italy are tributes to Shelley. Today it is probably safe to say that Casa Guidi attracts more British and American visitors than the sites traditionally associated with Dante.

Most of the English poets who lived in Florence were reformers or revolutionaries in politics and unorthodox in their religious views. Milton, Merry, Greatheed, Shelley, Landor, Hunt and the Brownings were all radicals of one type or another, and most of them were or became republicans. Walpole posed as a republican, not very convincingly, in his 'Inscription for the Neglected Column'. Shelley, Landor, the Brownings, Thedosia Trollope and Isa Blagden were passionate supporters of the Risorgimento; Greatheed had prophesied it in 'Ode to Apathy' and Milton had foretold the overthrow of the temporal power of the Pope in 'On the Late Massacre in Piedmont'. Lawrence's political position is more difficult to define. He was certainly neither a conservative nor a liberal, but in the 1920s he vacillated between the extreme left and the extreme right. In his last years he moved towards a more moderate socialism; at the time of the British elections of 1929 he wrote: 'Of course if I was in England I should vote Labour, without hesitation.'[1] What Greene called the 'old and stern republican renown' of pre-Medicean Florence probably helped to attract poets holding radical views to the city. Milton, Walpole and the *Florence Miscellany* group were aware of the city's republican past, and Sismondi's history exercised a potent influence on Shelley, Landor and their successors.

In religion few of the English poets who settled in Florence were Anglicans or Catholics. Milton, a member of the Puritan wing of the Church of England at the time of his visit, later worked out a theology of his own that differed from that of all the churches. Gray and Walpole conformed to the Established Church but were probably deists, and Robert Lytton, another nominal Anglican, seems to have been an agnostic. Robert and Elizabeth Browning were both Congregationalists. Frederick Tennyson rejected orthodoxy and developed a system of belief that combined Swedenborgianism, British Israelitism, spiritualism, freemasonry, millennarianism and astrology. For the rest, neither Merry, Shelley, Landor, Hunt, Lee-Hamilton nor Lawrence was a Christian. It would be a mistake, however, to draw too clear a dividing line between Dissenters and free thinkers; rather we are conscious of two traditions, one deriving from Puritanism, the other from the Enlightenment, between which a dialectical relationship existed. Milton's Puritanism – anti-Trinitarian, materialist, mortalist and antinomian – contained a strong rationalist element. Shelley's master, William Godwin, was a former Calvinist minister turned atheist, and his *Political Justice* reads like an exceptionally long Nonconformist sermon. Browning in early life was influenced both by Shelley's *Queen Mab* and by the works of Voltaire and other *philosophes* that he found in his father's library; to please his mother he repudiated his youthful atheism, and for the rest of his life he seems to have attempted in his poems to bully both his readers and himself into orthodoxy. Brought up as a Congregationalist, Lawrence 'got over the Christian dogma' by the time he was sixteen, yet he remained grateful for his upbringing among 'descendants of the Oliver Cromwell Independents'.[2]

Another characteristic common among the Anglo-Florentine poets is anticlericalism. Chaucer, good Catholic though he was, ridiculed ecclesiastical abuses so effectively in *The Canterbury Tales* that John Foxe could plausibly claim him as a secret follower of Wyclif. Distrust of the clergy, whether Catholic, Laudian or Presbyterian, is a thread that runs right through Milton's work, from 'In Quintum Novembris' and 'Lycidas' to *Of True Religion*. Walpole saw the Churches and monarchy as the sources of

323

most of the world's evils. There is a strong element of anticlerical satire in such poems of Gray's as 'Hymn to Ignorance', 'Inscription on a Portrait' and 'The Candidate'. To Shelley the Anglican clergy were 'the priests of the evil faith'.[3] The Risorgimento, so vigorously supported by English poets, in one of its aspects was an anti-papal and anticlerical movement, as a glance at Theodosia Trollope's *Socials Aspects of the Italian Revolution* will make obvious. Browning attacked the Catholic clergy in 'The Confessional', 'The Bishop Orders his Tomb' and 'Bishop Blougram's Apology', as Lee-Hamilton did in 'The Mandolin' and 'The Fiddle and the Slipper'. Even Acton, who as a Catholic and a conservative seems the odd man out in this company, unsparingly depicts in *The Last Medici* the evil consequences of clerical influence on the bigoted and priest-ridden Grand Duke Cosimo III. Perhaps it is true that a major poet – a Dante, a Milton, a Shelley, a Lawrence – is by nature a rebel and anticlerical, aware that he speaks with a higher authority than that of any Church or State.

It may seem paradoxical that so Catholic a city as Florence, with its scores of churches and its treasures of religious art, a city that produced the greatest of Catholic poets and such saintly figures as Sant' Antonino and Fra Angelico, should attract English Dissenters, anticlericals and unbelievers. Florentine Catholicism, however, has seldom been blind or unquestioning. The most devout Catholics, from Dante to Savonarola, have often been the fiercest in their condemnation of unworthy priests and Popes. The Guelf city twice waged war upon the Pope, in 1375–8 and again in 1478–80, in defiance of a papal interdict. When the Archbishop of Pisa was actively involved in the Pazzi conspiracy to murder Lorenzo and Giuliano de' Medici in the cathedral, the Florentines had no compunction about hanging him in all his vestments from a window of the Palazzo Vecchio. There has always been a strong element of scepticism in the Florentine temperament. When in 1235 the Dominican miracle-worker Fra Giovanni da Vicenza came to Florence the citizens refused to admit him, declaring that 'He'll only want to bring some more dead to life, and we've got enough people here already.'[4] In the first six tales of the *Decamerone* Boccaccio mocks at bogus saints, satirizes the corruption of the papal court and the hypocrisy of monks and friars and suggests that it is impossible to prove that Christianity is more true than Judaism or Islam. Throughout its history Florence has had its heretics and martyrs: Patarenes in the twelfth and thirteenth centuries, Fraticelli in the fourteenth, Savonarola in 1498, Galileo in 1633, Crudeli in 1739, the Madiai in 1852. It was among liberal-minded Catholics, sceptics and anticlericals – Dati, Cocchi, Pignotti, Niccolini, Orioli – that Milton, Gray and Walpole, Merry and his circle, Theodosia Trollope and Lawrence found their Florentine friends.

Many of the English poets who came to Florence were seeking an alternative society to the England that they had left behind. Some, such as Merry, saw in Italy a land of sexual freedom. Even Browning, normally so Victorian in his moral attitudes, deals sympathetically with adultery in *Men and Women*, and his friends Landor, Lytton and Isa Blagden write at times with an uninhibited sensuousness rare in Victorian verse. In Florence Lawrence enjoyed the freedom to publish *Lady Chatterley's Lover*, which he would have been denied in England. It was not only poets and novelists who took advantage of Italian tolerance; Merry's friends Lord and Lady Cowper were as unrestrained in their behaviour as he was. Others were able to indulge in practices then officially taboo in England. Florence was notorious as the home of an English homosexual colony in Horace Mann's day and again in the 1920s, when Douglas, Turner, Firbank, Scott Moncrieff and Acton were living there. According to Acton, at that time 'every other member of the foreign colony had had a purple past. Though the purple had faded, there was a piquancy in knowing that the suave Lord X had had to flee from the London police because he was "a Greek born out of due time".'[5]

In their search for an alternative society, some looked back into the city's past. Parsons, Theodosia Trollope, Isa Blagden, Wilde and Mary Robinson anticipated Lawrence in their enthusiasm for the Etruscans and their culture. Shelley and Browning found their ideal society in the medieval Florentine Republic, before it was betrayed by 'those flattered traiters and polished tyrants, the Medici' or, in Browning's phrase, 'Cosimo and his accursed son'. To Acton the Renaissance was the golden age of Florence, and the Medici, who 'preserved Florence as an oasis of culture amid the storm and strife of outer barbarism', and especially Lorenzo de' Medici, were the heroes of the story. In his essay on the history of Florence the three centuries of Medici rule occupy 33 of the 49 pages. But whatever the age of Florentine history from which they drew their inspiration, nineteenth-century English poets used it as a yardstick by which they measured English society and found it wanting. To them Italy was 'a country whose beauty, openness to life, and struggle for national liberty can be used to criticise the stiff conventionality, laissez-faire indifference, and industrial squalor of the country which had used to feel so superior'.[6]

The English poets have left their mark on Florence. There are plaques on Casa Guidi, the Villino Trollope and the house in the Via della Chiesa where Landor threw so many dinners out of the window. The Viale Milton, honouring the poet of freedom, runs east of the Fortezza da Basso, symbol of Medici tyranny. There is a Via Shelley in the Cascine, where the poet meditated the 'Ode to the West Wind'. The Villa La Pietra appears on Italian maps of Florence as the Villa Acton. At Vallombrosa a monument recalls that Milton, 'Studious of our classics, devoted to our civilization, in love with these trees and this sky',[7] stayed there in 1638, and visitors to the nearby skiing resort of Saltino can put up at the Albergo Milton. If so inclined, we can seek out the graves of Elizabeth Barrett Browning, Clough, Landor, Garrow, Theodosia Trollope and Isa Blagden in the old Protestant cemetery, and Eugene Lee-Hamilton's in the new one on the other side of the city.

In Florence it is not difficult for imagination to summon up the souls of poets dead and gone: Chaucer entering the Palazzo Vecchio for diplomatic negotiations; Milton conversing with Galileo in the garden of Il Gioiello; Gray and Walpole watching the Arno in flood from the windows of the Casa Ambrogi; Merry stealing out into the dusk for an assignation with Lady Cowper; Shelley striding through the Cascine in the rain; the octogenarian Landor tottering down the long road from the Villa Gherardesca; Elizabeth Barrett Browning listening to Pulcinella's squeaky voice through the open windows of Casa Guidi; Browning discovering his old yellow book on a stall in the Piazza San Lorenzo; Lytton talking spiritualism with Mrs Browning and Frederick Tennyson on the terrace of his villa at Bellosguardo; the frail Lawrence and his sturdy German *hausfrau* doing their weekly shopping in the markets. Let Henry James, the friend of Isa Blagden and Eugene Lee-Hamilton, have the last word:

> Strange and special the effect, in Italy, of the empty places (and there are many) that we stand and wonder in to-day for the sake of the vanished, the English poets; the irresistible reconstruction, to the all but baffled vision, of irrecoverable presences and aspects, the conscious, shining, mocking void, sad somehow with excess of serenity.[8]

Notes

1 Geoffrey Chaucer

1 David Wallace, *Chaucer and the Early Writings of Boccaccio* (Brewer, Woodbridge, 1985), Ch. 6.

2 Gene Brucker, *Renaissance Florence* (John Wiley, New York, 1969), p. 29.

3 Population statistics from David Herlihy and Christiane Klapisch-Zuber, *Tuscans and their Families* (Yale University Press, New Haven, 1985). Other scholars estimate the population of Florence in the 1340s at between 80,000 and 100,000, and the number of plague deaths at 50–60,000.

4 'The Prologue of the Clerk's Tale', 31. Quotations are from *The Complete Poetry and Prose of Geoffrey Chaucer*, ed. John H. Fisher (Holt, Rinehart & Winston, New York, 1977).

5 See James I. Wimsatt, *Chaucer and the Poems of 'Ch'* (D. S. Brewer, Cambridge, 1982).

6 *The Complaint of Venus*, 80; W. H. Auden, *Collected Poems* (Faber, London, 1976), p. 89.

7 'The Wife of Bath's Tale' 1125; 'The Monk's Tale' 2460; 'The Prologue of the Second Nun's Tale' 35–56.

8 *Paradiso* XXXIII.13–15; *Troylus and Criseyde* III.1262–3.

9 *Inferno* XXXIV.46–8; 'The Prologue of the Summoner's Tale' 1688.

10 *Inferno* XXXIII.49; 'The Monk's Tale' 2429–30.

11 Wallace, op. cit., p. 1; *Paradiso* XXII.133–8; *Troylus and Criseyde* V.1835–41; *Paradiso* XIV.28–30; *Troylus and Criseyde* V.1863–5.

12 Wallace, op. cit., p. 152; Boccaccio, *Opere in Versi*, ed. Pier Giorgio Ricci (Riccardo Ricciardi, Milan, 1965), p. 172; Horace, *Satires* I.ii.1.

13 'The Epilogue to the Parson's Tale' 1086.

14 J. A. W. Bennett in *Chaucer and the Italian Trecento*, ed. Piero Boitani (Cambridge University Press, 1983), p. 107.

2 John Milton

1 Logan Pearsall Smith, *Life and Letters of Sir Henry Wotton* (Oxford University Press, 1907), Vol. I, p. 281.

2 *Complete Prose Works of John Milton* (*CPW*), ed. Don M. Wolfe (Yale University Press, New Haven, 1953–82), Vol. I, p. 320.

3 Giuseppe Villaroel and Guido Davico Bonino, introduction to *La Divina Commedia* (Arnoldo Mondadori, Milan, 1991), p. xxxvii (trans. Charles Hobday); *CPW*, Vol. I, pp. 559, 890; *Acts and Monuments of John Foxe*, ed. Jeremiah Pratt (Religious Tract Society, London, 1877), Vol. II, pp. 707–8.

4 *CPW*, Vol. I, p. 327.

5 Sir John Reresby, *Memoirs and Travels*, ed. A. Ivatt (Kegan Paul, Trench, Trubner

& Co., London, 1904), p. 77.

6 *The Diary of John Evelyn*, ed. E. S. de Beer (Oxford University Press, 1955), Vol. II, p. 386; *CPW*, Vol. II, pp. 543–4.

7 Reresby, op. cit., p. 80.

8 Ibid., p. 75.

9 *CPW*, Vol. IV, pp. 615–16; *The Early Lives of Milton*, ed. Helen Darbishire (Constable, London, 1932), p. 210.

10 David Masson, *Life of Milton*, Vol. I (Macmillan, London, 2nd edn, 1881), p. 782; *CPW*, Vol. I, p. 809.

11 Lacy Collison-Morley, *Italy after the Renaissance* (Routledge, London, 1930), p. 298.

12 *CPW*, Vol. IV, p. 616; 'The Municipal Gallery Re-visited' in W. B. Yeats, *The Poems* (Everyman, London, 1992), p. 368.

13 John Arthos, *Milton and the Italian Cities* (Bowes & Bowes, London, 1968), p. 6; Masson, op. cit., Vol. I, p. 773; Evelyn, ed. cit., Vol. II, p. 415.

14 *Early Lives*, pp. 5, 6.

15 Ibid., pp. 6, 32, 204, 59; *The Poetical Works of John Milton*, ed. Helen Darbishire (Oxford University Press, 1952), Vol. II, p. 155.

16 *Dizionario Biografico degli Italiani*, ed. Alberto M. Ghisalberti (Istituto della Enciclopedia Italiana, Rome, 1960–), Vol. 27, p. 479; Arthos, op. cit., p. 11.

17 Eric W. Cochrane (ed.), *The Late Italian Renaissance 1525–1630* (Macmillan, London, 1970), pp. 43, 73, 131; *CPW*, Vol. II, p. 537–8.

18 *CPW*, Vol. II, p. 538.

19 Giorgio de Santillana, *The Crime of Galileo* (Heinemann, London, 1958), pp. 145–6.

20 *Paradise Lost* (*PL*) I.302–4. Quotations are from *The Poetical Works of John Milton*, Vol. I, ed. Darbishire.

21 *CPW*, Vol. II, p. 763.

22 Ibid., pp. 763–5.

23 Ibid., pp. 766, 772–3, 774–5.

24 Ibid., Vol. V, p. 558.

25 Ibid., Vol. I, pp. 813–14; *PL* III.588–90, 641–2; V.250, 261–3, 282–5; IV.266–71; *Purgatorio* XXVIII.49–51, 139–44.

26 *PL* I.287–91.

27 *CPW*, Vol. I, pp. 559–60.

28 *PL* III.418–20.

29 Ibid., 448–501 455–6, 474–5.

30 Ibid., III.573–5, 588–90; IV.591–5.

31 *PL* V.261–3, 419–20; VII.366; Galileo Galilei, *Dialogue Concerning the Two Chief World Systems*, trans. Stillman Drake (University of California Press, Berkeley, 1967), p. 70.

32 *PL* VIII.15–38, 66–178; X.668–78.

33 Galileo, op. cit., pp. 100–1; *PL* III.565–71; VII.620–22; VIII.140–58; Kvester
    Svendsen, *Milton and Science* (Harvard University Press, Cambridge, Mass.,
    1956), p. 237.

34 *CPW*, Vol. IV, p. 615; Vol. I, pp. 809–10, 809, Vol. II, p. **560**; 'To Mr Cyriack
    Skinner upon his Blindness'.

35 Masson, op. cit., Vol. I, p. 783.

3 Thomas Gray

1 *The Correspondence of Thomas Gray*, ed. Paget Toynbee and Leonard Whibley
   (Oxford University Press, 1935), Vol. I, p. 61.

2 *Purgatorio* VII.5–6; *Horace Walpole's Correspondence*, The Yale Edition (Oxford
   University Press, 1939–83), Vol. 29, ed. W. S. Lewis, Grover Cronin and
   Charles H. Bennett, p. 256.

3 *Gray's Correspondence*, Vol. I, pp. 125, 131–4.

4 *Walpole's Correspondence*, Vol. 17, ed. W. S. Lewis, Warren Hunting Smith and
   George L. Lam, p. 146; Vol. 37, ed. W. S Lewis, Lars E. Troide, Erwine M.
   Martz and Robert A. Smith, p. 68.

5 *Gray's Correspondence*, Vol. I, p. 136.

6 *Walpole's Correspondence*, Vol. 13, ed. W. S. Lewis, George L. Lam and Charles
   H. Bennett, p. 199.

7 Ibid., p. 200.

8 *Gray's Correspondence*, Vol. I, p. 144; *Walpole's Correspondence*, Vol. 13, p. 204.

9 *Walpole's Correspondence*, Vol. 37, p. 66.

10 *Gray's Correspondence*, Vol. I, p. 167; *Walpole's Correspondence*, Vol. 37, p. 78.

11 *Walpole's Correspondence*, Vol. 17, p. 107.

12 Ibid., p. 169.

13 Eric W. Cochrane, *Florence in the Forgotten Centuries 1527–1800* (University of
    Chicago Press, 1973), p. 378.

14 *A Collection of Poems by Several Hands* (R. Dodsley, London, 1748), Vol. II, pp.
    310, 320; *Gray's Correspondence*, Vol. I, p. 170.

15 Matthew Arnold, *Essays in Criticism, Second Series* (Macmillan, London, 1889),
    pp. 70, 91.

16 *Gray's Correspondence*, Vol. I, p. 178.

17 *Walpole's Correspondence*, Vol. 13, p. 237; *Gray's Correspondence*, Vol. I, p. 180.

18 *Gray's Correspondence*, Vol. I, p. 182.

19 *Walpole's Correspondence*, Vol. 28, ed. W. S. Lewis, Grover Cronin and Charles H.
    Bennett, p. 114; Vol. 13, p. 219; Vol. 37, p. 96.

20 Ibid., Vol. 28, p. 68.

21 Ibid., Vol. 17, pp. 31, 32.

22 Ibid., p. 50.

4 Robert Merry

1 H. E. Napier, *Florentine History* (Edward Moxon, London, 1847), Vol. VI, p. 88; Hester Lynch Piozzi, *Observations and Reflections Made in the Course of a Journey through France, Italy, and Germany*, ed. Herbert Barrows (University of Michigan Press, Ann Arbor, 1967), p. 153.

2 Arthur Young, *Travels in France and Italy* (J. M. Dent, London, 1915), pp. 272–3; Piozzi, op. cit., p. 137; Thomas Watkins, *Travels through Swisserland, Italy, Sicily [&c.]* (T. Cadell, London, 1792), p. 303; Tobias Smollett, *Travels through France and Italy*, ed. Frank Felsenstein (Oxford University Press, 1979), pp. 227–8.

3 Watkins, op. cit., pp. 287–8, 295; Kenneth Clark, *The Nude* (Penguin Books, Harmondsworth, 1960), pp. 79–80; Smollett, op. cit., p. 236.

4 Charles Dupaty, *Lettres sur l'Italie, en 1785* (L. Duprat-Duverger, Paris, 1812), p. 130; Piozzi, op. cit., p. 157.

5 H. C. B. Rogers, *Wellington's Army* (Ian Allan, London, 1979), p. 45. The muster rolls are now in the Public Record Office, Kew (WO 12, 3).

6 D. E. Baker, *Biographia Dramatica* (Longman, Hurst, Rees, Orme & Brown, London, 1812), Vol. II, p. 507.

7 *The Life and Times of Frederick Reynolds, written by himself* (Henry Colburn, London, 1826), Vol. II, p. 186.

8 Napier, op. cit., Vol. VI, p. 253 (trans. Charles Hobday).

9 Dupaty, op. cit., p. 162; *Autobiography, Letters and Literary Remains of Mrs Piozzi (Thrale)*, ed. A. Hayward (Longman, Green, Longman & Roberts, London, 1861), Vol. II, p. 35.

10 John Moore, *A View of Society and Manners in Italy* (W. Strahan and T. Cadell, London, 1781), Vol. II, p. 351; Reynolds, op. cit., Vol. II, p. 185.

11 *The Florence Miscellany* (G. Cam, Florence, 1785), p. 38. The poem is reprinted in *The New Oxford Book of Romantic Period Verse*, ed. Jerome J. McGann (Oxford University Press, 1993), p. 5.

12 *Horace Walpole's Correspondence*, The Yale Edition (Oxford University Press, 1939–83), Vol. 25, ed. W. S. Lewis, Warren Hunting Smith and George L. Lam, p. 540.

13 *Thraliana. The Diary of Mrs Hester Lynch Thrale (Later Mrs Piozzi) 1776–1809*, ed. Katharine C. Balderstone (Oxford University Press, 1942), p. 692; James L. Clifford, *Hester Lynch Piozzi (Mrs Thrale)* (Oxford University Press, 1952), pp. 307, 349.

14 *The Piozzi Letters*, ed. Edward A. and Lilian D. Bloom (University of Delaware Press, Newark, 1989), pp. 145, 151, 160–1.

15 *Thraliana*, p. 654; *The Piozzi Letters*, pp. 157, 169.

16 *The Piozzi Letters*, p. 161; *The Florence Miscellany*, p. 5.

17 *The Florence Miscellany*, pp. 9, 27.

18 Young, op. cit., pp. 273, 284; Watkins, op. cit., p. 299; *Thraliana*, p. 654.

19 *The Florence Miscellany*, pp. 212–13.

20 Ibid., p. 138; Coleridge, *Poetical Works*, ed. E. H. Coleridge (Oxford University Press, 1974), p. 224. 'Sir Roland' is reprinted in *The New Oxford Book of Eighteenth Century Verse*, ed. Roger Lonsdale (Oxford University Press, 1987), p. 720.

21 *The Florence Miscellany*, p. 183.

22 *Novelle Letterarie* (Florence, 1785), Vol. 16, cols. 673–4; *The Piozzi Letters*, p. 152.

23 *Journals and Correspondence of Thomas Sedgewick Whalley, D.D.*, ed. H. Wickham (Richard Bentley, London, 1863), Vol. I, p. 20; Merry, *Paulina* (J. Robson and W. Clarke, London, 1787), pp. 4–5.

24 Reynolds, op. cit., p. 186.

25 *Thraliana*, pp. 714, 740–1.

26 Ibid., pp. 848–9.

27 Ibid., pp. 993–4.

5 Percy Bysshe Shelley

1 *The Letters of Percy Bysshe Shelley*, ed. Frederick L. Jones (Oxford University Press, 1964), Vol. II, p. 33; 'Ode to Naples' 116–17.

2 Shelley, *Letters*, Vol. II, p. 184.

3 Ibid., p. 97; *The Letters of Mary W. Shelley*, ed. Frederick L. Jones (University of Oklahoma Press, Norman, 1944), Vol. I, p. 74.

4 Shelley, *Letters*, Vol. II, p. 117.

5 Helen Rossetti Angeli, *Shelley and his Friends in Italy* (Methuen, London, 1911), p. 90; Mary Shelley, *Letters*, Vol. I, p. 92; Shelley, *Letters*, Vol. II, pp. 126, 158.

6 Shelley, *Letters*, Vol. II, pp. 8, 335; *Shelley's Prose*, ed. David Lee Clark (Fourth Estate, London, 1988), pp. 289–90; Oscar Kuhns, *Dante and the English Poets from Chaucer to Tennyson* (Henry Holt, New York, 1904), pp. 196–7.

7 Joseph Forsyth, *Remarks on Antiquities, Arts, and Letters, during an Excursion in Italy, in the Years 1802 and 1803* (John Murray, London, 1835), pp. 365–6.

8 Shelley, *Letters*, Vol. II, p. 177.

9 Lady Morgan, *Italy* (Henry Colburn, London, 1821), Vol. II, p. 274n; Shelley, *Letters*, Vol. II, p. 332.

10 Mary Shelley, *Letters*, Vol. I, p. 89; Forsyth, op. cit., p. 375.

11 Shelley, *Letters*, Vol. II, p. 126; Lady Morgan, op. cit., Vol. II, pp. 174–5; *Shelley's Prose*, pp. 346–8.

12 Shelley, *Letters*, Vol. II, pp. 88, 322, 50, 112; *Shelley's Prose*, p. 350.

13 Giorgio Vasari, *Lives of the Artists: A Selection Translated by George Bull* [Vol. I] (Penguin Books, Harmondsworth, 1971), p. 260; Lady Morgan, op. cit., Vol. II, p. 177.

14 James E. Barcus (ed.), *Shelley: The Critical Heritage* (Routledge & Kegan Paul, London, 1975), p. 135; Thomas Medwin, *The Life of Percy Bysshe Shelley*, ed. H.

Buxton Forman (Oxford University Press, 1913), pp. 225–6.

15 Shelley, *Letters*, Vol. II, pp. 126, 128, 163.

16 Barcus, op. cit., p. 103; Shelley, *Letters*, Vol. II, p. 66.

17 Shelley, *Letters*, pp. 150, 109, 125.

18 Neville Rogers, *Shelley at Work* (Oxford University Press, 1967), p. 222; *The Revolt of Islam* IX.3649–89.

19 Shelley, *Letters*, Vol. II, p. 74; Rogers, op. cit., pp. 223–4.

20 Shelley, *Letters*, Vol. II, pp. 132, 150, 157.

21 Shelley, *Hellas* 66.

22 *Shelley's Prose*, p. 349; Shelley, *Letters*, Vol. II, p. 61.

23 *Shelley's Prose*, p. 240; Luke 12:49, *The Journals of Mary Shelley*, ed. Paula R. Feldman and Deana Scott-Kilvert (Oxford University Press, 1987), p. 302; Rogers, op. cit., p. 228.

24 Rogers, op. cit., pp. 217, 219; Wordsworth, 'Ode, 1815' 106–9; Byron, *Don Juan* VIII.70–71; Shelley, *Letters*, Vol. II, p. 135.

25 Shelley, *Letters*, Vol. II, p. 164; *Peter Bell the Third* 83–4, 478–9, 636–44, 56–65, 328–30, 147; 'Marenghi' 23–39; 'Ode to Liberty' 61–90.

26 Shelley, *Letters*, Vol. II, p. 191.

27 Ibid., p. 135.

28 Ibid., pp. 148, 164.

29 *Shelley's Prose*, p. 231.

30 Ibid., pp. 256, 234, 255, 248–9, 252–4; Shelley, *Letters*, Vol. II, p. 153.

31 Shelley, *Letters*, Vol. II, p. 167.

32 Ibid., p. 135; Mary Shelley, *Letters*, Vol. I, p. 84.

33 Mary Shelley, *Letters*, Vol. I, p. 88; Angeli, op. cit., pp. 97–8, 101. Sophia Stacey's diary has disappeared, but Mrs Angeli, who had seen it, quotes several passages from it.

34 Mary Shelley, *Letters*, Vol. I, p. 88.

35 Shelley, *Letters*, Vol. II, pp. 167, 165; *Prometheus Unbound* IV.372–5.

36 Mary Shelley, *Letters*, Vol. I, p. 87.

37 Shelley, *Letters*, Vol. II, p. 164.

38 Medwin, op. cit., p. 244.

6 Walter Savage Landor

1 Landor, *Complete Works* (*CW*) (Chapman & Hall, London), Vol. IX, ed. T. Earle Welby (1928), p. 128.

2 John Forster, *Walter Savage Landor* (Chapman & Hall, London, 1869), Vol. I, p. 197.

3 Ibid., p. 54. A servitor was a poor undergraduate who received a grant from college funds in return for performing certain menial services.

4 Ibid., pp. 172–3; Landor, *Gebir* VI.193.

5 Forster, op. cit., Vol. I, p. 323.

6 Ibid., p. 425.

7 R. H. Super, *Walter Savage Landor* (New York University Press, 1954), p. 157.

8 Ibid., p. 158; Giuliana Artom Treves, *The Golden Ring: The Anglo-Florentines 1847–1862* (Longmans, Green & Co., London, 1956), pp. 44–5; Forster, op. cit., Vol. II, pp. 218–19.

9 Super, op. cit., p. 156.

10 *CW*, Vol. XVI, ed. Stephen Wheeler (1936), p. 4.

11 *CW*, Vol. III, ed. T. Earle Welby (1927), pp. 131, 136, 114, 152, 151, 160, 133, 107, 99.

12 Ibid., pp. 196, 195, 216–17.

13 Forster, op. cit., Vol. II, p. 231.

14 Ibid., pp. 225–6, 231.

15 Super, op. cit., p. 243.

16 Treves, op. cit., p. 46.

17 *CW*, Vol. XVI, p. 9.

18 Lady Blessington, *The Idler in Italy* (Henry Colburn, London, 1839), Vol. II, pp. 506–8; R. W. Emerson, *English Traits* (George Routledge & Sons, London, 1883), pp. 10–11; Dickens, *Bleak House*, Ch. IX.

19 Forster, op. cit., Vol. II, p. 200; Leigh Hunt, *Lord Byron and Some of his Contemporaries* (A. & W. Galignani, Paris, 1828), Vol. III, p. 259.

20 Hunt, op. cit., Vol. III, p. 259; Malcolm Elwin, *Savage Landor* (Macmillan, London, 1941), p. 268; Super, op. cit., p. 258.

21 Super, op. cit., p. 278; *CW*, Vol. IV, ed. T. Earle Welby (1927), pp. 245–6.

22 Sir Austen Henry Layard, *Autobiography and Letters* (John Murray, London, 1903), pp. 24–5; Super, op. cit., p. 561.

23 Forster, op. cit., Vol. II, pp. 308–9.

24 Super, op. cit., p. 254; Forster, op. cit., Vol. II, p. 310.

25 *CW*, Vol. XVI, p. 19.

26 *CW*, Vol. III, p. 56; Vol. II, pp. 301–2.

27 *CW*, Vol. III, pp. 258–9.

28 Forster, op. cit., Vol. II, p. 239; *CW*, Vol. III, p. 15; Super, op. cit., p. 378.

29 *CW*, Vol. III, pp. 281–3, 279, 303.

30 Super, op. cit., p. 392.

31 Ibid., p. 466.

32 *CW*, Vol. XVI, p. 42.

33 Ibid., pp. 467, 463–4, 469; *King Lear* II.iv.249, I.i.295–8, IV.vii.60–1; Forster, op. cit., Vol. II, pp. 561–2.

34 Forster, op. cit., Vol. II, p. 425; Betty Miller, *Robert Browning: A Portrait* (John Murray, London, 1972), p. 210.

35 Forster, op. cit., Vol. II, pp. 565, 570.

36 Super, op. cit., pp. 605–6; *CW*, Vol. XVI, p. 45.

37 H. C. Minchin, *Walter Savage Landor: Last Days, Letters and Conversations*

(Methuen, London, 1934), p. 97; Forster, op. cit., Vol. I, p. 174n.

38 Minchin, op. cit., p. 171.

39 Super, op. cit., pp. 504, 612.

40 Minchin, op. cit., p. 172.

7 Robert Browning and Elizabeth Barrett Browning

1 Henry James, *William Wetmore Story and his Friends* (Blackwood, Edinburgh, 1903), Vol. I, p. 172; John Dryden, *Absalom and Achitophel* 156–7.

2 *The Letters of Elizabeth Barrett Browning*, ed. Frederick G. Kenyon (Smith, Elder & Co., London, 1897), Vol. I, pp. 326, 331; Vol. II, p. 258.

3 Ibid., Vol. I, pp. 331, 336, 343.

4 Ibid., p. 346.

5 Wordsworth, *The Prelude* VI.339–41.

6 Elizabeth Barrett Browning, *Casa Guidi Windows* I.1–3, 742–3, 762–3, 867–8, 1125–8, 1155–6, 1180–4, 1201–2.

7 *Letters*, ed. Kenyon, Vol. I, p. 357.

8 Elizabeth Barrett Browning, *Letters to her Sister, 1846–1859*, ed. Leonard Huxley (John Murray, London, 1929), p. 80.

9 *Letters*, ed. Kenyon, Vol. I, pp. 368, 374.

10 *Letters*, ed. Huxley, p. 87.

11 Ibid.

12 *Letters*, ed. Kenyon, Vol. I, pp. 384, 448; *Casa Guidi Windows* I.332; Lady Morgan, *Italy* (Henry Colburn, London, 1821), Vol. II. p. 102.

13 *Letters*, ed. Kenyon, Vol. I, p. 406.

14 Ibid., Vol. I, pp. 383, 386, 388, 400–1, 405–6; Vol. II, p. 98; *Letters*, ed. Huxley, p. 105.

15 *Casa Guidi Windows* II.65, 124–31, 145–7, 153–6, 299–306, 743.

16 Robert Browning, *Men and Women*, 'Old Pictures in Florence' 254, 'The Statue and the Bust' 38–9.

17 Ibid., 'Two in the Campagna' 36–40.

18 *Letters*, ed. Kenyon, Vol. I, p. 389; Vol. II, p. 42; *Letters*, ed. Huxley, pp. 84, 149, 310; Betty Miller, *Robert Browning: A Portrait* (John Murray, London, 1972), p. 165.

19 Edward C. McAleer, *The Brownings of Casa Guidi* (The Browning Institute, Inc., New York, 1987), p. 49; *Letters*, ed. Kenyon, Vol. II, pp. 104, 226; *Letters*, ed. Huxley, pp. 219–20.

20 *Letters*, ed. Kenyon, Vol. I, p. 204; *Letters*, ed. Huxley, p. 269.

21 Elizabeth Barrett Browning, *Aurora Leigh* VII.928–9, 901–4, 934–7, 1065–71, 1078–84, 1217–19, 1222–6, 1182–6.

22 *Letters*, ed. Huxley, p. 314.

23 *Letters*, ed. Kenyon, Vol. II, pp. 324, 328.

24 Elizabeth Barrett Browning, *Poems before Congress*, 'An August Voice' 37–45.

25 Elizabeth Barrett Browning, *Last Poems*, 'King Victor Emanuel Entering Florence, April 1860' 49–53.

26 Ibid., 'Bianca among the Nightingales' 64–72.

27 *Letters*, ed. Kenyon, Vol. II, pp. 388, 385; *Prince Hohenstiel-Schwangau* 14.

28 Robert Browning, *The Ring and the Book* I.472–87.

29 *Letters*, ed. Kenyon, Vol. II, p. 449; James, op. cit., Vol. II, p. 62.

30 *Letters*, ed. Kenyon, Vol. II, p. 451; James, op. cit., Vol. II, p. 64.

31 James, op. cit., Vol. II, p. 66.

32 Ibid., pp. 66, 279.

33 *The Ring and the Book* XI.3–13; XII.873–4.

34 James, op. cit., Vol. II, p. 284.

8 The Brownings' Circle

1 Thomas Adolphus Trollope, *What I Remember* (Richard Bentley, London, 1887), Vol. II, p. 150.

2 Ibid., Vol. II, pp. 155–6.

3 *The Gentleman's Magazine*, New Series, Vol. IV (1858), p. 112.

4 Theodosia Trollope's epitaph states that when she died in 1865 she was 'nonum agens lustrum', 'in her ninth lustrum', a lustrum being a period of five years (*Notes and Queries*, Tenth Series, Vol. X, 1908, p. 24). This suggests that she was born between 1820 and 1825. *The Dictionary of National Biography* gives 1825 as her birth-date, but this is improbably late.

5 T. A. Trollope, op. cit., Vol. II, p. 256.

6 Ibid., Vol. II, p. 261.

7 Ibid., Vol. II, pp. 156–8.

8 H. C. Minchin, *Walter Savage Landor: Last Days, Letters and Conversations* (Methuen, London, 1934), pp. 18–19; Giovanni Battista Niccolini, *Arnold of Brescia*, trans. Theodosia Garrow (Longman, Brown, Green & Longman, London, 1846), p. vii; *The Cornhill Magazine*, Vol. X (1864), p. 683; T. A. Trollope, op. cit., Vol. II, p. 361.

9 T. A. Trollope, op. cit., Vol. II, p. 153.

10 *The Letters of Elizabeth Barrett Browning*, ed. Frederick G. Kenyon (Smith, Elder & Co., London, 1897), Vol. I, pp. 17, 476; Vol. II, pp. 99, 177–8.

11 Theodosia Trollope, *Social Aspects of the Italian Revolution* (Chapman & Hall, London, 1861), p. 4.

12 Ibid., pp. 83–4.

13 Milton, 'Epitaphium Damonis', 128; George Dennis, *The Cities and Cemeteries of Etruria* (J. M. Dent, London, 1907), Vol. I, p. 70.

14 Theodosia Trollope, op. cit., pp. 84, 127–9, 286.

15 Ibid., p. 117; T. A. Trollope, op. cit., Vol. II, p. 371.

16 *Letters*, ed. Kenyon, Vol. II, pp. 97, 99, 125; Aurelia Brooks Harlan, *Owen Meredith: A Critical Biography of Robert, First Earl of Lytton* (Columbia University

Press, New York, 1946), p. 205.

17 Sir Guy Fleetwood Wilson, *Letters to Somebody* (Cassell, London, 1922), p. 9; Walberga, Lady Paget, *The Linings of Life* (Hurst & Blackett, London, 1928), Vol. II, p. 125; Harlan, op. cit., p. 90.

18 *Letters*, ed. Kenyon, Vol. II, p. 126; Robert Lytton, *Clytemnestra ... and Other Poems* (Chapman & Hall, London, 1867), p. 115.

19 *Letters*, ed. Kenyon, Vol. II, p. 134: Ifor Evans, *English Poetry in the Later Nineteenth Century* (Methuen, London, 1966), p. 330.

20 *Letters from Owen Meredith to Robert and Elizabeth Barrett Browning*, ed. Aurelia Brooks Harlan and J. Lee Harlan (Baylor University Press, Waco, Texas, 1936), pp. 100–1.

21 Elizabeth Barrett Browning, *Letters to her Sister, 1846–1859*, ed. Leonard Huxley (John Murray, London, 1929), pp. 276–7.

22 Robert Lytton, *The Wanderer* (Chapman & Hall, London, 1858), pp. 5–7.

23 *Letters from Owen Meredith*, pp. 162–7.

24 Harlan, op. cit., pp. 157, 45.

25 *Dearest Isa: Robert Browning's Letters to Isabella Blagden*, ed. Edward C. McAleer (University of Texas Press, Austin, 1951), p. xxi.

26 T. A. Trollope, op. cit., Vol. II, p. 173; *Letters*, ed. Huxley, p. 196; *Letters from Owen Meredith*, p. 123.

27 *Poems by the late Isa Blagden* (Blackwood, Edinburgh, 1873), pp. 6–7.

28 Henry James, *William Wetmore Story and his Friends* (Blackwood, Edinburgh, 1903), Vol. II, pp. 94–5.

29 *Dearest Isa*, p. 332; Clyde de L. Ryals, *The Life of Robert Browning* (Blackwell, Oxford, 1993), p. 203.

30 *Poems by the late Isa Blagden*, p. 32.

9 Eugene Lee-Hamilton

1 Peter Gunn, *Vernon Lee: Violet Paget, 1856–1935* (Oxford University Press, 1964), pp. 14, 48.

2 Ibid., p. 20.

3 Ibid., p. 21.

4 Lee-Hamilton, *Mimma Bella* (Heinemann, London, 1909), p. vii; *Dramatic Sonnets, Poems, and Ballads: Selections from the Poems of Eugene Lee-Hamilton* (Walter Scott, London and Newcastle, 1903), p. xviii; Edith Wharton, *A Backward Glance* (D. Appleton-Century Co., New York, 1934), p. 131; Gunn, op. cit., p. 21; Lee-Hamilton, *Sonnets of the Wingless Hours* (Elliot Stock, London, 1894), p. 60.

5 *The Complete Notebooks of Henry James*, ed. Leon Edel and Lyall H. Powers (Oxford University Press, 1987), p. 33.

6 Lee-Hamilton, *The New Medusa and Other Poems* (Elliot Stock, London, 1882), pp. 110, 99.

7   'Com' avesse l'inferno a gran dispitto' (*Inferno* X.36).

8   William Cowper, *Table Talk* 655.

9   Gunn, op. cit., p. 113; Lee-Hamilton, *Poems and Transcripts* (Blackwood, Edinburgh, 1878), p. 106; A. C. Swinburne, *Poems and Ballads (First Series)* (Heinemann, London, 1917), 'To Victor Hugo' 1–3; *Sonnets of the Wingless Hours*, p. 78.

10 Lee-Hamilton, *Imaginary Sonnets* (Elliot Stock, London, 1888), p. vi.

11 Lee-Hamilton, *The Fountain of Youth* (Elliot Stock, London, 1891), pp. 64, 67, 65.

12 Mario Praz, *The Romantic Agony* (Oxford University Press, 1933), pp. 380–1.

13 Gunn, op. cit., p. 22.

14 *Mimma Bella*, p. xi; Wharton, op. cit., p. 132.

15 Lee-Hamilton, *The Inferno of Dante* (Grant Richards, London, 1898), pp. 194–5; Gilbert F. Cunningham, *The Divine Comedy in English: A Critical Bibliography 1782–1900* (Oliver & Boyd, Edinburgh, 1965), p. 195.

16 Lee-Hamilton, *The Lord of the Dark Red Star* (Walter Scott, London, 1903), pp. 36–8.

17 *Dramatic Sonnets*, pp. 29–33, 193.

18 *Mimma Bella*, p. xiii.

10 D. H. Lawrence 1919–1921

1   Lawrence, *The Lost Girl* (Martin Secker, London, 1927), Ch. XIV, pp. 321, 327.

2   Lawrence, *Movements in European History* (Oxford University Press, 1971), pp. 164, 162.

3   Maurice Magnus, *Memoirs of the Foreign Legion* (Martin Secker, London, 1935 edn), p. 11; Lawrence, *Aaron's Rod* (Martin Secker, London, 1922), Ch. XV, p. 220.

4   *The Letters of D. H. Lawrence*, The Cambridge Edition (Cambridge University Press), Vol. III, ed. James T. Boulton and Andrew Robertson (1984), pp. 419–20, 424; Magnus, op. cit., p. 13.

5   *Dictionary of National Biography 1951–60*, ed. E. T. Williams and Helen M. Palmer (Oxford University Press, 1971), p. 308.

6   *Aaron's Rod*, Ch. XVI, p. 321; Richard Aldington, *Pinorman: Personal Recollections of Norman Douglas, Pino Orioli and Charles Prentice* (Heinemann, London, 1954), p. 187.

7   Magnus, op. cit., pp. 13, 17, 14, 12; *The Lost Girl*, Ch. VI, pp. 99, 100, 103, 108.

8   *Aaron's Rod*, Ch. XVI, pp. 228, 230.

9   Lawrence, *Sketches of Etruscan Places and Other Italian Essays*, ed. Simonetta de Filippis (Cambridge University Press, 1992), pp. 188–9.

10 *Aaron's Rod*, Ch. XVII, pp. 246–7.

11 *Letters*, Vol. III, p. 422; *Aaron's Rod*, Ch. XV, p. 220; Ch. XVI, p. 226.

12 *Letters*, Vol. III, pp. 417, 427, 450.

13 Ibid., pp. 450.

14 Ibid., p. 535.

15 Ibid., pp. 602, 603, 608; Derek Britton, *Lady Chatterley: The Making of the Novel* (Unwin Hyman, London, 1988), pp. 82–3.

16 *Letters*, Vol. III, pp. 592, 594; Aldington, op. cit., pp. 27–8.

17 *Movements in European History*, pp. 315–16; *Letters* Vol. III, pp. 593, 569–70.

18 'Red-herring', *The Complete Poems of D. H. Lawrence*, ed. Vivian de Sola Pinto and Warren Roberts (Heinemann, London, 1972), p. 490.

19 Tom Marshall, *The Psychic Mariner: A Reading of the Poems of D. H. Lawrence* (Heinemann, London, 1970), p. 125.

20 *Complete Poems*, p. 327.

21 Lawrence, *Fantasia of the Unconscious* (Martin Secker, London, 1923 edn), p. 9.

22 *Etruscan Places*, p. 19; *The Adelphi*, Vol. I, No. 5, p. 370; Giuseppe Orioli, *Adventures of a Bookseller* (Chatto & Windus, London, 1938), p. 234.

23 *Letters*, Vol. III, pp. 649, 677; Vol. IV, ed. Warren Roberts, James T. Boulton and Elizabeth Mansfield (1987), p. 226.

24 Ibid., Vol. IV, pp. 81, 83; *Complete Poems*, p. 342.

25 *Letters*, Vol. IV, pp. 84–5.

26 Ibid., pp. 85, 87.

11 D. H. Lawrence 1926–1929

1 *The Letters of D. H. Lawrence*, The Cambridge Edition (Cambridge University Press), Vol. V, ed. James T. Boulton and Lindeth Vasey (1989), pp. 413, 427.

2 Gaetano Salvemini, *The Fascist Dictatorship in Italy* (Jonathan Cape, London, 1928), Vol. I, p. 177.

3 Lawrence, *Movements in European History* (Oxford University Press, 1971), p. 317; *Letters*, Vol. V, pp. 433, 496, 570; Vol. VI, ed. James T. Boulton and Margaret H. Boulton with Gerald M. Lacy (1991), p. 308.

4 *Letters*, Vol. V, p. 447.

5 Francis King, *Florence: A Literary Companion* (John Murray, London, 1991), p. 62; *Letters*, Vol. V, pp. 477–8, 447.

6 Lawrence, *Sketches of Etruscan Places and Other Italian Essays*, ed. Simonetta de Filippis (Cambridge University Press, 1992), p. 291.

7 *Letters*, Vol. V, pp. 459, 568, 585.

8 Ibid., pp. 486, 491.

9 Frieda Lawrence, *'Not I, But the Wind ... '* (Heinemann, London, 1935), pp. 177–8.

10 *Etruscan Places*, pp. 226–7.

11 Ibid., pp. 211–12.

12 *Letters*, Vol. V, pp. 609–10; Frieda Lawrence, op. cit., p. 176; Richard Aldington, *Portrait of a Genius, But ...* (Heinemann, London, 1950), p. 320.

Letters, Vol. V, pp. 473, 465.

13 Ibid., pp. 452, 536, 515, 592, 519–20.

14 Ibid., Vol. VI, pp. 308, 321, 267.

15 Ibid., Vol. V, p. 560.

16 Ibid., pp. 570, 574, 576, 600; Keith Sagar, 'Lawrence and the Wilkinsons',

17 *Review of English Literature*, Vol. 3, No. 4 (October 1962), p. 67.
    Letters, Vol. V, pp. 619, 629; Vol. VI, p. 62.

18 Ibid., Vol. VI, p. 638; Lawrence, *The First Lady Chatterley* (Heinemann, London,

19 1972), p. 42.
    The First Lady Chatterley, p. 25; Lawrence, *John Thomas and Lady Jane*

20 (Heinemann, London, 1979), pp. 46–7, 190.
    Lawrence, *Lady Chatterley's Lover* (Heinemann, London, 1987), pp. 208, 276;

21 *Phoenix II: Uncollected, Unpublished and Other Prose Works by D. H. Lawrence*, ed.
    Warren Roberts and Harry T. Moore (Heinemann, London, 1968), pp. 564,
    606.
    Frieda Lawrence, op. cit., p. 178; *Letters*, Vol. V, p. 616.

22 *John Thomas and Lady Jane*, p. 150.

23 *Letters*, Vol. V, p. 651; Vol. VI, pp. 28, 33.

24 *Phoenix: The Posthumous Papers of D. H. Lawrence*, ed. Edward D. McDonald

25 (Heinemann, London, 1961), pp. 109, 129.
    Richard Aldington, *Life for Life's Sake* (Cassell, London, 1968), p. 342.

26 *Letters*, Vol. VI, pp. 65, 67; Vol. V, p. 474.

27 Frieda Lawrence, op. cit., p. 182.

28 *Letters*, Vol. VI, p. 212.

29 Ibid., pp. 217, 223, 250.

30 *Lady Chatterley's Lover*, p. 53.

31 Britton, op. cit., p. 232; *Lady Chatterley's Lover*, p. 153.

32 *Letters*, Vol. VI, p. 326; *Lady Chatterley's Lover*, p. 28.

33 *Lady Chatterley's Lover*, pp. 27–8.

34 *Letters*, Vol. VII, ed. Keith Sagar and James T. Boulton (1993), p. 274.

35 Frieda Lawrence, op. cit., p. 186.

36 *The Complete Poems of D. H. Lawrence*, ed. Vivian de Sola Pinto and Warren

37 Roberts (Heinemann, London, 1972), pp. 697, 719.
    Letters, Vol. VII, p. 585.

12 Natives, Residents and Visitors

38 *The Autobiography of Leigh Hunt*, ed. J. E. Morpurgo (Cresset Press, London,

1 1949), pp. 368–9.
    Ibid., p. 371.

2 Ibid., pp. 384–5.

3 *The Poetical Works of Leigh Hunt*, ed. H. S. Milford (Oxford University Press,

4 1923), p. 468.

Autobiography, p. 379.

5 G. A. Greene, *Dantesques* (Elkin Matthews, London, 1903), p. 5.

6 Harold Acton, *Memoirs of an Aesthete* (Methuen, London, 1948), p. 64; Émile

7 Legouis and Louis Cazamian, *A History of English Literature* (J. M. Dent, London, 1937), p. 1348.

   The Italian Journal of Samuel Rogers, ed. J. R. Hale (Faber, London, 1956),

8 p. 191.

   Ibid., p. 202.

9 Ibid., pp. 189, 201, 200.

10 Ibid., pp. 190, 192.

11 Ibid., p. 200.

12 Ibid., p. 202.

13 Ibid., p. 278.

14 *The Complete Letters and Journals of Lord Byron*, Vol. V, ed. Leslie A. Marchand

15 (John Murray, London, 1976), p. 210.

   P. W. Clayden, *Rogers and his Contemporaries* (Smith, Elder & Co., London,

16 1889), Vol. I, p. 320.

   Ibid., pp. 321, 324, 322.

17 *The Letters of William and Dorothy Wordsworth*, ed. Alan G. Hill, Vol. VI, Part III

18 (Oxford University Press, 1982), pp. 412, 411.

   The Poems of Tennyson, ed. Christopher Ricks (Longman, London, 1969),

19 p. 1020.

   The Letters of Oscar Wilde, ed. Rupert Hart-Davies (Rupert Hart-Davis, London,

20 1962), p. 6.

   Richard Ellmann, *Oscar Wilde* (Hamish Hamilton, London, 1987), p. 395n.

Epilogue

21 *The Letters of D. H. Lawrence*, The Cambridge Edition (Cambridge University

1 Press), Vol. VII, ed. Keith Sagar and James T. Boulton (1993), p. 327.

   Phoenix II: Uncollected, Unpublished and Other Prose Works by D. H. Lawrence, ed.

2 Warren Roberts and Harry T. Moore (Heinemann, London, 1968), pp. 599–600.

   Shelley, 'To William Shelley' 26.

3 Hélène Nolthenius, *In That Dawn* (Darton, Longman & Todd, London, 1968),

4 p. 120.

   Harold Acton, *Memoirs of an Aesthete* (Methuen, London, 1948), p. 102.

5 *Shelley's Prose*, ed. David Lee Clark (Fourth Estate, London, 1988), p. 231;

6 Robert Browning, 'The Statue and the Bust' 38–9; Harold Acton, *Florence* (Thames and Hudson, London, 1961), p. 48; Kenneth Churchill, *Italy and English Literature 1764–1930* (Macmillan, London, 1980), p. 103.

   J. M. French (ed.), *Life Records of John Milton* (Rutgers University Press, New

7 Brunswick, NJ), Vol. I (1949), pp. 381–2.

Henry James, *William Wetmore Story and his Friends* (Blackwood, Edinburgh, 1903), Vol. II, p. 4.

Bibliography

Florence

LADY BLESSINGTON, *The Idler in Italy* (Henry Colburn, London, 1839)

GENE A. BRUCKER, *Florentine Politics and Society 1343–1378* (Princeton University Press, 1962)

    Renaissance Florence (John Wiley, New York, 1969)

DINO CARPANETTO AND GIUSEPPE RICUPERATI, *Italy in the Age of Reason 1685–1789* (Longman, Harlow, 1987)

ERIC W. COCHRANE, *Florence in the Forgotten Centuries 1527–1800* (University of Chicago Press, 1973)

    Tradition and Enlightenment in the Tuscan Academies 1690–1800 (University of Chicago Press, 1961)

ERIC W. COCHRANE (ed.), *The Late Italian Renaissance 1525–1630* (Macmillan, London, 1970)

LACY COLLISON-MORLEY, *Italy after the Renaissance* (Routledge, London, 1930)

Dizionario Biografico degli Italiani, ed. Alberto M. Ghisalberti (Istituto della Enciclopedia Italiana, Rome, 1960–)

CHARLES DUPATY, *Lettres sur l'Italie, en 1785* (L. Duprat-Duverger, Paris, 1812)

JOSEPH FORSYTH, *Remarks on Antiquities, Arts, and Letters, during an Excursion in Italy, in the Years 1802 and 1803* (John Murray, London, 1835)

EDMUND G. GARDNER, *The Story of Florence* (J. M. Dent, London, 1900)

W. K. HANCOCK, *Ricasoli and the Risorgimento in Tuscany* (Faber & Gwyer, London, 1926)

HARRY HEARDER, *Italy in the Age of the Risorgimento* (Longman, Harlow, 1983)

DAVID HERLIHY AND CHRISTINE KLAPISCH-ZUBER, *Tuscans and their Families* (Yale University Press, New Haven, Conn., 1985)

JOHN LARNER, *Culture and Society in Italy 1290–1420* (B. T. Batsford, London, 1971)

JAMES LEES-MILNE, *The Last Stuarts* (Chatto & Windus, London, 1983)

JOHN MOORE, *A View of Society and Manners in Italy* (W. Strahan and T. Cadell, London, 1781)

LADY MORGAN, *Italy* (Henry Colburn, London, 1821)

H. E. NAPIER, *Florentine History* (Edward Moxon, London, 1847)

GAETANO SALVEMINI, *The Fascist Dictatorship in Italy* (Jonathan Cape, London, 1928)

TOBIAS SMOLLETT, *Travels through France and Italy*, ed. Frank Felsenstein (Oxford University Press, 1979)

GIOVANNI SPADOLINI, *Firenze Mille Anni* (De Monnier, Florence, 1984)

THEODOSIA TROLLOPE, *Social Aspects of the Italian Revolution* (Chapman & Hall, London, 1861)

THOMAS WATKINS, *Travels through Swisserland, Italy, Sicily [&c.]* (T. Cadell, London, 1792)

STUART WOOLF, *A History of Italy 1700–1860* (Methuen, London, 1979)

ARTHUR YOUNG, *Travels in France and Italy* (J. M. Dent, London, 1915)

Florence and English Poetry

KENNETH CHURCHILL, *Italy and English Literature 1764–1930* (Macmillan, London, 1980)

OLIVE HAMILTON, *The Divine Country: The British in Tuscany 1372–1980* (André Deutsch, London, 1982)

FRANCIS KING, *Florence: A Literary Companion* (John Murray, London, 1991)

OSCAR KUHNS, *Dante and the English Poets from Chaucer to Tennyson* (Henry Holt, New York, 1904)

GIULIANA ARTOM TREVES, *The Golden Ring: The Anglo-Florentines 1847–1862* (Longmans, Green & Co., London, 1956)

Geoffrey Chaucer

PIERO BOITANI (ed.), *Chaucer and the Italian Trecento* (Cambridge University Press, 1985)

D. S. BREWER, *Chaucer and his World* (Eyre Methuen, London, 1978)

W. F. BRYAN AND G. DEMPSTER, *Sources and Analogues of Chaucer's Canterbury Tales* (University of Chicago Press, 1958)

MARCHETTE CHUTE, *Geoffrey Chaucer of England* (Souvenir Press, London, 1977)

G. G. COULTON, *Chaucer and his England* (Methuen, London, 1908)

MARTIN C. CROW AND CLAIR C. OLSON, *Chaucer Life-Records* (Oxford University Press, 1966)

JOHN GARDNER, *The Life and Times of Chaucer* (Jonathan Cape, London, 1977)

R. K. GORDON, *The Story of Troilus* (J. M. Dent, London, 1934)

DONALD R. HOWARD, *Chaucer and the Medieval World* (Weidenfeld & Nicolson, London, 1987)

DAVID WALLACE, *Chaucer and the Early Writings of Boccaccio* (Brewer, Woodbridge, 1983)

HERBERT G. WRIGHT, *Boccaccio in England from Chaucer to Tennyson* (Athlone Press, London, 1957)

John Milton

ETTORE ALLODOLI, *Giovanni Milton e l'Italia* (C. & G. Spighi, Prato, 1907)

JOHN ARTHOS, *Milton and the Italian Cities* (Bowes & Bowes, London, 1968)

HELEN DARBISHIRE (ed.), *The Early Lives of Milton* (Constable, London, 1932)

GIORGIO DE SANTILLANA, *The Crime of Galileo* (Heinemann, London, 1958)

The Diary of John Evelyn, ed. E. S. de Beer (Oxford University Press, 1955)

J. M. FRENCH (ed.), *Life Records of John Milton* (Rutgers University Press, New Brunswick, NJ, 1949–58)

GALILEO GALILEI, *Dialogue Concerning the Two Chief World Systems*, trans. Stillman Drake (University of California Press, Berkeley, 1967)

CHRISTOPHER HILL, *Milton and the English Revolution* (Faber, London, 1977)

DAVID MASSON, *Life of Milton*, Vol. I (Macmillan, London, 2nd edn, 1881)

W. R. PARKER, *Milton: A Biography* (Oxford University Press, 1968)

SIR JOHN RERESBY, *Memoirs and Travels*, ed. A. Ivatt (Kegan Paul, Trench, Trubner & Co., London, 1904)

KVESTER SVENDSEN, *Milton and Science* (Harvard University Press, Cambridge, Mass., 1956)

Thomas Gray

The Correspondence of Thomas Gray, ed. Paget Toynbee and Leonard Whibley (Oxford University Press, 1935)

The Poems of Thomas Gray, William Collins and Oliver Goldsmith, ed. Roger Lonsdale (Longman, London, 1969)

R. W. KETTON-CREMER, *Horace Walpole: A Biography* (Duckworth, London, 1946)
    Thomas Gray (Cambridge University Press, 1955)

A. L. LYTTON SELLS, *Thomas Gray: His Life and Works* (Allen & Unwin, London, 1980)

JOSEPH SPENCE, *Letters from the Grand Tour*, ed. Slava Klima (McGill Queen's University Press, Montreal, 1975)

Horace Walpole's Correspondence, The Yale Edition, ed. W. S. Lewis et al. (Oxford University Press, 1939–83)

Robert Merry

JAMES L. CLIFFORD, *Hester Lynch Piozzi (Mrs Thrale)* (Oxford University Press, 1952)
    'Robert Merry – A Pre-Byronic Hero', *Bulletin of the John Rylands Library, Manchester*, Vol. 27 (1942–3)

W. N. HARGREAVES-MAWDSLEY, *The English Della Cruscans in their Time, 1783–1828* (Martinus Nijhoff, The Hague, 1967)

RODERICK MARSHALL, *Italy in English Literature 1755–1815: Origins of the Romantic Interest in Italy* (Columbia University Press, New York, 1934)

BRIAN MOLONEY, *Florence and England: Essays on Cultural Relations in the Second Half of the Eighteenth Century* (Leo S. Olschki, Florence, 1969)

Autobiography, Letters and Literary Remains of Mrs Piozzi (Thrale), ed. A. Hayward (Longman, Green, Longman & Roberts, London, 1861)

HESTER LYNCH PIOZZI, *Observations and Reflections Made in the Course of a Journey through France, Italy, and Germany*, ed. Herbert Barrows (University of Michigan Press, Ann Arbor, 1967)

The Piozzi Letters, ed. Edward A. and Lilian D. Bloom (University of Delaware Press, Newark, 1989)

Thraliana. The Diary of Mrs Hester Lynch Thrale (Later Mrs Piozzi) 1776–1809, ed. Katharine C. Balderstone (Oxford University Press, 1942)

ALASTAIR SMART, *The Life and Art of Allan Ramsay* (Routledge & Kegan Paul, London, 1952)

Percy Bysshe Shelley

HELEN ROSSETTI ANGELI, *Shelley and his Friends in Italy* (Methuen, London, 1911)

JAMES E. BARCUS (ed.), *Shelley: The Critical Heritage* (Routledge & Kegan Paul, London, 1975)

The Journals of Claire Clairmont, ed. Marion Kingston Stocking (Harvard University

Press, Cambridge, Mass., 1968)

MARIA LUISA GIARTOSIO DE COURTEN, *Percy Bysshe Shelley e l'Italia* (Fratelli Treves, Milan, 1923)

ROBERT GITTINGS AND JO MANTON, *Claire Clairmont and the Shelleys 1798–1879* (Oxford University Press, 1992)

RICHARD HOLMES, *Shelley: The Pursuit* (Weidenfeld & Nicolson, London, 1974)

THOMAS MEDWIN, *The Life of Percy Bysshe Shelley*, ed. H. Buxton Forman (Oxford University Press, 1913)

MICHAEL O'NEILL, *Percy Bysshe Shelley: A Literary Life* (Macmillan, London, 1989)

JAMES RIEGER, *The Mutiny Within: The Heresies of Shelley* (George Braziller, New York, 1967)

NEVILLE ROGERS, *Shelley at Work* (Oxford University Press, 1967)

The Journals of Mary Shelley, ed. Paula R. Feldman and Deana Scott-Kilvert (Oxford University Press, 1987)

The Letters of Mary W. Shelley, ed. Frederick L. Jones (University of Oklahoma Press, Norman, 1944)

The Letters of Percy Bysshe Shelley, ed. Frederick L. Jones (Oxford University Press, 1964)

Shelley's Prose, ed. David Lee Clark (Fourth Estate, London, 1988)

NEWMAN IVEY WHITE, *Shelley* (Secker & Warburg, London, 1947)

Walter Savage Landor

MALCOLM ELWIN, *Savage Landor* (Macmillan, London, 1941)

R. W. EMERSON, *English Traits* (George Routledge & Sons, London, 1883)

JOHN FORSTER, *Walter Savage Landor* (Chapman & Hall, London, 1869)

LEIGH HUNT, *Lord Byron and Some of his Contemporaries* (A. & W. Galignani, Paris, 1828)

SIR AUSTEN HENRY LAYARD, *Autobiography and Letters* (John Murray, London, 1903)

H. C. MINCHIN, *Walter Savage Landor: Last Days, Letters and Conversations* (Methuen, London, 1934)

R. H. SUPER, *Walter Savage Landor* (New York University Press, 1954)

Robert and Elizabeth Barrett Browning

The Letters of Elizabeth Barrett Browning, ed. Frederick G. Kenyon (Smith, Elder & Co., London, 1897)

ELIZABETH BARRETT BROWNING, *Letters to her Sister, 1846–1859*, ed. Leonard Huxley (John Murray, London, 1929)

MARGARET FORSTER, *Elizabeth Barrett Browning* (Chatto & Windus, London, 1988)

HENRY JAMES, *William Wetmore Story and his Friends* (Blackwood, Edinburgh, 1903)

EDWARD C. MCALEER, *The Brownings of Casa Guidi* (The Browning Institute, Inc., New York, 1987)

BETTY MILLER, *Robert Browning: A Portrait* (John Murray, London, 1972)

CLYDE DE L. RYALS, *The Life of Robert Browning* (Blackwell, Oxford, 1993)

Joseph Garrow

STEPHEN WHEELER, 'Landor and Dante', *Times Literary Supplement*, 27 May 1920, p. 336

Theodosia Trollope

ALFRED AUSTIN, *Autobiography* (Macmillan, London, 1911)

THOMAS ADOLPHUS TROLLOPE, *What I Remember* (Richard Bentley, London, 1887)

Robert Lytton

AURELIA BROOKS HARLAN, *Owen Meredith: A Critical Biography of Robert, First Earl of Lytton* (Columbia University Press, New York, 1946)

Letters from Owen Meredith to Robert and Elizabeth Barrett Browning, ed. Aurelia Brooks Harlan and J. Lee Harlan (Baylor University Press, Waco, Texas, 1936)

Isabella Blagden

Poems by the late Isa Blagden (Blackwood, Edinburgh, 1873). With a memoir by Alfred Austin.

Dearest Isa: Robert Browning's Letters to Isabella Blagden, ed. Edward C. McAleer (University of Texas Press, Austin, 1951)

Eugene Lee-Hamilton

GILBERT F. CUNNINGHAM, *The Divine Comedy in English: A Critical Bibliography 1782–1900* (Oliver & Boyd, Edinburgh, 1965)

PETER GUNN, *Vernon Lee: Violet Paget, 1856–1935* (Oxford University Press, 1964)

The Complete Notebooks of Henry James, ed. Leon Edel and Lyall H. Powers (Oxford University Press, 1987)

Dramatic Sonnets, Poems, and Ballads: Selections from the Poems of Eugene Lee-Hamilton (Walter Scott, London and Newcastle, 1903). With a memoir by William Sharp.

EUGENE LEE-HAMILTON, *Mimma Bella* (Heinemann, London, 1909). With a preface by Annie Lee-Hamilton.

D. H. Lawrence

RICHARD ALDINGTON, *Life for Life's Sake* (Cassell, London, 1968)

    Pinorman: Personal Recollections of Norman Douglas, Pino Orioli and Charles Prentice (Heinemann, London, 1954)

    Portrait of a Genius, But ... (Heinemann, London, 1950)

DEREK BRITTON, *Lady Chatterley: The Making of the Novel* (Unwin Hyman, London, 1988)

The Letters of D. H. Lawrence, The Cambridge Edition, Vols. III–VII (Cambridge University Press, 1984–93)

Phoenix: The Posthumous Papers of D. H. Lawrence, ed. Edward D. McDonald (Heinemann, London, 1961)

Phoenix II: Uncollected, Unpublished and Other Prose Works by D. H. Lawrence, ed. Warren

Roberts and Harry T. Moore (Heinemann, London, 1968)

D. H. LAWRENCE, *Sketches of Etruscan Places and Other Italian Essays*, ed. Simonetta de
Filippis (Cambridge University Press, 1992)

FRIEDA LAWRENCE, *'Not I, But the Wind ... '* (Heinemann, London, 1935)

MAURICE MAGNUS, *Memoirs of the Foreign Legion*, with an introduction by D. H. Lawrence
(Martin Secker, London, 1935)

GIUSEPPE ORIOLI, *Adventures of a Bookseller* (Chatto & Windus, London, 1938)

KEITH SAGAR, 'Lawrence and the Wilkinsons', *Review of English Studies*, Vol. 3, No. 4
(October 1962)

Leigh Hunt

EDMUND BLUNDEN, *Leigh Hunt* (Cobden-Sanderson, London, 1930)

The Autobiography of Leigh Hunt, ed. J. E. Morpurgo (Cresset Press, London,1949)

Sir Harold Acton

HAROLD ACTON, *Memoirs of an Aesthete* (Methuen, London, 1948)

More Memoirs of an Aesthete (Methuen, London, 1970)

Samuel Rogers

The Complete Letters and Journals of Lord Byron, Vol. V, ed. Leslie A. Marchand (John
Murray, London, 1976)

P. W. CLAYDEN, *Rogers and his Contemporaries* (Smith, Elder & Co., London, 1889)

The Italian Journals of Samuel Rogers, ed. J. R. Hale (Faber, London, 1956)

William Wordsworth

Henry Crabb Robinson on Books and their Writers, ed. Edith J. Morley (J. M. Dent, London,
1938)

The Letters of William and Dorothy Wordsworth, ed. Alan G. Hill, Vol. VI, Part III (Oxford
University Press, 1982)

Oscar Wilde

RICHARD ELLMANN, *Oscar Wilde* (Hamish Hamilton, London, 1987)

The Letters of Oscar Wilde, ed. Rupert Hart-Davies (Rupert Hart-Davis, London, 1962)

Index

Above: Walter Savage Landor in 1855, by Robert Faulkner
By courtesy of the National Portrait Gallery, London

Above left and right: Robert and Elizabeth Barrett Browning in 1859, by Field Talfourd
By courtesy of the National Portrait Gallery, London